Frederic Jesup Stimson

Glossary of Technical Terms

Phrases, and Maxims of the Common Law

Frederic Jesup Stimson

Glossary of Technical Terms
Phrases, and Maxims of the Common Law

ISBN/EAN: 9783744649353

Printed in Europe, USA, Canada, Australia, Japan

Cover: Foto ©Andreas Hilbeck / pixelio.de

More available books at **www.hansebooks.com**

GLOSSARY

OF

TECHNICAL TERMS, PHRASES, AND MAXIMS

OF THE

COMMON LAW.

BY

FREDERIC JESUP STIMSON.

BOSTON:
LITTLE, BROWN, AND COMPANY.
1881.

NOTE.

THIS book is the result of an attempt to produce a concise Law Dictionary, giving in common English an explanation of the words and phrases, English as well as Saxon, Latin, or French, which are of common technical use in the law. It is not a compilation of law, like the larger dictionaries, but consists purely of definition. Only such civil law, canon law, or Scotch terms have been introduced as are often used in the common-law courts. The writer has sought to give the popular and usual acceptation of each phrase, in much the same rough and general shape in which it would stand in the mind of the trained lawyer; only occasionally adding a hint of its more correct and exact meaning. More definite information must then be sought in the text-books. Unless otherwise mentioned, the definition is given according to the common law of England; and the date or present existence of the thing defined is only roughly indicated by the tense.

It has been impossible within the limits assigned to make the book exhaustive; but it is hoped that a judicious selection has been made of the more important catchwords, writs, courts, and maxims; and that, in seeking to compress the greatest amount of matter in the smallest possible space, the author has been concise, without being inaccurate and obscure.

The **black-faced** type is used for all terms defined under the present caption; the *Italic* is always used for reference, not emphasis. Thus the frequent use of abbreviations like "*v.*," "*see,*" and "*q. v.*" is avoided. The reader is desired always to refer to a term so Italicized, under the proper caption, as it will frequently be found to complete or modify the present definition. Literal translations, followed by explanations, are put in parentheses; paraphrases or explanatory additions, in brackets. The words of the captions are English unless otherwise indicated, and different spellings in the same language follow without a capital letter. Thus, **Gablum,** *l.,* **Gabel, gavel, Gafol,** *sax.: gabel* and *gavel* are the English forms, *gablum* the law Latin, and *gafol* the Saxon. Sometimes, to gain space, different words from the same root, as the noun and the verb, are put in the same paragraph; so, phrases beginning with the caption word. But when the word is found in different languages and begins very many phrases, it is otherwise; thus, the French, English, and Latin *in* begin each a separate paragraph.

BOSTON, February 21, 1881.

GLOSSARY OF LAW TERMS.

A.

A, ad, *fr.* Has (from *avoir, aver*).

A, ab, *l.* From; by; of; with; in; at. **A cancellis:** the Chancellor. **A cœlo usque ad centrum:** from the heavens to the centre of the earth. **A communi observantia non est recedendum:** there should be no departure from common observance. **A consiliis:** of counsel; a counsellor. **A contrario sensu:** on the other hand; in the opposite sense. **A fortiori:** by a stronger reason. **A jure suo cadunt:** they fall from (lose) their right. Applied to cases of loss of property by abandonment. **A latere:** collateral. **A me:** from me. A term used in grants expressing tenure by the grantee directly of the superior lord; opposed to **de me,** expressing tenure by the grantee of the grantor. **A mensa et thoro:** from bed and board. **A morte testatoris:** from the testator's death. **A non domino:** by one not the owner. **A non posse ad non esse sequitur argumentum necessarie negative, licet non affirmative:** from the impossibility of a thing you may infer its nonexistence; but not, from the possibility of a thing, its existence. **A piratis et latronibus capta dominium non mutant:** things taken by pirates or robbers do not change their ownership. **A posteriori:** applied to an argument founded on observation or experiment. The term **a priori** is used of such arguments as rest on analogy or abstract considerations. **A quo:** from which. The Court **a quo** is the court from which a cause has been removed to a higher court, which latter is called the Court **ad quem.** **A quo invito**

aliquid exigi potest: from whom something may be exacted against his will. The definition of a debtor in perfect obligation. **A retro**: behind; in arrear. **A tempore cujus contrarii memoria non existit**: from time of which there exists not memory to the contrary. **A verbis legis non est recedendum**: there should be no departure from the words of the law. **A vinculo matrimonii**: from the bond of marriage. A divorce which completely dissolves the marriage tie.

À, *fr.* At; to; with; in; for; by. **A aver et tener**: to have and to hold. **A causa de cy**: for this reason. **A ce**: for this purpose. **A fine force**: of pure necessity. **A large**: at large; free. **A l'impossible nul n'est tenu**: no one is bound to do what is impossible. **A pais**: to the country; at issue. **A prendre**: to take; v. *Profits à Prendre.* **A rendre**: to render, yield; v. *Profits à rendre.* **A savoir, à saver**: to know; to wit. **A terme**: for a term, for the term. **A tort**: wrongfully.

Ab, *l.* v. *A.* **Ab actis,** *l.* A notary; a registrar. **Ab agendo**: unable to act. **Ab ante**: in advance. **Ab antiquo**: of old. **Ab assuetis non fit injuria**: from things to which we are used, no legal wrong arises. **Ab extra**: from without. **Ab inconvenienti**: from what is inconvenient, or improper; v. *Argumentum.* **Ab inde**: from that time forward; thence. **Ab initio**: from the beginning. **Ab intestato**: from an intestate; used of property acquired from one dying without a will. **Ab invito**: unwillingly, by or from an unwilling person. **Ab olim**: of old.

Abactor, *l.* A cattle-stealer.

Abandonment. Desertion; surrender; relinquishment of property; as when an insured person makes over his rights in the goods to the insurer.

Abarnare, *l.* To detect or disclose a crime.

Abatamentum, *l.,* or **Abatement.** (A making less; a destroying.) Of a **nuisance,** when the party injured removes or destroys it. Of **freehold,** when a stranger enters, and keeps possession of, lands, after the death of the person last seised, and before the entry of the person next entitled. Of **legacies,** when there are not assets to pay all debts or legacies in full; in like manner, there is abatement of **debts** among creditors. Of a **suit,** when it is determined for want of proper parties, as by death, marriage, or bankruptcy; or by **Pleas in abatement**: these are pleas which only suspend the right to sue; or they defeat a particular action without affecting the right; v. *Plea*.

Abatre, abbatre, abater, *fr.* To abate, throw down, or destroy.

Abatre maison: to raze a house. **Abatus per vent**: thrown down by the wind.

Abbaiaunce, abbaizance. *Abeyance*.

Abbrocamentum, *l.*, **Abbrochment.** The forestalling of a market; buying up at wholesale all the goods, to sell at retail.

Abcariare, *l.* To carry away.

Abdite latet, *l.* He lies hid.

Abducere, *l.* To carry away a human being. **Abduxit,** he carried away.

Abduction. The forcible or fraudulent carrying away of a wife, child, or female servant.

Abearance. Behavior; carriage.

Abere-murder, *sax.* Wilful murder.

Abet. To aid or encourage. An abettor is present at the crime; an accessary is concerned in it either before or after.

Abeyance, *fr.* Expectation. An estate is in abeyance when there is no certain person living in whom it can vest.

Abiding by. In Scotch law, the judicial declaration of a party that he abides by a deed which has been attacked as forged, at his peril.

Abigeat. The crime of stealing cattle by driving them away in herds.

Abishersing. Immunity from, being quit of, *amerciaments*.

Abjuration of the Realm. Anciently a person accused of any crime, except treason or sacrilege, who took refuge in a church or other *sanctuary*, might save his life by confessing his offence and swearing to forsake the realm.

Abnormal. A term applied to law affecting persons not under natural relations or conditions, as if insane or under age; the law of persons; v. *Normal*.

Abroachment. v. *Abbrochment*.

Absolute. Unconditional; complete in itself; not relative; final. **Absolute conveyance**: one without condition or qualification. **Absolute estate**: one subject to no condition. **Rule absolute**: in English practice, an order or judgment of court to be carried immediately and unconditionally into effect; distinguished from a **rule nisi**, which is not to be carried into effect unless no cause be shown against it. A rule nisi, on being confirmed at the hearing, becomes absolute. **Absolute warrandice**: in Scotch practice, *warranty* against all the world.

Absolutum et directum dominium, *l.* Entire and right ownership.

Absque, *l.* Without. **Absque aliquo inde reddendo** (without rendering anything therefrom): without reserving any rent. **Absque hoc**: without this; v. *Traverse.* **Absque impetitione vasti** : without impeachment of *waste*, without liability for permissive waste. **Absque tali causa**: without such cause; v. *De injuria.* **Abstract of Fine** ; v. *Fine.* **Abstract of Pleas**: a short statement of the pleas a defendant intended to plead, attached to the summons for leave to plead several pleas. In English practice, and now obsolete. **Abstract of title**: a short statement of the grants, devises, and incumbrances affecting property, on which the title depends.

Abundans cautela non nocet, *l.* Plenty of care does no harm.

Abuttals. The bounds of land. The sides **adjoin,** the ends **abut on,** surrounding land.

Ac etiam, *l.* And also. **Ac etiam billæ**: and also to a bill. In English practice, in the K. B., words used to introduce the real cause of action in cases where it was necessary to allege a fictitious cause to give the court jurisdiction; v. *Bill,* 1, 8. **Ac si** : as if.

Acc., Accord., *fr.* Abbreviations of **accordant,** agreeing.

Accapitare, *l.* To do homage to a chief lord on taking a feud.

Accapitum, *l.* The relief money payable to a chief lord.

Accedas ad curiam, *l.* (That you go to the court.) An English common-law writ to remove a cause from an inferior court not of record to one of the higher courts.

Acceptance. 1. The agreement to pay a bill of exchange, made by the drawee when the bill is presented, as by writing his name on the face. **Acceptance supra protest** or **for honor**: an acceptance made by some friend of the drawer or indorser of a bill, when the drawee has refused to accept, by which the acceptor becomes liable if the drawee does not pay at maturity. 2. v. *Receipt.*

Acceptare, *l.* To accept. **Acceptavit:** he accepted.

Acceptilatio, *l.* Acceptilation; the verbal release of a debt, by declaring it paid when it has not been paid.

Acceptor. v. *Bill,* III. 4. The drawee or other persons *accepting* a bill.

Accessio, *l.* Accession; a mode of acquiring property by natural increase, or addition to what one already possesses; as land, by deposit of a river; or houses, when built on one's own land; or the young of animals.

Accessory, accessary. 1. That which is incident or subordinate to something else, called its principal. 2. v. *Abet.* **Accessorium non ducit sed sequitur suum principale** (the accessory does not lead, but follows its principal): the incident shall pass by grant of the principal, but not the principal by grant of the incident. **Accessorium sequitur naturam rei cui accedit:** the accessory follows the nature of that to which it relates. The spelling *accessary* is reserved for the second meaning.

Accion sur le case, *fr.* Action on the *case.*

Accomenda, *ital.* The contract between the owner of property and the master of a vessel, when the latter is to sell the goods on joint account and share the profits.

Accommodation paper. Notes or bills made, accepted, or indorsed by one person for another without consideration.

Accomplice. Any person concerned in a crime, whether principal or accessary.

Accompt. v. *Account.*

Accord. v. *Acc.*

Accord. An agreement between two persons in settlement of a claim which one of them has against the other. When performed, it is called **accord and satisfaction,** and is a bar to all actions upon that claim.

Account. An obsolete common-law action to compel a person to render an account and enforce settlement thereof. **Account current:** an open account. **Account stated:** an account balanced, which is considered accepted after a reasonable time.

Accouplé, *fr.* Married.

Accredulitare, *l.* To purge one's self of an offence by oath; v. *Purgation.*

Accretion. The increase of land by natural causes.

Accroach. To exercise power without authority.

Accusare nemo se debet, nisi coram Deo, *l.* No one is bound to accuse himself, except before God.

Accusator post rationabile tempus non est audiendus, nisi se bene de omissione excusaverit, *l.* An accuser should not be heard after a reasonable time, unless he has satisfactorily explained his delay.

Achat, achate, *fr.* A purchase or bargain.

Acknowledgment-money. Money paid in some. parts of England by copyhold tenants to the new lord on the death of the old.

Acquest. Property acquired newly, or by purchase.

Acquets, *fr.* Property acquired otherwise than by descent; profits or gains of property as between husband and wife.

Acquietandis plegiis, *l.* A common-law writ formerly lying for the surety against a creditor who refused to acquit him after the debt was paid.

Acquietantia, *l.* An acquittance; a release.

Acquietare, *l.* To acquit. **Acquietatus:** acquitted by a jury.

Acquittance. The discharge of a debt or obligation in writing. A **release** is a similar discharge under seal.

Acre fight. A camp fight; an ancient duel fought between the English and Scotch, in an open field.

Act of bankruptcy: an act for which a debtor may legally be adjudged bankrupt. **Act in pais:** an act out of court. **Act of God:** an occurrence which a man cannot foresee or prevent. **Act of settlement:** the 12 & 13 Will. III. c. 2, by which the Crown was limited to the present royal family. **Act of supremacy:** the 1 Eliz. c. 1, by which the supremacy of the Crown in matters ecclesiastical was established. **Acts of uniformity:** the 1 Eliz. c. 2, and 13 & 14 Car. II. c. 4, by which the public worship of the Church of England is regulated.

Acta, *l.,* **Actes,** *fr.* Acts, records, transactions. **Acta exteriora indicant interiora secreta** (outward acts show inward secrets): acts indicate the intention.

Actio, *l.* An action; cause. **Actio ex contractu:** an action based on contract; **ex delicto,** on tort. **Actio in personam,** against the person; **in rem,** against the thing, or property; v. *Ad rem.* **Actio mixta:** against both person and property.

Actio nominata: a named action; an action where there was a writ *de cursu*, existing before *Westminster II.*; v. *Trespass, Case, Action*. **Actio non, Actionem non**: words anciently beginning a special plea, averring that the plaintiff ought not to maintain his action. **Actio non accrevit infra sex annos**: the (plaintiff's) claim did not accrue within six years. **Actio non datur non damnificato**: no action is given to one who is not injured. **Actio personalis moritur cum persona**: a personal right of action dies with the person.

Action. The legal demand of one's right. **Ancestral action**: one brought to recover land, relying on the seisin or possession of an ancestor. **Civil action**: one to enforce a private right. **Droitural action**: an action brought upon the right, to determine the title, as distinguished from *possessory* actions. **Fictitious or feigned action**: one brought to settle a point of law, there being no real controversy. **Formed action**: one for which a set form of words is prescribed, *Actio nominata*. **Local action**: one which must be brought in a particular place, not *transitory*. **Mixed action**: one in which both damages are sought, and the recovery of real property. **Penal action**: one brought to enforce or recover a penalty. **Personal action**: brought to recover money, damages, or other personal property. **Petitory action**: one determining the title, *droitural*. **Popular action**: one which may be brought by any person for breach of a penal statute. **Possessory action**: one brought to recover possession, without necessarily determining the right. **Real action**: one brought to recover real property, obsolete except in a few States. **Rescissory action**: in Scotch law, one brought to avoid a deed or other instrument. **Qui tam action**: a *popular* action, brought on behalf of the sovereign and the informer. **Transitory action**: one which may be brought in any county, with any *venire*; not *local*. **Plea to the action of the writ**: one which went to show that the plaintiff had no cause to have the writ he brought; v. *Plea*. **Action upon the case**: an action so called because the plaintiff's whole case was set forth in the *writ*, there being no *original writ* to cover his cause of action. A remedy given by the Statute of Westminster II. in cases which were similar (**in consimili casu**) to those covered by the original writs, and usually employed in cases where there was no actual violence or immediate injury. The **actiones nominatæ** were those for which original writs then existed.

Acton Burnel. The statute 11 Ed. I. (1233), authorizing the *statute merchant.*

Actor, *l.* A plaintiff. **Actor sequitur forum rei** (the plaintiff follows the defendant's court): the plaintiff must sue where the defendant lives. **Actore non probante absolvitur reus**: the plaintiff not having proved his case, the defendant is discharged. **Actori incumbit probatio**: the burden of proof lies on the plaintiff.

Acts of Sederunt. The general rules and orders of the Scotch *Court of Sessions.*

Actum, *l.* Done; a deed.

Actus, *t.* An action, act. **Actus curiæ neminem gravabit**: an act of the court shall prejudice no one. **Actus Dei vel legis nemini facit injuriam**: an act of God or an act of the law injures no one. **Actus legis nemini est damnosus**: an act of the law is prejudicial to no one. **Actus me invito factus non est meus actus**: an act done by me against my will is not my act. **Actus non facit reum nisi mens sit rea**: an act makes no one guilty unless the intention be guilty.

Ad, *l.* To; for; at; until. **Ad admittendum clericum**: a writ in the nature of an execution, given to the successful plaintiff in *quare impedit*, commanding the bishop to admit his clerk. **Ad aliud examen**: to another tribunal. **Ad audiendum et terminandum**: to hear and determine; *Oyer and terminer.* **Ad captum vulgi**: suited to the common understanding. **Ad colligendum bona defuncti**: to collect the goods of the deceased. Special letters of administration granted to a person called the **collector** pending delay in the probate of a will or the appointment of an administrator or executor. **Ad communem legem**: at the common law. An obsolete writ of entry, brought by the reversioner after the death of the life tenant, to recover land wrongfully alienated by him. **Ad comparendum**: to appear. **Ad compotum reddendum**: to render an account. **Ad custagia, ad custum**: at the costs. **Ad damnum**: to the damage. That part of the declaration which states the plaintiff's money loss. **Ad diem**: at the day. **Ad ea quæ frequentius accidunt jura adaptantur**: the laws are adapted

to those cases which occur most frequently. **Ad effectum sequentem**: to the following effect. **Ad exitum**: at issue ; at
the end. **Ad fidem**: in allegiance. **Ad filum medium
aquæ** or **viæ**: to the middle line (thread) of the water *or* way.
Ad fin., ad finem litis: at the end, at the end of the suit.
Ad firmam: to farm. **Ad gaolas deliberandas**: to make
gaol-delivery, empty the gaols; v. *Commission*, 5. **Ad hominem**:
to the person, applied to a personal argument. **Ad idem**: to
the same point, or effect. **Ad inde requisitus**: thereunto required. **Ad infinitum**: indefinitely, to an infinite extent. **Ad
inquirendum**: to inquire. A judicial writ, commanding any
matter in a pending cause to be inquired into. **Ad interim**:
in the mean time. **Ad jungendum auxilium**: to join in aid ;
v. *Aid-prayer*. **Ad jura regis**: for the rights of the King. A
writ brought by one holding a Crown living against those seeking to eject him. **Ad Kalendas Græcas** (at the Greek Ka-
lends): never. **Ad largum**: at large. **Ad litem**: for the
purposes of the suit, during the suit. **Ad lucrandum vel per-
dendum**: for gain or loss. **Ad majorem cautelam**: for
greater caution, or security. **Ad mordendum assuetus**: accustomed to bite ; v. *Scienter*. **Ad nocumentum**: to the hurt,
or nuisance. **Ad ostium ecclesiæ**: at the church-door : v.
Dower. **Ad proximum antecedens fiat relatio, nisi im-
pediatur sententia**: reference (relation) should be made to
the next antecedent, unless the sense forbid. **Ad quæstionem
juris respondent juratores, ad quæstionem facti respondent judices**: jurymen answer questions of fact, judges those
of law. **Ad quem**: to which ; v. *A quo*. **Ad quod damnum** :
to what injury. A writ issuing before the grant of liberties by
the Crown, to see that no rights will thereby be injured. **Ad
quod non fuit responsum** : to which there was no answer.
Ad rationem ponere: to cite to appear, to arraign. **Ad rem** :
to the thing, to recover the thing, against the thing. Thus
actions are **ad rem**, or **in rem**, to recover the thing in whose
ever hands it may be, or **in personam** against some particular
person or persons. In the Roman law rights **ad rem** were personal rights, rights to recover the thing against some person, as
distinct from rights **in re**, rights or property in the thing which
might be asserted against all the world. **Ad reparationem et**

sustentationem : for repairing and keeping in proper condition. **Ad respondendum** : to answer; v. *Capias*. **Ad sectam**: at suit of. **Ad terminum annorum**: for a term of years. **Ad terminum qui præteriit**: for a term which has expired. A writ of entry which lay for the lessor or his heirs against the lessee or any one holding the land after the lease expired. **Ad tunc et ibidem**: then and there. The technical name for a part of an indictment specifying time and place. **Ad tristem partem strenua est suspicio**: suspicion lies heavy on the unfortunate side. **Ad unguem**: perfect, finished to the smallest detail. **Ad usum et commodum**: to the use and benefit. **Ad valentiam, valorem**: to the value; v. *Cape*. **Ad ventrem inspiciendum** ; v. *De ventre inspiciendo*. **Ad vitam aut culpam** (for life or until fault) : during good behavior. **Ad voluntatem domini**: at the will of the lord. **Ad waractum**: to fallow.

Additio probat minoritatem, *l.* An addition indicates minority, or inferiority.

Addition. The title or description added to the name of a person in legal writings for greater certainty.

Adeem. To take away, revoke.

Ademption. The withholding or extinction of a legacy caused by some act of the testator during life.

Adeprimes, *fr.* First; in the first place.

Aderere, *fr.* In arrear ; behind.

Adesouth, *fr.* Under, beneath.

Adherence. In Scotch law, an action by either party for the restitution of conjugal rights.

Adiratus, *l.* Strayed ; lost.

Aditus, *l.* A public road ; a way of entry.

Adjective law. The part of law establishing remedies.

Adjornare, *l.*, **Adjourner,** *fr.* To adjourn. **Adjornatur**: it is adjourned.

Adjudication. Judgment, decree. **Adjudication in implement**: in Scotch law, a grantee's action against a grantor who refuses to complete his title.

Adjunctio, *l.* Adjunction ; a method of accession, or gaining property, when one man's property is materially affixed to that of another.

Adjunctum, *l.* An incident ; an adjunct.

Adjustment. The termination, division, and settlement of a loss under a marine insurance policy.

Adlegiare, *l.,* **aleier,** *fr.* To purge one's self of crime by oath ; v. *Purgation.*

Admeasurement of Dower. A writ which lay for the heir against the widow holding more land than she was entitled to.

Admeasurement of Pasture. A writ for the adjustment of rights of pasture which lay against one of those who were entitled to common in favor of the others.

Adminicle. That which aids something else ; in Scotch law, a deed or document referring to and proving another. **Adminicular** : auxiliary to. **Adminiculum,** *l.* : adminicle.

Administrare, *l.,* **Administer.** To manage, take charge of.

Administration. Collecting the estate of a deceased intestate under legal appointment, paying his debts, and dividing the remainder among those entitled. Management of affairs generally. **Administration ad colligendum** : temporary administration granted to preserve perishable goods or property. **Ancillary administration** : subordinate administration, granted to collect assets in a foreign state. **Cum testamento annexo** : with the will annexed. Administration granted when there is a will, but no executor. **De bonis non** : of the goods not [administered]. Administration granted when the first executor or administrator dies before completing the work. **Durante absentia** : during the absence [of an executor]. **Durante minori actati** : administration granted when the executor is a minor, to continue until he attains the lawful age to act. **Pendente lite** : administration granted pending a suit about the will.

Administration Suit. A suit brought in Chancery, in English practice, by any one interested, for administration of a decedent's estate, when there is doubt as to its solvency.

Administrator. One who rightfully administers an estate.

Admiral, Lord High. The chief officer of the English navy, and theoretical head of the courts of admiralty. His naval duties are now performed by the *Lords Commissioners,* and his judicial, by the Judge of Admiralty ; v. *Court,* 90.

Admiralty. A court having jurisdiction of marine affairs and maritime causes, civil and criminal. Sometimes also of prize questions, in time of war ; v. *Court,* 90.

Admittance. Giving possession of a copyhold estate, whether upon grant of the lord, surrender by a former tenant, or descent.

Admittendo clerico; v. *De.*

Admonitio trina, *l.* The threefold warning given to a prisoner standing mute before subjecting him to the *paine forte et dure.*

Adnihilare, adnullare, *l.,* **adnihil.** To annul.

Adonques, adunque, adoun, *fr.* Then.

Adrectare, *l.* To do right, make amends.

Adscripti glebæ, *l.* Annexed to the soil; slaves who were sold with the land.

Adsm., ads., ats. Abbreviations of **ad sectam,** at suit of.

Adsecurare, *l.* To make secure; as by giving pledges.

Adult. In civil law, a person who has reached the age of fourteen, or twelve if female. In common law, a person aged twenty-one.

Adulterium, *l.* A fine anciently imposed for adultery or fornication.

Advancement. Money or property given to a child by a father, or other person *in loco parentis,* in anticipation of what the child might inherit.

Advenir, avener, aveigner, *fr.* To happen; come to; become.

Adventure. Goods sent to sea at the risk of the sender, to be sold at best advantage by the supercargo.

Advisement. Consultation; deliberation.

Advocate. A person privileged to plead for another in court; a name for counsel in ecclesiastical or admiralty courts. Also, the patron of a living.

Advocate, Lord. The chief Crown lawyer and public prosecutor in Scotland.

Advocatio, *l.* An advowson. An avowry in replevin. Advocation.

Advocation. The Scotch process of appeal.

Advover, *fr.,* **advow, avouch, avow, advocare,** *l.* To avow, admit; to acknowledge and justify.

Advowee. He who holds an advowson.

Advowry. v. *Avowry.*

Advowson. A right of presentation to a church or benefice, of appointing a clergyman to the living. **Advowson appen-**

dant: one annexed to a manor. **Advowson in gross**: one belonging to a person. **Advowson presentative**: when the patron presents to the bishop, and **collative** when the patron is himself the bishop. **Donative advowson**: when the patron could place his clerk in possession without *presentation, institution,* or *induction.*

Advowtry, advowterer. Adultery, adulterer.

Ædificare in tuo proprio solo non licet quod alteri noceat. It is not lawful to build upon your own land what may injure another.

Ædificatum solo solo cedit. What is built upon the land goes with it.

Æl, aieul, ayle, *fr.* A grandfather. v. *Aiel.*

Æquitas, *l.* Equity. **Æquitas sequitur legem**: equity follows the law. **Æquitas uxoribus, liberis, creditoribus maxime favet**: equity favors wives and children, creditors most of all.

Æquivocum, *l.* Of various or doubtful signification.

Æquus, *l.* Equal; fair; just. **Æquior est dispositio legis quam hominis**: the disposition of the law is fairer than man's.

Ærerer, airer, *fr.* To plough.

Æs alienum, *l.* *In civil law,* a debt.

Æstimatio capitis, *l.* The value of the head. A fine imposed for murder, varying in amount according to the rank of the person killed. **Æstimatio præteriti delicti ex postremo facto nunquam crescit**: the rating of a past offence is never aggravated by a later act.

Æstate probanda. v. *De.*

Affaire, *fr.* To do, make; to be made or taken.

Affectus punitur, licet non sequatur effectus, *l.* The intention is punished, though the consequences do not follow. **Affectum propter**; v. *Challenge.*

Affeere, affere ; afferer, *fr.; ***afferare,** *l.* To assess, appraise.

Affeeror, afferator, *l.* Persons appointed in courts-leet to assess fines and amerciaments, upon oath.

Affer, affri, affra, *fr.* Cattle, or beasts.

Affiant. One who makes affidavit.

Affidare, *l.* To swear to ; swear fealty; pledge one's faith. Hence **affidavit,** an oath in writing sworn before some person legally authorized; v. *Deposition.* **Affidavit of merits**: a formal statement that the defendant has good ground of defence. **Affidatus**: a tenant by fealty.

Affiert, afiert, affert, *fr.* It belongs, it behooves.

Affilare, *l.* To file. **Affiletur**: let it be filed.

Affiliation. The process of determining a man to be the father of a bastard child, whereby he is forced to maintain it.

Affinis, *l.* One related by marriage. **Affinis mei affinis non est mihi affinis**: one related by marriage to one related to me by marriage has no affinity to me.

Affinitas, *l.*, **Affinity.** Relation by marriage.

Affirmant. One who affirms; used in place of **deponent** (one making oath) where no oath is taken.

Affirmanti, non neganti, incumbit probatio. The proof lies upon the one affirming, not the one denying.

Affirmare, *l.*, **affirmer**, *fr.* To affirm; confirm; ratify; assert; state in pleading; give evidence not under oath. **Affirmance**: the ratification.of a voidable act or contract by the party who is to be bound thereby.

Affirmation. Testimony given without oath.

Afforciare, *l.*, **afforcer**, *fr.* To afforce; to add; to increase; to strengthen. **Afforcing the assize**: to obtain a verdict by adding jurors until some twelve of the jury agreed; or, later, by keeping the jury without food and drink.

Afforestare, *l.*, **afforest.** To make land into a forest; v. *Forest*.

Affranchir, *fr.* To affranchise; to make free.

Affray. A public fight between two or more persons, to the terror of others. There must be a blow or stroke given or offered, or a weapon drawn. It must be in a public place, thus differing from an *assault*; and it is unpremeditated, thus differing from a *riot*.

Affrectamentum, *l.*, **Affreightment.** The contract for the use of a vessel.

Aftermath. The second crop of grass; the right to such crop.

Agait, *fr.* Waiting; in wait. **Gist en agait**: he lies in wait.

Agard, *fr.* Award. **Agarder**: to award, to condemn.

Age. Capacity of legal action depends partly on age. Thus, of a man, after seven he may be capitally punished if proved consciously guilty; after fourteen, youth is no defence; after twelve, he may take the oath of allegiance; after fourteen, he may marry and choose his guardian, or make a will of personal property ; at twenty-one, he is of **full age** for all purposes. So a woman is dowable at nine ; may consent to marriage, or make a will of personal property, at twelve ; is of full age at twenty-one. These periods vary in civil and statute law.

Age prier, *fr.,* **Age-prayer.** A suggestion of *non-age,* made in a real action to which an infant is a party, with a request that the proceedings be stayed until the infant comes of age. This was called the plea of **parol demurrer.**

Agenhine, awnhin, *sax.* A guest, an inmate, one of the household, for whom the host is answerable if he break the peace.

Agent and Patient. A person is so called when both the doer of a thing and he to whom it is done. **General agent:** an agent authorized to perform a general class of acts, or employed as practising a certain trade or profession. **Agentes et consentientes pari poena plectentur:** those who act and those who consent are liable to the same punishment.

Ager, *l.* A field ; an acre.

Agere, *l.* To act ; to do ; to sue. **Agetur:** suit is brought.

Aggravation. Matters of aggravation are those which are inserted in the declaration to increase the damages, but not affecting the right of action.

Aggregatio mentium, *l.* The meeting of minds ; spoken of the moment when a contract is complete.

Agild, *sax.* Free from penalty ; not subject to the customary fine.

Agiler, *sax.* An observer, informer.

Agillarius, *l.* A hay-ward, herd-ward, the keeper of cattle in a common field.

Agio, *ital.* The term used in commerce to express the difference in value between one kind of currency and another.

Agiser, *fr.* To lie. **Agisant:** lying.

Agistare, *l.,* **Agistor.** *fr.,* **Agist.** To put, place, assign, apportion. To take in the cattle of strangers to feed in a royal forest. To take cattle to pasture at a certain rate of compensation.

Agistamentum, *l.,* **Agistment.** The taking in of cattle to feed at a certain rate per week ; also, the profit thereof. Also, a duty or tax for repairing banks, dikes, or sea-walls, levied on the owners of lands benefited thereby.

Agistator, *l.,* **Agister.** The bailee in agistment of cattle ; the officer of the forest who took account of cattle there agisted.

Agnates, Agnati, *l.* Aguates ; relatives by the father's side.

Agnatio, *l.*, **Agnation.** Relation or kinship through males.

Agniser, *fr.* To acknowledge.

Agnomen, *l.* An additional name, a nickname.

Agrarian. Relating to land, or the division or distribution thereof.

Agreare, *l.* To agree. **Agreavit:** he agreed. **Agreamentum:** agreement.

Aid. A service or payment due from tenants in chivalry to their lords ; usually either to ransom the lord's person ; **pur faire l'eigne fitz chivaler,** to make the eldest son a knight ; or **pur l'eigne file marier,** to marry the eldest daughter.

Aids. Extraordinary grants to the Crown by the Commons.

Aide-prier, *fr.*, **Aid-prayer.** A proceeding by which one sued for land in which he had a limited interest sought suspense of the action and aid of his lord or reversioner. So a tenant *in capite,* or a city or borough holding a fee-farm from the King, might pray in aid of the King.

Aider by Verdict. Where a defect or error in pleading which might have been objected to is, after verdict, no longer open to objection ; is " cured by the verdict."

Aider. Same as *Abettor,* qu. v.

Aie, *fr.* I have. **Ait:** he has. **Aiet:** he shall have.

Aiel, aieul, ayle, *fr.* A grandfather. A writ which lay for the heir to recover lands on the seisin of his grandfather, when a stranger had entered on the day of the grandfather's death.

Ailours, aylours, *fr.* Elsewhere ; besides.

Ainesse, *fr.* *Esnecy,* q. v. ; the right of the eldest born.

Ainsi, *fr.* Thus ; so. **Ainsi come:** even as it were. **Ainsi soit il:** so be it.

Airer, ærer, *fr.* To plow. **Aireau:** a plough.

Aisiamentum, *l.*, **Aisement,** *fr.* An easement.

Aisne, eigne, *fr.* Eldest, first-born. **Aisneese:** Esnecy ; v. *Ainesse.*

Ajant, *fr.* Having.

Ajourner, *fr.* To summon ; to adjourn.

Ajuger, *fr.* To adjudge, award. **Ajugé:** adjudged.

Al, *fr.* At the ; to the. **Al aid de Dieu:** with the aid of God. **Al huis d'esglise:** at the door of the church. **Al barre:** at the bar. **Al comon ley avant,** etc.: at the common law before, etc.

Ala, alast, alant, *fr.* v. *Aler.*

Alba firma, *l.* White rent; rent payable in silver, as distinguished from black rents, black mail, payable in corn, work, or the like. **Album breve**: a blank writ.

Aleatory; v. *Contract.* Hazardous, uncertain.

Aler. aller, *fr.* To go. **Ala, alast**: went, gone. **Alant**: going. **Aller à Dieu** (to go to God): to be dismissed the court, to go quit. **Aler sans jour** (to go without day): to be finally dismissed, without *continuance,* q. v. **Alé et tout defail**: gone and quite spoiled.

Alia enormia, *l.* (Other wrongs.) A general statement of injuries at the end of a declaration in trespass, under which matters of aggravation may be given in evidence.

Alias, *l.* Otherwise; at another time; formerly. **Alias dictus**: otherwise called. **Alias writ**: a second writ, issued after a previous one has been issued in the same cause without effect.

Alibi, *l.* Elsewhere. A defence in criminal law, showing that the accused was in another place when the offence was committed.

Alien. One born in a foreign country, not naturalized. **Alien amy**: the subject of a foreign nation at peace with our own. **Alien enemy**: the subject of a foreign nation at war with our own.

Alienare, *l.,* **Aliener,** *fr.,* **Alienate, Aliene.** To transfer, convey.

Alienatio, *l.,* **Alienation.** The transfer of ownership, conveyance. **Alienatio licet prohibeatur, consensu tamen omnium in quorum favorem prohibita est, potest fieri**: though alienation be forbidden, yet it may be made with the consent of all those for whose benefit it is forbidden. **Alienatio rei præfertur juri accrescendi** (alienation of property is preferred to the right of survivorship): the law favors a conveyance made in the owner's lifetime, rather than allow the property to descend or accumulate.

Alieni appetens, sui profusus, *l.* Greedy of others' property, wasting his own. **Alieni generis**: of another kind. **Alieni juris**: under the control of another, as of a parent or guardian. **Alieno solo**: on another's land.

Alien-nee, *fr.* An alien born.

Alienus, alienum, *l.* Another's, by or of another.

Aliment. In Scotch law, to give support to a person unable to support himself.

Alimony. An allowance made to the wife out of the husband's estate, during or at the termination of a suit, for her maintenance while separated from her husband.

Alio intuitu, *l.* In a different view ; with another purpose.

Aliqualiter, *l.* In any way.

Aliquid, *l.* · Somewhat ; something. **Aliquid conceditur ne injuria remaneat impunita, quod alias non concederetur** : something is conceded which otherwise would not be, lest an injury should go unredressed. **Aliquid possessionis et nihil juris** : somewhat of possession, but nothing of right.

Aliquis, *l.* Any one. **Aliquis non potest esse judex in propria causa** : no one can be judge in his own cause.

Aliter, *l.* Otherwise ; otherwise decided. **Aliter vel in alio modo** : otherwise, or in another way.

Aliunde, *l.* From another place, from another source.

Aliud est celare, aliud tacere, *l.* It is one thing to conceal, another to be silent.

Allegare, *l.* To allege, or state. **Allegans contraria non est audiendus** : one alleging contradictory things is not to be heard. **Allegans suam turpitudinem non est audiendus** : one alleging his own infamy is not to be heard. **Allegari non debuit quod probatum non relevat** : that ought not to be alleged which is not relevant if proved. **Allegata et probata** : things alleged and things proved.

Allegation. A pleading ; a statement of a fact ; the assertion of a party in a cause of what he intends to prove. **Allegation of Faculties** : the statement made by the wife of the property of her husband, in order to her obtaining alimony. **Allegatio contra factum non est admittenda** : an allegation contradicting the deed (or the fact) should not be admitted.

Allegiare, *l.* To clear one's self, defend, by due course of law ; to wage one's law.

Alleging diminution. The allegation of some error in a subordinate part of the *nisi prius* record.

Aller, *fr.* v. *Aler.* **Aller,** *germ.* The greatest possible.

Alleu, aleu, alieu, *fr.* An allodial estate.

Alleviare, *l.* To pay an accustomed fine or composition.

Allision. The running of one vessel into another.

Allocare, *l.* To allow. **Allocatur,** abb. **alloc.**: it is allowed.

Allocatio, *l.*, **Allocation.** An allowance made upon an account in the English Exchequer.

Allocatione facienda, *l.* (To make allowance.) A writ which lay for one of the Crown's accountants against the Exchequer, commanding them to allow him such sums as he had lawfully expended.

Allocato comitatu, *l.* v. *Exigent.*

Allocatur exigent, *l.* v. *Exigent.*

Allodial. Free; not held of any superior; the opposite of fendal.

Allodium, alodium, alodum, *l.* An estate held absolutely, of no superior; hence, owing no rent, fealty, or service.

Alloigner, alloyner, *fr.* To eloign; remove to a distance; delay.

Allonge, *fr.* A piece of paper annexed to a bill or note in which to write further indorsements, when there is no more room on the document itself.

Allotment note. An assignment by a seaman of a part of his wages to a near relative.

Alluvio, *l.*, **Alluvion.** Natural increase of land by deposit on a river or sea shore.

Alm, alme, *fr.* Soul. **Almes-feoh**: *Peter's pence.*

Almoigne, almoin, *fr.* Alms.

Alnage. Ell-measure. A duty on woollen cloth, paid for measuring and sealing by the **alnager.**

Alnetum, *l.* A place where alders grow.

Aloarius, *l.* The holder of an allodium.

Alodium, alode. v. *Allodium.*

Alors, *fr.* Then; there.

Als., *l.* For **Alios** and **Alias,** others.

Alt, *fr.;* **Altus, alta,** etc., *l.* High. **Alta proditio**: high treason. **Alta via**: highway.

Altarage. Offerings made upon the altar; the priest's profits; contributions; tithes.

Alter, *l.* Another.

Alternatim, *l.* Interchangeably.

Alternative. Giving an option of two things; as, to do an act or show cause, like a writ of Mandamus. **Alternativa petitio non est audienda** : an alternative prayer is not to be heard.

Alternis vicibus, *l.*   Alternately ; by turn.

Alterum non lædere, *l.*   Not to injure another.

Alteruter, *l.*   One of the two ; each.

Altius non tollendi, *l.*   The name of a servitude by which the owner of a house was restrained from building higher than a certain limit.

Alto et basso, *l.*   High and low.   A phrase applied to an absolute submission of all differences to arbitration.

Altre, altrei, *fr.*   Another.

Altum mare, *l.*   The high sea.

Amalphitan Code.   A collection of sea law compiled about the eleventh century by the people of Amalfi, and in force in the Mediterranean countries.

Ambactus, *l.*   A servant, messenger ; client.

Ambideux, *fr.*   Both.

Ambidexter, *l.*   One who has the use of both hands ; one who takes bribes from both parties to an action.

Ambiguitas, *l.*, **Ambiguity.**   Uncertainty of meaning in the words of a written instrument.   It is **patent,** when the doubt arises upon the face of the instrument itself ; **latent,** when the doubt arises from extrinsic matter or collateral circumstances. **Ambiguitas verborum latens verificatione suppletur, nam quod ex facto oritur ambiguum verificatione facti tollitur** : a latent ambiguity of words may be (supplied) helped by averment, for that ambiguity which arises from an [extrinsic] fact is [may be] removed by an averment of the fact [as it really is].   **Ambiguitas verborum patens nulla verificatione suppletur** : a patent ambiguity is helped by no averment. **Ambigua responsio contra proferentem est accipienda, Ambiguum placitum interpretari debet contra proferentem** : an ambiguous plea ought to be interpreted against the party pleading it.   **Ambiguum pactum contra venditorem interpretandum est** : an ambiguous contract is to be taken against the seller.

Ambulatoria voluntas, *l.*   An ambulatory, changeable, revocable will or intention.

Amenable, Amesnable.   Tractable ; responsible ; subject to the jurisdiction of the court.

Amende honorable, *fr.* A punishment by disgrace, infamy, or the doing an humble act. A satisfactory apology.

Amerciament, Amercement. A penalty, like a fine, but imposed by a court not necessarily of record, and of uncertain amount. The defendant was said to be in the mercy of the king or lord whom he had offended; and the amount was assessed by the affeerors; v. *Pledges to Prosecute.*

Ameaner, *fr.* To lead, drive; to cite; to bring the body of a party to court.

Ami, Amy, *fr.*, **Amicus,** *l.* A friend. **Amicus curiæ :** a friend of the court; an uninterested person who makes a suggestion, or gives information, in a case. **Amici consilia credenda :** the advice of a friend is to be trusted.

Amicable action. One brought by consent of both parties to settle a doubtful point of law, the facts being usually agreed upon.

Amittere liberam legem, *l.* To lose one's *frank-law.* **Amittere legem terræ :** to lose the law of the land. Both expressions used of an outlaw, one who has lost the privilege of bearing witness, or being juryman, or suing, in court. Part of the punishment of one who has become infamous; i. e. who has cried craven in the trial by battel. So, **Amittere curiam :** to lose the right to attend court.

Amont, amount, *fr.* Upwards; above.

Amortir, *fr.*, **Amortise.** To alien lands in *mortmain.*

Amortizatio, *t.*, **Amortisement.** Alienation in *mortmain.*

Amotion. Turning out; dispossession; carrying away.

Amour, *fr.* Grace; favor.

Amoveas manus, *l.* That you remove the hands; v. *Ouster-le-main.*

Ampliare, *l.*, **Amplier,** *fr.* To enlarge; extend; defer. **Ampli-.ation :** a deferring judgment till after further consideration.

Amy, *fr.* Friend. **Prochein amy :** *next friend.*

An, anne, ann, *fr.* A year. **An, jour et waste :** *year, day, and waste.*

Anatocismus, *gr.*, *l.*, **Anatocism.** Compound interest.

Ancestor. The person from whom an estate is inherited; not necessarily related lineally.

Ancestral action. v. *Action.*

Anchorage. A duty paid by ships for use of a harbor.

Ancient demesne or **domain.** A tenure existing in certain manors held by the Crown at the time of Edward the Confessor or William the Conqueror. A species of copyhold with fixed services and certain privileges. **A plea of ancient demesne** may be pleaded in abatement to real actions, or actions where the freehold may come in question; v. *Court*, 42. **Ancient house :** one which has stood long enough to acquire an easement of support against the adjoining land ; in England, twenty years. **Ancient lights :** windows which have been used in their present state for twenty years, giving, in England, a right to have them unobstructed. **Ancient writings :** deeds and other documents more than thirty years old, which do not require preliminary proof if coming from the person who might naturally possess them.

Ancillary. Attendant upon; auxiliary; subordinate.

Ancipitis usus, *l.* Of doubtful [legal or illegal] use.

Anecius, *l.* The eldest, first-born.

Angaria, *gr., l.* A forced or excessive service exacted by a superior of a vassal. The impressment of a vessel.

Angleterre, *fr.* England.

Anglice, *l.* In English.

Anichiler, adnichiler, anienter, anientir, aneantir, *fr.* To avoid, annul. **Anient,** etc. : void. **Anientisement :** destruction ; waste.

Animus, *l.* Mind ; will ; disposition ; design. **Animo :** with a mind, intention, etc. **Cancellandi :** of cancelling. **Custodiendi :** of keeping. **Defamandi :** of defaming. **Differendi :** of obtaining delay ; postponing. **Donandi :** of giving, making a gift. **Furandi :** of stealing. **Lucrandi :** of gaining. **Manendi :** of remaining. **Morandi :** of staying, delaying. **Possidendi :** of possessing, keeping. **Recipiendi :** of receiving. **Remanendi :** of remaining away. **Revertendi :** of returning. **Republicandi :** of republishing. **Revocandi :** of revoking. **Testandi :** of making a will. **Animo et corpore :** in intention and act. **Animo felonico :** with felonious intent. **Animus et factus :** intention and act. **Animus hominis est anima scripti :** the man's purpose is the spirit of the writing. **Animus domini :** the intention [of acting as] owner.

Annates, *l.* *First-fruits.*

Anni nubiles, *l.* A woman's marriageable years, the age of twelve.

Annuity. A yearly sum payable by the grantor, charging his person only.

Annulus et baculus, *l.* The ring and staff; used as symbols in feudal and ecclesiastical investitures.

Annus, *l.* A year. **Annus deliberandi**: the year of deliberation, allowed in Scotch law to the heir to decide whether he will accept the inheritance. **Annus et dies**: a year and a day. **Annus, dies et vastum**: *year, day, and waste.* **Annus inceptus pro completo habetur**: a year begun is held as completed. **Annus luctus**: the year of mourning, following the husband's death, and during which, in the Roman law, the widow could not marry. **Annus utilis**: an available year, one during which a right could be exercised or a prescription grow.

Annuus reditus, *l.* An annuity; a yearly rent.

Anoyer, *fr.* To trouble, annoy. **Annoysance**: a nuisance.

Answer. Any defensive pleading except a demurrer. The usual mode of defence in equity, corresponding to a plea at law.

Ante, *l.* Before. **Ante exhibitionem billæ** (before the exhibition of the bill) : before the commencement of the suit. **Ante litem motam**: before suit brought. **Ante occasum solis**: before sunset. **Ante omnia** : before all else, first of all.

Antejuramentum, *l.* A preliminary oath required of the accuser, to prosecute ; and of the accused, that he was not guilty ; in old English law.

Antenati, *l.* Persons born before a particular event.

Antichresis, *l.* A sort of mortgage, in which the debtor transfers the thing or estate to the creditor, who is entitled to retain the use and profits in lieu of interest.

Anique temps, Antic, *fr.* Old time, of old.

Antiqua statuta, *l.* The Acts of Parliament from Richard I. to Edward III. **Ut antiquum**: v. *Feudum.* **Antiquum dominicum**: ancient demesne. **Antiqua custuma** : v. *Custuma.*

Anuels livres, *fr.* The *Year books.*

Aore, *fr.* Now.

Aparelle, aparaile, *fr.* Ready.

Aperte, *fr.* Open ; plain. **Apertement**: openly.

Apertus, *l.* Open. **Aperta brevia**: open writs, unsealed. **Apertum factum** : an overt act.

Apex juris, *l.* A subtlety of law. **Apices juris non sunt jura** : the mere subtleties of law are not law.

Apostata capiendo, *l.* v. *De.*

Apostles. The papers forming the record on appeal, and transmitted, in civil or admiralty practice, from the lower to the higher court. Brief letters of dismissal, given the appellant, and stating that the record will be transmitted.

Apostille, apostyle, *fr.* An addition ; a marginal note.

Apparator, apparitor, *l.* A messenger who serves process in the ecclesiastical courts.

Apparent heir. One who will be the heir if he live until the ancestor's death. In Scotland, the heir after the ancestor's death and before he enters.

Apparere, *l.* To appear. **Apparitio** : an appearance.

Appeal. 1. The complaint, and removal of a cause, to a higher court, for error or informality, for the purpose of trial or review. 2. In English criminal law, the accusation, by one private person against another, of some heinous crime, demanding punishment on behalf of the party injured ; v. *Approver, Battel.*

Appearance. The coming of a party into court, in person or by attorney.

Appel, *fr.* An appeal ; a challenge.

Appellate. Having cognizance of appeals.

Appendant. Annexed, or belonging to anything, and going with it. Like **appurtenant,** except that rights appendant to land cannot be created by grant.

Appiert, appers, apierge, *fr.* It appears.

Application of payments. The appropriation of money, paid by a debtor, to some particular debt.

Appointment. v. *Power.*

Appreciare, *l.* To appraise, estimate.

Apprentice. A person, usually a minor, bound by indenture to serve another for a term of years, in consideration of being supported and taught a trade.

Apprenticii ad legem, *l.* Barristers at law.

Apprester, *fr.* To prepare. **Apprest** : ready.

Apprimes, *fr.* First.

Appris, apprise, *fr.* Learned, skilled.

Approbate and reprobate. To approve and reject; to take advantage of one part of a document and reject the rest.

Appropriation. The perpetual annexing of an ecclesiastical benefice to the use of a spiritual corporation sole or aggregate. **Appropriation of Payments**: v. *Application.*

Approver, *fr.,* **Approbare,** *l.,* **Approve.** To improve; to cultivate and enclose waste land.

Approver. A person indicted of a capital crime who confessed the crime before pleading and accused [appealed] another of the same crime. This latter was called the **appellee**; and if he was found guilty, the approver was acquitted **ex debito justitiæ**; otherwise the accuser was hanged upon his own confession. The accusation was called an **appeal**, and was triable by *battel,* like the ordinary appeal. This method of **approvement** is now superseded by *queen's* or *state's evidence.*

Appurtenant. Belonging to, accessory to; v. *Appendant.* A thing incident to something else and of a different nature. It may be either corporeal or incorporeal, and may be created by grant, accession, or prescription.

Appurtenances. Things appurtenant.

Apres, *fr.* After; afterwards. **Apres que**: after that. **Apres midi**: after noon. **Cy apres**: thereafter.

Apta viro, *l.* Marriageable.

Apud, *l.* Among; with; at. **Apud acta**: among the acts, among the recorded proceedings, in presence of the judge.

Aqua, *l.* Water. **Aqua cedit solo** (water follows the land): water goes with the land which it covers. **Aqua currit, et debet currere, ut currere solebat**: water runs, and ought to run, as it used to run. **Aquæ ductus**: the right of conducting water through the land of another. **Aquæ haustus**: the right of drawing water from the well or spring of another.

Aquagium, *l.,* **Aquage.** A water-course; toll paid for water carriage; *ewage.*

Arare, *l.,* **Arer,** *fr.* To ear, to plough. **Arabant**: they ploughed, applied to such vassals as held their land by service of ploughing the lord's manor lands. **Aralia, aratia**: plough-lands.

Aratum terræ, *l.* A plough-land, as much as can be tilled by one plough.

Arbitrament and Award. A plea that the matter has been referred to arbitration, and a decision given.

Arbitrement, *fr.*, **Arbitrium,** *l.* An award, in arbitration. **Arbitrium est judicium:** an award is a judgment.

Arbor, *l.* A tree. **Arbor civilis, consanguinitatis:** a family-tree. **Arbor dum crescit, lignum dum crescere nescit:** [called] a tree while it grows, wood while it cannot grow [i. e. when cut].

Arcana imperii, *l.* Secrets of state.

Archdeacon. The ecclesiastical officer next the bishop, appointed by him and having a court of concurrent jurisdiction in the diocese or a part of it. v. *Court,* 81.

Arches Court. v. *Court,* 83.

Archiepiscopus, *l.*, **Archievesque,** *fr.* Archbishop.

Arcta et salva custodia, *l.* In close and safe keeping.

Arer, *fr.* To plough. **Arer et semer:** to plough and sow.

Arere, *fr.*, **Aretro,** *t.* Behind; in arrear; back; again.

Arg., Arguendo, *l.* In arguing; by way of argument.

Argentum Dei, *l.* (God's money.) Earnest-money.

Argumentative. Indirect, inferential. Used of a plea, the important part of which is stated by implication only.

Argumentum, *l.* Argument. **Argumentum a communiter accidentibus in jure frequens est:** an argument from commonly occurring things is frequent in law. **Argumentum a divisione est fortissimum in lege:** an argument by division [of the subject] is of very great force in law. **Argumentum a similis valet in lege:** an argument from analogy is good in law. **Argumentum ab auctoritate:** au argument from authority [judicial decisions]. **Ab impossibili:** from an impossibility. **Ab inconvenienti:** from an inconvenience. **Ad crumenam:** to the purse. **Ad hominem:** to the person, personal. **Ad ignorantiam:** to ignorance [relying on a sophism which the hearers cannot detect]. **Ad verecundiam:** to modesty [appealing to the sense of decency].

Arma, *l.* Weapons offensive and defensive. **Arma libera:** free arms, a sword and lance given to a servant when set free. **Arma moluta:** sharpened weapons. **Arma reversata** (reversed arms): a punishment for treason or felony. **Arma in armatos jura sinunt:** the laws permit using arms against those armed.

Armiger, Armig., *l.* An esquire; one entitled to bear a coat of arms; a servant to a knight.

Arpen, arpent, *fr.* A measure of land.

Arra, arræ, arrhæ, *l.,* **arrhes,** *fr.* Earnest-money.

Arraign. To call one accused of crime before court to answer.

Array. The whole body of jurors summoned to attend court. The list of jurymen, arranged in the panel.

Arrears, arrearages. Money due on rents, accounts, or interest unpaid at the given time.

Arrect, arrette, *fr., l.* To accuse; accused.

Arrentatio, *l.* A renting; arrentation, licensing an owner of lands in a forest to enclose them with a low hedge and small ditch, under a yearly rent.

Arrer. v. *Arer.* **Arrere.** v. *Arere.*

Arrestare, *l.,* **Arrester,** *fr.* To arrest, to take into legal custody.

Arrest of Judgment. A staying of judgment after verdict for error apparent on the record.

Arrestandis bonis ne dissipentur, *l.* A writ which lay for one whose cattle or goods were taken by another who was likely to make away with them and unable to make amends.

Arrestment. Arrest. In Scotch law, a process of attachment or garnishment. **Arrestee**: the garnishee.

Arrettare, *l.,* **arretter,** *fr.* To accuse.

Arrha. v. *Arra.* Earnest-money. v. *Denarius Dei.*

Arriage and Carriage. Indefinite services formerly exacted from tenants.

Arser in le main. Burning in the hand; the punishment of those pleading their clergy; v. *Benefit of Clergy.*

Arson. The wilful burning of another's house.

Art and part. A term used in Scotch law of one who is accessary to a crime, or aiding and abetting in it.

Article. A species of pleading in the English ecclesiastical courts. The division or paragraph of a document. **Articles of faith, religion,** or **the thirty-nine articles**: a statement of the faith of the Church of England, formed by Cranmer, and revised by the Convocation of 1562. **Articles of the peace**: in English law, a complaint made before a court or justice of the peace against a person from whom the complainant fears injury to person or property, whereby the party complained of is forced to find *sureties of the peace.* Popularly termed **swearing the peace** against one.

Articled clerk. A person bound to serve with some practising attorney for his instruction until admitted himself to practice.

Articulus, *l.* An article; a point. **In articulo mortis**: at the point of death. **Articuli super Chartas**: the Stat. 28 Edw. III. st. 3.

Arura, *l.* A ploughing; a day's work at ploughing.

Asaver, asçavoir, *fr.* To wit; to say; to be understood.

Asceverer, *fr.* To affirm.

Ascient, *fr.* Knowing; knowingly.

Ascripticii, adscriptitii, *l.* Tenants by ancient demesne; in civil law, naturalized foreigners.

Ascun, *fr.* Any one, some one.

Asoyne, *fr.* v. *Essoin.*

Asportare, *l.* To carry away. **Asportavit**: he carried away. v. *De bonis asportatis.*

Ass. Abb. from **Assisa**, an assize.

Assaltus, *l.* An assault.

Assartare, *l.,* **Assart, essart.** To pull up trees by the roots, clear land in a forest. **Assartum, assart**: cleared land.

Assault. An attempt of one man to do physical injury to another, real or apparent, and coupled with real or apparent power to injure. v. *Battery.*

Assayer, *fr.* To essay, try. **Assaye, assaie**: an assay, an examination or trial.

Assecurare, *l.* To make secure; to assure; to confirm. **Assecuratio**: assecuration, assurance.

Assembly unlawful. The meeting of three or more persons to do an unlawful act.

Assensu patris. v. *Dower.*

Assertare, etc. v. *Assartare.*

Asses, assez, *fr.* Enough.

Assets. Property available for debts or legacies. **Assets entre mains**: assets in hand, property which comes at once into the hands of the executor or trustee for the payment of debts. **Assets per discent**: property which goes to the heir, chargeable only with the ancestor's specialty debts; otherwise called **real assets.** **Equitable assets**: those which creditors can reach only through a court of equity. **Legal assets**: those in the hands of the executor or administrator, which may be reached in an action at law. **Marshalling of assets**: an equitable doctrine, by which, when there are two classes of assets and some creditors can enforce their claims against both and others against only one, the former class of creditors are compelled to exhaust the assets against which they alone have a claim before having recourse to the other assets. Thus providing for the settlement of as many claims as possible.

Assignatus utitur jure auctoris: an assignee enjoys the rights of his principal [assignor].

Assignee, assign. A person to whom a right of property is transferred.

Assignment. A transfer of property. **Assignment of dower**: the ascertaining and setting out of a widow's share in her husband's estate. **Assignment of errors**: the statement of the case of the plaintiff in error, setting forth the errors complained of, and placed on the records; v. *New assignment*.

Assis, assys, *fr.* Situated; fixed; assessed.

Assisa, *l.,* **Assise,** *fr.,* **Assize.** A jury, inquest, summoned by a writ of assize. Also, a court; the sittings of a court; an ordinance or statute; a tax or tribute; an adjustment or measure; an action at law, a real action; a writ. **The assizes**: sessions of **courts of assize and nisi prius,** which are composed of two or more commissioners (in England) called judges of **assize** and **nisi prius,** who are sent, by special commission from the Crown, on circuits all around the kingdom, to try, by a jury of the respective counties, such matters of fact as are then under dispute at Westminster Hall. These judges are judges of the superior common-law courts, and the successors of the ancient "justices in eyre," **justiciarii in itinere**; they sit by virtue of several authorities, viz.: 1. Commission of **oyer and terminer,** to deal with treasons, felonies, etc. 2. Of **gaol delivery,** to try every prisoner in gaol, for whatever offence. 3. Of **nisi prius,** to try all questions of fact on cases in which issue has been joined in the courts of Westminster. 4. Of **peace,** by which all justices of the peace and sheriffs are bound to be present at their sittings. 5. Of **assize,** to take assizes and have **jurisdiction** of writs of assize. **Action of assize**: a writ

and real action, having for its object the recovery of lands
whereof the demandant or his ancestors had unjustly been disseised. It was not necessary, as in a writ of entry, to show the
unlawful beginning of the tenant's possession. **Rents of assize** : the certain established rents of the freeholders and ancient
copyholders of a manor, which cannot be departed from or
varied. Those of the freeholders are frequently called **chief-
rents,** *reditus capitales ;* and both sorts are called **quitrents,**
quieti reditus, because thereby the tenant goes quit and free of
other services. **Assisa cadere** (to fall from the assize) : to be
nonsuited. **Assisa cadit in juratam** (the assize falls to a
jury) : the assize is converted into a jury. **Assisa continuanda** :
an ancient writ directed to the justices of assize to continue a
cause, when time is desired for the production of records. **Assisa proroganda** : a writ to stay proceedings at the assizes
because one of the parties was engaged in the King's business.
**Assize of darrein presentment, Assisa ultimæ præsenta-
tionis,** *l.* An assize of last presentation. An action to determine who had the gift of a church living, superseded by **quare
impedit. Assize of fresh force, Assisa friscæ fortiæ,** *l.*
An action, assize, which lay by a custom of a city or borough for
the recovery of lands of which the demandant had been disseised
within forty days. **Assize of mort d'ancestor,** *fr.,* **Assisa
mortis antecessoris,** *l.* An assize to recover land of which the
demandant's father, mother, uncle, aunt, brother, sister, nephew,
or niece died seised, and a stranger abated. **Assize of novel
disseisin, Assisa novæ disseisinæ,** *l.* An assize to recover
land of which the complainant had been disseised since the last
circuit of the justices in eyre, i. e. within seven years. **Assize of
nuisance, Assisa de nocumento,** *l.* An assize to remedy a
nuisance, by having it abated and recovering damages. **Assize
of utrum, assisa juris utrum,** *l.* An assize sometimes called
the parson's writ of right, which lay for him or a vicar to recover
church lands alienated by his predecessors. **Grand assize.** A
peculiar jury, introduced by Henry II. and authorized in lieu
of battel for the trial of writs of right. The sheriff returned
four knights, who chose twelve others, making in all sixteen
recognitors. All these assizes are now obsolete.

Assisores, *l.,* **Assisors.** Assessors ; jurors.

Assistance. A writ issued by Chancery to execute a decree for the possession of lands.

Association. A writ or patent addressed to the justices of the assize, commanding and authorizing them to associate others with them as justices, usually learned sergeants at law or the clerks of the assize. Granted at suit of a party when a justice dies or is disabled from holding the assizes.

Assoil, Assoilzie, *sc.,* **Assoiler,** *fr.* To acquit, absolve; to deliver from excommunication.

Assumpsit, *l.* He assumed; he undertook. A promise, contract, undertaking. The name of an action on the case, which lies for the party injured by the non-performance of a parol contract. If the contract or promise is express, the action is called **special assumpsit; indebitatus assumpsit** or **general assumpsit,** if implied by law. This latter action generally applies only to contracts resulting in a debt; and judgment is given as damages for the detention of the debt, differing thus from the action of *Debt.* **Assumpserunt super se**: they undertook.

Assurance, Assurantia, *l.* An instrument used as evidence of the title to land. **Common assurances**: a man's title-deeds. Also, *Insurance,* q. v. The word has lately been applied to *life insurance* to distinguish it from *fire* and *marine.*

Assythment, assithment. An action in Scotch law, brought by the relatives or personal representatives of a murdered person against the guilty person before the trial of the latter. Damages were awarded called an assythment, whence the name of the action.

Astitution. An arraignment.

Astre, *fr.,* **Astrum,** *l.* A hearth; a house. **Astrer, Astrarius,** *l.* : a householder; belonging to, or born in, the house. v. *Hæres.*

Astrihilthet, *sax.* A penalty of double the damage for breach of the King's peace.

At, *fr.* Hath; and.

At arm's length. Out of another's undue influence or control. **At bar**: before the court. **At large**: not limited to any particular matter, place, or person; not under physical restraint.

Atia, acya, etc., *l.* Malice; hatred.

Atilium, *l.* Tackle; rigging. **Atilia**: the harness of a horse or plough.

Atrium, *l.* A court before a house; a church-yard.

Attach, Attachiare, *l.* To take a person or goods by command-ment of a writ or precept, and keep for presentment in court. Differing from an **arrest** in that the latter term is only used of persons; and a person **arrested** is handed over to a higher authority for keeping.

Attachiamenta bonorum. A distress formerly levied by bailiffs upon the goods of one sued for a personal debt, as a security to answer to the action.

Attachment, Attachiamentum, *l.* 1. A process of taking into custody a person or property; it issues from courts of record in cases of contempt. If issuing only against the person, it is called **personal attachment.** 2. **Attachment of goods,** taken either as security or to give jurisdiction of an action against a foreigner, in which latter case it was called **Foreign attachment.** This existed in old English law, and is now common in some of the Eastern States. 3. **Foreign attachment:** a process, arising out of a custom of London, by which the debtor's goods or debts were reached by the creditor in the hands of a third person. Called also **Factorizing** or **Trustee Process,** or **Garnishment.** All these writs of attachment were issued at the institution or during the process of an action in a court of record. **Attachment of privilege:** a process whereby a man privileged to litigate in a certain court (as attorneys and officers in their own court) calls another into that court to answer to some action. Also, a writ issued to apprehend a person in a privileged place. **Attachments, Court of:** v. *Court,* 75.

Attainder. The extinction of civil rights and capacities which resulted upon judgment of death or outlawry for treason or felony. It included forfeiture of property; **corruption of blood,** so that nothing could pass by inheritance to the heirs of the person attainted, nor could he himself inherit from others; and inability to bear witness in a court of law, to sue or be sued, or even to be put on trial again for felony.

Attaint. An old writ brought for the reversal of an improper ver-dict. The action was tried by a jury of twenty-four men; and if the first verdict was found false, the twelve men of the first jury were adjudged infamous.

Atteindre, *fr.* To attaint, convict. **Atteynte, Atteintz:** attaint, attainted; convicted; found guilty.

Attendant terms. Long leases or mortgages, held by the owner or his trustee as a distinct and additional title, to make his estate more secure.

Attentare, *l.* To attempt. **Attentat** (he attempts): a wrong motion or act in a cause made by the judge *a quo* pending an appeal.

Atterminare, *l.,* **Atterminer,** *fr.* To attermine; to delay; to grant time for the payment of a debt.

Attestation. Evidence. Testimony. The act of witnessing the execution of a legal document and subscribing one's own name as testimony of the fact. **Attest:** to witness, a witness.

Attile, attilamentum, *l.* Tackle; v. *Atilium.*

Attingere, *l.* To touch; to amount to. **Atting', attingent:** they amount to, attain. **Attincta:** an attaint. **Attinctus:** attainted.

Attornare, *l.,* **Attorner,** *fr.,* **Attorn.** To transfer; to consent to a transfer; to put in one's place; to make attornment. **Attornment:** the act of a tenant in consenting to the transfer of the reversion, with its rents and services, to a new lord, and in acknowledging the new landlord.

Attornatus, *l.,* **Attorney.** One who has authority to act for another. If in conducting suits, he is termed **attorney-at-law**; v. *Barrister.* If by special authority for one act, or, more broadly, in matters *in pais* generally, attorney **in factum** [in fact]. **Attorney-general:** the chief law officer of the government.

Au, *fr.* At the; to the; until. **Au besoin** (in case of need): a phrase used in the direction of a bill of exchange, pointing out some person to whom application may be made for payment in case of the refusal of the drawee to pay. **Au ces temps:** at that time. **Au dernier:** at last. **Au plus:** at most. **Au quel:** to which. **Au tiel forme:** in such manner.

Auceps syllabarum, *l.* (A catcher of syllables.) A quibbler.

Auctor, *fr., l.* A plaintiff; a principal; a vendor.

Aucun, *fr.* Some; some one; any one. **Aucune foits:** sometimes. **Aucunement:** somewhat.

Audi alteram partem, *l.* Hear the other side.

Audience Court. v. *Court*, 83.

Audiendo et terminando, *l.* *Oyer et terminer ;* v. *Assize.*

Audita querela, *l.* (The complaint having been heard.) A writ which lies for a defendant who is in danger of execution, to recall or prevent the execution for some cause which has happened since judgment.

Auditor, *l.*, **Auditor.** One who examines accounts. In practice, a person appointed by the court to take and state an account.

Auditus, *l.* Hearing; oyer.

Augmentation. The increase of crown revenues arising from the suppression of religious houses, 27 Hen. VIII., and the appropriation of their revenues. A court erected by Henry VIII. to determine controversies about the lands of such houses; v. *Court*, 43.

Aujourd'huy, *fr.* To-day.

Aula, *l.* A hall, court. **Aula regia, regis :** the supreme court of England established by William the Conqueror, afterwards divided into three common-law courts and Chancery ; v. *Court*, 4.

Aumone, Almoign, *fr.* Alms.

Auprès, *fr.* Near; nigh; about.

Aurum reginæ, *l.* *Queen's gold.*

Aussi, ausint, etc., *fr.* Also; in this manner.

Aut, *l.* Either; or. **Aut eo circiter :** or thereabouts.

Autant, *fr.* As much; so much; like as.

Auter, autre, *fr.* Another; other. **Auter action pendant** (another action pending) : a plea in abatement stating that a prior suit has been begun for the same cause. **En autre droit :** in right of another. **Pur auter vie :** for the life of another. **Auterment :** otherwise. **Autrefois :** at another time ; formerly ; heretofore. **Autrefois acquit** (formerly acquitted) : a plea of a criminal in bar to an indictment, that he has once before been acquitted of the same offence ; v. *Plea.* So also **Autrefois convict,** that he has been once before convicted; and **Autrefois attaint,** once before attainted ; v. *Attainder.*

Auxi, *fr.* Also ; so. **Auxybien :** as well.

Auxilium *l.* Aid ; an aid. **Auxilium curiæ :** an old precept of the court citing one person to warrant something, at the suit of another.

Avail, aval, *fr.* Downwards ; below. v. *Amont.*

Availe, *fr.* Profit; proceeds. **Avail of marriage** : value of marriage ; v. *Valor maritagii, Marriage.*

Aval, *fr.* The guaranty of a bill of exchange, or note.

Avaler, *fr.* To descend ; lower; put down ; swallow.

Avant, *fr.* Before; forward. **Issint avant** : so on. **Avant dit** : aforesaid.

Avanture, Aventure, *fr.* Chance ; mischance ; adventure.

Avec, avecques, *fr.* With.

Aveigner, avener, *fr.* To come, become; happen.

Avenage, *fr.* Oats, given a landlord in lieu of rents or services.

Aver. To state ; to plead ; to avouch or verify.

Aver, avoir, *fr.* To have ; v. *À.*

Average. 1. A service with cattle, due to a lord by his tenant. 2. A medium, mean. 3. A loss or damage to ship or cargo at sea. 4. The adjustment or apportionment of such loss among the owners and underwriters. 5. A small duty paid the master for care of the cargo, over and above his freight. **General average** : when part of a ship's cargo is destroyed or injured in order to save the ship, the loss is apportioned among the proprietors in general or their underwriters. Also called **Gross average.** **Particular average** : partial loss or damage to goods which must be borne by the owner, and is settled by the underwriters according to the ratio which the goods lost bore to the whole goods insured. This is called an **Average, or partial loss.** **Petty average** : small charges paid by the master for the benefit of the ship and cargo, such as pilotage, towage, anchorage, etc.

Aver-corn. A reserved rent in corn, paid to religious houses by their tenants. **Aver-land** : land ploughed and manured by the tenants. **Aver-peny** : money paid to be freed from doing the King's averages or carriages. v. *Average,* 1.

Averium, *l.,* **averia.** A working beast, an heriot ; cattle. **Averia carucæ** : beasts of the plough. **Averia elongata** : cattle eloigned, carried away. **Averiis captis in withernam** (cattle taken in withernam) : same as *Capias in withernam.*

Averment. The ending part of a plea in confession and avoidance, or any affirmative pleading, which offers to verify the plea; the **verification.** v. *Aver.*

Avers, *fr.* Cattle, beasts ; cf. *Affer.*

Aversio periculi, *l.* A turning away of peril; used of the contract of insurance.

Avisare, *l.*, **aviser,** *fr.* To advise; consult; deliberate. **Avisamentum,** *l.* : counsel. **Avis,** *fr.*. advised, instructed.

Avoidance. A making void; an evading or escaping; the state of being vacant. v. *Confession*, *Plea.*

Avoir, *fr.* To have. Property; means; estate.

Avoucher, *fr.* The calling into court, by a tenant, of a person bound to warrant, to defend the title or yield him other lands.

Avouterie, *fr.*, **Avowtry.** Adultery.

Avow, Avowson, etc. v. *Advow*, etc.

Avowry. A pleading in replevin whereby the defendant avows [confesses] the taking, and seeks to justify it on his own right; v. *Conusance, Cognizance.*

Avulsion. Earth suddenly removed by water and placed on the land of another; or land joined to another's land by change in the bed of a stream. Such land remains the property of its original owner.

Award. The decision of an arbitrator, referees, or commissioners.

Away-going crop. A crop sown during the last year of a tenancy, but not ripe until after the end of the term.

Ay. In the beginning of French words; v. *Ai.*

B.

Bacberend, *sax.* (Carrying on the back.) A term used of a thief caught with the stolen goods.

Back-bond. In Scotch law, a declaration of trust.

Backing. Indorsement. **Backing a warrant:** the indorsement of a warrant, issued in one county, by a justice of the peace of another, which enables it to be served in the latter county.

Backside. A yard behind a house.

Bail, Baila, *l.*, **Baile, baille,** *fr.* Delivery; livery; custody; guardianship. The setting at liberty of a person in custody upon others becoming sureties for his appearance at a day and place assigned. Also, the persons who become such sureties; differing from *mainpernors* in that **bail** may confine and keep the person bailed. **Bail below,** or **to the sheriff:** when a

bail-bond is given to the sheriff to secure the appearance of a person arrested on mesne process. **Bail above** or **to the action**: when a recognizance is entered into that the defendant in an action shall pay the costs and judgment, or be surrendered into custody. **Common bail**: bail with fictitious sureties, amounting only to entering an appearance. **Special bail**: bail with *bona fide*, responsible sureties. **Justifying bail**: ascertaining the sufficiency of the bail. **Bail Court**: v. *Court*, 9.

Bailee. The person to whom a bailment is made.

Bailie. In Scotch law, a magistrate, alderman, bailiff; v. *Court*, 92.

Bailiff. A keeper; a sheriff's officer; a land steward.

Bailiwick, Ballivia, *l.* A sheriff's jurisdiction; or a liberty exempted therefrom; a county.

Bailment. A delivery of goods by one person to another for a purpose or trust; the contract resulting therefrom.

Bailor. The person making a bailment.

Bailpiece. A memorandum of special *bail* signed by the judge and filed in court.

Ban, Banns. A proclamation; edict; the announcement in church of a proposed marriage. The spiritual judge might dispense with these by giving a marriage license; but a marriage without either banns or license was void and a penal offence.

Banc, Bank, Bancus, *l.* A bench; the full bench; the full court, as distinguished from the sitting of a single judge at **nisi prius.** **Communis Bancus,** abb. **C. B.**: the Common Bench, the English *Court of Common Pleas*. **Bancus Regis,** abb. **B. R.**: the King's Bench; v. *Court*, 8. **Banci narratores**: sergeants at law who enjoyed the monopoly of practice in the C. B.

Bank-note, Bank-bill. A promissory note issued by a bank and payable to bearer on demand, intended for circulation as money.

Bankruptcy Courts: v. *Court*, 50.

Bar. A partition running across a court-room, separating the public and outer barristers from the court, attorneys, sergeants, Queen's counsel, officers, and parties appearing in person. **At bar**: before court; before the full court, as distinguished from *nisi prius*. **Pleas in bar**: pleas attacking the right of action on grounds of fact; v. *Plea*. **To bar**: to defeat, end, cut off.

Bargain and sale. A method of conveying land without livery of seisin, under the statute of uses, for a *valuable* consideration.

Barmote. v. *Court*, 73.

Baro, *l.,* **Baron,** *fr.* A freeman; a baron. **Baron et feme**: husband and wife. **Court Baron**: v. *Court*, 11, 34.

Baron. 1. A vassal holding directly of the King. 2. The fifth and lowest English degree of nobility. 3. A judge of the Court of Exchequer.

Barra, *l.,* **Barre,** *fr.* A plea in bar; the bar of a court.

Barratry. Fraudulent, negligent, or wilfully injurious conduct on the part of the master and crew of a ship, to the damage, and without the knowledge of, the owner.

Barretry. The offence of frequently exciting groundless suits.

Barrister. In England, a counsel admitted to plead at the bar. **Outer or utter barristers**: those who appear without the bar, as distinguished from **inner barristers** (sergeants, or Queen's counsel). Barristers conduct cases in court, while **attorneys** prepare the pleadings and see to matters out of court.

Bas, *fr.* Low. **Bas cur**: an inferior court, not of record. **Bas chevaliers**: inferior knights holding by base tenure.

Base fee. 1. A fee with a qualification; determinable upon some collateral event. 2. A tenure in fee at the will of the lord. **Base tenure**: by base services, as by villenage or customary services.

Bastard. In the common law, a person born out of matrimony, or under circumstances which render it impossible for him to have been the son of the husband. **Bastard-eigné,** *fr.*: the son of two unmarried persons who afterwards intermarry and have another son. The latter was called **mulier puisné. Bastardus nullius est filius; aut filius populi**: a bastard is no man's son; or the son of the people.

Bastardy process. The statutory method of procedure against the putative father to secure the bastard's maintenance.

Baston, *fr.* A staff or club; an officer, tipstaff.

Battel, Bataile, *fr.* Combat; duel. **Wager of battel**: a method of trial by personal conflict which prevailed in the courts of chivalry; on appeals and approvements for felony; and on writs of right, in which last case the parties might fight by champions. If the appellee was vanquished, he was hanged; if he killed the appellant or maintained the fight from sunrise to star-rise he was acquitted. If the appellant became recreant and pronounced the word *craven* (to beg) he lost his *liberam legem* and became infamous; and the appellee recovered damages and was forever quit.

Battery. The physical injury of one person by another; usually employed, in connection with assault, of *unlawful* injury.

Beasts of the chase. The buck, doe, fox, marten, and roe. **Beasts of the forest**: the hart, hind, boar, and wolf. **Beasts of the warren**: the hare, coney, pheasant, and partridge.

Bedel. A crier; an apparitor; a bailiff; a beadle.

Bellum, *l.* War. **Bello parta cedunt reipublicæ**: things acquired in war go to the state.

Bench. A seat of judgment; a court; the judges; v. *Court,* 5, 18. **Bench warrant**: a warrant issued by the judge or court itself for the arrest of a person indicted, or for contempt; a justice's warrant being issued by a justice of the peace or magistrate.

Benchers. The governing members of the English Inns of Court.

Bene, *l.* Well; sufficiently; in due form.

Benedicta est expositio quando res redimitur a destructione: that is a blessed interpretation when a thing is saved from destruction [by which effect is given to the instrument].

Benefice. In England, a church living.

Beneficiary. The *cestui que trust.*

Beneficium. A benefice. **Beneficium clericale**: benefit of clergy.

Benefit of Clergy. A privilege of exemption from capital punishment, granted to all who could read. The prisoner was then handed over to the Court Christian, where he cleared himself upon his oath and that of twelve persons as his **compurgators.** Later, it could be claimed by laymen only once; and they were burned in the hand. The privilege only applied to capital felonies; and was gradually removed by statutes.

Beneplacitum, *l.* Good pleasure. **Durante beneplacito ipsius**: during his good pleasure.

Benevolence. An extraordinary aid granted by freemen to the sovereign, nominally voluntary.

Benigne faciendæ sunt interpretationes, propter simplicitatem laicorum, ut res magis valeat quam pereat; et verba intentioni, non e contra, debent inservire, *l.* Interpretations are to be made liberally, by reason of the ignorance of laymen, that the instrument may have effect rather than be void; and words ought to be made subject to the intention, not the contrary. **Benignior sententia in verbis generalibus seu dubiis est præferenda**: the more liberal meaning of general or doubtful words is to be preferred.

Bequeath. To give personal property by will.

Berenica, bernita, *l.* A manor; part of a manor; a hamlet appurtenant to a manor; a town.

Berghmote. The old name of the *Barmote Court;* v. *Court,* 73.

Beria, *l.,* **Berg.** 1. A plain, an open field. 2. A berg; a manor; a burgh.

Bernet, *sax.* Arson; any capital offence.

Besael, Besayle, etc., *fr.* A great-grandfather. A writ like *Aiel,* brought on the seisin of a great-grandfather; v. *Aiel.*

Bestes, bestiales, etc., *fr.* Beasts; cattle.

Betterment. A permanent improvement or addition made to lands or houses by the occupant; something more than repairs.

Beyond sea, beyond the four seas. Out of the kingdom of Great Britain and Ireland. Out of the United States. Out of the State.

Bien, *fr.* Well; advisable; lawfully. **Del bien estre**: *de bene esse,* q. v.

Biennium, *l.* The period of two years.

Biens, *fr.* Goods; goods and chattels; property in general. **Biens meubles**: *bona mobilia,* movable goods.

Bigamy. The offence of having two wives or husbands at the same time. In the civil and canon law, having them either at the same time, or one after the death of the other.

Bilagines, bilagæ, *l.* By-laws; laws of towns.

Bilateral. Two-sided. v. *Contract.*

Biline. Collateral.

Bilinguis, *l.* Double-tongued; one speaking two languages. Applied to a jury **de medietate linguæ,** allowed in England in cases between an Englishman and a foreigner, where half the jury were of the latter's nation; a jury of the **half-tongue.**

Bill. A written statement or declaration; a complaint; a record; an account. The word has many special and limited meanings.

I. In legal procedure. (**Bill for cancellation**: v. *To perpetuate,* I. 13.) 1. **Bill in chancery or equity**: the complaint of a suitor in chancery, in the form of a petition, stating the case and praying relief or discovery. It is the usual mode of beginning a chancery suit, and corresponds to the declaration in an action at law. 2. **Bill of conformity**: a bill in equity filed by an executor or administrator against the creditors when the estate is so much involved that he cannot safely administer it without the direction of a court of chancery. 3. **Bill of costs**: an itemized statement of the costs awarded the plaintiff or defendant in an action. 4. **Bill of discovery**: a bill in equity praying for the disclosure of books, writings, or facts lying within the defendant's knowledge; and claiming no other relief except delay of a process or suit; v. *Discovery*. 5. **Bill of exceptions**: a statement of the directions given by the judge, or his decisions on points of law, to which the party excepting objects. When signed by the judge, the bill becomes part of the record, and may be brought before the court in banc, or a superior court, for review. 6. **Bill of indictment**: a written accusation of one or more persons of a crime or misdemeanor, presented to a grand jury. If they decide the accused ought to be tried, the return is made a "**true bill**," and thenceforward it is called the **indictment**. Otherwise the return is made "not a true bill," "not found," or "**ignoramus**" (we do not know). 7. **Bill of interpleader**: when a person possesses goods or money under no claim of title, and two or more parties make such claim, he being in danger of a suit from one or both of them; he may have this bill in equity to force them to interplead, that is, to litigate the title among themselves, and get judgment which is conclusive upon all. In England, there is a summary process of interpleader at law. 8. **Bill of Middlesex**: a civil process by which the Court of King's Bench sitting in Middlesex assumed jurisdiction in civil cases without an original writ from the Crown. It was founded on a fictitious trespass committed within the county, of which the K. B. always had jurisdiction; and was a kind of **capias**. If the defendant was not in Middlesex, a writ of **latitat** issued on the return of **non est inventus** (he has not been found) directed to the sheriff of the county where he was, alleging that the defendant *lurks* and wanders about in such county. The true cause of action was introduced, in both writs, by au **ac etiam**, q. v. 9. **Bill for a new trial**: a bill in equity praying for an injunction after a judgment at law, on grounds of fraud in obtaining the judgment.   10. **Bill** or **Origi-nal Bill** : the old method of commencing an action in the K. B., without a writ.   It resembled a declaration, and was in the form of a complaint, alleging a fictitious trespass to give jurisdiction; v. *Bill of Middlesex*.   11. **Bill of particulars** : the itemized statement of the demand or debts for which an action is brought, or of the defendant's set-off.   12. **Bill of peace** : a bill in equity brought by one threatened with a number of suits by one or more persons based on the same claim, or involving the same contro-versy, to obtain a perpetual injunction of such suits.   13. **Bill to perpetuate testimony** : a bill in equity brought to obtain and preserve the testimony of witnesses with reference to some mat-ter which is not in litigation, nor can be put in litigation by the plaintiff.   The converse of a **Bill for cancellation**, which is brought to destroy evidence which may affect the plaintiff injuri-ously at some future time.   So **Bills to remove cloud upon title**, to settle and confirm a title which is really good, when the possessor fears possible injury from evidence or deeds in posses-sion of another, who has not brought action.   All these bills may be called (14.) **Bills quia timet** (because he fears), which last title also includes bills filed by a remainderman of realty, or a person having a future interest in personalty, to prevent injury to such property or his rights thereto from the neglect or default of another.   15. **Bill of privilege** : the old method of proceed-ing against any attorney or officer of the court, who was not liable to arrest.   16. **Bill of review** : a bill to review a judg-ment in chancery, either for error or by reason of new evidence. 17. **Bill of revivor** : one brought to continue a suit in equity which abated, as by death, or marriage of the (female) plain-tiff, before its proper consummation.   18. **Supplemental bill** : one filed in addition to an original bill in equity, to supply some defect by new matter which cannot be introduced by amend-ment.   19. **Bill to take testimony de bene esse** : a bill brought to get the testimony of an aged or infirm witness, or one about to leave the country, to a suit already begun ; v. *De bene esse*.   20. **True bill** : v. *Bill*, I. 6.

II.   In legislation or constitutional law.   The draft of a law sub-mitted to a legislative body for enactment.   A special act.   The solemn declaration of a legislature.   1. **Bill of attainder** : an act of Parliament or a legislature attainting a person; v. *Attainder*. 2. **Bill of indemnity**: an act of Parliament passed every session for the relief of those who have, unwittingly or unavoidably, not taken the necessary oaths of office. 3. **Bill of mortality**: the list of deaths and births in a municipal district. These records were introduced in London about the time of the Plague; hence the expression was used to designate the city limits. 4. **Bill of rights**: a legislative declaration of popular rights and liberties, especially that of 1 W. & M., st. 2, c. 2.

III. In mercantile law: the written statement of a debt, demand, or contract. 1. **Bill of adventure**: a writing signed by a merchant or ship-owner to the effect that the property and risk in goods shipped in his own name belong to another, to whom he is accountable for the proceeds; v. *Adventure*. 2. **Bills of credit**: paper issued by the authority of a state, on the faith of the state, designed to circulate as money. Also, a letter giving a person credit on the agents or correspondents of the maker for goods or money. 3. **Bill of debt**: the old general term for a written engagement of a merchant to pay money on demand or at a specified time. It included bonds and negotiable paper. 4. **Bill of exchange**: a written order from one person to another to pay a certain sum of money to a third person, or his order, or bearer. The first person is the **drawer**; the second, the **drawee**, who, when he accepts it, becomes the **acceptor**; the third, the **payee**; the person to whom the payee indorses the bill, the **indorsee**; and the person in actual legal possession of the bill, whether indorsee, payee, or bearer, the **holder**. 5. **Bill of lading**: a receipt issued by the master of a ship, or other common carrier, to the shipper of goods, containing the contract of conveyance. It is also a symbol of the goods themselves, property in which will pass, subject to certain liens, by proper transfer of the bill of lading. 6. **Bill of sale**: an assignment in writing of personal chattels. 7. **Bill single**: a bill of debt without penalty, superseded by bills of exchange and notes. If with a penalty it was called a **Bill penal**, and corresponds to a bond or obligation.

Billa, *l.* A bill; a declaration. **Billa cassetur**: that the bill be quashed. **Billa excambii**: bill of exchange. **Billa exonerationis**: a bill of lading. **Billa vera**: a *true bill*; v. *Bill*, I. 20.

Bis, *l.* Twice. **Bis petitum:** twice demanded. **Bis dat qui cito dat:** he gives twice who gives quickly.

Black Book of the Admiralty. An ancient repository of admiralty law, containing the laws of Oleron with many ordinances and commentaries. **Of the Exchequer:** an ancient book of charters, conventions, etc., kept in the Exchequer.

Black mail. 1. A tribute paid by the inhabitants of the northern counties of England to some border chieftain to be protected from the depredations of the Scotch border-thieves and moss-troopers. 2. **Black rents:** rents reserved in cattle, provisions, or labor, as distinguished from **white rents,** payable in silver.

Blada, *l.* Corn or grain; **crescentia,** growing.

Blanc, blanche, *fr.,* **Blancus,** *l.* White; blank; smooth. **Blanch ferme:** white rents; v. *Black mail,* 2. **Blanch holding:** a Scotch tenure like *free and common socage,* q. v.

Blank bar. *Common bar;* a plea in trespass which forced the plaintiff to assign a certain place for the injury. **Blank indorsement:** v. *Indorsement.*

Blees, blé, *fr.* Corn, grain. **Blees scies:** grain cut.

Blench holding. v. *Blanch holding.*

Blodwite, *sax.* An amerciament for the shedding of blood.

Bloody hand. When a person was caught trespassing in a forest, was evidence of his having killed deer. v. *Backberend.*

Boc, *sax.* A book, writing; deed; charter.

Boc-land. In Saxon law, land held by deed, and allodial; like free socage. **Folc-land** was held by the people without written evidence of title, and more resembled villenage.

Bois, boys, *fr.* Wood. **Haut bois:** high wood. **Sub bois:** underwood.

Bon, bonne, *fr.* Good. **Bones gents** (good men): persons qualified.

Bona, *l.* Goods; property. **Bona et catalla:** goods and chattels. **Bona felonum:** goods of felons. **Bona forisfacta:** goods forfeited. **Bona fugitivorum:** goods of fugitives. **Bona mobilia, immobilia:** goods movable, immovable. **Bona notabilia:** goods worthy of notice, i. e. of the value of £5. If a decedent left goods worth £5 in more than one diocese, administration had to be taken out before the metropolitan of the province, by way of special prerogative, to avoid having two or more administrators appointed by the different ordinaries of the diocese. **Bona peritura**: perishable goods. **Bona utlagatorum**: goods of outlaws. **Bona vacantia**: goods without an owner; goods found, or goods belonging to a person dying without successor or heir. **Bona waviata**: goods waived; goods stolen and thrown away by the thief in his flight.

Bona, bonus, bonum, *l*. Good. **Bona fide**: in good faith. **Bona fides non patitur ut bis idem exigatur**: good faith does not suffer the same thing to be twice sued for. **Bonæ fidei emptor**: a purchaser in good faith. **Bonæ fidei possessor in id tantum quod ad se pervenerit tenetur**: a person holding property in good faith is liable [to the real owner] only for those [profits] which have actually come to him.

Bond. An instrument under seal, wherein the maker or obligor expresses that he owes or will pay a certain sum of money to the obligee; usually with a condition added, that, in the event of his performing a certain act or paying another sum, the instrument is to be void. **Bond and disposition in security**: the Scotch term for a mortgage of land. **Bond tenants**: copyholders and customary tenants.

Boni et legales homines: good and lawful men. **Boni judicis est ampliare jurisdictionem**: it is the duty of a good judge to construe his jurisdiction liberally. **Boni judicis est judicium sine dilatione mandare executioni**: it is the duty of a good judge to put the judgment into execution without delay. **Boni judicis est lites dirimere, ne lis ex lite oriatur**: it is the duty of a good judge to put an end to suits, lest suit should grow out of suit.

Bonis non amovendis, *l*. (The goods not to be removed.) A writ directing the sheriff to hold the goods of a person against whom judgment has been obtained, pending the prosecution of a writ of error.

Bono et malo. v. *De*.

Bonus, *l*. A premium given for a loan. v. *Bona*. **Bonus judex secundum æquum et bonum judicat, et æquitatem stricto juri præfert**: a good judge decides according to what is just and good, and prefers equity to strict law.

Book-lands. v. *Boc-lands*.

Boon-days. Certain days in the year when copyhold tenants did base services for their lord.

Boot. v. *Bote.*

Booty. Property of the enemy captured in war *on land.*

Bordage, Bordagium, *l.* A species of base tenure by finding the lord in provisions, or perhaps by carrying timber.

Bordarii, bordimanni, *l.* Cottagers; tenants in *bordage.*

Bordlands. Lands held in *bordage ;* the demesne lands which the lord reserved to supply his table.

Borgh, *sax.* A pledge; a surety. **Borghbrech:** breach of the mutual pledge existing among the members of a *tithing* for their good behavior.

Borough, burg, Bourg, *fr.* A walled town; a town sending a burgess to Parliament. **Borough-court:** v. *Court,* 35, 57.

Borough English. A custom of burgage tenure, prevailing in some old English boroughs or manors, whereby land descended to the youngest son, instead of the eldest.

Borsholder: *Head-borow,* the chief pledge.

Bote, boot, *sax.* Compensation; reparation; an allowance; an estover. **Housebote:** an allowance of wood to the tenant for repairing the house; **haybote or hedgebote,** for his hedges; **ploughbote or cartbote,** for his implements of husbandry; **firebote,** for fuel.

Bottomry, bummaree. A contract by which money is loaned at a high rate of interest (*fœnus nauticum*) upon the mortgage or hypothecation of a ship. The loan is repayable only upon the safe return or arrival of the ship; and is made to enable the master to make or continue his voyage. v. *Respondentia.*

Bouche, *fr.* Mouth. **Ne gist en le bouche** (it does not lie in the mouth): it is not for one to say.

Bought and sold notes. Memoranda of a contract made through a broker, signed by him, and given, one to the buyer and the other to the seller, when they become binding on both.

Bourg, *fr.* A walled town; a village; v. *Borough.*

Bovata terræ, *l.* An *oxgang, oxgate.*

Brachium maris, *l.,* **Brace de la mer,** *fr.* An arm of the sea.

Bracton. The writer of the treatise *De Legibus et Consuetudinibus Angliæ ; tempo* Henry III.

Breach of close. Unlawful or unlicensed entry on another's land. **Breach of peace:** the term includes assaults, batteries, forcible entry, criminal libel, public threatening, and turbulent and indecorous conduct. **Breach of privilege**: an act or default in violation of the privilege of a parliament or legislature.

Brehon law. The old Irish law existing before the conquest by Henry II., so called from **brehon**, a judge.

Breve, *pl.,* **brevia,** *l.,* **Bref, brefe,** *fr.,* **Brieve,** *sc.* A writ. A precept of the King, in writing, issuing out of a court. **Breve de recto**: a writ of *right.* **Breve originale**: an original writ ; v. *Writ.* **Brevia anticipantia**: writs of prevention, at common law ; v. *Writ.* **Brevia formata** or **de cursu**: formed writs, or writs of course; v. *Writ.* **Brevia judicialia**: judicial writs ; v. *Writ.* **Brevia nominata**: named writs, writs specifying the circumstances of the case ; *formed writs.* **Brevia innominata**: writs making only a general complaint. **Brevia magistralia**: writs prepared by the masters in chancery in cases where there were no *brevia formata,* the writ being varied to suit each case. The necessity for them was removed by Stat. West. II., c. 24, authorizing writs upon the case ; v. *Action on the case, Writ.* **Brevia testata**: short written memoranda of conveyances by livery or hand grants, from which the modern *deed* has grown. They were not signed, but contained the names of the witnesses to the conveyance.

Brief. In England, a statement of a client's case, prepared by the attorney for the convenience of the barrister, containing the facts, pleadings, names of witnesses, and suggestions. In America, a written or printed argument of counsel submitted to the court.

Brigbote, brugbote, *sax.* A contribution for the repair of bridges.

Brocage, brokerage. A broker's pay, commission.

Broker, brogger, Broccator, *l.* An agent employed to buy, sell, or make contracts.

Brutum fulmen, *l.* An empty threat.

Burg. A *borough.* **Burgbrech**: v. *Borghbrech.* **Burghmote**: v. *Court,* 35.

Burgage. A tenure by which houses, or lands formerly covered with houses, in an ancient borough, are held of the King or lord of the borough. It is a kind of socage, affected by some old Saxon customs. v. *Borough English.*

Burgbote. A tribute towards repairing the walls of a town.

Burgess, Bourgeois, *fr.* The freeman of a borough ; a magistrate ; an elector ; a representative in Parliament.

Burglar, Burgator, *l.* One who breaks and enters the dwelling-house of another by night, with felonious intent. (This definition has been much changed by statute.)

Burking. Murder for the purpose of selling the bodies for dissection.

Butts and bounds. The lines separating a piece of land from the land surrounding; v. *Abuttals. Butts* also means the corners or angles of such lines.

Buying of titles. The purchase of land or claims to land from one not in possession. The transfer was void, and an offence at common law. v. *Champerty.*

By-laws. Local laws of towns or courts. Laws made by a corporation for itself.

By the bye. (*l., obiter.*) Incidentally; without special process. Used of a declaration filed, against a person already in custody, by another plaintiff, or for a new cause of action.

C.

C. B. For *Common Bench.* **C. P.** For *Common Pleas.*

Çà, *fr.* Here. **Çà et là:** here and there.

Ca. resp., Ca. sa. v. *Capias ad respondendum, ad satisfaciendum.*

Cablish, Cablis, *fr.* Brush-wood; wind-fallen boughs.

Cadere, *l.* To fall; end; cease; fail; abate. **Cadit quæstio:** there is an end of the question. **Cadere a** or **ab:** to fall from, fail in, lose. **Cadere assisa:** to be cast, nonsuited. **Cadere in:** to fall into, change into, become liable to.

Caducus, *l.* Falling. **Caduca:** escheats.

Caducary. Relating to escheats or forfeitures.

Cætera desunt, *l.* Other things [the rest] are wanting. **Cæteris paribus:** other things equal. **Cæteris tacentibus:** the others silent [expressing no opinion].

Cæterorum, *l.* Administration *cæterorum* is given as to the rest of the estate, after a limited power has been exhausted.

Calcetum, calcea, *l.* A causey.

Call. *To call,* in land law, is to require a point of surveying to correspond with some natural object. Such objects, or bases of survey, are termed the **calls. Calling the plaintiff:** a formal nonsuiting, when the plaintiff desires to abandon the case, effected by his nonappearance at the *call* of the crier. **Calling to the bar**: the making a student barrister at law.

Calumniare, *l.* To claim; object to; challenge.

Cambipartia, *l.* *Champerty.*

Cambist. A dealer in notes and bills of exchange.

Camera, *l.* A chamber, judge's chamber; a treasury; v. *Chamber.* **Camera regis** (a chamber of the king): a harbor or place of commercial privilege. **Camera scaccarii**: the Exchequer Chamber. **Camera stellata**: the Star Chamber; v. *Court,* 44.

Campus, *l.* A field. Campfight, battel. **Campi partitio**: *Champerty.*

Cancellaria, *l.* Chancery. **Cancellarius**: the chancellor. **Cancelli**: bars, lattice-work, whence the name of the Court of Chancery; v. *A.*

Canon. 1. A law. 2. A prebendary, member of a chapter. **Canon law**: the law of the Church of Rome as to matters in its jurisdiction; and partly preserved in English ecclesiastical law and admiralty.

Cantred. In Wales, a *hundred.*

Capax, *l.* A taker or holder; capable of. v. *Doli.*

Cape, *l.* (Take.) A writ judicial, issued in real actions for the recovery of land, directing the sheriff to take and hold the land when the tenant or defendant made default. The **grand cape, cape magnum,** was awarded when the defendant had never appeared to the summons, and required an answer to the default and the demand; the **petit cape** issued after appearance, and required an answer to the default alone. **Cape ad valentiam**: a kind of *grand cape,* awarded a defendant in a real action when the person whom he called to warrant made default and the demandant recovered. It commanded the sheriff to *take* land of the vouchee *to the value* of the land recovered.

Capias, *l.* (That you take.) The general name for a writ of attachment or arrest. 1. The **capias ad respondendum,** called commonly **capias,** was a judicial writ issuing from the C. P. or K. B., supposed to be founded on an original, directing the sheriff to arrest the person of the defendant, and have him before court on the return day to answer the plaintiff in his suit. If the sheriff returned **non est inventus,** or the defendant lived

in another county, a **testatum capias** issued from the C. P. to
the sheriff of that county, reciting such fact, and ordering his arrest as before; so, in the K. B., a **Bill of Middlesex**; v. *Bill*,
I. 8.   2. **Capias ad satisfaciendum**: a writ of execution of
the highest nature, commanding the sheriff to have the defendant
before court on a certain day to *satisfy judgment*; its effect was
to imprison the defendant until he made satisfaction.   3. So, **ad
computandum**, on a judgment that the defendant account.
4. **Capias ad audiendum judicium**: a writ to bring in a defendant, who has been found guilty of a misdemeanor in his absence,
to *hear judgment*.   5. **Capias in withernam**: a writ of reprisal
granted one whose cattle or goods have been distrained and carried out (*eloigned*) of the county so they cannot be replevied.
It directed the sheriff to take other cattle or goods of the dis-
trainor, of equal value. v. *Withernam*.   6. **Capias pro fine**: an
obsolete writ ordering the arrest of an unsuccessful defendant in
cases where a *fine* was due from him to the King.   7. **Capias
utlagatum** (that you take the outlaw): a writ for the seizure of
the goods or person of an absconding defendant who has been
outlawed; v. *Exigent*.

Capiatur pro fine, *l.* Let him be taken for the fine; v. *Capias*, 6.

Capita, *l.* Heads; persons. **Per capita**: by heads, per head, in
distinction from **per stirpem**, by stock, by way of representation. v. *Caput*.

Capital, Capitalis, *l.* Chief; principal; affecting the head or life.
Capitalis dominus, plegius, debitor, baro, etc.: the chief
lord, surety, debtor, baron. **Capitalis justitiarius**: in old
English law the chief *justiciar* or justice.

Capitaneus, *l.* A person holding an estate **in capite**; a captain.

Capitation. A poll or personal tax.

Capite, in. v. *Caput*.

Captio, *l.*, **Caption**. 1. A taking; a seizure; an arrest. 2. The
heading of a document.

Caput, *l.* A head; a person. A chief; beginning, principal. **Caput anni**: the first day of the year. **Caput baroniæ**: a nobleman's mansion-house, which descended to the eldest daughter if
no son. **Caput lupinum** (a wolf-head): an outlaw. **Caput,
principium et finis**: the head, beginning and end. **In capite**:

in chief; directly of the King or chief lord. **Capitis deminutio**: loss of condition or rank.

Car, *fr.* For; because. **Car entant**: forasmuch.

Carcare, *l.* To load. **Carcata**: freighted.

Carcer, *l.* A gaol. **Carcer ad homines custodiendos (continendos) non puniendos haberi debet**: a gaol ought to be kept to guard (confine) men, not to punish them.

Carnaliter cognovit, *l.* [He] carnally knew.

Carrier. One who carries goods for hire. v. *Common carrier.*

Carta, charta, *l.* A deed, charter. v. *Charta.*

Carte blanche, *fr.* A white sheet of paper; a blank instrument. Used of a signature, given with authority to fill up as desired.

Cartel. A written challenge. An agreement between two hostile states relating to the exchange of prisoners. **Cartel ship**: a ship of truce, unarmed, employed to carry messages, exchange prisoners, etc. between two hostile states.

Carucata, *l.* From **caruca,** a plough. A plough-land, a carve of land; as much land as one plough could cultivate.

Carvage, carucage. A tax imposed on each plough, or carve of land.

Cas, *fr.* Case. **Cas fortuit**: an inevitable event.

Case. 1. v. *Action upon the case, Trespass on the case.* 2. An action or suit at law. **Case agreed or stated**: a statement of the facts agreed on by the parties, or by another court, and submitted to the court without trial for decision of a point of law. So, **case reserved,** or **made, special case,** where points of law are reserved by the judge or parties for the decision of the court in banc, and a nonsuit or verdict is given subject to such decision.

Cassare, *l.,* **Casser,** *fr.* To break; to annul, quash. **Cassatio,** *l.*: a quashing, an abatement. **Cassation,** *fr.*: the annulling or appeal of a judgment; the French highest court of appeal. **Cassetur billa or breve**: let the *bill* or *writ* be quashed; the form of judgment for the defendant on a plea in abatement.

Cast. To allege, proffer; to overthrow, defeat. **Cast an essoign**: to put in an excuse for non-appearance in an action.

Caste, *l.* Chastely.

Castigatory. v. *Common scold.*

Castle guard or **ward.** A feudal service or tenure. An imposition laid on dwellers within a certain distance of a castle to maintain the garrison.

Casu consimili, *l.* 1. In a similar case; v. *Action on the case.*
2. An old writ of entry which lay for a reversioner to recover land alienated by a tenant for life or by the courtesy, for a greater estate than he held; so called because like the writ of **Casu proviso,** which was a similar writ brought against a tenant in dower. Both could be brought during the life of the tenant, thus differing from *Ad communem legem.*

Casual ejector. The fictitious defendant in *ejectment.*

Casus, *l.* Case; event; chance. **Casus fœderis:** a case within a treaty, to which it applies. **Casus fortuitus:** an inevitable event; a chance occurrence. **Casus fortuitus non est sperandus, et nemo tenetur divinare:** a chance event is not to be expected, and no one is bound to foresee it. **Casus major:** an extraordinary casualty. **Casus omissus:** a case omitted, unprovided for. **Casus omissus et oblivioni datus dispositioni juris communis relinquitur:** a case omitted and forgotten is left to the disposal of the common law.

Catalla, *l.* Chattels; all goods except fees and freeholds. **Catalla odiosa:** dead goods [not animals]; idle cattle [not beasts of the plough].

Catallis reddendis. v. *De.*

Catchpole. A sheriff's deputy, bailiff.

Cattle-gate. A right of pasturing cattle in another's land.

Causa, *l.* Cause; occasion; reason; a suit. **Causa causans or remota:** the original or remote cause. **Causa causata or proxima:** the immediate or next cause. **Causa mortis, adulterii, impotentiæ:** by reason of death, adultery, impotence. **Causa proxima, non remota, spectatur:** the immediate cause is considered, not the remote. **Causa et origo est materia negotii:** the cause and origin of a thing are material parts of it. **Causa matrimonii prælocuti:** an old writ of entry which lay for a woman who had given a man lands in fee with intent that he should marry her, and he refused. **Causa jactitationis maritagii:** in ecclesiastical law, a suit of jactitation of marriage, to enjoin silence on one claiming to be married to the libellant.

Causam nobis significes, *l.* (That you signify to us the reason.)

A writ that lay against the mayor of a town who had refused to deliver seisin to the grantee of the King.

Cautio, *l.*, **Caution.** Security; bail; a bond given by way of surety.

Caveat, *l.* (Let him beware.) A formal notice to a court or a judicial or ministerial officer not to do some act, or not without notice to the "caveator." It is filed by the party having interest in the matter, to prevent the enrolment of a decree in Chancery when an appeal is contemplated, to prevent the probate of wills, granting letters of administration, letters patent, a patent for lands, and in other cases. **Caveat emptor** : let the purchaser take care. [In the absence of warranty or special covenant, the seller guarantees neither title nor quality of the goods or lands.] **Caveat emptor, qui ignorare non debuit quod jus alienum emit** : let the buyer take care, who ought not to be ignorant that he is buying another's right.

Cayagium, *l.* Kayage, a duty paid for landing goods at a wharf.

Ce, Cecy, Ceo, *fr.* This.

Ceans, *fr.* Here within.

Ceapgild, *sax.* Payment, or forfeiture, of an animal.

Cel, celle, celuy, *fr.* That.

Cenegild, *sax.* A mulct paid by the slayer to the kin of a person slain.

Centena, *l.* A *hundred.*

Central Criminal Court. v. *Court,* 47.

Ceo, *fr.* v. *Ce.*

Ceorl, carl, churl, *sax.*, **Ceorlus,** *l.* A freeman of inferior rank ; a tenant at will by rents or services ; a husbandman.

Cepi corpus, *l.* I have taken the body. **Cepi corpus et paratum habeo** : I have taken the body and have it ready. These were the returns of a sheriff to a writ of *capias* when the party arrested was out on bail. If in actual custody, the return was **cepi corpus et est in custodia.**

Cepit, *l.* He took. Replevin **in the cepit** : when brought for the taking only, not the keeping; v. *Replevin, Detinet.* **Cepit in alio loco** (he took in another place) : the plea in replevin when the defendant intended to avow and claim a return. **Cepit et abduxit** (he took and led away) : emphatic words in a writ of trespass brought for animals ; **cepit et asportavit** (he took and carried away), if brought for goods.

Cert money. Head-money paid by tenants to the lords of manors for the keeping of the court-leet.

Certificate, trial by. When an action was determined by the written evidence of some person best informed, which is final. **Certificate into chancery:** the opinion of a common-law court on a matter arising in a chancery suit.

Certification of assize. An old writ for review of a matter tried by assize.

Certified check. A check as it were accepted, by having the bank's teller or cashier write his name across the face, thereby admitting that the bank has funds to meet it.

Certiorari, *l.* (To be made more certain, to be informed.) A writ issuing from a superior court to an inferior, before verdict, requesting the latter to send up the proceedings or record for review or trial. It was an original writ issuing from Chancery or the K. B. in civil or criminal cases. It was also auxiliary to a writ of error. It lies, in the U. S., to courts not of record, or tribunals proceeding not according to the common law; and *after* judgment. A **bill of certiorari** was a bill in chancery, praying relief, and the removal into chancery of a suit in an inferior court of equity, for reason of incompetency or hardship.

Certum est quod certum reddi potest, *l.* That which can be made certain *is* certain.

Cessare, *l.* To cease; to stay, stop. **Cessante causa, cessat effectus:** the cause ceasing, so does the effect. **Cessante ratione legis, cessat et ipsa lex:** the reason of the law ceasing, so does the law itself. **Cessavit per biennium:** the writ of an obsolete real action for the recovery of land, which lay for a lord against a tenant in fee who *ceased during two years* to pay rent or perform services; also against a religious house who held lands by spiritual services or alms, when there was not enough goods and chattels on the land for a distress. **Cesset executio,** or **processus:** let the execution *or* process be stayed; the old formal order, and entry on the record, for such delay.

Cesser, cessure. Neglect; omission.

Cessio bonorum, *l.* The abandonment or assignment by a debtor of all his property for the benefit of his creditors.

C'est asçavoir, asaver, *fr.* That is to say, to wit.

Cestui, cestuy, *fr.* He. **Cestuy que doit enheriter al père**

doit enheriter al fitz: he who would be heir to the father shall be heir to the son. **Cestuy que trust** (he who trusts): the beneficiary under a trust. **Cestuy que use**: he to whose use or profit another is enfeoffed or seised of lands. **Cestuy que vie**: he whose life determines an estate for life.

Cet, cettuy, *fr.* That. **Ceux, ceulx**: those.

Chacea, *l.*, **Chace,** *fr.* A *chase*.

Chalenger, *fr.*, **Challenge.** To object; except to; to claim, demand; to dispute. **Challenge to the array**: an objection to the whole panel of jurors. **Challenge to the polls**: an objection to a juror or jurors singularly and personally. There are four kinds of this challenge: **propter honoris respectum,** *on account of honor*, as if a lord of Parliament be called; **propter defectum,** *for defect*, lack, of estate or other qualification; **propter affectum,** *for partiality* or bias; **propter delictum,** for some crime or misdemeanor that renders him infamous, or affects his credit. These are all **challenges for cause** in distinction from **peremptory challenges,** which are usually allowed in criminal cases. They are also **principal challenges,** in distinction from **challenges for favor,** a weaker kind of *challenge propter affectum*, as for acquaintance, probable opinion, or the like.

Chamber. A court; a treasury. **Chambers**: the private room of a judge; any place where he does business when not sitting in court. **Chambers, the King's chambers**: parts of the sea, included within lines drawn from one point of land to another, over which the nation claims jurisdiction, and where all hostilities must cease.

Champarty, champerty. The offence of aiding another man in his suit upon condition to have part of the thing in suit when recovered or preserved. It included the purchasing of the thing pending the action, and the *buying of titles ;* and was a kind of *maintenance.*

Chancellor. The judge of a court of equity. The highest officer of a university, usually an honorary position. A president, or judicial officer. **Chancellor of a diocese**: he assists a bishop in law matters, and holds his consistory court. **Chancellor of the Duchy of Lancaster**: he presides over the Duchy Court. **Chancellor of the Exchequer**: he formerly presided in the Exchequer, with the barons of that court, over whom he took precedence, and looked out for the interests of the Crown; and sat also in the equity side under the *Lord High Treasurer*. Now the principal finance officer of the government. The **Lord High Chancellor** is the highest judicial officer of the realm, supreme judge of the Court of Chancery, Keeper of the Great Seal, privy councillor, and Prolocutor of the House of Lords.

Chance-medley. Accidental killing in self-defence, on a sudden, unpremeditated attack.

Chancery. Equity; a court of equity. v. *Court*, 15.

Chanter, chaunter, *fr.* To sing; to declare aloud; to find a verdict.

Chantry, Chauntry. A church, chapel, or altar endowed with lands for the maintenance of priests to do spiritual service, or sing masses for the repose of the soul of the donor.

Charge. 1. A burden, incumbrance, or lien; as when land is charged with a debt. 2. A claim, demand. 3. The summing up, or final address of a judge to a jury. 4. The **charging part** of a bill in equity, either alleging evidence, or matters in anticipation of the defence, or to which the plaintiff wishes the defendant's answer. **Charge and discharge:** the old method of taking accounts in chancery, where the plaintiff delivers his account to the master, and the defendant his *discharge,* his objections, or counter-claim. **Charging order:** an order obtained under English statutes by a judgment creditor to have the stock of the debtor in any public company or funds charged with the debt.

Charta, *l.* A charter; a deed; an instrument under seal. **Charta communis:** an indenture, a deed with mutual covenants; so **charta cyrographata:** a deed executed in two parts. **Charta de non ente non valet:** a deed of a thing not in existence is void. **Charta partita:** a charter-party. Charta *Magna,* de *Foresta,* see those titles.

Charter-land. *Boc-land;* land held by written evidence; freehold land.

Charter-party. The contract for hire of a vessel.

Chartis reddendis. v. *De.*

Charue, *fr.* A plough.

Chascun, *fr.* Each; every.

Chase, chace. 1. A tract of wild land, in size between a forest and a park, unenclosed, and not subject to forest law, privileged for game and wild animals. 2. A franchise granted to a subject empowering the latter to have a chase. 3. The right of hunting wild animals; **common chase,** where every one has such right.

Chatel, chatelle, *fr.,* **Chattel.** A chattel; any article of property not a freehold or fee in land. **Chateux, cateux,** *fr.,* **Chattels, catals:** plural, v. *Catalla.* **Cateux meubles, immeubles:** goods movable, immovable. **Chattels real:** such as are annexed to, or arise from, real property, but yet do not amount to a freehold, such as a lease for years. **Chattels personal:** movable goods, or interests concerning them, not annexed to the realty. **Chattel interest:** an interest in realty not amounting to a freehold, and which is usually governed by the law of personal property.

Chaud-medley. Killing a man in an affray in the heat of passion.

Chaunter, Chauntry. v. *Chanter,* etc.

Check, Cheque. A check resembles an inland bill of ʻexchange. It is an order on a bank or banker for the payment of money to the drawer, or a third person, order, or bearer. There is, however, no distinct *acceptance;* no days of grace are allowed; and it is not a matter of credit, but an appropriation of money in the hands of the bank.

Cheser, cheir, chaier, etc., *fr.* To fall. **Chaye:** fallen. **Chet, chiet:** it falls, happens. **Cheaunce:** an accident, chance.

Chef, *fr.* The head; chief; beginning.

Chemin, chimin, *fr.* A way, road; a journey.

Chescun, *fr.* Each; every.

Chet. v. *Cheser.*

Chevage, chivage, *fr.,* **Chevagium,** *l.,* **Chiefage.** A sum of money paid yearly by villeins to their lord in acknowledgment of bondage. A poll-tax paid to the King by the Jews.

Chevisance, *fr.* A bargaining, contract. A usurious agreement.

Chief. Head; lord; principal. **Chief justice:** the oldest, or presiding judge of a court. The **chief justice of England** is the chief justice of the K. B. **Chief lord:** the ultimate or highest lord of the fee, of whom the mesne lords held, before Stat. *Quia Emptores.* A tenant **in chief** is one holding directly of the chief lord, of the King. **Chief rents:** quitrents, rents paid by the freeholders of a manor in discharge of all services. v. Rents of *assize.* **Chief-pledge:** a head-borow, borsholder;

the head of a *decennary*. **In chief, tenure in**: v. *Chief lord.*
Examination in chief: the first examination of a witness, as
distinguished from cross-examination.

Chiltern Hundreds. The hundreds of Stoke, Desborough, and
Bonenham, the stewardship of which is a nominal office in the
gift of the Crown. As acceptance of an office under the Crown
vacates a seat in the House of Commons, this office is given to a
member wishing to retire, to evade the principle that a member
of Parliament cannot give up his seat.

Chimin, *fr.* A way. **Chiminage**: a toll paid for having a way
through a forest.

Chirgemote, chirchgemote, *sax.* A synod; an ecclesiastical
court.

Chirograph. A deed, indenture; a fine of lands. The word was
written between the two parts of an indenture in the place where
the parchment was cut. **Chirographum apud debitorem
repertum præsumitur solutum**: a bond found with the
debtor is presumed to have been paid.

Chivalry. *Knight-service.* v. *Tenure.*

Chose, *fr.* A thing. **Chose in action**: a personal right to a
thing not actually in possession, but recoverable in a suit at law;
or to the performance of a contract. **Chose in possession**:
a thing actually possessed and enjoyed.

Christianitatis curia. The Court Christian. v. *Court,* 79.

Churl. *Ceorl.*

Ci, cy, si, *fr.* So. Here. **Ci devant**: heretofore. **Ci bien**: as
well. **Ci tost**: as soon as. **Cy gist**: here lies.

Cinque ports. Five (now seven) ports on the S. E. coast of England having privileges of their own, with a governor called Lord
Warden, and an exclusive jurisdiction of their own, for which
they were bound to furnish a certain number of ships and men-
at-arms to the King, — Romney, Dover, Sandwich, Hastings,
Hythe, Winchelsea, and Rye.

Cippi, *l.,* **Cipps, ceps,** *fr.* The stocks.

Circa, *l.* About; concerning.

Circuit. A division of the country into judicial districts. The
journey of a judge around the country for the purpose of holding courts, v. *Assize.* **Circuit court**; v. *Court,* 105.

Circuitus, *l.* A going round; a roundabout way; a more indirect way than is needful. **Circuitus est evitandus**: circuity of action is to be avoided.

Citatio, *l.* Citation; a summons to court; the first process in an ecclesiastical cause.

Civil. Used in contradistinction to *criminal*, or *ecclesiastical*, or *military*, or *political*, or *barbarous*. **Civil action**: one grounded on a private right, seeking to enforce it, or to obtain compensation for a private injury. **Civil corporation**: a lay corporation not eleemosynary; municipal or trading corporations. **Civil death**: the privation or extinction of a person's legal rights and capacities, as when a man became outlawed, attainted, or entered a monastery. **Civil injury**: the private wrong resulting from a breach of contract, a tort, or a crime. **Civil law**: 1. The Roman law, as expressed by Justinian and his successors; v. *Corpus juris civilis*. 2. Municipal law, the law of a nation as distinguished from the law of nations. 3. Not criminal law. **Civil liberty**: a man's liberty as restrained by law. **Civil list**: in England, the sum appropriated for the expenses of the royal household and establishment. In the U. S., the general expenses of the government, except for the army and navy.

Civiliter, *l.* Civilly. **Civiliter mortuus**: dead in law; v. *Civil death*.

Clam, *l.* Secretly.

Clamare, *l.* To cry out; claim. **Clamor**: a complaint, claim; an outcry.

Clarendon, Constitutions of. Statutes made at Clarendon in the reign of Henry II., whereby the power of the Pope and clergy was checked, and their immunity from secular jurisdiction limited.

Clause. Close, sealed; used of writs not open or **patent**.

Clausula, *l.* A clause, a sentence. **Clausula generalis non refertur ad expressa**: a general clause does not (refer to) cover things (expressed) specially mentioned. **Clausula quæ abrogationem excludit ab initio non valet**: a clause forbidding (abrogation) repeal is void from the beginning. **Clausulæ inconsuetæ semper inducunt suspicionem**: unusual clauses always arouse suspicion.

Clausum, *l.* 1. *Clause.* 2. A close. **Clausum fregit**: he broke the close; v. *Trespass*.

Clearance. A certificate given by the collector of a port to a ship about to sail, that she has complied with the law, and is duly authorized to depart.

Clergy. Persons in holy orders; hence, persons who could read. v. *Benefit of clergy.*

Clericale privilegium, *l. Benefit of clergy.*

Clerici prænotarii, *l.* The *Six clerks* in chancery.

Clerico admittendo, etc. v. *De.*

Clericus, *l.* A priest; a clerk.

Clerimonia, *l. Clergy.*

Clerk. A person in ecclesiastical orders. Anciently, a person who could read. For *Six clerks,* clerks of the *Hanaper, Petty bag,* see those titles.

Clerus, *l.* The clergy.

Close. 1. A piece of land held as private property. 2. *Clause;* sealed. **Close writs**: the opposite of letters patent. Writs directed to the sheriff, not the lord; or to a particular person, not people generally. **Close rolls**: rolls preserved among the public records in England, containing the record of close writs and other documents. **Close copies**: not office copies, which required to have a certain number of words to each sheet, but copies written *close,* or not, at pleasure.

Cloud on title. v. *Bill,* I. 13.

Clough. A valley.

Coadunatio, *l.* A uniting together; a conspiracy.

Cocket. The seal of a custom-house. A certificate that the duties have been duly paid on goods.

Code. A general system of the law, embodied and authorized by legislative enactment. **Code civil** or **Code Napoléon**: a code of the law of persons and property, established in France under Napoleon I.

Codex, *l.* A code; a volume, roll, or book.

Codicil. An addition to a will, executed at a later time.

Cogitationis pœnam nemo patitur, *l.* No man suffers punishment for his thoughts.

Cognati, *l.* Cognates; relations on the mother's side.

Cognitio, *l.* The ackowledgment of a *fine; cognizance;* jurisdiction.

Cognizance, cognisance, conusance. Acknowledgment, recognition, jurisdiction. 1. **Conusance of pleas**: an exclusive right to try causes; a privilege of trial granted certain cities and corporations which may be pleaded by "**claim of conusance**," to oust the jurisdiction of another court. 2. The acknowledgment of a *fine*, q. v. 3. A pleading in replevin justifying the taking as servant or bailiff of some third party; v. *Avowry*.

Cognizor, conusor. A person levying a fine. **Cognizee, conusee**: the person to whom the fine was levied.

Cognoscere, *l.* To acknowledge. **Cognovit actionem** (he has acknowledged the action), or **cognovit**: a written confession of the justice of an action at law, signed by the defendant or his attorney after the declaration, authoriziug the plaintiff to enter judgment for a sum named. If after plea, it contained an agreement to withdraw the plea, and was called a **cognovit actionem relicta verificatione** (the plea being abandoned), or a **relicta**.

Coif. The badge of a sergeant at law; a lawn cap formerly worn.

Collateral. On the side, by the side. Relationship by blood not lineal. **Collateral limitation**: a limitation which makes the duration of the estate depend, not alone on the life or blood of the grantee, but on some' other event. **Collateral warranty**: warranty made by a person not having the title, and who could not at any time have held it.

Collatio bonorum, *l.* A bringing together of goods into a common fund; bringing into *hotchpot*.

Collation to a benefice. The conferring a benefice by a bishop who has himself the *advowson*.

Collegialiter, *l.* In a corporate capacity.

Colligendum bona defuncti, *l.* v. *Ad*.

Colloquium, *l.* A conversation. That part of the declaration in slander, which averred that the words were spoken concerning the plaintiff. When the words were not in themselves actionable, it was preceded by the explanatory **inducement,** a traversable statement of certain facts, and followed by the **innuendo** (meaning) which connected the words with these facts, and showed them to be defamatory to the plaintiff.

Color, *l.,* **Colour.** Apparent or *prima facie* right. To **give colour**: to confess sufficiently the truth of the declaration for the purposes of a plea in confession and avoidance; not to deny.

To give express colour: to allege in the plea some fictitious fact which enables the defendant to set up his defence by confession and avoidance. It gives the plaintiff an apparent right, and so does away with the necessity of pleading by traverse. **Colour of office**: the false pretence of authority or official duty. **Colore officii**: under colour of office.

Combat. Trial by *Battel.*

Combe. A narrow valley.

Combustio domorum, *l.* Burning of houses; arson.

Come, comme, *fr.* As; so; whereas. **Come semble**: as it appears.

Comen, *fr.* Common.

Comes, *l.* A companion, follower; a count, earl.

Comitas, *l.* Courtesy, comity. **Comitas inter gentes**: the **Comity of nations**: the courtesy by which one state recognizes or follows the law of another.

Comitatus, *l.* A county, shire; an earldom; the county court; a suite or body of attendants. v. *Posse.*

Commandité, *fr.* Special or limited partnership.

Commendam, in, *l.* 1. Partners *en commandité.* 2. A living or benefice commended to a clerk to hold until a pastor is provided; a living which a bishop is allowed to hold for life, besides his bishopric.

Commendatio, *l.* Praise, recommendation.

Commercium, *l.* Commerce; traffic. **Commercia belli**: compacts of war; truces; contracts between hostile nations or their subjects.

Commissary. An officer anciently exercising a bishop's jurisdiction in out-places, where there were no archdeacons.

Commission. A warrant; authority; writ. 1. **Commission of assize**: v. *Assize.* 2. **Commission of bankrupt** was granted by the Lord Chancellor to examine into the affairs of bankrupts, and given to some five persons, who were called commissioners, and had authority to proceed generally according to the statutes. Later, these commissioners constituted a permanent court of one judge and six commissioners. 3. **Commission to examine witnesses**: issues for the purpose of taking testimony out of court. 4. **Commission of lunacy** was issued out of chancery, authorizing certain persons to inquire whether a person represented *non compos* was so in fact. It is now directed to the masters in lunacy, and is usually made before a jury. If found affirmatively, the lunatic's person or estate was committed to the charge of a person or persons called his **committee. 5. Commission of gaol delivery**: v. *Assize*. 6. **Commission of nisi prius**: v. *Assize*. 7. **Commission of the peace**: v. *Assize, Justice of the peace*. 8. **Commission of rebellion.** One of the processes for contempt in chancery; it was directed to four commissioners, and authorized them to attach the party as a rebel and contemner of laws and bring him to court on a day assigned. 9. **Commission of review**: v. *Court*, 88.

Commissioners of bankrupt. v. *Commission*, 2.

Commitment. The sending a person to prison for crime or contempt; the warrant therefor; the *mittimus*.

Committee. v. *Commission*, 4.

Committitur, *l.* (He is committed.) A minute of a defendant's surrender by bail, and commitment.

Commixtio, *l.* Mixing together of things solid or dry, belonging to different persons; v. *Confusio*.

Commodatum, *l.* A thing loaned; a gratuitous loan of a specific chattel.

Commodum, *l.* Advantage, profit. **Commodum ejus esse debet cujus periculum est**: he who runs the risk ought to have the profit. **Commodum ex injuria sua nemo habere debet**: no one ought to profit by his own tort.

Common. A profit which one man has in the land of another, a *profit à prendre*, usually common of pasture. 1. **Common appendant**: an immemorial right of tenants in a manor to feed commonable cattle on other lands of the same manor. 2. **Common appurtenant**: a right of feeding cattle on the land of another, enjoyed by the holder of certain land. It is created by grant, and may extend to cattle not commonable. 3. **Common because of vicinage (pur cause de vicinage,** *fr.***)**: where inhabitants of two adjoining townships have mutually permitted their cattle to feed in either. 4. **Common in gross or at large**: common vested in a person or corporation, not annexed to land. 5. **Common sans nombre**: common without stint, a right to common an indefinite [not unlimited] number of cattle.

6. **Common of estovers**: a liberty of taking wood necessary for use or repairs. 7. **Common of piscary**: liberty of fishing. 8. **Common of turbary**: liberty of digging turf. 9. **Common in the soil**: liberty of mining or quarrying. 10. **Common de Schack**: a kind of *Common pur cause de vicinage* existing by special custom in the east of England, after harvest, among occupiers of land in the same common field.

Common assurances. v. *Assurance.* **Common bail**: v. *Bail.* **Common bar**: *Blank bar.* **Common Bench**: the Bench, as distinguished from the King's Bench, the Court of *Common Pleas;* v. *Court.* **Common carrier**: a carrier who carries indifferently for all the world; one who undertakes to carry persons or goods without special contract; v. *Carrier.* **Common counts**: certain general forms of declaration in actions to recover money due when a debt has been incurred. They are usually added to the special counts, to prevent the possibility of a *variance,* and cover the ordinary cases of contracts which result in an implied promise to pay money. **Common day**; v. *Day.* **Common fine**: like *Cert money.* **Common form**: proof of a will by the executor on his own oath; as opposed to proof **per testes** (by witnesses) when the will was disputed. **Common intendment**: natural sense, a simple, not strained, construction. **Common jury**; v. *Jury.* **Common law**: 1. English law, as distinguished from foreign, civil, or canon law; 2. That part of English law which does not depend on statutes; 3. Law administered in the common-law courts, not equity or admiralty; 4. General customs, as distinguished from special or local. **Common nuisance**: one affecting, or which may affect, the public or people generally, not a particular person or persons. **Common place**: *common pleas.* **Common pleas**: civil cases; v. *Court, Plea.* **Common recovery**: v. *Recovery.* **Common scold**: a woman of this kind was considered a nuisance at common law, and was punished by the castigatory or cucking-stool, a species of chair on the end of a pole. She was placed thereon, and immersed in a pond of water. **Common traverse**; v. *Traverse.* **Common vouchee**; v. *Recovery.*

Common, tenancy in. When there are two or more owners for the same land, holding in distinct undivided shares. Only " unity of possession" is necessary; hence, they hold under different titles; or under the same title accruing at different times; or under the same instrument by words importing that the grantees are to take in distinct shares. There is no right of survivorship, and estates in common are subject to both dower and courtesy. v. *Coparcenary, Joint tenancy*.

Commonable. Beasts of the plough, or beasts which manure the land.

Commonalty. v. *Commons*, 2. The people, not holding office.

Commons. 1. Land set apart for the public; or over which people have rights of common of pasture. 2. The freeholders of England not peers of the realm.

Commorant, *l.* Dwelling; temporarily abiding.

Commorientes, *l.* Persons dying at the same place and time, as in an accident.

Communicare, *l.* To common.

Communis, commune, *l.* Common. **Commune consilium regni**: the common council of the realm [Parliament]. **Commune placitum**: a common plea, a civil action. **Commune vinculum**: a mutual bond. **Communia**: common things, common. **Communia piscariæ, turbariæ, pasturæ**: *common* of piscary, turbary, pasture, which see. **Communia placita**: common pleas, as opposed to **placita coronæ**, criminal actions, pleas of the crown. **Communis error facit jus**: common error makes law. **Communis rixatrix**: a *common scold*. **Communis strata**: a common way. **Communibus annis**: in common years, on an average of years. **Communem legem**: v. *Ad*.

Communio bonorum, *l.* Community of goods.

Communitas regni Angliæ, *l.* Parliament.

Communiter usitata et approbata, *l.* Things commonly used and approved.

Commutation of tithes. Their conversion into a money payment.

Comparatio literarum, *l.* Comparison of handwritings.

Comparere, *l.* To appear. **Comperuit ad diem**: he appeared at the day, a plea to the action on a bail-bond.

Compensatio criminis, *l.* (Set-off of crime.) A plea of recrimination in a suit for divorce.

Compensation: set-off.

Compester, *l.* To manure.

Competere, *l.* To be proper, available. **Competit assisa**: an assize lies.

Componere lites, *l.* To settle, compromise suits.

Compos mentis, *l.* Sound in mind.

Composition. An agreement, compromise.. **A real composition**: an agreement made between the parson and land-owner, with consent of the ordinary and patron, that certain lands shall be discharged of tithes, for some real recompense given in lieu thereof.

Compotus, computus, *l.* An account. **De computo**: the old action of *account*.

Compound larceny. v. *Larceny*.

Compurgatores, *l.* The eleven ₁persons who swore with the defendant, in a trial by wager of law, that he was not guilty, or did not owe the plaintiff anything; the twelve persons who swore with the defendant that he was not guilty, in the trial of a clerk for felony. v. *Wager of law, Benefit of clergy*.

Concedere, *l.* To grant. **Concedo**: I grant. **Concessi**: I granted.

Concessio, *l.* A grant by deed, one of the common assurances.

Conclude. To end, determine; to estop. **Conclusion to the country**: the tender of issue to be tried by jury, at the end of a plea of traverse.

Concord, concordia, *l.* An agreement, accord. v. *Fine*.

Conculcavit et consumpsit, *l.* He trampled and destroyed.

Condere, *l.* To make, establish. **Condidit** (he made): a plea on a suit attacking a will, that the testator made it and was of sound mind.

Conditio, *l.* A condition. **Affirmative condition**: which requires something to happen, or be done, like **positive condition**; **negative** or **restrictive**, one which requires something not to be done. **Condition casuelle,** *fr.*: one which depends on chance, as opposed to **potestative**, which depends on the will of the party, or **mixte**, which depends on the will of the party and some third person, or some other event, conjoined. **Copulative condition**: one requiring all of several things to happen or be done, as opposed to **disjunctive**, one requiring only one of several things. **Condition compulsory** or **single** : one absolutely requiring some special thing to be done. **Condition expressed, in deed, in fact** : one made by special words, particularly expressed, as opposed to **condition in law,** or **implied** by common intendment. **Condition inherent**: one previously existing, not now created ; as to pay the rent anciently reserved by the chief lord on a modern grant of land. **Condition insensible, repugnant** : one contradictory to the main act, or inconsistent with the object ; impossible. **Condition precedent** or **suspensive** : one which is to happen before the main act or obligation, as distinguished from **subsequent** or **resolutory.** **Condition:** v. *Conditional limitation.*

Conditional fee. One limited to descend to a particular class of heirs ; changed by the Statute *de Donis* into fee-tail. v. *Fee.*

Conditional limitation. The limitation of an estate by deed under the Statute of Uses to a third person on the happening of a certain event, thereby cutting short the previous estate in the grantee. Distinguished from an **estate on condition,** or *base fee,* where the grantor or his heirs could alone take advantage of the breach of condition, and the estate reverted to them ; and also from a **limitation,** where the estate was only expressed to be granted until the happening of a certain event, and hence was not cut short, but reverted to the grantors as upon a natural determination ; v. *Limitation.*

Conditionem testium tunc inspicere debemus cum signarent, non mortis tempore : we ought to consider the competency of the witnesses as at the time when they subscribed, not at the [testator's] death.

Condonatio, *l.* Condonation, forgiveness. In cases of divorce, the forgiveness, either express or implied from actions, of a breach of marital duty, on condition that the fault shall not be repeated.

Conduct-money. Money paid a witness for his travelling expenses and maintenance.

Conductio, *l.* A hiring. v. *Locatio.*

Cone and key. (Accounts and keys.) A woman was deemed fit to receive cone and key — that is, to assume the cares of housekeeping — at fourteen or fifteen, by the Saxon law.

Coneu, conu, *fr.* Acknowledged ; known.

Confeccion, *fr.,* **Confectio,** *l.* The making or execution of a written instrument or deed.

Confessio in judicio omni probatione major est, *l.* A confession made in court is greater than all proof.

Confession and avoidance. Pleas are so termed which impliedly admit the facts alleged in the declaration, but aver more facts which obviate their legal effect; the ordinary *special plea;* v. *Plea.*

Confesso, pro, *l.* v. *Pro.*

Confirmare nemo potest prius quam jus ei acciderit, *l.* No one can confirm [release] a right before it has fallen to him. v. *Confirmation.* **Confirmat usum qui tollit abusum:** he vindicates the use of a thing who forbids its abuse.

Confirmatio perficiens, *l.* A confirmation which makes good a defeasible estate, or makes a conditional estate absolute. **Confirmatio crescens:** one which enlarges a rightful estate. **Confirmatio diminuens:** one which releases part of the services whereby the estate is held. **Confirmatio est nulla ubi donum præcedens est invalidum:** a confirmation is void where the grant preceding it is void. **Confirmatio omnes supplet defectus, licet id quod actum est ab initio non valuit:** a confirmation supplies all defects, although the deed was faulty at the beginning.

Confirmatio Chartarum, *l.* The Stat. 25 Ed. I., confirming *Magna Charta* and the Carta de *Foresta.*

Confirmation. A deed of confirmation may be either by way of ratification, or perfecting grant, of a previous estate.

Conformity. v. *Bill,* I. 2.

Confusio, *l.* The mixing of goods (properly liquid) belonging to different persons. v. *Commixtio.*

Congé d'accorder, *fr.* Leave to accord ; v. *Fine.* **Congé d'emparler:** leave to imparl ; v. *Imparlance.* **Congé d'eslire:** the King's license to a dean and chapter to choose a bishop.

Congeable, *fr.* Lawful, licensed ; done with leave.

Conjunctim, *l.* Jointly ; — **et divisim,** and severally.

Conquerer, *fr.* To gain, acquire ; **conquereur,** the *conqueror,* or first purchaser of an estate.

Conquestus, conquisitio, *l.* Conquest; acquisition.

Consanguineus, *l.* Related by blood. **De consanguineo:** a writ of *cosinage*. **Frater consanguineus**: a half-brother on the father's side.

Consanguinity. Relationship by blood, as opposed to *Affinity*.

Conscience, courts of. v. *Court*, 63.

Conscientia rei alieni, *l.* (Scotch law.) Knowledge that property held by one belongs to another. If the possessor knows this, he is liable for *violent profits*, being *in mala fide*.

Consensual. v. *Contract*.

Consensus facit jus, *l.* Consent makes law. **Consensus, non concubitus, facit matrimonium**: consent (agreement of marriage), not consummation, makes marriage. **Consensus tollit errorem**: consent removes error [the acquiescence of a party who might take advantage of an error obviates its effect].

Consent rule. A proceeding filed by the defendant in an action of ejectment, by which he bound himself to admit all the necessary fictions.

Consentientes et agentes pari pœna plectentur, *l.* Those who consent (to an act) and those who act shall be punished equally.

Consentire videtur qui tacet, *l.* Silence gives consent. **Consentire matrimonio non possunt infra annos nubiles**: they cannot consent to marriage under the age of twelve.

Consideratio curiæ, *l.* The judgment of the court.

Consideration. Compensation; a *quid pro quo*. **Good consideration**: one founded on natural affection, blood relationship, as opposed to **valuable consideration**: a profit or loss capable of being estimated in money. **Express consideration**, when stated in the contract; **implied**, when arising from the law; **executed**, when performed prior to the promise founded upon it; **executory**, when to be performed after the promise is made.

Consideratum est per curiam, *l.* It is adjudged by the court.

Consimili casu, in, *l.* v. *Casu consimili*.

Consistory. v. *Court*, 80.

Consolato del mare. A code of sea laws in force about the Mediterranean from the eleventh century.

Consolidation rule. A rule for uniting several actions brought by the same parties on the same cause, whereby the parties are bound in all the actions according to the verdict in one.

Consols, consolidated annuities. The English funded debt.

Consortium *l.* A union of fortunes; marriage. v. *Per quod.*

Conspiracy. An unlawful combining together of two or more persons to accomplish an unlawful act, or a lawful act by unlawful means.

Constat, *l.* It is clear, evident. **Constat de persona:** there is no doubt as to the person.

Constitutio, *l.* An act, ordinance, statute; a constitution. v. *Clarendon.*

Constructio legis non facit injuriam. The construction of the law works [must so be made as to work] no wrong.

Constructive. (v. *Trust.*) Made out; deduced by construction; inferred, construed, or interpreted by law.

Construe. To explain and apply, even to vary the sense; a stronger word than **Interpret:** to explain or render intelligible.

Consuetudo, *pl.* **consuetudines,** *l.* Custom, customs; usage, practice. **Consuetudinibus et servitiis:** v. *De.* **Consuetudo debet esse certa; nam incerta pro nullis habentur:** a custom should be certain; for uncertain things are held as naught. **Consuetudo est altera lex:** custom is another law. **Consuetudo est optimus interpres legum:** Custom is the best interpreter of laws. **Consuetudo ex certa causa rationabili usitata privat communem legem:** an established custom with a certain reasonable cause supersedes the common law. **Consuetudo loci, manerii, est observanda:** the custom of the place, the manor, is to be observed. **Consuetudo semel reprobata non potest amplius induci:** a custom once disallowed cannot again be set up.

Conte, *fr.* A statement, plea. **Conter:** to count. **Contamus,** *l.;* we count, we declare.

Contemporanea expositio fortissima in lege, *l.* A contemporaneous exposition is in law the strongest.

Contentious. Litigious. The proceedings in ecclesiastical courts upon matters disputed are so called, as distinguished from its **voluntary jurisdiction,** probate, etc., where there is no dispute.

Contestatio litis, *l.* Pleading; joinder of issue; v. *Litis.*

Contingency with a double aspect. A contingent remainder limited in substitution of another contingent remainder.

Contingent. Dependent on the happening of some other event, which may or may not happen. v. *Use, Remainder.*

Continual claim. A sort of attempt at entry, made by a party disseised, as near the land as possible. It worked as an actual entry to keep alive his right if made once every year and day.

Continuance. Adjournment, postponement, of an action. It was formerly entered on the record; and, if made before declaration, was by **dies datus,** a *day given* to proceed; if after declaration, by **imparlance,** leave to talk with the plaintiff, to plead; if after issue, by **vicecomes non misit breve,** *the sheriff hath not sent the writ;* and after verdict, by **curia advisari vult,** *the court wishes to consult,* where the point of law was novel or difficult.

Continuando, *l. By continuing:* an allegation in declaration for trespass, whereby the plaintiff recovered damages for a succession of like or repeated trespasses, without bringing more than one cause of action.

Contra, *l.* Against; contrary to. **Contra bonos mores**: against good morals. **Contra formam doni**: against the form of the grant; v. *Formedon.* **Contra formam collationis** (against the form of the gift): an old writ which lay for the grantor of lands to be held by divine service, when they were wrongfully alienated. **Contra formam feoffamenti** (against the form of the feoffment): an old writ which lay for a tenant distrained for more services than his ancestor was, by the charter of feoffment, required to perform. **Contra formam statuti in hoc casu nuper edict' et provis'**: against the form of the statute in such case lately made and provided. **Contra jus belli**: against the law of war. **Contra jus commune**: against common right. **Contra negantem principia non est disputandum**: you cannot argue with one who denies principles. **Contra non valentem agere nulla currit præscriptio**: no prescription runs against one unable to act. **Contra omnes gentes**: against all the world. **Contra pacem domini regis**: against the peace of our lord the King. **Contra proferentem**: against the one putting it forth.

Contractus, *l.,* **Contrat,** *fr.* Contract. **Aleatory contract**: one the performance of which on either or both sides depends on an uncertain event. **Bilateral contract**: one consisting of two promises, one made on each side, mutually consideration for each other; in contradistinction from a **unilateral contract**, where one party only makes a promise. **Consensual contract**: one complete by the mere agreement of the parties, as distinguished from a **real contract**, where some object is delivered by way of sale, pledge, or bailment. **Executed contract**: one which is completed at the time it is made, like a sale for cash, as distinct from **executory contract**, one where some further act remains to be done. The former conveys a *chose in possession;* the latter creates a *chose in action.* **Oral, Parol**, or more properly **Simple contract**: one created by words or writing not under seal, as distinguished from **Special contract**, **Covenant**, or **Specialty**: a contract under seal, and requiring no consideration. **Contract of beneficence**: one by which only one of the parties is benefited, as a *loan, deposit*, or *mandate.* **Contracts of record**: those evidenced by matter of record, as *judgments* or *recognizances.* **Contractus ex turpi causa, vel contra bonos mores, nullus est**: a contract founded on a base consideration, or against good morals, is void. **Contractus legem ex conventione accipiunt**: contracts take their law from the agreement of the parties. **Contractus est quasi actus contra actum**: a contract is, as it were, act against act.

Contramandatio placiti, *l.* (Countermand of a plea.) The respiting a defendant, giving him a longer time to answer.

Contraplacitum, *l. Counter-plea.*

Contrapositio, *l.* A plea or answer.

Contrarotalator, *l.* Controller. An auditor; a keeper of accounts.

Contre, conter, *fr.* Against.

Contrectatio rei alienæ, animo furandi, est furtum, *l.* The touching another's property with intent to steal is theft.

Contribution. 1. A suit in equity, brought by one who has discharged a debt or liability, to compel those jointly liable to pay their share. 2. Ratable division of losses or liabilities.

Contributione facienda. v. *De.*

Contributory. A present or past member of a company now being wound up, who may be compelled to contribute to the assets for the purpose of paying creditors.

Contumace capiendo. v. *De.*

Contumacy. Contempt of court; persistent disobedience.

Conusance, Conusor, Conusee, etc. v. *Cognizance, etc.* **Conusans,** *fr.*: acknowledgment. **Conusant:** knowing. **Conus:** known. **Cognustre:** to acknowledge. **Conusor:** the party entering into a recognizance for debt. **Conusee:** the party to whom it is given.

Convalescere, *l.* To gain strength; to become valid.

Convenable, *fr.* Suitable; agreeable; fitting.

Convenire, *l.* To sue; to prosecute; to covenant. **Convenit:** it is (or was) agreed. **Conventio:** an agreement, covenant.

Conventio vincit legem, *l.* [Express] agreement prevails over law. **Conventio privatorum non potest publico juri derogare:** the agreement of private persons cannot injure the public right.

Conversantes, *l.* Conversant; acquainted; commorant.

Conversion. 1. Wrongful appropriation of another's property to one's own use. 2. In equity, that change in the nature of property by which, for certain purposes, real estate is considered as personal, and personal estate as real, and transmissible and descendible as such.

Convey, Conveer, *fr.* To transfer. **Conveyance:** a document effecting a transfer of property, usually real estate, other than a will, a lease for a short term, or an executory contract of sale. It is **original** or **primary,** if by it an estate or interest first is created or arises, as in the case of feoffments, gifts, grants, leases, exchanges, and partitions; **derivative** or **secondary,** if it presupposes, or depends upon, some other conveyance, which it enlarges, confirms, executes, or modifies, as in the case of releases, confirmations, surrenders, assignments, and defeasances; **tortious,** if it conveys a larger estate than the grantor holds, as in feoffments, which worked a forfeiture; **innocent,** if it only conveys the estate the grantor actually has, as in the case of bargains and sales, covenants to stand seised, and releases. By statute all conveyances are now *innocent,* and even a feoffment will have no tortious operation. **Conveyancing:** the law of the alienation of real property. **Conveyance by record:** one evidenced by the authority of a court of *record,* as fines and recoveries.

Coopertus, *l.* Covered; covert.

Coparcenary. Land is held in coparcenary when there is "unity of title, possession, and interest." It happens when land falls to two or more persons by descent *ab intestato;* as to two or more women, at common law, or men, in gavelkind tenure; and is subject to courtesy and dower. On alienation by one coparcener, it becomes tenancy in *common;* there is no right of survivorship, and on the death of one coparcener his heirs hold the same estate in coparcenary as before. v. *Common, tenancy in, Joint tenancy.*

Copia, *l.* 1. Opportunity; means of access. 2. A copy.

Copulatio verborum indicat acceptationem in eodem sensu, *l.* The coupling together of words shows that they are to be understood in the same sense.

Copyhold. Tenure of manor lands by copy of court roll, at the will of the lord, according to the custom of the manor. Originally pure villeinage, it has gradually become divested of its base services and approached a state resembling socage, and the lord cannot evict without cause or against custom.

Coram domino rege ubicunque tunc fuerit Angliæ, *l.* Before [our] lord the King, wherever he shall then be in England. **Coram ipso rege** (before the King himself): in the K. B. **Coram nobis**: before us; a name given to a writ of error on a judgment in the K. B. If on a judgment in other courts it was **coram vobis,** before you. Hence, the latter term is used when the proceedings of another court are to be reviewed; the former, when the proceedings of a court are to be reviewed by itself. v. *Error.* **Coram me vel justiciariis meis**: before me or my justices. **Coram non judice** (before one not a judge): in a court having no jurisdiction. **Coram paribus de vicineto**: before the [his] peers of the neighborhood. **Coram sectatoribus**: before the suitors.

Co-respondent. The person charged with adultery with the husband or wife in a suit for divorce.

Cornage. Tenure by winding an alarm-horn; a species of grand *serjeanty.*

Corodium, *l.,* **Corody.** An allowance of victuals, clothing, or money due from a religious house to its founder for the support of such person as he should appoint.

Corona, *l.* Crown. **Placita coronæ**: pleas of the crown, criminal actions.

Coronator, *l.*, **Coroner.** A magistrate authorized to inquire concerning sudden deaths, shipwrecks, and treasure-trove. They were also conservators of the peace, in certain cases replacing the sheriff.

Corporal oath. An oath taken by laying hand on the Gospels; a solemn oath.

Corporalis injuria non recipit æstimationem de futuro, *l.* A personal injury cannot receive satisfaction from a future course of proceedings.

Corporation. An artificial legal person, persisting through the change or succession of its members. It has power to act or contract, usually under a common seal, and to regulate its actions by by-laws. It is a **corporation sole** if consisting of one person; **aggregate,** if of more than one person at the same time; **ecclesiastical,** if constituted of religious persons for spiritual purposes; **lay,** if constituted for secular purposes. **Lay** corporations are divided into **civil corporations,** existing for purposes of profit, and **eleemosynary,** or charitable. The former include **municipal corporations,** as counties, townships, villages, and **public corporations,** which exist for the public interest or advantage, and **private corporations.**

Corpus, *l.* Body. The capital of a fund. **Corpus comitatus**: all the inhabitants of a county, the county at large. **Corpus cum causa**: v. *Habeas corpus.* **Corpus delicti** (the substance of the fault): the fact that a crime has actually been committed; the subject of the crime, or its visible effect. **Corpus humanum non recipit æstimationem**: the human body is not susceptible of valuation. **Corpus juris civilis** or **canonici**: the body of the civil *or* Roman canon law. The former includes the Institutes, the Pandects, or Digest, the Code, and the Novels of Justinian. The latter includes Gratian's Decree, Gregory's Decretals, the Sixth Decretal, the Clementine Constitution, and the Extravagants of John and his successors. v. *Civil Law, Canon Law.*

Correi credendi, debendi, *l.* Joint creditors, debtors; creditors or debtors *in solido.*

Corruptive, *l.* Corruptly.

Corruption of blood. v. *Attainder.*

Corsepresent. A mortuary offering, generally the second-best beast of a person to be buried, taken along with the corpse and presented to the priest. v. *Mortuary.*

Corsned, *sax.* The morsel of execration; a piece of barley bread given to an accused with solemn oaths and incantations. If it stuck in his throat, he was deemed guilty.

Cosinage, *fr.* Collateral relationship. An old writ lying for an heir against one who entered the land of a great-great-grandfather (*tresayle*) or distant collateral relation. cf. *Aiel.*

Costs "de incremento," *l.* Costs of increase; adjudged by the court in addition to those found by the jury.

Cota, Cotagium, *l.* A cot, cottage. **Cotarius** : a cottager.

Cotland. Land held by a cottager in socage or villeinage.

Cottage. A dwelling-house, with a garden.

Couchant et levant, *fr.* Lying down and rising up; v. *Levant.* **Coucher de soel**: sunset.

Count. A distinct statement of the cause of action in a declaration, or of the charge in an indictment. In real action, the declaration.

Counter, *fr.*, **Count.** To declare; to plead orally. **Countamus** : we declare.

Counterplea. A plea answering some matter incidental to the main object of the suit; as in answer to *Aid-prayer, Oyer, Voucher.*

Counter-roll. A roll or account kept by one officer as a check upon another.

Countez, *fr.* (Count ye.) A direction given by the clerk of the court to the crier to count the jury.

Countour, *fr.*, **Countor.** An advocate or sergeant at law.

Countre, *fr.* Against.

Country. The inhabitants of a district from which a jury is to be summoned. **To put one's self on the country** is to claim jury trial. **Country cause** : a cause out of London and Middlesex.

County corporate. A city or town with land annexed, privileged to be a county by itself. **County court**: v. *Court,* 29, 41. **County Palatine** : a county where the owner had royal privileges, as of pardoning offences or issuing writs; there were formerly three such counties, — Chester, Durham, and Lancaster.

Coupable, *fr.* Guilty.

Courir, *fr.* To run. **Courge, court**: he runs, it runs.

Court, Courts. — I. **English.** A. The **superior common-law courts** were anciently as follows : — 1. **Witenagemote.** This court or assembly existed in Anglo-Saxon times, and was an "assembly of the wise men" of the nation, who met to make laws for the nation at large and to provide for the general welfare and protection. Incidentally, they adjudged upon disputes of the King's thegns and great men, cleric and lay. Its functions were legislative and judicial, chiefly the former. It was succeeded in the Anglo-Norman period by a similar body called both (2.) The **King's Court** and (3.) the **Great Council**, which must not be confounded with the *King's Court* proper (*Court,* 5), and was the original of Parliament. 4. The **Thenningmannagemot,** or **Thegnmen's Court**, in Saxon times was an aristocratic court of original jurisdiction, open only to the King's *thegns* or tenants *in capite ;* and under Edward the Confessor was called the **Aula Regis** or **Regia.** 5. The **King's Court** and the **Exchequer** (*Court,* 11) were the two *royal* courts of the Norman period. The *King's Court* consisted of a body of great men attendant on the King, and was, in a sense, the successor of the *Aula regis,* but with much wider jurisdiction. By the use of writs it usurped the jurisdiction of the *popular* courts; and, differing in this respect also from the *Aula regis,* had appellate jurisdiction from them. In the twelfth century, a smaller *King's Court* was created, five persons being appointed to hear complaints; and in 1179, its justiciars were appointed to act both on circuit and in the presence of the King as the **Bench.** The earlier and larger *King's Court,* now called (6.) the **King's Council,** followed the King's person and had appellate jurisdiction over the smaller *King's Court.* The former was the origin of the **Privy Council** (*Court,* 14); the latter, of the **King's Bench** (*Court,* 8).

In modern times, up to the passing of the *Judicature Act,* the three (7.) **Superior courts of common law,** which, with the **Court of Chancery** (*Court,* 15), formed the four **Superior courts of the kingdom,** were (8.) the **King's Bench**; (10.) the **Common Pleas**; and (11.) the **Exchequer.** The *King's Bench* or *Queen's Bench, l.* **Bancus Regis,** in theory followed the King's person (*coram ipso rege*), but in fact sat at Westminster. It was the

highest court of common law in England ; had four puisne justices and a chief justice, who was the **Chief Justice of England**; took cognizance of criminal cases on the **crown side** or '
crown office, and of civil cases on the **plea side**.   Formerly,
its civil jurisdiction was confined to trespasses *vi et armis*, on
the theory that they were an offence against the King's peace;
but by the fictions of the *Bill of Middlesex* and *Latitat* (v. *Bill*,
I. 8), it usurped jurisdiction over all *personal actions*.   See also
Court, 5.   9. The **Practice** or **Bail Court** was a court auxiliary to the King's Bench, presided over by each puisne judge
in rotation.   10. The **Common Pleas** or **Common Bench**,
l. **Communis Bancus, Communia Placita**, is also derived
from the old King's Court, by a clause in *Magna Charta* fixing
the hearing of *common pleas* (civil cases, pleas between subject
and subject) at Westminster.   It had the exclusive jurisdiction
of *real actions*, and universal jurisdiction, for a long time also
exclusive, of *personal actions* between subject and subject.   There
were four puisne justices and a chief justice.   Appeals were
anciently taken to the K. B.; but in the present century only to
the judges of the K. B. and the barons of the Exchequer in the
Exchequer Chamber (*Court*, 12), and thence to the **House of
Lords** (*Court*, 13).   11. The **Exchequer** was originally the royal
treasury; and its functions were to keep the royal accounts, to
collect the royal revenues and debts, and escheats.   Common
pleas were anciently held there as matter of favor, the court
affording peculiar advantages by its records, which included the
Domesday book, and its permanent location at Westminster.   The
holding of common pleas was, however, forbidden by the *Ar-
ticula super Chartas* in 1290; and the Exchequer became a
purely fiscal court, until it regained its jurisdiction by use of the
fiction that the plaintiff was a debtor to the King.   In modern
times, there were two divisions of this court; the **receipt**, which
managed the revenue and such matters, and the **court** or **plea
side**, which had jurisdiction of all personal actions between subject and subject.   The *court* had both an equity and a common-
law side, until 1842, when the equity jurisdiction was transferred
to Chancery.   The Exchequer was the lowest of the three superior courts, and had four puisne **barons** and one **chief baron**.
12. The **Exchequer Chamber** was an intermediate court of ap-

peal between the three superior courts of common law and the House of Lords. When sitting on an appeal from any one court, it was composed of the judges of the two other courts. 13. The **House of Lords** was the supreme court of judicature in England, having appellate jurisdiction over the common-law courts, and probably also over the Court of Chancery; and it has now appellate jurisdiction over the Court of Appeal (*Court*, 26). Its original jurisdiction is now obsolete, except as a court of impeachment. It is presided over by the Lord High Chancellor, and only such peers as have performed judicial functions take part. 14. **The Judicial Committee of the Privy Council** had jurisdiction in certain colonial causes, and appellate jurisdiction from the courts of admiralty and the commissioners in lunacy. See also *Court*, 26, 83, 87, 89.

B. The **Superior Courts of Equity** were as follows : — 15. The **Court of Chancery, *l*. Cancellaria,** was the court of the Lord High Chancellor, who in theory exercises such judicial powers as reside in the Crown; v. *Court*, 19. Originally, such powers were invoked as a favor of the King, but were long since crystallized into the system of **Equity.** The Court of Chancery was the highest court of equity, and reckoned one of the four modern **superior** courts. Its ordinary jurisdiction, long since practically obsolete, consisted chiefly in the issuing of royal *writs*, writs under the great seal, *original;* which were all framed in Chancery as the (**officina justitiæ**) mint of justice. The extraordinary jurisdiction was what is now known as Equity. Besides this, the Court of Chancery and the Chancellor had certain statutory powers. In modern times, there have been six superior courts of equity, over which the Court of Chancery proper, just mentioned, had appellate jurisdiction; the (16.) **Court of the Master of the Rolls,** and (17.) three **Vice-Chancellor's Courts,** each presided over by a **Vice-Chancellor.** Also, by the 14 and 15 Vict. c. 83, was established (18.) the **Court of the Lords Justices of Appeal,** of whom there were two; and who, with the Lord Chancellor, formed the (18.) **Court of Appeal in Chancery.**

By the 36 & 37 Vict. c. 66, usually known as the **Judicature Act,** is established one (19.) **Supreme Court of Judicature.** Into this the *High Court of Chancery*, the *King's Bench, Common*

Pleas, and *Exchequer,* the *High Court of Admiralty,* the *Court of Probate,* and the *Divorce Court,* are united and consolidated. The **London Court of Bankruptcy** (*Court,* 48) remains an independent court, though the office of chief judge in bankruptcy is filled by a judge of the High Court of Justice (*Court,* 20), and the decisions of the court are subject to review by the High Court of Appeal (*Court,* 26). This Supreme Court of Judicature consists of two divisions, one to be called (20.) **Her Majesty's High Court of Justice,** and the other **Her Majesty's Court of Appeal** (*Court,* 26). The jurisdiction of the former is chiefly original; and includes in general that previously exercised by the Courts of *Chancery, King's Bench, Common Pleas, Exchequer, Admiralty, Probate, Divorce, Common Pleas at Lancaster, Pleas at Durham,* and by the *Assize courts. Except,* however, the appellate jurisdiction of the *Court of Appeal in Chancery* (*Court,* 18), or of the same court sitting as a court of appeal in bankruptcy; the jurisdiction of the *Court of Appeal in Chancery of* the *County Palatine of Lancaster;* the jurisdiction, whether of the Lord Chancellor or Lords Justices, over idiots, lunatics, and persons of unsound mind; the jurisdiction of the Lord Chancellor in the matters of letters patent and commissions under the great seal, or over colleges and charities; the jurisdiction of the Master of the Rolls over records in England. The members of the High Court of Justice are the Chief Justice of England, the Master of the Rolls, the Chief Justice of the *Common Pleas,* the Chief Baron of the *Exchequer,* the Vice-Chancellors of the *High Court of Chancery,* the Judge of the Court of *Probate,* and of the *Court for Divorce and Matrimonial Causes,* the puisne judges of the *King's Bench* and *Common Pleas,* the junior barons of the *Exchequer,* and the Judge of the *High Court of Admiralty.* The Lord Chief Justice of England is President of the Court, which is divided into five divisions: the (21.) **Chancery Division;** (22.) **King's [Queen's] Bench Division;** (23.) **Common Pleas Division;** (24.) **Exchequer Division;** (25.) **Probate, Divorce, and Admiralty Division.** To each of these, as a general rule, are assigned the judges of the corresponding old court, similarly named, with substantially the same jurisdiction. Legislation is now in process having for its object the fusion of the Common Pleas and Exchequer Divisions in the Queen's Bench Division, and the abolition of the offices of Chief Baron of the Exchequer and Chief Justice of the Common Pleas. 26. The **High Court of Appeal** has a jurisdiction chiefly appellate. It includes the appellate jurisdiction of the Lord Chancellor, and of the *Court of Appeal in Chancery,* and of the same court when sitting as a court of appeal in bankruptcy; the jurisdiction of the *Court of Appeal in Chancery of the County Palatine of Lancaster,* and of the Chancellor of the Duchy and County Palatine of Lancaster when sitting alone or apart from the Lords Justices of Appeal in Chancery as a judge of rehearing or appeal from decrees or orders of the Lancaster chancery courts; the jurisdiction of the Lord Warden of the *Stannaries* and his assessors, of the *Exchequer Chamber,* of the King or Queen in council, and the *Judicial Committee of the Privy Council* in admiralty and lunacy; and general appellate jurisdiction from the *High Court of Justice.* Appeals lie from this court to the House of Lords. The judges of the Court of Appeal are the Lord Chancellor, the Chief Justice of England, the Master of the Rolls, the Chief Justice of the Common Pleas, the Chief Baron of the Exchequer, who are styled the *ex officio* judges of the court; also the Lords Justices of Appeal in Chancery, and an additional judge appointed. These latter are the *ordinary* judges of the court, and are styled *Justices of Appeal.* The Lord Chancellor is President of the court.

C. The **inferior English common law courts** which existed generally throughout the kingdom, and were not of a local or special nature, are as follows: — 27. The courts of **Assize and Nisi Prius** (v. *Assize, Nisi Prius*), or **Gaol Delivery, Oyer and Terminer,** succeeded the ancient courts of the justices in *eyre.* These **Assizes** are the ordinary courts for the trial of jury cases by a jury of the county; and are held twice a year, formerly in the vacations after Trinity and Hilary terms, in every county except Middlesex; two judges of the Superior Court being appointed for each circuit, under four, formerly five, commissions (v. *Assize*), and all England being divided into six circuits, and Wales into two. The court for London and Middlesex is within no circuit, and is termed the (28.) **London and Westminster sittings.** These courts are now part of the High Court of Justice (*court,* 20). 29. The **County courts** were held by the sheriff once a month or oftener to try small cases, not exceeding 40 *s.* in amount (though larger cases and real actions might be brought under a *justicies*), and for certain other purposes. The freeholders of the county were the judges and members of the court; and being a popular court, not of record, it early lost its jurisdiction, causes being removable into the Superior Courts by writs of *recordari facias loquelam, false judgment,* and *pone.* For the new County Courts, see *Court,* 41. 30. The **Hundred courts** were similar and inferior to the County Courts (*Court,* 29) held by the steward, with the freeholders of the *hundred* as judges. It is not to be confounded with the (31.) **Hundred gemote** of Saxon times, which had larger civil and criminal jurisdiction. 32. The **Court-leet** or **View of frankpledge** was a court of record in a particular lordship, hundred, or manor, held once a year before the steward of the leet. It existed by royal charter or franchise; and was a court of small criminal jurisdiction, long since superseded by the *Quarter Sessions.* They also took *view of frankpledge,* and made *presentment* by jury of crimes. 33. The **Sheriff's Tourn** was a court similar to that last mentioned, held by the sheriff twice a year in various parts of the county, being the great court-leet of the county. 34. The **Court Baron (manorial courts)** was a court, not of record, incident to every manor. In one sense, it is a *customary* court, having jurisdiction over copyhold lands, surrenders, and admittances; in another, it was a common law court, similar in jurisdiction and nature to the hundred courts, sometimes independent both of them and even of the county courts. 35. The **Burghmotes, borough courts,** or **Hustings** existed by special franchise, and resembled the county courts (*Court,* 29) in nature and jurisdiction. 36. The courts of **Pie-poudre,** *fr.,* **Pedis pulverizati,** *l.,* **Pipowders,** were courts of record held by the steward, or him that had the toll, of every fair or market. They had cognizance of all cases of contract and minor offences arising during that particular fair or market; and were courts of speedy and summary process, so called from the *dusty feet* of the suitors, or from the French word *pied pul-dreaux,* a pedlar. 37. The court of the **Clerk of the Market** had authority to punish misdemeanors and try weights and measures; they existed in every fair or market throughout the kingdom. 38. The **Coroner's** and (39.) **Sheriff's courts** were of record, and are more properly termed inquests, being inquisitions into the property of treasure-trove, on violent deaths, boundaries of lands, damages, and other matters. 40. The **Quarter Sessions,** or **County Sessions** : a minor criminal court, or general sessions of the peace, held in each county four times a year before two justices of the peace, one of whom must be of the *quorum,* or the recorder in boroughs. 41. The new **County courts** were established by the 9 & 10 Vict. c. 95; they are over five hundred in number, and have a common-law jurisdiction up to £50; also of all consent actions, ejectments, attachments, interrogatories; and an equity jurisdiction up to £500; as well as some jurisdiction in probate, admiralty, and bankruptcy. Appeals lie from them to the divisions of the High Court of Justice.

D. The **more important** English courts of **special** or **local** nature or jurisdiction are as follows:—42. The courts of **Ancient Demesne** were anciently held by a bailiff appointed by the King; in them alone the tenants of the King's demesne could be impleaded; v. *Ancient demesne.* 43. The **Court of Augmentations** was established by the 27 Hen. VIII. c. 27, for protecting the King's interests as to suppressed monasteries, and dissolved in the reign of Mary. 44. The **Star Chamber, Camera Stellata,** *l.,* was an ancient court, remodelled under Henry VII. and Henry VIII. It consisted of divers lords spiritual and temporal, being privy councillors, together with two judges of the courts of common law; and tried, without the intervention of a jury, matters of riots, perjury, misbehavior of sheriffs, and other high misdemeanors. By usurpation of jurisdiction it became also a court of civil matters and revenue; and, owing to great abuses, was abolished under Charles I. 45. The **Court of Wards and Liveries** was founded under Henry VIII., to inquire into matters arising from tenures in chivalry, as concerning the wardship, marriage, and lands of the King's tenants *in capite ;* and abolished by the 12 Car. II. c. 24. 46. The **Court of the Lord High Steward** is a court of peers, instituted during the recess of Parliament for the trial of a peer for treason or felony or misprision of either. 47. The **Central Criminal Court** was established by the 4 & 5 Will. IV. c. 36, for the trial of offences committed in London, Middlesex, or Surrey; and succeeded the (48.) **Old Bailey.** 49. The **Court of Criminal Appeal, or Court for the Consideration of Crown Cases reserved**, was established by the 11 & 12 Vict. c. 78, and was composed of the judges of the superior courts, or such as could attend, for deciding any question of law reserved by any judge or magistrate of any court of oyer and terminer, gaol delivery, or quarter sessions, before which a prisoner had been found guilty by verdict. Its judgment is final; and its jurisdiction is now transferred to any five judges of the High Court of Justice. 50. **Courts of Bankruptcy.** There have been courts of bankruptcy in different districts from which an appeal usually lay to the **London Court of Bankruptcy,** v. *Court,* 19, established by the 1 & 2 Will. IV. c. 56. The county courts (*Court,* 41) have now a bankruptcy jurisdiction. 51. The 20 & 21 Vict. c. 77 established a **Probate Court,** to be held in London, which court exercised the testamentary jurisdiction previously belonging to the ecclesiastical courts. It is now consolidated into the Probate, Divorce, and Admiralty divisions of the High Court of Justice (*Court,* 25). Into the same division was also consolidated the (52.) **Court for Divorce and Matrimonial Causes,** which by the 20 & 21 Vict. c. 85 exercised the matrimonial jurisdiction of the ecclesiastical courts, decided on the validity of marriages, and granted divorces *a vinculo.*

E. The **inferior** English courts of a **local** nature or **special** jurisdiction are as follows: — 53. The **Court of Lord Steward of the King's Household,** established by the 33 Henry VIII. c. 12, and long obsolete, had jurisdiction of treason, blows, and homicides within the limits (two hundred feet from the gate) of any palace or house where the King might reside. 54. There was also a **Court of the Lord Steward, Treasurer, or Comptroller of the King's Household** established by 3 Henry VII. c. 14, to inquire of felony by a servant of the household; also obsolete. 55. The **Court of Marshalsea** held plea of trespasses or debts where a servant within the King's household was concerned. Its jurisdiction extended to the *verge,* twelve miles around the royal residence. It was derived from the old *Aula règis,* and a writ of error lay to Parliament only. It being ambulatory, Charles I. created the (56.) **Curia Palatii,** *l.,* or **Palace Court,** to succeed it. This court had jurisdiction of all personal actions whatever arising within twelve miles of the royal palace at Whitehall, not including the city of London, and was abolished in 1849. 57. There were many **Borough Courts**, and (58.) **Courts of Hustings** in the old English cities; and particularly, in London, the (59.) **Sheriffs' Courts**, holden before their steward or judge, from which a writ of error lay to the (60.) **Court of Hustings**, before the mayor, recorder, and sheriffs; and thence to justices appointed by the King's commission, who sat in the church of St. Martins-le-Grand; thence to the House of Lords; v. *Court*, 34. This (61.) **Court for the City of London**, as it was later called, has now become the county court for London. 62. The **Lord Mayor's Court** in London has both equity and common-law jurisdiction; and is presided over by the Recorder, or, in his absence, the Common Sergeant. The (63.) **Courts of Conscience or Requests** were tribunals, not of record, established in London and other towns, for the recovery of small debts; they are succeeded by the county courts, and mostly abolished. 64. The **Court of Policies of Assurance** was established under Elizabeth, for determining summarily all cases concerning policies of insurance on merchandise in London. Abolished in 1863, although long before obsolete. 65. The **Universities Courts** were established in Oxford and Cambridge; the (66.) **Chancellor's Court** had jurisdiction of personal actions and minor offences of members of the University; the (67.) **Court of the Lord High Steward** had jurisdiction of treasons, felonies, and mayhems committed by members of the University. They were formerly governed by the rules of the civil law; but now their jurisdiction, particularly in Cambridge, is in great part obsolete. 68. The courts of the **Counties Palatine.** That of **Chester,** a court of mixed jurisdiction, has been abolished. The (69.) **Court of Common Pleas at Lancaster** and (70.) **of Pleas at Durham** have lost their jurisdiction under the Judicature Act of 1873; but the **Chancery courts** of these counties are retained. 71. The **Courts of the Principality of Wales** were private courts of extensive jurisdiction, abolished by the 11 Geo. IV. and 1 Will. IV., when Wales was divided into two circuits for the judges of assize. 72. The **Stannary Courts** administered justice among the tin-miners of Devonshire and Cornwall. They were presided over by the *Vice-Warden*, with appeal to the *Lord Warden, of the Stannaries.* This appellate jurisdiction is now transferred to the High Court of Appeal; and the plaintiff may, in the first instance, sue in the county court. In like manner, there are two (73.) **Barmote** or **Berghmote Courts** in Derbyshire, called respectively the **Great** and **Small**, which administer justice among the miners of the Peak. 74. The **Forest Courts** existed for the government of the King's *forests*, to punish injuries to the *vert, venison,* or *covert.* They comprised the courts of (75.) **Attachments, Wood-mote**, or **Forty-days Court**, held by the verderors of the forest, to inquire into offences against the vert and venison; the (76.) **Court of Regard**, for the *lawing* of dogs; of (77.) **Sweinmote**, held by the *sweins* or freeholders in the forest, to inquire into grievances committed by the officers of the forest, and to try presentments certified from the Court of Attachments; and of (78.) **Justice-seat**, held before the Chief Justice in Eyre to determine all trespasses, claims of franchise, and other causes. All these courts were obsolete before the Restoration.

F. **Ecclesiastical Courts.** 79. The **Ecclesiastical Courts, or Courts Christian.** In Norman times, these courts consisted of councils, or synods, composed entirely or partly of the clergy, and had jurisdiction of crimes or delicts, and even of causes concerning land. These councils were national, provincial, or diocesan; the first resembled the lay *Witenagemote;* the last was the origin of the ecclesiastical court of modern times. This last has jurisdiction of matters ecclesiastical or pecuniary (withholding of tithes, etc.), matrimonial (affecting the relations of the sexes, legitimacy, divorce, etc.), and testamentary (the probate of wills, legacies, etc.). The last two kinds of jurisdiction were transferred to the Court of Probate and the Court for Divorce and Matrimonial Causes (*Court*, 51, 52), and are now vested in the Supreme Court of Judicature. The law of ecclesiastical courts was founded in the civil and canon law; and they are not courts of record. They are seven in number: the Archdeacon's Courts, the Consistory Courts, the Court of Arches, the Court of Peculiars, the Prerogative Courts of the two archbishops, the Court of Faculties, and, on appeal, the Privy Council, formerly the Court of Final Appeal, or Court of Delegates. There was also the Convocation, and the Court of High Commission. 80. The **Consistory** or **Diocesan Court** was held by each bishop, or his chancellor, in his diocese, with appeal to the archbishop. 81. The **Archdeacon's Court** was a minor court of concurrent or delegated jurisdiction in some part of the diocese, with appeal to the bishop. Both these were termed (82.) **Ordinary's Courts.** 83. The **Court of Arches,** so called because held in the church of St. Mary-le-Bow (*Sancta Maria de Arcubus,* l.), by the Dean of the Arches, later held in Doctors' Commons, now in Westminster Hall, was the principal consistory court of the Archbishop of Canterbury, with appeal from all other ecclesiastical courts in his province, and extensive original jurisdiction by means of *letters of request.* The **Audience Court** was similar, but of inferior jurisdiction. An appeal formerly lay to the Pope; afterwards to the *Court of Delegates,* now to the *Judicial Committee of the Privy Council.* 84. The **Court of Peculiars** is a branch of the Court of Arches, and has jurisdiction over all those parishes of the province of Canterbury which are exempt from the ordinary's jurisdiction and subject to the metropolitan only. An appeal lies to the Court of Arches. 85. The **Prerogative Courts** were courts held in the provinces of York and Canterbury before a judge appointed by the Archbishop, which had jurisdiction over testamentary matters where the decedent left *bona notabilia,* goods to the value of £5 in two distinct parishes. This jurisdiction is now transferred; v. *Court,* 79. 86. The **Court of Faculties,** a tribunal belonging to the archbishop, grants various licenses, creates rights to pews, monuments, burial, etc. 87. The **Court of Delegates** was created under Henry VIII., and was the great **Court of Final Appeal** in ecclesiastical and admiralty causes; succeeded by the *Judicial Committee of the Privy Council.* The decree of the Court of Delegates was sometimes revised by (88.) **Commissioners of Review.** 89. The **Judicial Committee of the Privy Council** has now practically ceased to be a court of appeal, even in ecclesiastical matters; such jurisdiction being transferred to the High Court of Appeal; v. *Court,* 14.

G. **Courts of Admiralty.** 90. The **High Court of Admiralty.** In theory the court of the Lord High Admiral;

presided over by his deputy, the Judge of Admiralty, and held in Doctors' Commons. It was a court not of record, having civil and criminal jurisdiction over maritime affairs. The criminal jurisdiction was conferred upon the *Central Criminal Court*, upon its establishment. The civil jurisdiction is twofold; and there are two courts, the (91.) **Instance Court**, for ordinary marine contracts, and the (92.) **Prize Court**. The Court of Admiralty now forms part of one division of the High Court of Justice; and the Instance Court has jurisdiction of assaults, batteries, collisions, restitution of ships, piratical or illegal takings, at sea; and of contracts between part owners of ships, seamen's wages, pilotage, bottomry bonds, salvage, tonnage, ship provisions, and mortgages. The county courts have also some admiralty jurisdiction.

H. **Military Courts.** 93. **Courts-martial.** The earliest was the **Court of Chivalry**, an ancient court not of record, held before the Lord High Constable or Earl Marshal of England, touching contracts or deeds of war and arms, both without and within the realm, coats of arms, precedency, etc.; its jurisdiction being criminal as well as civil, but of vague and indefinite extent. It became obsolete in the eighteenth century. The modern Courts-martial date from the Revolution. They are naval or military, and from their judgment there is no appeal. They have jurisdiction of offences against the mutiny act and the articles of war.

II. **Scotch Courts.** 94. The **Court of Session** is the supreme civil court of Scotland. There are two divisions; the first presided over by the Lord-President, the second by the Lord Justice-Clerk. Besides these two, there are eleven Lords Ordinary. making thirteen judges. Before the Union, there was a (95.) **Court of Exchequer**, now merged in the Court of Session. The judges of the Court of Session, having the power formerly exercised by the **Commissioners of Teinds** (Tithes), now sit also as the (96.) **Teind Court**, having jurisdiction of parish matters, valuations and sales of teinds, etc. An appeal lies from this court, as also from the Court of Session, to the House of Lords. 97. The **Justiciary Court** is the supreme criminal court, and is composed of five Lords of Session, with the Lord-President or Justice-Clerk as President. There are three circuits of the judges of this court; and appeal lies to the House of Lords. 98. The **Sheriff's Courts** are county courts of large civil and criminal jurisdiction, and formerly proceeded without a jury. There are also (99.) **Bailie's courts** in burghs, and (100.) **Justice of the Peace** courts. The **High Court of Admiralty** and **Commissary Court** or **Consistorial Court** are now obsolete.

III. 101. **Irish Courts.** Until the year 1877, when the **Judicature Act for Ireland** (40 & 41 Vict., c. 57) was passed, Ireland had the following courts : — Queen's Bench, Exchequer, Exchequer Chamber, Court for Crown Cases Reserved, Consolidated Chamber and Registry Appeals, Court of Chancery, of Appeal in Chancery, Rolls Court, Vice-Chancellor's Court, Landed Estates Court, Court of Bankruptcy and Insolvency, of Admiralty, of Probate, and Ecclesiastical Courts. By the Judicature Act, the Courts of Chancery, Queen's Bench, Common Pleas, Exchequer, Probate, the Court for Matrimonial Causes and Matters, and the Landed Estates Court, were fused into a **Supreme Court of Judicature** for Ireland. There is a **High Court of Justice,** with five divisions, and a **Court of Appeal,** as in England, with appeal from the latter to the House of Lords ; and law and equity are concurrently administered.

IV. **American Courts.** 102. **Courts of the United States.** They have jurisdiction exclusive of the State courts in the following cases : crimes cognizable under the authority of the United States ; suits for penalties and forfeitures incurred under United States laws ; civil causes of admiralty and maritime jurisdiction ; seizures on land or on waters not within admiralty and maritime jurisdiction ; cases arising under patent-right or copyright laws ; matters and proceedings in bankruptcy ; controversies of a civil nature, where a State is a party, except between a State and its citizens, or between a State and citizens of other States, or aliens ; suits and proceedings against ambassadors or public ministers, or their domestics or domestic servants, or against consuls or vice-consuls. 103. The **Senate** sits as a court of impeachment to try the President, Vice-President, and civil officers of the United States for treason, bribery, and other high crimes and misdemeanors. 104. The **Supreme Court** consists of one chief and eight associate justices ; and sits at Washington. It has exclusive jurisdiction in nearly all civil cases where a State is a party, and in suits or proceedings against an ambassador or his servants; original jurisdiction, not exclusive, in cases between a State and its citizens, or between a State and citizens of other States, or aliens; in suits by an ambassador or his servants, or in which a consul or. vice-consul is a party; it has power to issue writs of prohibition to the District Courts when proceeding in admiralty, and writs of mandamus in certain cases; it has appellate jurisdiction from the final judgment of any Circuit Court, or District Court acting as Circuit Court, in civil actions at law when $2,000 is involved, by writ of error, and in cases of equity, admiralty, and maritime jurisdiction, by appeal; and in case of division of opinion between the circuit judge and the district judge, by review; and, without regard to the amount involved, in all patent, copyright, or revenue cases; and in cases of deprivation of rights of citizenship, suits for conspiracy against "civil rights," cases tried by the Circuit Court without a jury; and from the final judgment of Territorial courts or the Supreme Court of the District of Columbia where $1,000 is involved, or where United States statutes or treaties are brought in question; and from the Court of Claims from all judgments adverse to the United States, and on behalf of the plaintiff, where $3,000 is involved. 105. The **Circuit Courts.** There are nine Circuits. The first includes the districts of Maine, New Hampshire, Massachusetts, and Rhode Island; the second, Vermont, Connecticut, and New York; the third, Pennsylvania, New Jersey, and Delaware; the fourth, Maryland, the Virginias, and the Carolinas; the fifth, Georgia, Florida, Alabama, Mississippi, Louisiana, and Texas; the sixth, Ohio, Michigan, Kentucky, and Tennessee; the seventh, Indiana, Illinois, and Wisconsin; the eighth, Nebraska, Minnesota, Iowa, Missouri, Kansas, Arkansas, and Colorado; the ninth, Oregon, Nevada, and California. Each court is composed of a member of the Supreme Court as *Circuit Justice*, a *Circuit Judge*, who shall reside within his circuit, and the district judge of the district where the circuit court is held; and may be held by any one of the three sitting alone, or by any two sitting together; but a district judge cannot vote on appeal or error from his own decision. The Circuit Courts have original jurisdiction in civil suits at common law or equity where $500 is involved and an alien is a party, or the suit is between a citizen of the State where it is brought and a citizen of another State, or of suits in equity involving $500, where the United States are petitioners, or at common law where the United States, or any officer thereof suing under the authority of any act of Congress, are plaintiffs; of suits under import, internal revenue, and postal laws; of patent and copyright suits, suits against national banks, suits in bankruptcy, and in divers other cases. They have appellate jurisdiction from the District Courts in cases involving $50, of equity, admiralty, or maritime jurisdiction. The Circuit Court meets at least twice a year in every district. 106. The **District Courts.** There is one or more district in every State, for which a District Judge is appointed. These courts are the lowest of the United States courts, and have original jurisdiction of certain crimes and offences cognizable under the authority of the United States; of piracy, when no Circuit Court is held in the district; of suits for penalties and forfeitures incurred under United States laws; of suits brought by the United States or an officer thereof authorized to sue; of suits in equity to enforce internal revenue taxes; of suits for penalties or damages for frauds against the United States; of suits under postal laws; of all civil causes of admiralty and maritime jurisdiction, and of seizures on land, or waters not subject to admiralty jurisdiction; of suits against conspirators, as for deprivation of "civil rights"; of suits to recover offices in certain cases, or for the removal of officers; of suits against national banks; and of proceedings under national bankruptcy laws; besides some other less common proceedings. 107. The **Court of Claims** consists of one chief justice and four judges, and holds one annual session at Washington. It has jurisdiction of all claims founded upon any law of Congress, or upon any regulation of an Executive Department, or upon any contract, expressed or implied, with the government of the United States, and all claims which may be referred to it by either House of Congress; and of all set-offs or counter claims made by the United States; of all claims by a disbursing officer for relief from responsibility for government funds or papers put in his charge; and of all claims for captured or abandoned property.

108.   The **State courts.** Generally, in each of the States, there is a **Supreme Court, Supreme Court of Appeals, of Er-**

rors, or **Supreme Judicial Court,** having both original and appellate jurisdiction, the judges of which sit at stated times in the various county seats at *nisi prius,* and at the State capital *in bank.* These courts have usually power to issue remedial writs, such as *error, supersedeas, certiorari, habeas corpus;* and particularly the higher writs, like the English *prerogative* writs, such as *quo warranto, mandamus, prohibition,* and *ne exeat regno (republica).* Frequently, they are the only courts exercising equity powers, or having jurisdiction of appeals from courts of probate, of awards of land damages, and of divorce or matrimonial causes. In some States the jurisdiction of the supreme courts is appellate only; in others, an appellate court above the supreme has been established, called the **Court of Appeals,** or **Court of Errors.** There is generally also a court (109.) called the **Court of Common Pleas, County Court, Circuit Court for the County,** or **Superior Court,** having large original jurisdiction, and some appellate jurisdiction from minor courts or tribunals. Usually this court has also sittings *in bank.* In some States there are **Courts of Chancery** or **Equity,** exercising general equity powers and distinct from the courts of common law. There are usually (110.) district courts exercising powers over the probate of wills, matters testamentary, guardianship, and occasionally trusts; called **Courts of Probate, Ordinary, Orphans'** or **Surrogate's** courts. Sometimes there is a State court of criminal jurisdiction or a criminal branch of a court of general jurisdiction, termed the (111.) **Court of Oyer and Terminer.** 112. There are generally many minor courts, of inferior, limited, local, or special jurisdiction, both civil and criminal, termed **City** Courts, **Municipal** Courts, **Police** Courts, **District** Courts, **Justice of the Peace** Courts, Courts of **Hustings,** Courts of **Sessions, Parish** Courts, etc.

113. **Territorial Courts.** These are created under the authority of the United States government; and usually consist of a Supreme Court, with a chief and two associate justices; a District Court, of which one of the Supreme Court justices is judge, both these courts having equity as well as common-law jurisdiction; probate courts, and justice of the peace courts. There is an appeal from the Territorial Courts to the Supreme Court of the United States in cases where $1,000, or, in Washington, $2,000, is involved.

114. There is a **Supreme Court for the District of Columbia**, having the jurisdiction of the Circuit Courts of the United States ; and any one of its justices, holding a special term, has the power and jurisdiction of the District Courts of the United States. This court has also jurisdiction of cases arising under the copyright and patent laws, bankruptcy, and other special cases. There is an appeal to the Supreme Court of the United States, where $1,000 is involved.

115. The term **Royal courts** is applied to the *King's courts*, established by the Conqueror or his successors, on the Norman theory that all justice flows from the King, of which the jurisdiction rested directly on royal authority. 116. The term **Popular courts** is usually applied to such courts as existed before the Conquest (except the *Witenagemote*), which were national, popular, or social tribunals ; such as the hundred, county, and borough courts. 117. A **Court of Record** is one which has power to fine or imprison for contempt of its authority. The records of a court of record were formerly kept on parchment, and written in Latin ; they are received in other courts as conclusive evidence of their own genuineness ; and these records are in many cases conclusive evidence of the matters therein contained.

Court-lands. The *demesne* land of a manor. **Court-rolls** : the rolls of a manor, the record of surrenders and admittances, wills, grants, and other matters affecting the lands of the manor.

Coustum, coutum, *fr.* Toll, tribute.

Coututlaugh, *sax.* A person who knowingly receives an outlaw.

Covenable, *fr. Convenable.*

Covenant. An agreement, a promise, or an express statement, made by a deed, or contained in a deed, between two or more persons, and sealed by one or more of them. Covenants are **dependent** on some prior act or condition, or **independent**; or **concurrent**, when each is dependent on the other, and either party must aver performance of his own or readiness to perform it, before seeking to enforce the other against the other party. They are also **in deed**, expressed in the deed, or **in law**, implied by law. They are **inherent** when relating directly to the land granted, or **collateral**, when affecting some other matter. They **run with the land** into the hands of other grantees, or they exist **in gross**. Covenants of title are divided into six common classes: of **seisin**, that the grantor is duly seised; of **right to convey**; **against incumbrances**; **for further assurance**; **of quiet enjoyment**; and **warranty**. These are sometimes called **real covenants**; more particularly the last three, which run with the land. The first three are more properly **personal**, and cannot be enforced by an assignee of the land.

Covenant. The action brought to recover damages for breach of a contract under seal.

Covenant to stand seised. A conveyance under the statute of uses, in which, in consideration of blood relationship, a man covenants to stand seised to the use of a wife or relative, whereby the possession is vested in such person by the statute. Now obsolete.

Covert. Covered; protected. **Feme covert**: a married woman. **Coverture**: the condition of marriage. **Covert baron**: under the protection of a husband.

Covin. Secret combination to effect fraud.

Crassus, *l*. Large; gross. **Crassa negligentia**: gross negligence.

Crastino, *l*. On the morrow. **Crastino animarum**: on the morrow of All Souls.

Craven, *sax*. To beg. v. *Battel*.

Creditors' bill. In England, a bill in equity filed by one or more creditors for an account of the assets and ratable settlement of the estate of a deceased, among such creditors as come in under the decree. A kind of *Administration suit*.

Crepare oculum, *l*. To put out an eye.

Crepusculum, *l*. Twilight.

Cresser, *fr*. To grow. **Cressant**: growing.

Cribler, *fr*. To argue. **Furent criblés**: were debated.

Crier, *fr*. To proclaim. **Crie de pays**: hue and cry. **Criez la peez**: rehearse the concord. An order given by the justice to the sergeant in the process of levying a fine. v. *Fine*.

Crim. Con. *Criminal conversation.*

Crimen falsi, *l*. The crime of falsifying. It includes counterfeiting, forgery, and perjury, and other cases of fraud. **Crimen furti**: theft. **Crimen incendii**: arson, burning. **Crimen læsæ majestatis** (the crime of injured majesty): high treason. **Crimen raptus**: rape. **Crimen roberiæ**: robbery.

Criminal conversation. Adultery. **Criminal information:** v. *Information.* **Criminal Appeal, Court of:** v. *Court,* 49.

Croft. A small piece of land by a dwelling-house.

Cross bill. A bill relating to a suit in equity, brought by the defendant in the previous suit against the plaintiff or other parties. **Cross examination:** the examination of a witness by the party opposed to the party producing him, to test the truth of his evidence given in chief. **Cross remainders:** when each of two or more grantees of an estate, usually tenants in common, has reciprocally a remainder in the shares of the others.

Crossed cheque. (In England) a cheque crossed by two lines enclosing a banker's name, whereby the cheque is made payable only to a certain banker. Sometimes the words *and company* only are written, and the payee is expected to prefix his banker's name.

Crown law. Criminal law. **Crown side:** the criminal side of the K. B.; v. *Court,* 8. **Crown Cases Reserved, Court for the Consideration of:** v. *Court,* 49. **Crown office:** a department in the crown side of the K. B. where cognizance is taken of criminal causes, and informations are filed.

Cry de pais, *fr.* (The cry of the country.) Hue and cry.

Cucking-stool. v. *Common scold.*

Cui ante divortium, *l.* (To whom before the divorce.) A writ of entry brought by a woman divorced to recover lands of hers which the husband had alienated during coverture. **Cui in vita:** a similar writ brought by a widow to recover lands alienated by her husband in his lifetime. **Cui bono:** for whose good, frequently mistranslated "for what good." **Cui licet quod majus, non debet quod minus est non licere:** he to whom the greater [act or power] is lawful, ought not to be prohibited from the less.

Cuicunque aliquis quid concedit, concedere videtur et id sine quo res ipsa esse non potuit, *l.* Any one who grants anything to another is held also to grant that without which the thing itself could not exist.

Cuilibet in arte sua perito credendum est, *l.* Any skilled person is to be believed in his own art.

Cujus est commodum, ejus debet esse incommodum, *l.* He who enjoys the profit ought to bear the loss. **Cujus est**

dare, ejus est disponere (whose it is to give, his it is to dispose): a giver can regulate the application of his gift. **Cujus est divisio, alterius est electio**: whichever has the division, the other has the choice [of shares]. **Cujus est dominium ejus est periculum**: he who has the ownership bears the risk. **Cujus est solum, ejus est usque ad cœlum et ad inferos**: he who owns the ground possesses also to the sky and the centre of the earth, i. e. all things above and below it.

Cul, culp., *l.* (Culpabilis.) Guilty. **Cul. prit.**: guilty; ready, etc. A reply of the clerk, on behalf of the Crown, to a prisoner's plea of not guilty, in criminal cases.

Culpa, *l.* Fault; negligence; guilt. **Culpa lata dolo æquiparatur**: gross negligence is held equivalent to intentional wrong.

Cum, *l.* With. **Cum grano salis** (with a grain of salt): allowing for exaggeration. **Cum onere** (with a burden): subject to a charge. **Cum pertinentiis**: with the appurtenances. **Cum testamento annexo**: with the will annexed; v. *Administration.*

Cum, quum, *l.* When. **Cum duo inter se pugnantia reperiuntur in testamento, ultimum ratum est**: when two things repugnant to each other are found in a will, the last prevails. **Cum quod ago non valet ut ago, valeat quantum valere potest**: when what I do is of no effect as I do it, it shall have as much effect as it can [in some other way]; v. *Cy-près.*

Cumulative. Additional, increasing. v. *Legacy.*

Cur. For *Curia,* q. v.

Cura, *l.* Care. **Cura animarum**: *Cure of souls.*

Curate. v. *Rector.*

Curator ad hoc, *l.* A guardian for this [purpose]. **Curator bonis**: the guardian of a minor or lunatic.

Cure of souls. The spiritual charge of a parish; the duties of an officiating clergyman. **Cure by verdict**: v. *Aider.*

Curge, *fr.* Runs. **Curgera ove la terre**: shall run with the land.

Curia, *l.,* **Cur, Cour,** *fr.* *Court.* **Curia advisari vult**: the court wishes to deliberate. **Curia admiralitatis**: the court of admiralty. **Curia baronis** or **baronum**: the court baron. **Curia christianitatis**: the ecclesiastical court. **Curia comitatus**: the county court. **Curia cancellariæ est officina**

justitiæ: the court of chancery is the workshop of justice. **Curia domini**: the lord's court. **Curia magna** (the great court): Parliament. **Curia majoris**: the mayor's court. **Curia Palatii**: the *Palace Court*. **Curia pedis pulverizati**: *Piedpoudre* court. **Curia regis**: the king's court; v. *Aula Regis*.

Curialitas, *l.* Curiality; *curtesy*.

Currere, *l.* To run. **Currit quatuor pedibus**: it runs upon all fours.

Cursitors. Clerks of chancery, whose duties were to make out the original writs, or writs *de cursu*.

Cursus, *l.* Course; practice. **Cursus curiæ est lex curiæ**: the practice of the court is the law of the court.

Curtesy, Curtesy of England. The life estate which a husband has on the death of his wife in any lands of which she was seised, in fee simple or fee tail, during coverture, if he had lawful issue by her born alive and capable of inheriting.

Curtilage, *fr.* The enclosed land about a dwelling.

Curtis, *l.* A court, a yard; a dwelling; a household; a court or tribunal; a residence.

Custagium, custagia, Custantia, *l.* Cost; costs.

Custode admittendo, amovendo. v. *De*.

Custodia. Ward, keeping, guardianship, custody.

Custom of merchants. The *law merchant*. **Custom**; v. *Prescribe*.

Customary estate. An estate existing by the custom of a manor, evidenced by copy of court roll. **Customary freehold**: a copyhold tenure held not at the will of the lord, resembling freehold.

Custos, *pl.* **custodes,** *l.* A guard, keeper, warden, magistrate. **Custos brevium**: the keeper of the writs, a principal clerk of the C. B. **Custos maris** (warden of the sea): admiral. **Custos placitorum coronæ**: keeper of the pleas of the Crown. **Custos rotulorum**: keeper of the rolls; the principal justice of the peace of a county, the first civil officer, as the lord lieutenant is the first military officer. **Custos spiritualium**: guardian of the spiritualities, he that exercised ecclesiastical jurisdiction during the vacancy of a see, while the **custos temporalium**, guardian of the temporalities, looked after the material interests and accounted for the rents and profits to the King.

7

Custuma antiqua sive magna, *l.* An old export duty on wool and hides. **Custuma parva et nova:** old duties on goods exported or imported by aliens.

Custus, *l.* Costs; charges; expense.

Cy, *fr.* Here. **Cy-après:** bereafter. **Cy-devant:** heretofore.

Cy, si, etc., *fr.* So, as. **Cy-près:** as near [as possible]; the doctrine of construing instruments as near the intention of parties as possible; and, particularly, the equitable doctrine by which, when it would be impossible or unreasonable to carry out the directions of a testator literally, his intention is carried out so far as practicable; applied to charitable bequests.

Cynebote, *sax. Cenegild,* q. v.

Cyrographum, *l.* v. *Chirographum.*

D.

D. P. (Domus Procerum, *l.*). The House of Lords.

Da, oui da, *fr.* Yes.

Damage-clere, *fr.* A fee formerly due the chief clerk from a plaintiff recovering damages in the K. B. and C. P. **Damage-feasant:** doing damage, a term applied to cattle trespassing.

Damages. The sum claimed by the plaintiff or assessed by the jury in a personal or mixed civil action. **Exemplary, punitive,** or **vindictive damages:** damages more than the actual damage given by way of punishment for fraud, malice, or oppression; smart-money. **General damages:** such as necessarily result from the injury complained of; not **Special damages,** which must be specified in the declaration. **Liquidated damages:** a sum agreed upon by the parties as compensation for a breach of contract.

Dame, *fr.* A wife of a knight or baronet; lady.

Damnatus, *l.* Condemned; unlawful.

Damnosa hæreditas, *l.* A burdensome inheritance.

Damnum, *pl.* **damna,** *l.* Harm, loss; damages.

Damnum absque injuria, *l.* A damage without a [legal] wrong. **Damnum fatale** (fatal damage): unavoidable loss.

Danelage. The Danish law anciently prevailing in the eastern counties of England.

Dans, *fr.* In ; within.

Dans et retinens nil dat, *l.* One who gives and retains [possession] gives nothing ; i. e. the title does not pass.

Darrein, dareyne, darraign, etc., *fr.* Last; v. *Continuance, Puis darrein continuance.* **Darrein presentment :** v. *Assize.* **Darrein seisin.** An old plea for the tenant in a writ of *right.*

Dat', data, datum, *l.* " Given," executed ; the date of instruments.

Datio in solutum, *l.,* **Dation en paiement,** *fr.* (Giving in payment.) A species of accord and satisfaction by transfer or assignment of property in lieu of money.

Dative. In one's gift; appointed by public authority ; removable at pleasure.

Days in bank. The days in the C. B. on which writs were returnable; v. *Bank ;* also called **common days. Days of grace :** three days allowed persons summoned in the English courts for appearance, after the return day ; the fourth day being the **quarto die post.** In mercantile law, days (usually three) after the day upon which bills or notes are expressed to be payable on the last of which the bill becomes legally due. **To go without day :** to be dismissed finally from court; v. *Continuance.*

De, *l.* Of; from; about; out of; concerning; among; for; to. **De admensuratione dotis :** a writ of *Admeasurement of dower,* q. v. **De admittendo clerico :** a writ commanding the bishop to admit the clerk presented by a patron of a living who has established his right thereto in *quare impedit* or *darrein presentment.* **De ætate probanda :** a writ to determine whether the heir of a tenant *in capite* was of full age. **De alto et basso :** v. *Alto.* **De annuo reditu :** a writ to recover an annuity. **De apostata capiendo :** a writ for the arrest of a person professing some religious order who left his abbey or other residence and wandered about the country. **De arrestandis bonis ne dissipentur :** v. *Arrestandis.* **De averiis replegiandis :** a writ to replevy cattle. **De audiendo et terminando** (*fr.* **oyer et terminer**) : to hear and determine, v. *Assize.* **De averiis captis in withernamium :** v. *Capias in withernum, Withernam.* **De avo :** a writ of *aiel.* **De banco :** of the bench, of the Court of Common Pleas. **De bene esse** (*fr.* **del bien estre**) : for what it is worth, provisionally, v. *Bill,* I. 19. Spoken of evidence taken, but which is to be used only upon certain conditions, as if the witness be unable to attend at some future time; also of a verdict found subject to the opinion of the court, etc. **De bonis asportatis**: the action, brought *for goods carried away*, of trespass to personal property. **De bonis non**: of the goods not [administered], v. *Administration*. **De bonis non amovendis**: v. *Bonis*. **De bonis propriis**: of his own goods, spoken of a judgment against an executor or administrator to be satisfied from his own property, not **de bonis testatoris** or **intestati**, out of the goods of the testator or intestate. **De bono gestu**: for good behavior; v. *Good abearing*. **De bono et malo** (*fr.* **de bien et de mal**): 1. For good or evil. 2. The name of a special writ of gaol delivery. **De cartis reddendis**: a writ to secure the specific returns of deeds; **de catallis reddendis**: a similar writ for chattels generally. **De champertia**: a writ to enforce the statute of champerty. **De chimino**: a writ to enforce a right of way. **De clauso fracto**: of breach of close. **De clerico admittendo**: v. *De admittendo clerico*. **De combustione domorum**: concerning house-burning, a kind of *appeal*; v. *Appeal*, 2. **De computo**: v. *Compotus*. **De consanguineo**: a writ of *Cosinage*. **De consilio**: of counsel. **De conspiratione**: a writ of *Conspiracy*. **De consuetudinibus et servitiis**: a writ by landlord against tenant to enforce customs and services. **De contributione facienda**: an old writ to compel coparceners or tenants in common to contribute their share of rents or services. **De contumace capiendo**: a writ issuing from Chancery to arrest a defendant in contempt of an ecclesiastical court. **De conventione**: a writ of covenant. **De corpore**: of the body; v. *Corpus*. **De curia claudenda**: a writ directing the defendant to fence in his land. **De cursu**: of course; v. *Writ*. **De custode admittendo**: a writ to admit a guardian; **amovendo**, to remove one. **De custodia terræ et hæredis**: writ of ward, a writ for a guardian in chivalry or socage to recover the possession of the land and infant heir. **De debito**: a writ of debt. **De die claro** (by clear day): by daylight. **De die in diem**: from day to day. **De dolo malo**: concerning fraud. **De domo reparanda**: a writ to compel a man to repair his house when dangerous to the neighbors. **De donis conditionalibus**: of conditional gifts; the title of the statute establishing fees tail, 13 Edw. I., st. 1, c. 1. **De dote assignanda**: a writ for the widow of a tenant *in capite*, commanding the King's escheator to assign her dower. **De dote unde nihil habet** (of dower whereof she has nothing): a writ for a widow commanding the tenant to assign her dower. **De ejectione custodiæ** (for ejectment of ward): a writ for the guardian to recover the ward's land or person. **De ejectione firmæ**: a writ to recover damages for ejectment, which lay for a term tenant against the reversioner, remainderman, lessor, or a stranger; v. *Ejectment*. **De escæta**: a writ of *escheat*. **De essendo quietum de theolonio**: a writ which lay for the burgesses of a town exempt from toll to enforce such right of exemption. **De essonio de malo lecti**: a writ to authorize an examination into the truth of an *essoin* of *malo lecti*. **De estoveriis habendis**: a writ for a wife divorced *a mensa et thoro* to recover her alimony or estovers. **De estrepamento**: a writ to prevent *estrepement* by the tenant during a suit about the possession of land. **De et super præmissis**: of and upon the premises. **De excommunicato capiendo**: a writ to arrest a person excommunicated, now superseded by *de contumace capiendo*. **De executione facienda in withernamium**: a writ of execution in withernam, a species of *capias in withernam*. **De exitibus terræ**: out of the profits of the land. **De exoneratione sectæ**: a writ to privilege the King's ward from suit in all courts lower than the C. B. **De facto**: in fact, in deed; actual; distinguished from **de jure**, in law, of right. **De feodo**: in fee, of fee. **De fide et officio judicis non recipitur quæstio, sed de scientia, sive sit error juris, sive facti**: the good faith and honesty of purpose of a judge cannot be questioned, but his decision may be impugned for error either of law or fact. **De fine capiendo pro terris**: a writ which lay for a juror who had been attainted for giving a false verdict, to obtain release of his person, land, and goods on payment of a fine to the King; v. *Attaint*. **De furto**: of theft, a kind of criminal *appeal*. **De futuro**: for the future, regarding the future. **De gratia**: of grace, by favor. **De gratia speciali, ex certa scientia, et mero motu**: of special grace, certain knowledge, and mere motion. **De hærede deliberando illi qui habet custodiam terræ**: a writ for delivering the heir to

him who has custody of the land. **De hærede rapto et abducto** : a writ for a guardian in chivalry or socage to recover his
ward when abducted. **De hæretico comburendo** : a writ to
burn a heretic who had abjured his heresy and again relapsed.
De homine capto in withernamium : a writ to take in *withernam* him who had led any bondman or bondwoman out of
the county, so he or she could not be replevied according to law.
De homine replegiando : a writ to replevy a man out of custody, on giving security to the sheriff that he will appear to answer
any charge against him. **De incremento** : of increase ; v. *Costs.*
De idiota inquirendo : a writ to inquire whether a man be an
idiot or not. **De infirmitate** : of infirmity ; v. *Essoin.* **De ingressu** : writ of entry. **De injuria sua absque tali causa,** or
absque residuo causæ : of his own wrong without such cause,
or without the rest of such cause ; a replication, traversing, in
general terms, a plea of excuse or justification in an action
of tort. **De integro** : anew ; a second time ; as it was before.
De intrusione : a writ of *intrusion.* **De jure** : of right, by
law. **De jure communi** : at common law. **De jure judices,
de facto juratores, respondent** : the judges answer as to the
law, the jurymen to the fact. **De latere** : from the side, collat-
erally. **De libertatibus allocandis** : a writ for burgesses entitled to certain liberties to enforce their rights. **De lunatico
inquirendo** : a writ to inquire about lunacy ; v. *Commission,* 4.
De magna assisa eligenda : a writ to choose the *grand assize.*
De malo lecti, veniendi, villæ : v. *Essoin.* **De manucap-
tione** : writ of *mainprise.* **De manutenendo** : a writ of *maintenance.* **De me** : v. *A me.* **De medietate linguæ** : of
half-tongue, a jury half natives, half aliens ; v. *Bilinguis.* **De
medio** : a writ of *mesne.* **De melioribus damnis** (for the
better damages) : a term applied to the election by a plaintiff,
who has had the damages assessed severally against the defendants, of one defendant against whom he will proceed while he
enters a *nol. pros.* as to the others. **De mercatoribus** (of
merchants) : the statute of *Acton Burnel,* 11 Edw. I., 1233,
and the statute 13 Edw. I., st. 3, which established the recognizance by *statute merchant.* **De minimis non curat lex** :
the law concerns not itself about trifles. **De modo decimandi** : [a prescription] of a *modus* of paying tithes. **De morte**

hominis nulla est cunctatio longa: as to the death of a man no delay is long. **De non apparentibus et non existentibus eadem est ratio**: the rule as to things which do not appear is the same as the rule as to things which do not exist. **De non decimando** (of not paying tithes): a prescription to be entirely discharged of tithes. **De novo**: anew, a second time. **De odio et atia** (by hatred and malice): an old writ, issuing as of course and gratis, similar in purpose to the *habeas corpus*, which lay for a person imprisoned on charge of homicide commanding the sheriff to inquire whether there was just cause of suspicion against him. If it was found that he was accused *de odio et atia*, or that he committed the deed *se defendendo*, or *per infortunium*, a writ of **tradas in ballium** might issue commanding the sheriff to admit him to bail if he could find twelve good and lawful men of the county as *mainpernors*. **De onerando pro rata portionis**: a writ for a joint tenant or tenant in common, distrained for more than his share of the rent, to charge the other tenants proportionately. **De pace et legalitate tuenda**: for keeping the peace and good behavior. **De pace et plagis**: of breach of the peace and wounds, a kind of criminal *appeal*. So **De pace et roberia** (robbery) or **imprisonamento** (imprisonment). **De pace infracta**: of breach of the peace. **De parco fracto**: a writ of *pound breach*. **De partitione facienda**: a writ for making partition of lands held by tenants in common, joint tenants, or coparceners. **De perambulatione facienda**: a writ to ascertain the boundaries of lands. **De placito**: of a plea, in an action. **De plano**: summarily; clearly; by covin; forthwith. **De plegiis acquietandis**: a writ for a surety, who has been compelled to pay a debt, against his principal. **De pone**: a writ of *Pone*. **De post disseisina**: a writ of *Post disseisin*. **De praesenti**: for the present, as of the present. **De proprietate probanda**: a writ directing the sheriff to inquire by inquest into the ownership of goods distrained. **De quibus sur disseisin**: an old writ of entry. **De quodam ignoto**: from a certain person unknown. **De raptu haeredis**: a writ for a guardian in tenure against one who abducted his ward. **De raptu virginum**: of the rape of maids, a kind of criminal appeal. **De rationabili parte bonorum** (of a reasonable part of the goods): an old writ enabling the wife and children of a man deceased to recover the thirds of his personal property which he could not, by common law, or county customs, bequeath away from them. **De rationabili parte**: a writ of right for one coparcener against another usurping the entire possession. **De recto**: writ of *right*. **De recto de advocatione**: writ of *right of advowson*. **De recto de dote**: writ of right of *dower*. **De recto deficere**: to fail of right. **De recto [breve] patens**: the patent writ of right. **De redisseisina**: writ of *redisseisin*. **De replegiare**: writ of *replevin*. **De rescussu**: writ of *rescous*. **De retorno habendo**: to have a return, a judgment for the defendant in replevin. **De rigore juris**: by strict law. **De salva guardia**: writ of *safeguard*. **De salvo conductu**: writ of safe-conduct. **De scutagio habendo**: a writ to recover escuage from tenants by knight's service who failed to serve the King in war. **De se bene gerendo**: for his good behavior. **De secta ad molendinum**: a writ to enforce one to continue grinding at the plaintiff's mill as by custom. **De servitio regis**: for the King's service; v. *Essoin*. **De similibus idem est judicandum**: of like things the same judgment is to be made. **De statuto mercatorio**: a writ of *statute merchant*. **De statuto stapulæ**: writ of *statute staple*. **De superoneratione pasturæ**: a writ of *surcharge of pasture*. **De supersedendo**: a writ of *supersedeas*. **De tempore cujus**, etc.: v. *A tempore*, etc. **De tempore in tempus et ad omnia tempora**: from time to time and at all times. **De terra sancta**: of the holy land; v. *Essoin*. **De theolonio**: a writ to recover toll. **De transgressione**: a writ of trespass. **De ultra mare**: of beyond sea; v. *Essoin*. **De una parte**: unilateral, a deed where one party only binds himself. **De uxore rapta et abducta**: a writ for a man to recover damages for the abduction of his wife. **De vasto**: a writ of *waste*. **De ventre inspiciendo** (for examining the belly): a writ which a presumptive heir might have to examine whether the widow was pregnant or not; a writ to examine into the pregnancy of a woman sentenced to death. **De verbo in verbum**: word for word. **De vicineto**: from the neighborhood. **De warrantia chartæ**: a writ of warranty of charter, given a defendant in assize or other action, where he could not *vouch to warranty*, against the feoffor or his heir to compel them to warrant.

De warrantia custodiæ: a writ for one who had purchased lands in knight-service, or his heir, against the grantor warranting them free of *wardship*, or his heir, when wardship was claimed by a third party. **De warrantia diei**: a writ to prevent default where a man had a day given him to appear in court, and was absent on service of the King.

De, *fr.* Of; about; from; concerning; out of; in; at; in order to; on; with. **De bone memorie** (of good memory): of sound mind. **De comon droit**: at common law, of common right. **De cornes et de bouche** (with horns and mouth): an expression applied to hue and cry. **De coste**: on the side, collateral. **De cy en avant**: from now henceforth. **De defaute de droit**: for failure of right; an old appeal in feudal law. **De droit**: *de jure*. **De fine force**: of pure necessity. **De haut en bas**: of high and low, a term expressing the unlimited power of taxation enjoyed by a lord. **De la pluis beale**: v. *Dower*. **De mot en mot**: word for word. **De non sane memorie**: of unsound mind. **De pleine age**: of full age. **De ques en ça**: from which time until now. **De quoy**: of which, wherewith. **De rien culpable**: guilty of naught. **De son tort demesne sans tiel cause**: of his own wrong without such cause; v. *De injuria sua*, &c. **De sa vie**: for his life, not *pour auter vie*. **De son done**: by his gift. **De son grée**: of his own accord. **De temps dont memorie ne court**, etc. . from time of which memory runneth not [to the contrary]; v. *A tempore*.

Dead freight. The amount paid by a charterer for that part of the vessel's capacity which he does not occupy, though he has contracted for it.

Dead man's part, Death's part. That part of the personal effects of a decedent which by the custom of London and York went to the administrator. In Scotch law, **Dead's part** meant such of his personalty as remained beyond the shares of the widow and children, which the decedent could dispose of by will. **Dead pledge**: a mortgage.

Deafforest. To discharge from being a *forest* and subject to forest law.

Dean and Chapter. The council of a bishop, a spiritual corporation. **Dean of the Arches**: the presiding judge of the *Court of Arches*. v. *Court*, 83.

Debas, debassa, *fr.* Below, downwards.

Debent, *l.* They owe. **Debet:** he owes, he ought. **Debet et detinet:** he owes and withholds, words applied to an action of debt brought by one of the original contracting parties. If by or against an assignee, the original writ contained the word **detinet** alone. **Debet et solet:** he ought and has been used [to do], words in a writ of right, importing that the plaintiff sues for a thing now for the first time withheld; if he sued for a right of which his ancestor was deprived, the writ contained the word **debet** alone. v. *Debet.*

Debentures. The bonds of English public companies.

Debet esse finis litium, *l.* There ought to be an end of suits. **Debet quis juri subjacere ubi delinquit:** one ought to be subject to the law of the place where one offends ; v. *Debent.*

Debile fundamentum fallit opus, *l.* A weak foundation spoils the whole work.

Debita, *l.* Debts. **Debita fundi:** debts secured upon land. **Debita sequuntur personam debitoris:** debts follow the person of the debtor.

Debito modo, *l.* In due manner.

Debitor non præsumitur donare, *l.* A debtor is not presumed to make a gift [to intend a conveyance as a gift].

Debitum, *l.* Debt; a thing due or proper. **Debitum et contractus sunt nullius loci:** debt and contract are of no place [they may be enforced in any jurisdiction]. **Debitum in præsenti, solvendum in futuro** (owed now, to be paid in future): a debt or obligation, complete when contracted, to be performed subsequently.

Debitor, *l.* A debtor. **Debitorum pactionibus creditorum petitio nec tolli nec minui potest:** a claim of creditors can neither be lost nor modified through agreements made among debtors.

Debt. 1. An old action having for its object the recovery of a specific sum of money; v. *Debent.* 2. **Indebitatus assumpsit:** v. *Assumpsit.* **Debt of record:** a judgment or recognizance debt. **Debt by specialty:** a debt acknowledged by writing under seal.

Debuit, *l.* He owed. **Debuit reparare:** he ought to repair.

Deça, decha, *fr.* On this side.

Decanus, *l.* A dean. **Decania, decanatus:** his jurisdiction, a deanery; also, a *tithing.*

Deceder, *fr.,* **Decedere,** *l.* To die. **Decedens,** *l.,* **Decedent:** a person deceased.

Deceit. 1. An old judicial writ in the C. B. brought to recover lands lost in a real action by default of the tenant through collusion. 2. An original writ to recover damages for deceit by way of forgery, collusion, or fraudulent misrepresentation. 3. The modern similar action in trespass on the case.

Decem tales, *l.* (Ten such.) A writ to summon ten jurors to make up a deficiency.

Decenna, *l.* A decennary, a *tithing.* **Decennarius:** a deciner.

Deceptis, non decipientibus, jura subveniunt, *l.* The laws assist the deceived, not those deceiving.

Decern, *sc.* To decree.

Decet, *l.* It is fit, becoming.

Decies tantum, *l.* (Ten times as much.) A species of popular action against a juror who had been bribed, to recover ten times the amount of the bribe; also against the *embraceour.*

Decimæ, *l.,* **Dismes,** *fr.* 1. Tenths; the tenth part of the profit of church livings formerly claimed by the Pope, now part of the royal revenue. 2. Tithes.

Deciner, desiner, dozyner, etc. One of a *tithing,* a *hand-borow.*

Declaration. The first *pleading* of the plaintiff in a civil action at law; the written statement of his case; formerly, when oral, called the *count.* **Declaration of intention:** a declaration made by an alien before a court of record that he intends to become a citizen of the United States. **Declaration of trust:** an act showing, or instrument stating, that the donor grants, or the owner holds, certain property in trust for certain purposes; such act or instrument being made or assented to by the donor or holder.

Declare. To prepare, file, and serve a declaration. To state solemnly before witnesses.

Declinatory plea. The plea of *sanctuary,* or *benefit of clergy.*

Declination, declinature. A Scotch plea to the jurisdiction. **Decline:** to object to, *ibid.*

Decree, Decreet, *sc.* The judgment of a court of equity or admiralty, which, if **final,** disposes of the suit; if **interlocutory,**

disposes not of the main question, but of some plea or issue
arising in the cause. **Decree nisi**: one which will be made
absolute on motion, *unless* some cause to prevent intervene.
Decreet absolvitor, a decree for the defendant; **condemna-
tor**, for the plaintiff.

Decretal order. An order, like a decree, made by the Court of
Chancery on motion.

Decretales, *l.,* **decretals.** The second division of the canon law.
v. *Corpus juris.*

Dedi, *l.* I have given. The operative word in conveyances by
grant, anciently held to imply a warranty. **Dedi et concessi:**
I have given and granted.

Dedication. The appropriation of property, usually land, by the
owner to public uses; as of a right of way, when a private land-
owner lays out a road, and it is accepted by the public or public
authorities.

Dedicere, *l.* To deny. **Dedictum**: denied.

Dedimus, *l.* A commission to take testimony. **Dedimus et
concessimus**: we have given and granted. **Dedimus potestatem** was an old English writ, issuing out of Chancery, empowering the persons named in it to perform certain judicial or
ministerial acts; as to make an attorney, take oaths, take the
acknowledgment of a fine, etc.

Dedire, *fr.* To deny. **Dedit**: denied.

Dedit et concessit, *l.* He hath given and granted. v. *Dedi.*

Deed. A written agreement or grant, sealed and delivered; usually
the term is applied only to conveyances of real estate. A **deed
indented** is one executed in two parts, or as many parts as
there were parties, which formerly were separated by cutting
in a curved or indented line; a *chirograph*. A **deed poll**
is one executed in one part; by one party only; having the
edge *polled* or cut even, not indented. The terms are still used
to distinguish deeds in which there are agreements of more than
one party, from those which are the acts of a single party, like
simple grants or appointments. **Deeds to lead,** or to **declare
uses**: a deed made *before* or *after* a fine or common recovery, to
show the object thereof.

Defalcatio, *l.* Deduction, abatement.

Defalta, *l.,* **Default.** Omission, failure; failure to appear, or plead,
in court.

Defeasance. A collateral deed, accompanying or annexed to another, providing that the latter is to be void upon the happening or performance of certain conditions.

Defectus, *l.* Defect, imperfection. v. *Challenge, Escheat.*

Defendre, *fr.*, **Defendere,** *l.*, **Defend.** To deny; prohibit. **Defendant, defender:** the party denying, against whom an action is brought. **Defendemus,** *l.* (we will defend): a phrase in ancient grants binding the grantor and his heirs to defend the grantee against the imposition of servitudes or incumbrances other than those mentioned in the grant. **Defendendo,** *l.*: v. *Se defendendo.* **Defendere se per corpus suum** (to defend himself by his body): to wage *battel.* **Defendere se unica manu:** to *wage his law.* **Defendit vim et injuriam,** *l.*: he denies the force and injury.

Defensa, defensum, *l.* An enclosure, fenced land; a deer park.

Defensio, *l.*, **Defense,** *fr.* Defence; prohibition.

Defensive allegation. In ecclesiastical courts, the plea of the defendant stating the facts upon which he relies and to which he may have the plaintiff's answer under oath.

Defensor, *l.* A defendant; guardian, protector; warrantor.

Deficiente uno sanguine, non potest esse hæres, *l.* One blood wanting, he cannot be heir.

Definitive sentence. The final judgment of an ecclesiastical court.

Deforce, Deforciare, *l.*, **Deforcer,** *fr.* To withhold wrongfully, to act in deforcement. **Deforciant, deforcians, deforceor:** one who deforces. **Deforcement:** the withholding of lands or tenements from another who has a right to them, including *intrusion, abatement, disseisin,* or *discontinuance;* in a restricted sense, such detainer of the freehold from him that hath the right, but never had any possession, as falls within none of these, the deforciant having originally gained possession rightfully.

Degaster, *fr.* To waste.

Degree of relationship. In the *canon* law, we reckon by the number of steps from the person farthest from the common ancestor to him; in the *civil* law, we reckon by the number of steps from one person up to the common ancestor and down to the other. Thus, a grand-uncle is related to his grand-nephew in the third degree by the canon law, in the fourth degree by the civil.

Dehors, *fr.* Out of; beyond; foreign to.

Dei gratia, *l.* By the grace of God. **Dei judicium** (the judgment of God): trial by *ordeal.*

Deins, *fr.* Within. **Deins age:** under age.

Delate, *sc.* To accuse.

Del bien estre, *fr.* *De bene esse.*

Del credere, *ital.* Of belief or warranty. An agreement made by a factor or broker for an additional commission, to warrant the solvency of the parties to whom he sells; a kind of guaranty or suretyship.

Delectus personæ, *l.* Choice of the person; a term expressive of the right of a partner to have no person admitted into the partnership against his will.

Delegare, *l.* To delegate; assign; appoint; depute. **Delegata potestas non potest delegari:** a delegated authority cannot be re-delegated. **Delegatus non potest delegare:** an agent (delegate) cannot delegate [his authority].

Delegates, Court of. v. *Court,* 87.

Delegatio, *l.,* **Delegation.** 1. The changing of one debtor for another, by which the first is discharged and the second put in his place; a kind of *novation;* if the first debtor be not discharged, it is **imperfect delegation.** 2. The act of transferring, or the transfer, of authority.

Deliberandum est diu quod statuendum est semel, *l.* That which is to be resolved once for all [enacted] should be long considered.

Delictum, *l.* A crime, offence, fault. v. *Challenge.* **Ex delicto:** from tort or wrong, as distinguished from breach of contract.

Deliverance. The verdict of a jury.

Delivery. 1. The act by which the possession of goods is transferred, as from the seller to the buyer. It may be **actual,** or **symbolic,** as by key or bill of lading. 2. The transfer of a deed to the grantee or his agent. If to a third person, to hold until the performance of some condition, the delivery is by way of *escrow.*

Dem. For *demise,* on the demise of.

Demain, *fr.* 1. To-morrow. 2. *Demesne.*

Demandant. The party suing in a real action, the plaintiff.

Demens, *l.* One who has lost his mind; **amens:** a person wholly mad. **Dementia:** such insanity as comes from weakness or loss of mind.

Dementenant en avant, *fr.*   From this time forward.

Demesne, *fr.*   1. Lordship, seigniory.   2. Lands held absolutely, or used directly, by the lord, as distinguished from lands held by a superior lord; *bordlands*, not lands demised to tenants. 3. Own, original.

Demi, *fr.*   Half.   **Demi-sangue**: half-blood.

Demise.   1. A conveyance for life, years, or at will.   2. Death.

Demise and re-demise.   Mutual leases of the same land, by which a rent-charge is effected in favor of the person not owner; the lease to him being for a nominal rent.

Demisi, *l.*   (I have demised.)   Words in a lease importing that the lessor had full power and authority.

Demissio, *l.*   A lease; a transfer.   **Demittere**: to lease, transfer.

Demonstratio, *l.*   Description; designation.

Demonstrative legacy.   The bequest of a certain sum to be paid out of a specific fund.

Demorage.   v. *Demurrage*.

Demorari, *l.*, **Demorer, demurer,** *fr.*   To wait, stay; to demur.

Dempster.   The officer who pronounced the sentence in a Scotch court.

Demur.   To wait, stay.   v. *Demurrer*.

Demurrage.   1. Detention of a ship by a freighter beyond the time allowed in the charter-party.   2. The allowance for such detention.

Demurrer.   A pleading objecting that the adversary's last pleading is insufficient or bad in law, and asking judgment thereon.   A **special demurrer** states the causes of objection.   **Demurrer to the evidence**: an objection by one of the parties to an action that the evidence produced by the other was insufficient in law to maintain his case; whereby the jury were dismissed and the court called upon to give judgment on the facts as alleged. Nearly obsolete.   **In equity,** a pleading by the defendant praying judgment whether he is bound to answer on the face of the bill; if alleging new matter, it is called a **speaking demurrer.**

Demy, *fr.*   Half.   **Demy-sangue**: half-blood.

Den, dene, dena, *l.*   A valley, vale; a low woody hollow.

Denarius, *l.*   A penny.   **Denarius Dei**; **Denier à Dieu,** *fr.* (God's penny.)   Earnest-money; it was not, however, part of the consideration, like *Arrha*, but was paid to the poor.

Denizen. An alien born, made a subject by letters patent of the King. He could take land by purchase, not inheritance.

Denominatio est a digniori, *l.* Denomination is from the more worthy.

Deodand. Any personal chattel, animate or inanimate, which was the immediate occasion of the death of any reasonable creature; it was formerly forfeited to the Crown, to be applied to pions uses by the high almoner; thus, a sword, a horse, a platform from which a man fell, might be deodand.

Departure. A shifting of ground in pleading; as when a man sets up one defence in the plea and a different one in the rejoinder.

Depone. To make oath in writing, to **depose.**

Deposit. A species of bailment for safe keeping without reward.

Deposition. Evidence taken in writing, under oath, before a judicial officer, in answer to interrogatories. An **affidavit** is *ex parte*, with no adverse interrogatories.

Depuis, *fr.* Since.

Deputy. An agent authorized to do certain acts in the name of another.

Deraign, deregn; Derationare, *l.;* **Desrener,** *fr.* To prove; to disprove; to refute; to refuse.

Derechief, derchef, *fr.* Moreover; again.

Determine. To end, come to an end on the happening of a contingency; to **expire** is, properly, to end by natural causes, by limitation.

Derelict. Left; deserted; abandoned. v, *Abandonment.*

Derivativa potestas non potest esse major primativa, *l.* A derived power cannot exceed the original. **Derivative:** v. *Conveyance.*

Dernier ressort, *fr.* The last resort.

Des, *fr.* From; of. **Desmaintenant:** from now. **Desormes:** from now henceforward.

Descender, *fr.* To descend. v. *Formedon.*

Descensus tollit intrationem, *l.* A *descent* (cast) tolls the entry.

Descent. Succession to an estate by inheritance, or by act of law, as distinguished from *purchase.* **Descent cast** was where the heir of an abator, disseisor, or intruder took the estate by inheritance from him; in which case the rightful owner could no longer perfect his estate by mere *entry*, but was driven to his right of *action.*

Descriptio personæ, *l.* Description of the person.

Designatio unius est exclusio alterius, *l.* The special mention of one is [implies] the exclusion of the other.

Desoubs, dessous, desouth, *fr.* Under; underneath; below.

Desus, dessus, *fr.* Above.

Detainer. 1. The keeping of a person against his will, or withholding property or land from another. 2. A process for the commencement of an action against a person already in custody.

Determine. To cease; to end, in the happening of a contingency, as distinguished from **expire,** to end by natural limitation.

Detinet, *l.* He detains. v. *Debent, Replevin, Cepit.*

Detinue, *l.* An old real action for the specific recovery of a personal chattel unlawfully detained.

Deus solus hæredem facere potest, non homo, *l.* God alone can make an heir, not man.

Devant, *fr.* Before. **Devant le roy** : before the King.

Devastavit, Devastaverunt, *l.* (He *or* they have wasted.) The waste or misapplication of the assets of a decedent by the executor or administrator. On return of *devastavit,* a judgment debtor may sue out execution *de bonis propriis* against the executor.

Devenio vester homo, *l.* (I become your man.) Words used in doing homage. **Devenit**: comes or falls to. **Devenerunt** (they fell to) : an old writ which directed the escheator to inquire what lands held *in capite* fell to the King by the death of the tenant, and of the heir while under age.

Dever, deyver, *fr.* To owe. **Deit**: he owes.

Devest. To take away, deprive of.

Devier, devyer, *fr.* To die. **Devi, devie,** etc. : dies.

Devisavit vel non? *l.* (Did he devise or not?) An issue directed by a court of equity in a court of law to try the validity of a will.

Devise. A gift of real property by will. **Executory devise**: v. *Executory.*

Di colonna, *ital.* The contract between the owner, master, and mariners of a ship when all share the profits of the voyage; as in whaling or fishing voyages in New England.

Dict, dit, etc., *fr.* Said; a saying.

Dictum, *pl.* **dicta.** A saying or remark. **Obiter dictum**: a re-

8

mark thrown out by the way; an assertion of law not necessary to the decision of the case.

Diem clausit extremum, *l.* 1. An old writ lying for the heir on the death of a tenant *in capite* directed to the King's escheators, to ascertain of what lands he died seised and reclaim them into the King's hands until such time as the heir should be of age. 2. An old writ of *Extent* issuing from the Exchequer on the death of a Crown debtor, directing the sheriff to seize his chattels, debts, and land into the hands of the crown.

Dies, *l.* A day. **Dies amoris**: a day of indulgence; v. *Day of Grace*. **Dies a quo**: the day from which; **ad quem,** to which. **Dies communes in banco**: common days in bank; v. *Day*. **Dies inceptus pro completo habetur**: a day begun is taken as completed. **Dies datus**: a day given [to proceed]; v. *Continuance;* **prece partium,** on the prayer of the parties. **Dies dominicus**: the Lord's day. **Dies dominicus non est juridicus**: Sunday is not a court day. **Dies gratiæ**: a *day of grace*. **Dies interpellat pro homine**: the day makes demand for the man. When the fulfilment of an obligation is due on a certain day, the occurrence of the day is of itself deemed sufficient demand on the part of the creditor. **Dies juridicus**: a court day, a day for legal purposes. **Dies legitimus** (a lawful day); a term day. **Dies non** (for **dies non juridicus**): not a court day. **Dies utiles**: available days; days on which an act might be done.

Dieta, *l.* A day's journey, twenty miles; a day's work.

Dieu et mon droit, *fr.* God and my right. **Dieu son acte**: the act of God.

Digesta, *l.,* **Digests,** abb. **Dig.** The Pandects of Justinian.

Dignity. An honour, a title; a species of incorporeal hereditament.

Dilapidation. Ecclesiastical *waste;* waste committed or permitted on the lands or buildings of a church living.

Dilationes in lege sunt odiosæ, *l.* Delays in law are odious.

Dilatory plea. A plea which tends to delay the action, or abate this particular action without impeaching the right or denying the injury. v. *Abatement, Jurisdiction, Plea.*

Diligence. In Scotch law, a process of execution for debt.

Dillonques, *fr.* From thence; after that time.

Dimidium, *l.* Half; an undivided half.

Diminution of the record. In proceedings for the reversal of judgment, if the whole record be not certified or not truly certified to the superior court, the party suing out the writ of error may *allege diminution* and have the whole record brought up on *eertiorari*.

Dimisi, *l.* I have demised; v. *Demisi.* **Dimisi, concessi, et ad firmam tradidi:** I have demised, granted, and to farm let.

Dimittere, *l.* To send away, release, let go.

Diocese. The see of a bishop. **Diocesan court:** v. *Court,* 80.

Diriment impediments. Actual bars to marriage, which make it null *ab initio,* though consummated.

Disability. Legal incapacity or inability to do an act.

Disafforest. v. *Deafforest.*

Disbar. To expel a barrister from the bar.

Discharge. Setting free; acquittance. v. *Charge, Plea.*

Disclaimer. A denial, abandoment; a waiver of a claim, a refusal to accept an estate or trust. A **disclaimer of tenure,** made by a tenant in a suit for rent or services, forfeited his estate. In equity pleading, an abandonment of all claim to the subject of the plaintiff's demand.

Discontinuance. 1. The grant by a tenant in tail of a larger estate than he was entitled to, whereby the heir or reversioner was driven to his right of action and could not enter; a species of *ouster.* 2. Of plea, when all parts of a pleading are not answered. If the plaintiff failed to take judgment by *nil dicit* for such part as was unanswered, it was a discontinuance of the action. 3. Of process or action, when the plaintiff failed to take some necessary step for continuing the action. Actions are frequently ended by voluntarily entering a discontinuance and paying costs.

Discontinuous servitude. One which is made up of repeated acts of man, such as that of drawing water.

Discoöperta, *l.,* **Discovert.** Uncovered; unprotected; unmarried.

Discovery. Evidence given by the defendant in equity under oath in answer to the plaintiff's bill. v. *Bill,* I. 4.

Discretio est discernere per legem quid sit justum, *l.* Discretion is to determine what is just by the law.

Disentailing deed. A deed by which a tenant in tail is enabled in England to alienate his estate absolutely. It must be enrolled within six months after execution.

Disgavel. To free lands from the custom of *gavelkind.*

Dishonor. To refuse to accept or pay a bill or note on presentation.

Disjunction, *l.* Separately; severally.

Dismes, dimes, *fr.* Tithes.

Disparagement. An unequal alliance; an injury by inequality, unsuitableness.

Dispone, *sc.* To grant, convey.

Disseisin. Wrongfully putting a man out of possession of a freehold; a kind of *ouster.*

Distincte et aperte, *l.* Distinctly and openly.

Distrain. To take another's property in satisfaction of an injury or claim; or in pledge, to enforce the performance by him of some duty. v. *Distress.*

Distress. The act of distraining; usually to enforce the payment of rent in taxes, or to enforce compensation for damage done by the trespassing of cattle. **Distress infinite**: a distress unlimited as to quantity, which may be repeated from time to time until satisfaction is made.

Distribution. The division of the personal property of an intestate among his next of kin. In England, the **Statutes of Distributions** are the 22 & 23 Car. II. c. 10, and the 29 Car. II. c. 3.

District Courts. v. *Court*, 106.

Districtio, *l.* A distress; the right of distress; the thing distrained.

Districtus, *l.* A distress; a district.

Distringas, *l.* (That you distrain.) 1. A writ directing the sheriff of the county to distrain a defendant's goods, in order to enforce his appearance. 2. A writ to enforce a judgment for the plaintiff in *detinue* by repeated distresses. 3. An old writ of the K. B. commanding the sheriff to bring in the bodies of those jurors who did not appear, or distrain their lands and goods. 4. A process in equity against a body corporate refusing to obey the summons of the court. 5. An order of the Court of Chancery in favor of a party claiming to be interested in Bank of England stock, directing the bank not to transfer or pay dividends. **Distringas nuper vice comitem** (that you distrain the late sheriff): a writ to distrain the goods of a sheriff now out of office for non-performance of a duty while in office.

Disturbance. Interference with the enjoyment of some incorporeal hereditament.

Dit, ditz, etc., *fr.* Said; a word, decree.

Dites ouster. Say over; the form of awarding a *respondeas ouster.*

Dittay, *sc.* The matter or charge of an indictment or criminal information.

Diversis diebus et vicibus, *l.* At different days and times.

Diversity. A plea by a prisoner in bar of execution, that he is not the same person who was convicted or attainted; upon which a jury was formally impanelled to try his identity.

Diverso intuitu, *l.* With a different purpose; by a different process; in another view.

Divest. An estate, vested in a man or his heirs, may become *divested,* or cease to be so vested, by conveyance, forfeiture, determination by the terms of the grant, or the order of the court.

Divinatio, non interpretatio est, quæ omnino recedit a litera, *l.* That is guessing, not interpretation, which altogether departs from the letter.

Divine service. v. *Tenure.*

Divisa, *l.* A division; a boundary.

Divisim, *l.* Severally; separately.

Divisum imperium, *l.* A divided empire; a jurisdiction shared by two tribunals.

Divorce, Divortium, *l.* The legal separation of husband and wife, by decree of court. Divorce **a vinculo matrimonii,** (from the tie of marriage): absolute divorce, where the wife has no dower and the parties can marry again. If for a cause existing prior to marriage, the children are bastards. Divorce **a mensa et thoro,** (from bed and board): a legal separation, but the parties may not marry again. There are various kinds of these divorces under modern statutes, frequently called **absolute** and **limited** divorce respectively, or **total** and **partial.**

Divorce Courts. v. *Court,* 25, 52.

Do, *l.* I give. v. *Dedi.* **Do, lego:** I give and bequeath. **Do ut des:** I give that you may give. **Do ut facias:** I give that you may do. Words descriptive, in the civil law, of different kinds of contracts; v. *Facio.*

Doarium, dotarium, etc., *l. Dower.*

Docket. An entry, brief, or abstract in writing; the book containing such entries. **Striking a docket**: the entry (in England) of a petitioning creditor's affidavit and bond.

Doctors' Commons. A place, near St. Paul's churchyard, where the ecclesiastical and admiralty courts used to be held; courts and offices of the doctors of law who had received a degree from Oxford or Cambridge, and been admitted to practice as advocates. They formed a college, of which the Dean of the Arches was President. v. *Court*, 82, 90.

Doli capax, *l.* Capable of malice; a term applied to a child between the ages of seven and fourteen, who has sufficient understanding to he criminally responsible for his actions, contrary to the ordinary presumption. **Doli incapax**: incapable of malice. v. *Malitia*.

Dolus, *l.* Fraud; malice. **Dolus malus**: evil design. **Dolus auctoris non nocet successori, nisi in causa lucrativa.** the fraud of the author does not affect the successor, except [when he acquires] by a lucrative title [gratuitously]. **Dolus circuitu non purgatur**: fraud is not purged by circuity [the taint is not removed by elaborate device, which makes the fraud remote]. **Dolus versatur in generalibus**: a person acting with fraudulent intent deals in general terms.

Dom. Proc., *l.* For **Domus procerum**, the House of Lords.

Dombec, domboc, *sax.* A code of laws; the **Dome-book,** a code of laws and precedents compiled under King Alfred.

Dome, doom, *sax.* Judgment, sentence. **Domesday-book**: an ancient survey or inquisition of all the lands in England, taken under William the Conqueror, and preserved in the Exchequer. v. *Court*, 11.

Domesmen. Inferior judges, as in a manor court.

Domicil of origin. The place of a man's birth.

Dominant tenement. That which enjoys a servitude, distinct from the **servient tenement,** which suffers it.

Dominicum, *l.* A demesne; the demesne lands; a lordship, seigniory; the estate of a free tenant; a church.

Dominium, *l.* Ownership; property. **Dominium directum**: legal ownership; the ownership of a superior lord, as distinguished from that of a vassal; allodial ownership. **Dominium utile**: equitable or beneficial ownership. **Dominium plenum**: full ownership, the union of *dominium directum* with *dominium utile.* **Dominium eminens**: eminent domain. **Dominium non potest esse in pendenti**: the ownership cannot be in abeyance.

Dominus, *l.* Lord; master; principal. **Dominus litis** (the master of a suit): the party interested, the one having control.

Domitæ naturæ, *l.* Of a tame nature; domesticated.

Domus, *l.* A house; dwelling; home. **Domus sua cuique est tutissimum refugium**: a man's house is his safest refuge.

Domo reparanda, *l.* v. *De.*

Don, *fr.*, **Donum,** *pl.* **dona,** *l.* A gift. **Dona clandestina sunt semper suspiciosa**: secret gifts are always suspicious.

Donare, *l.* To give. **Donari videtur quod nullo jure cogente conceditur**: that is considered a gift which is granted under compulsion of no law.

Donatio, *l.* A gift, grant, donation. **Donatio causa mortis** (a gift by reason of death): a gift of personal property made by a person about to die, and which is valid only in the event of his death, coupled with manual or symbolical delivery to the donee, or some person for him. **Donatio inter vivos**: a gift between living people. **Donatio propter nuptias**: a gift in consideration of marriage. **Donatio non præsumitur**: a gift is not presumed [it is not presumed that a gift was intended]. **Donatio perficitur possessione accipientis**: a gift is perfected by the possession of the person receiving. **Donatio velata**: a veiled gift, a gift which pretends to be something else.

Donative. v. *Advowson.*

Donator nunquam desinit possidere, antequam donatorius incipiat possidere, *l.* The donor never ceases to possess until the donee begins to possess.

Done, doun, *fr.* A gift. **Done, grant et render**; v. *Fine.*

Donec, *l.* Until; while.

Donor. Properly, a grantor of an estate tail. A grantor generally. The party conferring a power. **Donee**: a grantee; the party exercising a power, the *appointor.*

Donque, donc, dunques, etc., *fr.* Then.

Dont, *fr.* Whereof, whence, whereby.

Doresnavant, *fr.* From henceforth.

Dormant partners. Partners who have no power in the firm, in which their names do not appear, but who partake of the profits.

Dormiunt aliquando leges, nunquam moriuntur, *l.* The laws sometimes sleep, but never die.

Dos, *l.,* **Dot,** *fr.* 1. A dowry; a woman's marriage portion. 2. Dower. **Dos de dote peti non debet:** dower ought not to be claimed of dower. **Dos rationabilis:** reasonable dower. v. *Dower.* **Doti lex favet; premium pudoris est, ideo parcatur:** the law favors dower; it is the reward of modesty, therefore it should be spared. **Dote assignanda, etc.;** v. *De.*

Double bond. In Scotch law, a bond with a penalty. **Double costs:** the ordinary single costs of a suit, and one half that amount in addition. **Double damages:** twice the actual damages, as assessed by the jury. **Double fine:** a *fine sur done grant et render.* **Double plea:** a plea which sets up more than one defence. **Double voucher:** a voucher over; v. *Recovery.* **Double waste:** where a tenant suffers a house to fall out of repair and then cuts timber on the estate to repair it.

Dower. The life estate which the widow has in her husband's lands on his death; usually one third part of any lands of which he was seised in an estate of inheritance at any time during the marriage, if the husband's estate in such lands was such that the common issue might have inherited. **Dower ad ostium ecclesiæ,** *l.* (at the church door,) was anciently where the husband specifically endowed his wife with certain of his own lands; or of his father's lands, **Dower ex assensu patris.** If this was not done, she was asssigned her **Reasonable dower, Dos rationabilis,** *l.,* **Dower by the common law,** a third part of the husband's land. **Dower by custom:** varied in amount according to local usage. **Dower de la pluis belle,** *fr.* (of the fairest part): where the wife was endowed of socage lands held by her as guardian. **Writ of dower** or **Writ of right of dower:** an old real action lying for a widow against a tenant who had deprived her of part of her dower. **Dower unde nihil habet,** *l.*: a similar writ which lay for a widow to whom *no* dower had been assigned.

Dowry. A marriage portion; property which the wife brings the husband; *dos, dot.*

Drawer, Drawee. v. *Bill,* III. 4.

Droit, droict, dreit, *fr.* Right, justice; the law; a writ of right. **Droit droit:** a double right; the right of possession united with that of property. **Droit ne done pluis que soit de-**

manndé: the law gives no more than is asked. **Droit ne poet pas morier**: right cannot die. **Droits of Admiralty**: goods found abandoned at sea; property captured in a time of war by non-commissioned vessels; the goods of the enemy claimed by the Crown. **Droit d'Aubaine**: a right or prerogative claimed by some European sovereigns of seizing the goods and estate of an alien dying within their dominions. **Droit close**: an old writ for a tenant in *ancient demesne* against the lord. **Droit patent**: a writ of *right patent*. **Droit d'eignesse**: v. *Esnecy*.

Droitural. Concerning right or title. v. *Action*.

Dry Exchange. A term invented to disguise usury. **Dry rent**: v. *rent seck*.

Dubitatur, abb. Dub., *l*. It is doubted. **Dubitante**: doubting. **Dubii juris**, *l*. Of doubtful law.

Duces tecum, *l*. (Bring with you.) A term applied to writs where a party summoned to appear in court is required to bring with him some evidence, or something that the court wishes to view; v. *Subpœna*. **Duces tecum licet languidus**: an old writ ordering the sheriff to bring the prisoner to court despite his illness.

Duchy Court of Lancaster. v. *Court*, 69.

Ducking-stool. v. *Common scold*.

Due-bill. A written acknowledgment of debt without a promise to pay.

Dum, *l*. While. **Dum fervet opus** (while the work glows): in the heat of action. **Dum fuit in prisona** (while he was in prison): an old writ of entry to recover lands which a man had aliened under duress. **Dum fuit infra ætatem** (while he was under age): a similar writ to recover lands aliened when an infant. So **Dum fuit non compos mentis**: a writ to recover lands aliened *while he was of unsound mind*. **Dum recens fuit maleficium**: while the offence was fresh. **Dum se bene gesserit**: while he conduct himself well [during good behavior]. **Dum sola**: while unmarried. **Dum sola et casta vixerit**: while she live single and chaste.

Dummodo, *l*. Provided that. **Dummodo constat de persona**: so that it be clear as to the person meant.

Duo non possunt in solido unam rem possidere, *l*. Two cannot possess the same thing in entirety.

Duodecima manus, *l.* (Twelfth hand.) The oath of twelve men.

Duplex querela, *l.* (Double complaint.) A kind of appeal, in an ecclesiastical court, from the *ordinary* to his superior. **Duplex valor maritagii:** double the value of the marriage; v. *Marriage.*

Duplicity. The fault of pleading a *double plea.*

Durante, *l.* During. **Durante absentia, beneplacito, itinere, furore, minore ætate, viduitate, vita,** etc.: during absence, good pleasure, the journey, insanity, minority, widowhood, life, etc.

Duress "per minas," *l.* Constraint by threats.

Durham, Courts of County Palatine of. v. *Court,* 70.

Dusty foot, Court of. The Court of *Pipowders.* v. *Court,* 36.

Dying without issue. At common law a person is said to die without issue if his issue fail at any time after or before his death. By statute, and in wills, the words are construed according to their popular meaning, dying without issue at the time of decease.

E.

E. g., abb. for *Exempli gratia.*

E, ex, *l.* From; out of; v. *Ex.* **E converso:** conversely. **E contra:** on the other hand. **E mera gratia:** of mere favor.

Ea intentione, *l.* With that intent.

Easement. A right, without a profit, enjoyed by an owner of land over land held by another; not an estate or interest in the land itself.

Easter term. In England, begins on the 15th of April and ends on the 8th of May.

East Greenwich. A royal manor in Kent; mentioned in grants by the King as descriptive of the tenure of free socage.

Eat inde sine die, *l.* "Let him go thence without day," words used in recording judgment for the plaintiff. v. *Days.*

Eau, eawe, ewe, etc., *fr.* Water.

Eberemord, *sax.* Open killing; *abere murder.*

Ecce, *l.* Behold; look.

Ecclesia, *l.* A church; a parsonage. **Ecclesia ecclesiæ decimas solvere non debet:** the church ought not to pay tithes to the church. **Ecclesia non moritur:** the church does not die.

Ecclesiastical Corporations, Courts. v. *Corporation, Court,* 79.

Ecclesiastical law: the law administered by the English ecclesiastical courts, now applying chiefly to church matters. It is derived largely from the canon and civil law.

Editus, *l.* Put forth; brought forth; promulgated.

E'e, *fr.* Abb. for **Estre,** to be, or **este,** been.

Effractores, *l.* Burglars; housebreakers.

Effusio sanguinis, *l.* The shedding of blood; a mulct therefor.

Egetter, *fr,* To eject. **Ejettement**: ejectment.

Egglise, église, *fr.* Church; a church.

Ego, talis, *l.* I, such a one.

Egrediens et exeuns, *l.* Going forth and issuing.

Egressus, *l.* A going forth; an issue, exit.

Ei incumbit probatio qui dicit, non qui negat, *l.* The burden of proof lies upon him who affirms, not him who denies.

Eide, *fr.* Aid; relief.

Eigne, eisne, aisne, etc., *fr.* The eldest; the first born. **Eignesse, Einecia,** *l.*: eldership, *esnecy.*

Einetia, *l.* The share of the eldest son.

Eins, *fr.* In; in possession. **Eins ceo que**: inasmuch as.

Eire. v. *Eyre.* A journey. **Eirant**: errant, wandering.

Eit, *fr.* Has.

Ejectione firmæ, custodiæ, etc. v. *De ejectione, Ejectment.*

Ejectment. An action employed to try title to land; originating in the old mixed action of **ejectment of farm,** wherein a tenant dispossessed recovered his term and damages for the trespass. This modern action of ejectment contained many legal fictions, such as a lease by the real to the fictitious plaintiff, with entry, and ouster by a fictitious defendant called the *casual ejector.*

Ejectment of ward, Ejettement de garde, *fr.* v. *De ejectione custodiæ.*

Ejectum, *l.* Things cast up by the sea; wreck.

Ejus nulla culpa est cui parere necesse sit, *l.* No guilt attaches to him who has to obey.

Ejusdem generis, *l.* Of the same nature. **Ejusdem negotii**: of the same transaction.

Electio est creditoris, debitoris, *l.* The creditor *or* debtor has the election. **Electio semel facta non patitur regressum**: an election once made does not admit of recall.

Eleemosyna, *l.* Alms. **Eleemosynarius**: an almoner.

Eleemosynary. Charitable; v. *Corporation.*

Elegit, *l.* (He has chosen.) A writ of execution given on judgments for debt or damages, commanding the sheriff to deliver all the defendant's goods and chattels, except beasts of the plough, to the plaintiff; and if these were not sufficient, a moiety of the defendant's lands to hold until the debt was satisfied. The plaintiff then had actual possession of the lands as **tenant by elegit.** The plaintiff had his choice (*elegit*) of this writ or *fieri facias*, which ran against the defendant's goods only.

Elisors. Persons appointed to name a jury, in lieu of the sheriff or coroner, when they were objected to.

Eloign, Elongare, *l.*, **Eloigner,** *fr.* To remove; send away. **Eloignment of goods**: removal out of the county of goods so they could not be distrained. **Elongatus**: eloigned. **Elongavit**: he hath eloigned.

Emanare, *l.* To issue; award. **Emanavit**: it issued.

Embezzlement. The fraudulent appropriation to his own use of money or property intrusted to an agent or servant, not actually or legally in the master's possession; v. *Larceny.*

Emblements. The annual profits of sown land; such crops as are sown anew each year; the right to gather such crops.

Embler, *fr.* To sow; to steal.

Embracery. The offence of corrupting, or seeking to influence, a jury. v. *Decies tantum.*

Emendare, *l.* To make amends or satisfaction; to correct.

Eminent domain. The right of a state to use private property for public purposes.

Emparler, *fr.* To imparl. **Emparlance**; v. *Imparlance.*

Emphyteusis. A species of indefinite lease for improvement; in which the tenant paid rent, and had all but the nominal ownership of the land, like a fee-farm.

Emprompter, *fr.* To borrow.

Emptio et venditio, *l.* Purchase and sale. **Emptor**: a purchaser. **Emptor emit quam minimo potest, venditor vendit quam maximo potest**: the purchaser buys for as little, the seller sells for as much, as he can.

En, *fr.* In; into. **En apres**: hereafter. **En ariere**: in time past. **En autre droit**: in another's right. **En autre soile**: on land of another. **En avant**: in future. **En banke**: in the bench.

En barre: in bar. **En bonne foy**: in good faith. **En ce**: in this. **Enchemin**: on the way. **En certein**: in certain. **En chiefe**: in chief. **En coste**: on the side, collateral. **En court**: in court. **En demeure**: in delay, default. **En demeyne**: in demesne. **En fet, fait**: in fact. **En gros**: in gross. **En juge-ment**: in court. **En le mercie**: *in mercy*. **En le per**; v. *Entry, writ of*. **En mort meyne**: in *mortmain*. **En oultre**: furthermore. **En owel main**: in equal hand. **En pais**: in the country. **En plein vie**: in full life. **En poigne**: in hand. **En prender, render**; v. *in prender, render*. **En primes**: in the first place. **En son damage**: in his damage, damage feasant. **En son demeyne come de fee**: in his demesne as of fee. **En suspence**: in abeyance. **En tesmoignance**: in testimony. **En ventre sa mere**: in its mother's womb. **En vie**: in life, alive.

Enabling Statute. The 32 Hen. VIII. c. 28, which enabled ten-ants in tail, husbands seised in right of their wives, and ecclesi-astical persons or corporations seised in right of their churches, to make leases for twenty-one years, so as to bind their heirs. widows, issue, or successors.

Enbler, *fr.* To sow.

Enceinte, *fr.* Pregnant.

Encheson, *fr.* Cause; reason; occasion.

Encroach. To take more than one's right; v. *Accroach*.

Endorser, endosser, *fr.* To indorse; to write on the back.

Endorsement. v. *Indorsement*.

Endowment. The assigning of dower. The setting apart a por-tion of lands for the vicar's maintenance. Any permanent pro-vision for collegiate, religious, or charitable purposes.

Enfeoff. To give in fee; to invest with an estate by feoffment.

Enfranchisement. Making free; granting rights or privileges; incorporating a man into a society or body politic. **Of copy-hold**: its conversion into freehold.

Engager, *fr.* To pledge.

Engin, enghein, engyn, *fr.* Deceit; fraud; ill design.

Engetter, *fr.* To eject; cast out.

Englecery, Engleshire. The proving a person slain to be an Eng-lishman, or the fact thereof, whereby the heavy fines imposed upon the hundred for the death of a Dane or Norman for *mur-drum*, were avoided.

Engleterre, *fr.*   England.   **Engleys**: English.

Engross.   To make a fair copy.   To buy up all of a certain commodity with intent to sell at a forced price; formerly a criminal offence.

Enitia pars, *l.*   The part of the eldest; the share chosen by the eldest coparcener on partition of land, she having first choice.

Enlarge.   To set at large, release from custody; to extend, to grant further time.

Enlarger l'estate, *fr.*   To enlarge an estate; as when the next remainder-man releases all his interest to the tenant.   v. *Release.*

Enormia, *l.*   Wrongful acts.   **Enormis**: immoderate, excessive.

Enparler, *fr.*   To talk together, to *imparl.*

Enquet, enquest, *fr.*   An inquest, inquiry; a jury.

Enroll.   To enter, record, transcribe.

Ens, *l.*   A being, existence.   **Ens legis**: a being of the law.

Ensemble, *fr.*   Together.

Ensement, *fr.*   Also; in like manner.

Ensy, ensi, *fr.*   Thus; so; in like manner.

Entail.   To create an estate *tail.*   **Entailed**: settled in *tail* or *strict settlement.*   The word as commonly used means the latter.

Entencion, Entente, *fr.*   A plaintiff's count, declaration.

Entendement, entente, *fr.*   Understanding.

Enter, entre, *fr.*   In; within; among.   **Entre mains**: at hand, in his hands.

Enterlesse, *fr.*   Left out; omitted.

Entry.   1. A record in writing, in a book or account.   2. The taking possession of lands by going into them.   **Right of entry**: a right to actually enter and take possession, thereby regaining or perfecting an estate, without suit at law.   **Writ of entry**: an old real action to regain the possession of land. Writs of entry were **in the quo** or **quibus** when brought against the wrong-doer himself; **in the per,** when against his alienee or heir; **in the per and cui,** when there had been two alienations or descents; **in the post,** if more than two.   There were also writs of entry **sur disseisin, alienation, intrusion,** etc., according to the circumstances of the case.   For writs of entry **ad communem legem, ad terminum qui præteriit, cui ante divortium, cui in vita, dum fuit in prisona, dum fuit infra ætatem, dum fuit non compos mentis,**

casu consimili, casu proviso, quare ejecit, see respective titles.

Enumeratio unius est exclusio alterius, *l.* The enumeration of the one is [amounts to] the exclusion of the other.

Envers, *fr.* Against.

Eo instante, *l.* At that instant. **Eo intuitu**: with that view or intent. **Eo ipso**: by the thing itself. **Eo nomine**: under that name.

Eod'. For eodem, *l.* The same. **Eodem modo quo quid constituitur, dissolvitur**: a thing is [may be] destroyed in the same way in which it is created. **Eodem ligamine quo ligatum est, dissolvitur**: a deed is released by the same formalities with which it is contracted.

Eques, *l.* A knight.

Equitable assets. The assets which a creditor can only reach through a court of equity. **Equitable estate**: one existing or cognizable originally only at equity, as a trust or interest of a mortgagor. **Equitable mortgage**: a pledge or lien arising by rules of equity, as when a loan is made on deposit of title deeds. **Equitable plea** or **defence**: a defence to a legal action in cases where an injunction would be granted in equity, resting on equitable grounds or doctrines. **Equitable waste**: extreme or excessive waste, or injury to the inheritance, forbidden even to a tenant without impeachment of waste; wilful destruction; which could only be remedied by courts of equity. v. *Waste*.

Equity. That system of jurisprudence administered first by the English Court of Chancery; a jurisdiction originally resident in the Crown and exercised by the Chancellor. **Courts of Equity**: v. *Court*, 15, 109. **Equity of a statute**: the sound interpretation of a statute, taking into consideration its reason and spirit. **Equity of redemption**: 1. The estate of a mortgagor in mortgaged land. 2. The mortgagor's right of redeeming after breach of conditions or foreclosure. **Equity side of the Exchequer**: v. *Court*, 11. **Equity to a settlement** or **Wife's equity**: the right which a wife has in equity to have a portion of her equitable estate (usually one half) settled upon herself and children. It may now be claimed by her; but was originally granted only when the husband sued in equity for the purpose of reducing her property into possession.

Erer, arer, *fr.* To plough.

Ergo, *l.* Therefore. **Ergo hic**: therefore here.

Erigimus, *l.* We erect; words used in granting a charter.

Errant, *fr.* Wandering about; itinerant. **v.** *Eyre.*

Erraticum, *l.* A waif; an estray.

Erronice, *l.* Erroneously; through mistake.

Error. An original writ which lies after judgment in an inferior court of record to review the judgment and inquire into errors of fact, or errors of law apparent on the record. In England, an erroneous judgment as to fact in the K. B. may be reversed in the same court by a writ of error **coram nobis.** A similar writ in the C. B. is called **coram vobis.** **v.** *Coram nobis.*

Error juris nocet, *l.* An error of law injures [i. e. the party committing it must suffer the consequences]. **Error nominis nunquam nocet, si de identitate rei constat**: an error in the name does no harm, if it be clear as to the identity of the thing itself. **Error qui non resistitur, approbatur**: an error which is not objected to is approved. **Error scribentis nocere non debet**: a mistake of the scribe should work no injury. **Errore lapsus**: an error through mistake; a false step.

Error, Court of. **v.** *Court,* 108.

Escæta, *l.* An *escheat.* **Escætor**: the *escheator.* **v.** *De.*

Escambio, *l.* A license in the form of a writ to a merchant to draw foreign bills of exchange. **Escambium**: exchange.

Escape. An escape from lawful arrest or imprisonment, whether violent or by collusion, **negligent** or **voluntary.**

Escape warrant. A warrant addressed to all the sheriffs of England, authorizing the arrest of a person who has escaped from imprisonment on execution or mesne process.

Escheat. 1. The falling back of land into the hands of the lord on failure of the blood of the tenant; which may be **propter defectum sanguinis** (for failure of blood, as if the tenant died without heirs) or **propter delictum tenentis** (for fault of the tenant) if he be attainted. 2. The lands so escheating. 3. Things falling, falling to the ground. Escheat was a consequence of tenure, and happened on account of the failure of the tenant to perform services to his lord, who might or might not be the King, thus differing from *Forfeiture.*

Escheator. An officer in every county whose duty was to inquire by sheriff's jury into escheats falling to the Crown.

Eschier, eschoir, *fr.* To fall; to happen; to escheat.

Escoce, Escosse, *fr.* Scotland.

Escrier, *fr.* To proclaim. **Felons escries:** notorious felons.

Escript, escrit, *fr.* A writing; a written instrument.

Escrow. A scroll; a deed; v. *Delivery.* A deed delivered to a third person, who is to hand it to the grantee when he performs some act, or some condition is fulfilled.

Escuage. (Service of the shield.) A kind of knight's service whereby the tenant was bound to follow his lord into wars at his own charge. Later a certain money commutation was paid instead, called escuage certain. v. *Scutage.*

Eskipper, *fr.,* **Eskippare,** *l.* To ship. **Eskippamentum,** *l.*: tackle of ships.

Eslier, *fr.* To choose. **Eslisors:** v. *Elisors.*

Esloigner, *fr.* To remove; eloign; adjourn.

Esnecy. The privilege of the eldest. v. *Enitia pars.*

Esplees. The full profits of land, including all crops, rents, issues, and services.

Essartum, *l.,* **Essart.** Woodland turned into tillage.

Esse. To be; being. **In esse:** in being. **Essendum:** being.

Essendi quietum de theolonio. v. *De essendo.*

Essentialia negotii, *l.* The essential parts of a transaction.

Essoign, essoin. An excuse for not appearing in court in answer to process. To **cast an essoin:** to essoin, to allege an excuse. **Essoin day:** the first day of the term, on which the court sat to receive essoins. There were several essoigns; as the essoign **de servitio regis,** *l.,* **de service del roy,** *fr.,* that the party was absent on the King's service; **de terra sancta, de terre seynte,** absent in Palestine; **de ultra mare, de outre mer,** absent beyond sea; **de infirmitate** or **de malo lecti, de mal de lit,** ill in bed; **de malo veniendi, de mal de venue,** that he had met with an accident in coming.

Est, *l.,fr.* It is; there is. **Est à sçavoir:** it is to be understood, to wit. **Est boni judicis ampliare jurisdictionem:** it is [the duty] of a good judge to enlarge [construe liberally] his jurisdiction.

Estate. 1. An interest in land. 2. Property in general. 3. *Status,* or condition of life. **Estate in common, coparcenary; by curtesy, dower, elegit; executory, equitable, legal; in fee; of joint tenancy; on condition;** see those titles. **Estate for**

life: a freehold interest, not of inheritance, which a man has for his own life, or for the life of another or others. If the latter, it is an estate **pur auter vie**. **Estate in possession**: where there is a right of present entry and enjoyment. **Estate in remainder, reversion, severalty**: see those titles. **Estates of the realm**: in England, the lords spiritual, the lords temporal, and the commons. **Estate by statute merchant, statute staple**, estate **tail, tail special**, etc.; see those titles. **Estate for years**: an interest, less than a freehold, for a fixed or determinable time. **Estate at will**: an interest less than freehold, which may be ended at the will of the lessor. **Estate at sufferance**: where a tenant is allowed to hold over after his term. **Estate from year to year**: a lease for a year, which, unless terminated by the lessor or lessee, will arise anew by implication, at the end of the year, for another year. **Estate in vadio**: in gage or pledge.

Ester in jugement, *fr.* To appear in court as a party.

Este, *fr.* 1. Summer. 2. Been, from **Ester, etre,** to be.

Esto, *l.* Be it. **Esto perpetua**: be it eternal.

Estop. To stop; bar; prevent; impede; preclude.

Estoppel. An impediment, by which a man is precluded in law from alleging or denying a fact, in consequence of his own previous action, inaction, allegation, or denial. An **estoppel by deed** is where it arises from a recital or statement contained in a previous deed of the party estopped; **in pais** (in the country), when it arises from an open act, or a verbal representation or declaration upon which another has acted. **Estoppel by record** is where it arises from an admission of the party made in the record of a court, in pleading or otherwise; or from a judgment against the party or some one to whom he is privy in blood, law, or estate; v. *Res judicata*. **Collateral estoppel**: the collateral determination of a question by a court having general jurisdiction of the subject; v. *Plea*.

Estoverium, *l.*, **Estovers.** 1. An allowance made to a person out of an estate, whether of money or other things; a *bote*, q. v. 2. An allowance made to a man arrested for felony for the support of his family. 3. The alimony allowed a wife divorced **a mensa et thoro**. **Estoveriis habendis**; v. *De*.

Estray. A wandering domestic animal.

Estre, *fr.* To be. **Del bien estre** : v. *De bene esse.*

Estreat. A copy or extract from a record. A forfeited recognizance estreated [extracted] from the records to be prosecuted.

Estrepe. To strip; lay bare; waste. **Estrepamentum,** *l.,* **Estrepement**: an aggravated waste, to the injury of the reversioner; especially when committed during a suit to recover possession. The writ of **estrepement** was formerly auxiliary to a real action, and sought to prevent strip during the pendency thereof; now superseded by an injunction in chancery.

Et, *l.* And. **Et al., et alii**: and others. **Et alii e contra** (and others on the other side): words used to describe a joinder of issue. **Et adjournatur**: and it is adjourned. **Et ad huc detinet**: and he still detains. **Et allocatur**: and it is allowed. **Et curia consentiente**: and the court agreeing. **Et de hoc ponit se super patriam**: and of this he puts himself upon the *country*. **Et ei legitur in hæc verba**: and it is read to him in these words [when a prayer for *oyer* is allowed]. **Et habeas ibi tunc hoc breve**: and have you then there this writ. **Et habuit**: and he had [obtained] it. **Et hoc paratus est verificare** : and this he is ready to verify. **Et hoc petit quod inquiratur per patriam**: and this he prays may be inquired of by the country. **Et inde petit judicium**: and thereof he prays judgment. **Et inde producit sectam**: and thereupon he brings suit. **Et modo ad hunc diem**: and now at this day. **Et non**: and not, *absque hoc.* **Et non allocatur**: and it is not allowed. **Et petit auxilium**: and he prays aid. **Et prædictus A. similiter**: and the said A. likewise. **Et sic** : and so. **Et semble**: and it seems. **Et sic ad judicium** : and so to judgment. **Et sic ad patriam**: and so to the *country.* **Et sic fecit**: and he did so. **Et sic pendet**: and so the matter rests.

Et, *fr.* And. **Et de ceo se mettent en le pays** : and of this they put themselves on the *country.* **Et issint**: and so.

Eundo, morando, et redeundo. In going, staying, and returning.

Evasio, *l.* An *escape.*

Evesque, *fr.* A bishop. **Evesche**: his diocese.

Eviction. Dispossession by process of law; recovery of lands; ouster; a notice to quit.

Ewe, *fr.* Water.

Ex, *l.* From; of; out of; by or with; according to. **Ex abundanti cautela**: from excessive caution. **Ex abuso non arguitur ad usum**: from the abuse of a thing you cannot argue as to its use. **Ex adverso**: on the other side. **Ex æquitate**: in equity. **Ex æquo et bono**: according to what is just and good. **Ex assensu patris**: from the father's consent; v. *Dower*. **Ex antecedentibus et consequentibus fit optima interpretatio**: the best interpretation is made by means of what precedes and follows. **Ex arbitrio judicis**: from the discretion of the judge. **Ex auditu**: from hearsay. **Ex bonis**: of the goods. **Ex bonis maternis, paternis**: from the goods inherited through the mother, the father. **Ex capite doli** *or* **fraudis**: on the ground of fraud. **Ex causa**: from cause, by title. **Ex causa lucrativa**: by a lucrative title [gratuitously]. **Ex certa scientia**: of certain knowledge. **Ex comitate**: by comity, courtesy. **Ex commodato**: from a loan. **Ex comparatione scriptorum**: by comparison of handwritings. **Ex concessione**: by grant. **Ex concessis**: from the granted [premises]. **Ex consultu**: from consultation. **Ex continenti**: immediately. **Ex contractu**: from contract. **Ex culpa levissima**: from the slightest fault. **Ex debito justitiæ** (from a debt of justice): as a matter of right. **Ex debito naturali**: from natural obligations. **Ex defectu juris**: for a defect in right. **Ex defectu sanguinis**: for a failure of blood. **Ex delicto**: from fault or crime. **Ex dem., demissione**: on the demise. **Ex dicto majoris partis**: according to the voice of the majority. **Ex directo**: immediately. **Ex diurnitate temporis, omnia præsumuntur solemniter esse acta**: on account of the lapse of time, all things are presumed to have been done in due form. **Ex dolo malo, non oritur actio**: out of fraud, no action arises. **Ex empto**: from purchase. **Ex eo quod plerumque fit**: from that which frequently happens. **Ex facie**: on the face. **Ex facto**: from an act, actual. **Ex facto jus oritur**: the law (arises) depends on the fact. **Ex fictione juris**: by a fiction of law. **Ex gratia**: by favor. **Ex gravi querela** (on grievous complaint): an old writ that lay for one to whom lands were devised by special custom by will, and the heir retained them. **Ex hypothesi**: according to the hypothesis. **Ex improviso**: without preparation. **Ex incontinenti**: summarily. **Ex industria**: with design, on purpose. **Ex insinuatione**: on the information [of]. **Ex integro**: anew, afresh. **Ex intervallo**: after an interval. **Ex jure naturæ**: by the law of nature. **Ex justa causa**: by a just cause. **Ex latere**: on the side, collateral. **Ex lege, legibus**: according to law. **Ex licentia regis**: by the King's license. **Ex locato**: from a letting, a hiring. **Ex maleficio, non oritur contractus**: from misconduct, no contract can arise. **Ex mero motu**: of mere motion. **Ex mora debitoris**: on account of the debtor's delay. **Ex more**: according to custom. **Ex natura rei**: from the nature of the thing. **Ex necessitate**: by necessity; **legis**, of law. **Ex nudo pacto non oritur actio**: from a bare agreement [parol and without consideration] no action arises. **Ex officio**: by virtue of office. **Ex pacto illicito non oritur actio**: from an illegal agreement no action arises. **Ex parte**: 1. from, of, or by one side, one party; hence, partial, done for or by one party. 2. On the application of. **Ex parte materna, paterna**: on the mother's, father's side. **Ex paucis**: from few (things or words). **Ex post facto**: by matter happening afterwards, from a later act or event. **Ex post facto law**: an act or statute changing the law as to previous events or contracts. **Ex præcogitata malitia**: of malice aforethought. **Ex præmisses**: from the premises. **Ex proprio motu**: of his own accord. **Ex proprio vigore**: of their own force. **Ex provisione viri**: lands settled on the wife in tail *by provision of the husband;* or on both husband and wife, by his ancestor. **Ex quasi contractu**: arising as if from a contract. **Ex rel, relatione**: on the relation, or information. **Ex rigore juris**: according to the rigor of law. **Ex scriptis olim visis**: from writings formerly seen. **Ex speciali gratia**: of special favor. **Ex tempore**: by lapse of time; without preparation. **Ex testamento**: by a will. **Ex transverso**: across. **Ex turpi causa non oritur actio**: on a bad [illegal] consideration no action can arise. **Ex una parte**: from one side. **Ex utraque parte**: on both sides. **Ex vi aut metu**: by force or fear. **Ex visitatione Dei**: by the visitation of God. **Ex visu scriptionis**: from sight of the writing [from having seen the person write]. **Ex vi termini**: by the force of the term.

Exaction. The collection of a fee by an officer, where none is due.

Excambium, *l.* Exchange; *exchange* of lands.

Exceptio, *l.* An exception; a plea; a defence; an objection; a contradictory allegation. **Exceptio ad breve prosternen-dum:** a plea in abatement. **Exceptio doli mali:** a plea of fraud. **Exceptio ejus rei cujus petitur dissolutio nulla est:** a plea of the same matter the dissolution of which is sought [in the action] is of no effect. **Exceptio firmat regulum in casibus non exceptis:** the exception strengthens the rule in cases not excepted. **Exceptio rei adjudicatæ:** a plea that the matter has been previously adjudged. **Exceptio semper ultima ponendo est:** an exception should always be placed last.

Exceptions, Bill of. v. *Bill,* I. 5.

Exchange. An original common-law conveyance for the reciprocal transfer of landed interests of the same degree. So, when the warrantor was to give the warrantee lands of equal value with those of which he has been dispossessed.

Exchequer. In England, the revenue department; also, the **Court of Exchequer:** v. *Court,* 11, 95.

Exchequer Chamber. v. *Court,* 12. **Exchequer Division:** v. *Court,* 24.

Excommengement, *fr.* Excommunication.

Excusable homicide. That which involves so little fault that the law excuses it from the guilt of felony. It includes homicide **per infortunium,** by accident in doing a lawful act, and **se defendendo,** in self-defence.

Excusat aut extenuat delictum in capitalibus quod non operatur idem in civilibus, *l.* That excuses or extenuates a fault in capital cases which would not so operate in civil.

Executed. Done; finished; effected; fully performed; accomplished; now existent; now in force; past; the reverse of **executory. Executed consideration, contract:** v. *Consideration, Contract.* **Executed estate:** an estate in possession, by which a present interest passes, as distinguished from an **executory estate,** one depending on some future contingency. An **executed trust** is one fully created and exactly defined; an **executory trust** is where some further instrument remains to be executed, the author of the trust having given only his general intent. **Executed use:** one created and "executed" by the

Statute at the time of the conveyance. **Executory use**: a springing use, one to arise at some future time, not dependent on a preceding estate in the land. **Executory devise**: a devise of a future estate in land which would not be valid by the rules of the common law.

Executio bonorum, *l.* Administration of goods. **Executio est finis et fructus legis**: execution is the end and fruit of the law. **Executio juris non habet injuriam**: the execution of the law does not work a wrong.

Execution. 1. The carrying into effect a judgment or decree. 2. A judicial writ issued for that purpose. 3. The completion of an instrument in such a way as to make it legally valid.

Executor. The person named in a will to take charge of the testator's property and carry the will into effect. **Executor de son tort,** *fr.:* one who interferes and acts as executor *of his own wrong,* without lawful authority.

Executory. Unfinished; to be completed; future; v. *Executed.*

Exemplary. v. *Damages.*

Exemplification. A certified copy, under seal, of a record.

Exemplum, *l.* An example; a copy. **Exempli gratia**: for purpose of example, for instance. **Exempla illustrant non restringunt legem**: examples illustrate, but do not restrict, the law.

Exequatur, *l.* An order for the home department of a government to recognize a consul or commercial agent of a foreign nation.

Exercitor maris, *l.* The employer of a ship; ship's husband.

Exfrediare, *l.* To break the peace.

Exhæredatio, *l.* Disherison; an injury or loss of inheritance.

Exhibitio billæ, *l.* (The exhibition of the bill.) The commencement of the suit.

Exigent or **Exigi facias,** *l.* A judicial writ in process of outlawry, when the defendant could not be found; issuing on the return *non est inventus* to a *ca. sa.,* directing the sheriff to *demand* the defendant at five successive county courts. If there were not five courts between the *teste* and return, an **allocatur exigent** was issued to extend the time so as to make up that number. **Allocato comitatu**: a new writ of exigent allowed before any county court had been holden, the previous writ having failed. On the defendant's failure to appear, he was outlawed; and a *capias utlagatum* might issue.

Exire, *l.* To go out; to issue. **Exitus** : issue, offspring.

Exlex, *l.* An outlaw. **Exlegare** : to outlaw.

Exonerare, *l.* To discharge, disburden. **Exoneretur** : let him be discharged.

Expedit reipublicæ, *l.* It is for the public advantage. **Ne sua re quis male utatur** : that no one should make ill use of his property. **Ut sit finis litium** : that there should be an end of suits.

Expeditio brevis, *l.* The service of a writ.

Expensæ litis, *l.* Costs of suit.

Expire. v. *Determine.*

Explees. v. *Esplees.*

Expressio falsi, *l.* A false statement. **Expressio eorum qui tacite insunt nihil operatur** : the express mention of those things which are implied avails nothing. **Expressio unius est exclusio alterius** : the express mention of one thing is the exclusion of another.

Expressum facit cessare tacitum, *l.* A thing expressed puts an end to the thing implied.

Extend. To appraise the yearly value of lands of a debtor forfeited upon statute or recognizance, so that it may he known how long the creditor is to retain possession to extinguish the debt.

Extendi facias, *l.* (That you cause to be extended.) A writ of *Extent.*

Extent. A writ of execution upon a debt due the Crown, or due a creditor upon recognizance, statute merchant or staple, directing the sheriff to appraise the debtor's lands and goods; they were then delivered to the creditor upon his suing out a *liberate.* **Extent in chief** was at suit of the Crown; **extent in aid,** of a Crown debtor against his private debtor. There was also a special writ called *Diem clausit extremum.*

Extortion. v. *Larceny.*

Extra, *l.* Without; out of; beyond; except. **Extra feodum** : out of his fee. **Extra judicium** : out of court. **Extra jus** : beyond the law. **Extra præsentiam mariti** : out of the husband's presence. **Extra legem** : out of the law, the law's protection. **Extra quatuor maria** : beyond the *four seas.* **Extra regnum** : out of the kingdom. **Extra territorium jus dicenti impune non paretur** : you cannot safely obey one exercising jurisdiction out of his own territory. **Extra viam** : out of the road.

Extracta, *l.* v. *Estreat.*

Extradition. Delivery of a fugitive by one state to another.

Extrahura, *l.* An estray.

Extraneus, *l.* A foreigner; a stranger.

Extremis probatis media præsumuntur, *l.* The extremes proved, the things between are presumed. **In extremis**: at the last extremity.

Extrinsic. Outside, from outside sources.

Extum, *l.* Thence; from then.

Ey. Water; a watery place.

Eyder, *fr.* To aid, help. **Eyde**: aid. **Eyes eid**: have relief.

Eygne, *fr.* Eldest.

Eyott. A little island.

Eyre. A way, journey; the journey of a justice about his circuit; v. *Assize.* The **Justices in eyre** were established in 1176 with a delegated power from the *aula regia,* and made their circuit around the kingdom once in seven years for the purpose of trying various causes; they were superseded by the justices of *Assize* and *Nisi prius.*

Ez arts, *fr.* At arts, of arts.

F.

Fabric lands. Lands given for the maintenance of churches.

Fabricare, *l.,* **Fabricate.** To forge; coin; create falsely.

Facere, *l.* To do, make, act, cause. **Facias**: you cause. **Faciendo**: doing, paying. **Facio ut des**: I do that you may give; **facio ut facias,** I do that you may do; v. *Do.* **Facit**: he does, he acts.

Factor. An agent employed to buy and sell goods on commission in his own name, intrusted with their possession and control.

Factum, *pl.* **facta,** *l.* A thing done; a deed; a fact. **De facto**: in fact.

Factorizing process. Attaching the goods of a debtor in the hands of a third party. v. *Attachment,* 3.

Factum a judice quod ad officium ejus non pertinet ratum non est, *l.* An act done by a judge which does not belong to his office is held null.

Faculties, Court of. v. *Court*, 86.

Fæstingmen. Vassals; persons of wealth; *frank-pledges*.

Failing of record. Failure of a party pleading a record to produce it when required.

Faint action, Feigned action. v. *Action*. **Faint pleading:** false or collusory pleading, to the injury of a third person.

Faire, fere, *fr.* To make; to do. **Faisant, feasant:** doing. **Fait:** a thing done; a deed, act, fact. **Fair à sçavoir:** to make to know.

Faitours, *fr.* Evil-doers; idle vagabonds.

Falcare, *l.* To mow, cut. **Falcatura:** a day's mowing.

Faldage. Foldage; the privilege of setting up a movable sheepfold, to manure the land.

Falsa demonstratio non nocet, cum de corpore constat, *l.* False description does no harm, when it is clear as to the [thing or] person. **Falsa grammatica non vitiat chartam:** bad grammar does not vitiate a deed.

False imprisonment. Any unlawful restraint of the person. **False judgment:** an English writ issuing from one of the superior courts to correct error in a court not of record; v. *Court*, 29. **False pretences:** v. *Larceny*.

Falsify. In equity practice, to disprove an item in an account.

Falso retorno brevium. A writ which lay against a sheriff for a false *return* of writs.

Falsus in uno, falsus in omnibus, *l.* False in one, false in all.

Fama, *l.* Character; fame; reputation.

Famosi libelli, *l.* Libellous books; libels.

Farm. 1. The rent of land leased; anciently, provisions; **white farm:** if money. 2. A term of years in lands.

Fas, *l.* Right, justice; the divine law.

Fatetur facinus qui judicium fugit, *l.* He who flies from judgment confesses his guilt.

Fauces terræ, *l.* Headlands enclosing an arm of the sea.

Fautor, *l.* A favorer; supporter; abettor.

Faux, fausse, *fr.* False; counterfeit. **Fauxer, faucher:** to forge.

Favorabiliores rei potius, quam actores, habentur, *l.* The defendants are held to be favored rather than the plaintiffs.

Feal, *fr.* Faithful; **Fealte:** fealty.

Fealty. The faith which every tenant owes his lord; his obligation to perform due obedience and service. The **oath of fealty** was a ceremony performed on the admission of every tenant, except those in frankalmoign.

Feasance, *fr.* A doing, a making. **Feasor**: a doer. **Feasant**: doing.

Fee. 1. A freehold estate held of, and granted by, a superior lord, on the condition of performing some service in return for it. It was originally granted as a reward. 2. An estate of inheritance in land; an estate granted to a man and his heirs. 3. A *Fee simple*. **Fee-farm**: land held in fee at a rent, but without other services (except they be specified in the deed of feoffment). **Fee-farm rent**: that reserved on granting lands in fee-farms, one fourth or one third their value. **Fee simple**: an unlimited estate in land, descendible to a man's heirs generally. **Fee simple conditional**: the old estate which arose when land was granted to a man and a limited class of heirs before the statute *de Donis*, which turned them all into estates tail. **Fee tail**: a restricted fee, descendible to certain classes of heirs only; one which can only pass to the *heirs of his body*, the direct descendants; v. *Tail*.

Feigned issue. An issue produced in a pretended action for the purpose of trying a single question of fact. Such an issue was formerly frequently directed out of the Court of Chancery, and rested on a fictitious wager. **Feigned action**: v. *Action*.

Felagus, *l.*, **Felawe.** A companion or friend, bound in the *decennary* for the good behavior of the others. v. *Tithing*.

Felo, *l.* A felon. **Felo de se**: a self-murderer.

Felony. 1. An offence for which the criminal forfeited his fee. 2. A serious offence; one punishable with death or the state prison.

Feme, femme, *fr.* A woman. **Feme covert**: a woman (protected) married. **Feme sole**: a spinster.

Feod, Feodum, *l.* A fee. v. *Feudum, Fee*. **Feodi firma**: fee-farm.

Feoffare, *l.* To enfeoff. **Feoffamentum**: a feoffment. **Feoffatus**: a feoffee. **Feoffator**: a feoffor. **Feoffavit**: he enfeoffed.

Feoffee to uses. He in whom the legal estate was vested, the beneficial owner being the *cestui que use*.

Feoffment. 1. The conveyance of a fee by livery of seisin. 2. The deed or charter in which such conveyance was perpetuated.

Feoh, *sax.* A stipend; wages, reward; a fee.

Feorme, ferme, *sax.* Provisions, rent; a manor; a farm; a lease on rent. v. *Farm.*

Feræ naturæ, *l.* (Of a wild nature.) A term applied to animals not usually tamed, as distinguished from those **domitæ naturæ,** domestic.

Ferdfare, *sax.* A summoning to military service; **ferdwite,** an acquittance therefrom, by fine; **ferdsocne:** exemption therefrom.

Feria, *l.* A week day; a holiday; a fair.

Ferme, *fr.* v. *Feorme, Farm.*

Fesaunt, *fr.* Doing. **Fesour:** a doer; v. *Faisant,* etc.

Festinatio justitiæ est noverca infortunii, *l.* Hurrying justice is stepmother to misfortune.

Festingman. A surety; frank-pledge. v. *Faestingmen.* **Festing-penny:** earnest given to servants when hired.

Festinum remedium, *l.* A speedy remedy.

Fet, *fr.* Done, made; v. *Fait.* **Fet assavoir:** a thing to be known; v. *Fleta.*

Feu, *fr.* A hearth, fireplace. **Feu, few,** *sc.:* a fee.

Feudal. Having the quality of a feud; held of another, as opposed to *allodial.* **Feudal system:** the system of *fiefs.*

Feudum, *l.* A *fief, feud, fee;* v. *Fee.* **Feudum antiquum:** an ancient fee, one which hath descended to a man from his ancestors, as distinguished from **feudum novum,** a fee acquired by the man himself. A **feudum ut novum antiquum:** a *new fee* granted *like an old one,* so that it might descend to any of the purchaser's heirs and not be restricted to his issue. At an early period, all fees were granted in this way; otherwise a *feudum novum,* though a fee simple, would resemble a fee-tail. **Feudum individuum:** one which could only descend to the eldest son. **Feudum laicum:** a lay fee, as opposed to one held by spiritual service. **Feudum ligium:** a liege fee, held directly of the Sovereign. **Feudum maternum** or **paternum:** one descended from the mother *or* father. **Feudum militare:** a military fee. **Feudum militis:** a knight's fee. **Feudum proprium:** a proper fief; an original, purely military fee, as distinguished from **feudum improprium,** a later variety. **Feudum simplex:** fee simple. **Feudum talliatum:** fee-tail. **Feudum sine investitura nullo modo constitui potest:** a fee can by no method be created without livery of seisin.

Fi. fa. *Fieri facias.*

Fiar, *sc.* The proprietor; the owner of the fee.

Fiat, *l.* (Let it be done.) A short order or warrant. **Fiat in bankruptcy**: an order of the Lord Chancellor that a commission in bankruptcy should issue; v. *Commission*, 2. **Fiat justitia, ruat cœlum**: let there be justice, though the heavens . fall. **Fiat ut petitur**: let it be, as is demanded.

Fictio, *l.* A fiction. **Fictio cedit veritati**: a fiction yields to truth. **Fictio juris**: a fiction of law. **Fictio legis inique operatur alieni damnum vel injuriam**: a legal fiction should not work to any person wrong or injury.

Fidei-commissa, *l.* The civil law expression for *trusts* created by last will.

Fidelitas, *l.* Fidelity; *fealty.*

Fides, *l.* Good faith; trust; honesty. **Fides servanda est**: faith must be kept.

Fiduciary. Relating to a *trust ;* founded upon confidence.

Fief, *fr.* A fee; v. *Fee, feudum.* **Fief d'haubert**: a fee held by knight-service.

Fieri facias, *l.* (That you cause to be made.) A writ of execution directing the sheriff to levy the amount of a judgment from the lands and goods of the defendant; it is usually enforced against the goods only; v. *Elegit.* **Fieri feci**: the return of the sheriff to a *fi. fa.* that he has satisfied the judgment. **Fieri non debet sed factum valet**: it ought not to be done; but, when done, it is valid.

Fifteenths. A tax or aid anciently imposed on cities and towns in England of one fifteenth of their valued personal property.

Fightwite, *sax.* A fine for a quarrel or disturbance.

Filacers, filizers. (From **Filace,** *fr.*, a file.) Officers in the C. P. and other superior courts who *filed* and issued writs.

File, fille, *fr.* A daughter.

Filiation. 1. The relation of a son to his father. 2. The adjudging a bastard to be the child of some man.

Filius, *l.* A son. **Filius est nomen naturæ, sed hæres est nomen juris**: *son* is the name of nature, but *heir* is the name in law. **Filius mulieratus**: a *mulier.* **Filius nullius** (the child of nobody): a bastard; so, **filius populi,** a son of the people.

Fils, fitz, *fr.* A son.

Filum aquæ, *l.* (The thread of the water.) The water line or edge; the middle line of a stream. **Filum viæ**: the middle line of a street.

Fin, *fr.* End. **En fin, al fine**: at last, at the end.

Final. Complete, finishing, as opposed to *interlocutory.* v. *Decree, Process.* **Final appeal court**; v. *Court,* 87.

Finalis concordia, *l.* A final concord; a *fine* of lands.

Fine. 1. A sum of money paid by an offender as punishment. 2. A price paid for a privilege. 3. **Fine for alienation**: a price paid the lord by the tenant in chivalry for permission to alien his lands. 4. **Fine of lands**: a conveyance of lands by acknowledgment of record, which had the effect of barring an estate tail by excluding the issue of the one levying the fine, the **cognizor.** The **cognizee** sued out a writ of præcipe on a fictitious covenant of the cognizor to convey the land in question, upon which a **primer fine** of one tenth the annual value of the land was due the King. The court then granted a **licentia concordandi, congé d'accorder,** or leave to agree, upon which the **post fine,** or three twentieths the annual value of the land, became due the King. Then followed the acknowledgment, the concord itself, made by the cognizor in open court or before commissioners appointed by *dedimus potestatem,* that the lands were the property of the cognizee. Then followed the **note** of the fine, an abstract of the writ of covenant and the concord, which was enrolled in the proper office; and the **foot** of the fine, containing the whole matter, engrossed in **indentures** by the **chirographer** and delivered to the cognizor and cognizee. There were four kinds of fines, **sur cognizance de droit come ceo que il ad de son done** (*fr.*), *a fine upon the acknowledgment of the right which the cognizee hath by gift,* a feoffment of record; **sur cognizance de droit tantum,** *upon acknowledgment of right merely;* **sur concessit,** *upon grant,* by acknowledgment of a grant *de novo,* but of no precedent right; and **sur don, grant et render,** *upon gift, grant, and render,* a combination of the first and third kinds.

Fine force, *fr.* Absolute necessity.

Finis, *l.* An end, limit; a *fine.*

Firdfare, Firdwite. v. *Ferdfare.*

Fire bote. v. *Bote.* **Fire ordeal**: trial by red-hot iron, either by taking a piece in the hand or by stepping blindfold and barefoot over nine red-hot ploughshares.

Firma, *l.* A farm, rent; v. *Farm.* **Firmarius**: a fermor. **Firma alba**: white rent.

First-fruits. The first year's profits of a spiritual living, due anciently to the Pope.

Fisc. The treasury of a prince or state. **Fisk,** *sc.*. the revenue; the forfeited goods of a rebel.

Fish royal. Whale, porpoise, or sturgeon; which, when thrown ashore, belonged to the King.

Fistuca, *l.* A staff; a wand delivered as a symbol of property.

Fitz, *fr.* Son; a son.

Fitzherbert. A law writer, *tempo* Henry VIII., author of a Grand Abridgment of the year-books and of the new **Natura Brevium** [F. N. B.], a treatise on the writs then existing. v. *Registrum brevium, Natura brevium.*

Fixture. A chattel so fixed or fastened to the land or building as to become real property.

Flagrante bello, *l.* During actual war. **Flagrante delicto**: in the heat of the offence, in the very act.

Fledwit, Flightwite. 1. A fine paid by an outlaw for pardon. 2. A discharge from amerciaments when an outlawed fugitive came to the King's peace of his own accord.

Fleet. A prison in London; formerly of the Courts of Chancery and the C. P.

Flem, *sax.* An outlaw, a fugitive. **Flemenesfirinthe**: receiving a fugitive. **Flemeneswite**: a fine imposed on an outlaw.

Fleta. A treatise on the law founded chiefly on Bracton, and supposed to have been written *tempo* Edward I. by some learned lawyer at that time confined in the Fleet prison. Appended to it is a small French tract entitled **Fet assavoir.**

Fleth, Flet, *sax.* Land; a house.

Float, *am.* A certificate authorizing the occupation of land.

Flotsam. Goods floating on the water, lost from a wreck. **Jetsam**: goods thrown from the ship. **Ligan**: goods sunk and buoyed.

Focale, *l.* Firewood; fuel.

Fœnus nauticum, *l.* Marine interest; a high rate paid on ship loans. v. *Bottomry.*

Fois, foitz, *fr.* Time; times.

Folc land, *sax.* Land of the people. v. *Bocland.* **Folcmote folcgemote:** a popular assembly; a county court.

Folio. A leaf. A page containing seventy-two, or, in Chancery, ninety words; in America, usually one hundred.

Foot. v. *Fine.*

For, fors, *fr.* Out; without.

Forbannitus, *l.* Banished; outlawed.

Forbarrer, *fr.* To bar out; preclude; estop.

Force majeure, *fr.* *Vis major,* superior force.

Forcible entry or **detainer.** Violently or illegally taking possession or keeping lands or tenements. A criminal offence. Also, the civil action therefor.

Foreclosure. The process of barring the equity of redemption of a mortgagor; forfeiting the mortgagee's title.

Foreign attachment. v. *Attachment.* **Foreign Plea:** v. *Plea.* **Foreign bill:** a bill of exchange drawn or payable abroad.

Forejudge. To expel from court; to deprive of a thing by judgment.

Forest. A waste tract of land, belonging to the King, reserved for wild beasts of forest, chase, and warren, and having certain laws and courts of its own. **Forest courts;** v. *Court,* 74.

Forestall. To obstruct a highway. **Forestall the market:** to buy up provisions on the way to a market, with intent to sell at a higher price; a conspiracy to enhance the price of provisions.

Forgavel. A small money rent; a quit-rent.

Forgery. The fraudulent making or alteration of a written instrument to the prejudice of another's right.

Forinsecus, *l.* Outward; external; foreign.

Foris, *l.* Abroad; without; out of doors.

Forisfacere, *l.* To forfeit. **Forisfactura:** a forfeiture.

Forisfamiliated. Portioned off; provided for.

Forisjurare, *l.,* **Forjurer,** *fr.* To forswear; renounce.

Forma pauperis, *l.* v. *In.* **Forma non observata infertur adnullatio actus:** where due form is not observed, the nullity of the act is inferred.

Formata brevia, *l.* Formed writs. v. *Writ.*

Formed action. v. *Action.*

Formedon. An old writ of right or real action which lay for a tenant in tail. **Formedon in the descender,** when brought by the heir against his ancestor's alienee or disseisor; **in the remainder,** when brought by a remainder-man; **in the reverter,** when brought by the donor or his heirs.

Foro, *l.* In the forum, or jurisdiction. **v.** *Forum.*

Forprise. A reservation or exception.

Forsque, *fr.* Only; but.

Fortescue. A judge of the time of Henry VI., author of a book, *De Laudibus Legum Angliæ,* written in praise of the English common law.

Forthcoming bond. A bond to the sheriff, conditioned to deliver property levied on when demanded.

Fortia, *l.* Force. **Fortia frisca**: fresh force.

Fortior et potentior est dispositio legis quam hominis, *l.* The disposition of the law is stronger and more powerful than that of man [i. e. overrules that of man in certain cases].

Fortuit, *fr.* Accidental. **Fortuitment**: by chance.

Forty-days court. v. *Court,* 75.

Forum, *l.* A court; a jurisdiction; a tribunal; a *forum,* or place where legal redress is sought. **Forum actus,** the forum of the place where the thing was done; **contractus,** where the contract was made; **conscientiæ,** the tribunal of conscience, a court of equity; **domesticum,** a domestic jurisdiction; **domicilii,** that of the domicile; **domicilii actoris** or **rei,** that of the plaintiff's *or* defendant's domicile; **ecclesiasticum,** a spiritual court; **ligeantiæ rei** or **actoris,** the forum of allegiance of the defendant *or* plaintiff [of the country to which he owes allegiance]; **litis motæ,** or **fortuitum,** the forum where the suit happens to be brought; **originis,** the forum of a person's nativity; **regium,** the King's court; **rei** or **rei sitæ,** the forum where the property is; **rei gestæ,** of the place where the act was done; **sæculare,** the secular court.

Fos, fosse, *fr.,* **Fossa,** *l.* A dyke or ditch.

Founderosa, *l.* Founderous, out of repair.

Four seas. The four seas lying around England.

Fourcher, *fr.* To divide the essoin; to cause delay in a real action by casting essoins in turn where there was more than one tenant.

Foy, *fr.* Faith; oath; fidelity.

Fractio, *l.* A division; breaking. **Fractionem diei non recipit lex**: the law does not regard the fraction of a day.

Franc, fraunk, *fr.* Free. **Franc aleu :** free, allodial land.

Franchise. A liberty ; a privilege granted by the Crown to a private person.

Francigena, *l.* A Frenchman ; an alien.

Franclaine, franklyn. A freeholder.

Francus, *l.* Free ; a freeman. **Francus bancus :** *free bench.*

Francus homo : a freeman. **Francus plegius :** a *frank-pledge.*

Frankalmoign. *Free alms ;* a kind of tenure by spiritual services, without fealty, in land held by a religious corporation, to themselves and their successors forever. **Tenure by divine service** was where certain specified services were required, and the lord might distrain ; whereas in frankalmoign he could only complain to the ordinary. **Frank bank :** free bench. **Frank chase :** free chase. **Frank fee :** 1. The reverse of ancient demesne, lands in fee simple. 2. Lands held free of all services except homage. 3. Lands held by the lord of a manor in ancient demesne of the Crown. **Frank ferme :** an old kind of socage tenure, changed from knight's service by a new feoffment. **Frankfold :** free fold, a privilege of the lord to fold the tenant's sheep on his lands to manure them. **Frank law :** the rights and privileges of a citizen ; as to be a juror, witness, etc. **Frankmarriage :** an estate in tail special, given by the donor to a donee who married the donor's female relative, descendible to them and the heirs of their bodies, free of all services except fealty until the fourth generation of their descendants. **Frank-pledge :** a *tithing,* or a *decennary.* Also, the bond or pledge mutually entered into by the members of a tithing to answer for one another's transgressions or to produce the offending member. A system of suretyship for good behavior required of each free-born man on arriving at the age of fourteen. **Frank tenant :** a freeholder. **Frank tenement :** freehold.

Frassetum, *l.* A wood ; woody ground.

Frater, *l.* Brother. **Frater consanguineus :** a brother by the father's side ; **uterinus,** by the mother's side. **Frater fratri uterino non succedet in hæreditate paterna :** a brother shall not succeed a uterine brother in the paternal inheritance. **Frater nutricius :** a bastard brother.

Frauds, Statute of. The 29 Car. II. c. 2, making written memoranda necessary in many cases of contracts and grants.

Fraunche, fraunke, *fr.* Free. **Fraunk homo:** a freeman.

Fraus, *l.* Fraud. **Fraus est celare fraudem:** it is fraud to conceal fraud. **Fraus est odiosa et non præsumenda:** fraud is odious, and will not be presumed. **Fraus et dolus nemini patrocinari debent:** fraud and deceit ought to avail no one. **Fraus latet in generalibus:** fraud lurks in general phrases.

Frectare, *l.* To freight. **Frectum:** freight.

Free alms: *Frankalmoign.* **Free bench:** dower in copyhold lands; usually a third or fourth part of the land, to be held *dum sola et casta vixerit.* **Free fold;** v. *Frankfold.* **Freehold:** 1. Such an estate as a freeman might accept, i. e. an estate for life or inheritance, not a leasehold. 2. An estate in free socage, not copyhold or villeinage. **Freeman:** 1. A freeholder, not a villein. 2. One enjoying full privileges of citizenship. **Free pledge:** v. *Frank-pledge.* **Free services:** such as a soldier or freeman might perform, not base, uncertain, or villeinous. **Free ships:** ships of a neutral nation in time of war. **Free socage:** a tenure by free and certain services, not military; v. *Socage.* **Free tenure:** freehold; tenure by free services. **Free warren:** a regal franchise granted a subject to preserve beasts of warren.

Freight. The price paid for transporting goods.

Frendlesman, *sax.* An outlaw. **Frendwit:** a fine for succoring or harboring an outlaw.

Freneticus, *l.,* **Frentike,** *fr.* A madman.

Freoborgh, *sax.,* **Free burrow** or **borow.** A *frank-pledge.*

Frequentia actus multum operatur, *l.* The frequency of the act effects much [continual usage establishes the right].

Fresh disseisin. Recent disseisin; during the time of fresh disseisin (fifteen days) a man might right himself by force. **Fresh fine:** a fine of lands levied within a year past. **Fresh force:** deforcement or disseisin committed within thirty days past; v. *Assize of fresh force.* **Fresh suit:** immediate pursuit or prosecution.

Friborgh. A *frank-pledge.*

Friscus, *l.* Fresh; uncultivated. **Frisca fortia:** fresh force.

Fructus, *l.* Fruit; fruits. **Fructus rei alienæ:** the fruits of another's property. **Fructus civiles:** revenues and recompenses, profits, rents. **Fructus industriales**: the fruits of industry, emblements; as crops of grain, etc., distinguished from **fructus naturales**: the natural products of the soil or increase of animals, like the fruit of trees, wool, etc. **Fructus pendentes**: hanging fruits, things not severed from the land, as distinguished from **fructus separati. Fructuum perceptio**: the rightful taking of the produce of property by a person not the owner of the property; one of the methods of acquiring property with an act of possession.

Frustra, *l.* In vain, to no purpose. **Frustra est potentia quæ nunquam venit in actum**: a power which is never exercised is useless. **Frustra fit per plura, quod fieri potest per pauciora**: it is vain to employ many means when fewer are enough. **Frustra legis auxilium quærit qui in legem committit**: he who transgresses the law vainly seeks its aid. **Frustra petis quod statim alteri reddere cogeris**: it is useless to ask what you will immediately have to hand over to another. **Frustra probatur quod probatum non relevat**: it is useless to prove that which, being proved, is not relevant.

Frustrum terræ, *l.* A piece, or single tract, of land.

Frythe, *sax.* A wood; a plain between woods; an arm of the sea.

Fuage, fumage. A tax on chimneys.

Fuer, *fr.* To fly; flight.

Fugam fecit, *l.* He has made flight; whereby the goods of a person indicted for felony were forfeited.

Fugitation, *sc.* Outlawry.

Full age. In common law, twenty-one years; in civil law, twenty-five. **Full blood**: descent from both of two parents or married pair of ancestors; **half-blood**, descent from one only. **Full court**: a court in banc, with all the judges. **Full life**: life both in fact and law, legal capacity. **Full proof**: in civil law, proof by two witnesses or a public instrument. **Full right**: title conjoined with possession.

Fullum aquæ, *l.* A stream of water; a flume.

Functus, *l.* One who has performed or accomplished; discharged; **Functus officio**: one who has served his term of office; one whose authority has ceased.

Fundamus, *l.* We found [a corporation].

Fundus, *l.* Land. **Fundo annexa**: annexed to the soil.

Fungible. Consumable; measurable; that may be replaced in kind.

Fur, *l.* A thief. **Fur manifestus**: an evident thief, one caught in the act.

Furca, *l.* A gallows. **Furca et flagellum**: gallows and whip. **Furca et fossa**: gallows and pit.

Furcare, *l.* To fork or divide. v. *Fourcher.*

Furiosi nulla voluntas est, *l.* A madman has no will [is not criminally responsible]. **Furiosus absentis loco est**: a madman is as if absent [his presence is of no effect]. **Furiosus solo furore punitur**: a madman is punished by his madness alone.

Further assurance. v. *Covenant.* A covenant that the grantor will execute any further deeds which may prove necessary to complete the title.

Furtum, *l.* Theft. **Furtum grave**: aggravated theft, punishable with death. **Furtum conceptum, oblatum**: receiving stolen goods. **Furtum manifestum**: open theft, detected in the act, *bacberend.* **Furtum non est ubi mittimus habet detentionis per dominium rei**: there is no theft where the detention begins on grounds of ownership [authority].

Fustis, *l.* A staff; delivered as a symbol of land.

Futuri, *l.* Persons not yet in being.

G.

Gabel, gavel; Gablum, *l.;* **Gafol,** *sax.* A tax, duty, rent, or impost.

Gage. Security; a pledge.

Gager, *fr.* To find security; to wage. **Gager del ley**: wager of law.

Gaignage, *fr.,* **Gainage.** Wainage; profits of tillage; farm tools.

Gales, *fr.* Wales.

Gaol delivery. The emptying of a gaol by trying the prisoners. v. *Assize, De bono et malo.* **Gaol liberties**: a district around a gaol through which prisoners are allowed to go at large, on giving security to return.

Garaunt, garaunter, *fr.* Warrant; to warrant.

Garba, *l.* A bundle; a sheaf of corn.

Gard, garde, *fr.* Ward; custody; guardianship.

Garene, *fr.*, **Garrena,** *l.* A warren.

Garner, Garnir, *fr.* To warn; to summon; to garnish.

Garnishee. A person warned, as not to deliver goods. **Garnishment, garnishing process:** warning a debtor not to pay a debt or deliver goods to his creditor, but to answer the plaintiff's suit and keep the goods till judgment; v. *Attachment.*

Garrant, *fr.* Warrant. **Garrantie:** warranty.

Garth. A yard; a little close.

Gast, *fr.* Waste. **Gaster:** to waste.

Gate. A right in land for the use or passage of cattle.

Gavel. Custom; toll; tax; rent. **Gavelbred:** rent payable in provisions, in kind.

Gavelkind. A species of socage tenure, common in Kent, where the lands descend to all the sons, or heirs of the nearest degree, together; may be disposed of by will; do not escheat for felony; may be aliened by the heir at the age of fifteen; and dower and curtesy is given of half the land.

Gavelet. Rent. A process for the recovery of rent in gavelkind tenures; a kind of *cessavit.*

Geld, gild, *sax.* A payment, tribute, or fine. Money.

Gemote, *sax.* A public meeting or assembly; a court; a *moot* or *mote.*

Gen', for **Generosus,** *l.* A gentleman.

General agent. An agent in a particular business or employment, for which he has general and usual powers. **General assumpsit, average, damages, demurrer, imparlance, legacy, lien, occupant, partnership, tail, verdict:** see those titles. **General issue:** a short plea denying in general terms the whole declaration, indictment, or cause of action, without offering new matter. **General ship:** a ship open generally for conveyance of goods, not chartered.

Generale dictum generaliter est interpretendum, *l.* A general expression is to be interpreted generally. **Generale nihil certum implicat:** a general expression implies nothing certain. **Generalia specialibus non derogant:** general words do not derogate from special. **Generalia verba sunt generaliter intelligenda:** general words are to be understood generally. **Generalis clausula non porrigitur ad ea quæ**

antea specialiter sunt comprehensa: a general clause is not extended to cover things previously specially mentioned.

Generosus, *l.,* **Gentilhome,** *fr.* **Gentleman.** A man entitled to bear arms; above the rank of yeoman.

Gents, gentz, *fr.* People; folk.

Gerefa, *sax.* A reeve; an officer.

Gerere, *l.* To bear, to act, to behave. **Gerere pro hærede:** to act as heir.

Germanus, *l.* Of the whole blood; of the same stock.

Gersuma, *sax.* & *l.* A price; fine; reward; amerciament.

Gestio pro hærede, *l.* Behavior as heir.

Gestum, *pl.* **Gesta,** *l.* A deed; things done; transactions.

Getter, *fr.* To throw; bring; cast.

Gift. A gratuitous transfer; a conveyance in tail.

Gild, *sax.* v. *Geld.* Also, a fraternity; corporation; *friborgh.* **Gilda mercatoria,** *l.:* a mercantile company.

Gildale. A compotation where every one paid his scot and lot; *vulg.* a "Dutch treat."

Gilour, *fr.* A cheat; a deceiver.

Giser, *fr.* To lie. **Gisant:** lying. **Gist en le bouche:** it lies in the mouth. **Cy git:** here lies. **Le action bien gist:** the action well lies.

Glanvill. The author of the treatise *De Legibus et Consuetudinibus Angliæ,* the most ancient book in the English law, written about 1181, and containing the forms of writs as they then existed.

Gleba, *l.* A glebe; church land; the minister's land; a portion in addition to the parsonage. **Gleba terræ:** a clod of earth.

Glossa, *l.* A gloss; an interpretation or explanation.

Gloucester. The statute of this name was made in the sixth year of the reign of Edward I. (1278), providing for costs in actions; giving a writ of *cessavit* to lessors of tenants in *fee-farm,* and to the heir an immediate writ of entry in cases where a doweress alienated the land (*in casu proviso*); providing that no suit for *trespass de bonis* under 40 *s.* should be brought in the *superior* courts, that an appeal of murder should not abate for default of *fresh suit,* that no waste should be committed pending a suit about the lands, that a citizen of London, disseised of land, and suing therefor, should recover damages as well, etc., etc.

Glyn. A valley, glen.

Go. To be dismissed the court; to issue. v. *Day.*

God bote. A fine for a spiritual offence. **God's penny:** earnest-money; v. *Denarius dei.*

Goldsmiths' notes. Bankers' notes.

Good abearing. A species of probation; a man bound to good abearing was bound more strictly than if bound to keep the peace; he was bound also to **good behaviour,** to refrain from acts *contra bonos mores,* as well as *contra pacem.* **Good consideration:** v. *Consideration.*

Gors, gorce, *fr.* A wear; a fish-pool.

Gradatim, *l.* By degrees; by steps.

Grammatica falsa non vitiat chartam, *l.* False grammar does not vitiate a deed.

Graffarius, *l.* A graffer; a notary. **Grafium:** a register.

Grand assize. An extraordinary jury of sixteen knights employed to try *writs of right,* introduced by Henry II.; such actions being previously triable only by *battel.* **Grand bill of sale:** an instrument whereby a ship is transferred to the first purchaser; a bill of sale of a ship at sea. **Grand cape, cape ad valentiam, jury, larceny, serjeanty:** see those titles. **Grand days:** *dies non juridici,* holidays in court. **Grand distress:** a distress more extensive than the ordinary distress, running to all the goods and chattels of the party distrained within the county, which lay when he made default after being attached.

Grange. A barn, granary; a farm.

Grant. A gift; a conveyance; especially of a fee-simple; a conveyance without livery, as of an incorporeal hereditament.

Granum crescens, *l.* Growing grain.

Grassum. A sum paid in anticipation of rent; a fine paid for a lease; a customary fine due from a copyhold tenant on the death of the lord.

Gratis, *l.* Freely, gratuitously. **Gratis dictum:** a voluntary assertion.

Gravamen, *l.* Injury; grievance; the gist of complaint.

Great Seal. The emblem of royal authority, intrusted to the Chancellor or Lord Keeper.

Great tithes. *Predial* tithes; corn, hay, and wood. **Great council;** v. *Court,* 3.

Gree, *fr.* Satisfaction; agreement; consent; grace. **Per le gree**

ou sans le gree: with or without consent. **Bon gre mal
gre**: with good will or bad.

Gremium, *l.* Bosom. **In gremio legis**: in the lap of the law.

Gressume. v. *Grassum.*

Grith-brech, *sax.* Breach of the peace.

Gros, *fr.* Large; substance. **En gros**: at large; in substance.
Grosse avanture: bottomry. **Gros bois**: *timber.*

Gross average. v. *Average.*

Ground rent. Rent paid on a building lease; fee-farm rent.

Guaranty. A promise to answer for the payment or performance
of another; a warranty; to warrant. v. *Surety.*

Guardia, *l.* Ward; guardianship.

Guardian. A keeper, protector. **Guardian in chivalry**: the
superior lord, who, when the heir was under twenty-one, if male,
or fourteen, if female, in knight-service, was entitled to the
wardship and marriage of the heir and the profits of the land.
Guardian by statute: a kind of guardian appointed by the
father's deed or will, under the 12 Car. 2, c. 24. **Guardian by
appointment of the Court of Chancery**: when the father
fails to appoint, or is an improper person. **Guardian by custom**: in copyhold, the next of blood; in London, the mayor
and aldermen. **Guardian by deed or will**: i. e. of the father.
Guardian ad litem: a person representing the interests of a
minor in a suit at law, appointed by the court. **Guardian by
nature**: the father, and, on his death, the mother. **Guardian
for nurture**: the father or mother, but guardians of the person only, and until the age of fourteen. **Guardian in socage**:
the next of blood, in socage tenure, to whom the inheritance
cannot possibly descend; he has the custody of the infant heir's
lands and person up to the age of fourteen. **Guardian of the
Spiritualities, Temporalities**: v. *Custos spiritualium, temporalium.*

Guarra, guerra, *l.*, **Guerre,** *fr.* War.

Guerpi, *fr.* Abandoned; deserted.

Guet, *fr.* Watch. **Guet apous**: an ambush.

Gule of August. The first of August.

Gwabr merched, *brit.* Maid's fee; a payment made to the lord
of a manor upon the marriage or incontinency of the daughter
of a tenant.

H.

Habeas corpus, *l.* (That you have the body.) A name given to a number of writs having for their object to bring 'a person to court, and particularly the **Habeas corpus ad subjiciendum:** a writ directed to a person detaining the body of another, to inquire into the cause of the detention, and have him *submit* to whatever the court shall direct. **Habeas corpus ad faciendum et recipiendum:** a writ to remove the cause, as well as the body of the defendant, to the jurisdiction of a superior court; also called **habeas corpus cum causa.** **Habeas corpus ad prosequendum, testificandum, deliberandum,** etc.: to remove the body of the prisoner to be prosecuted or to testify in the higher court, in the proper jurisdiction. So **ad satisfaciendum,** to charge him, upon judgment in an inferior court, with execution in the superior. **Habeas corpora juratorum:** a writ for the sheriff to compel attendance of jurymen in the C. P., like a **distringas juratores** in the K. B.

Habeas Corpus Act. The 31. Car. II. c. 2, providing the remedy by *habeas corpus* for a violation of personal liberty.

Habemus optimum testem confitentem reum, *l.* We have the best witness, a confessing defendant.

Habendum, *l.* (To be held.) The clause of a deed defining the estate granted, containing the words of *limitation.* **Habendum et tenendum:** to have and to hold; to be had and held.

Habentes homines, *l.* (Having men.) Rich men.

Habere facias possessionem, *l.* (That you make him have possession). A writ of execution, for the successful plaintiff in ejectment to recover possession of the lands. **Habere facias seisinam:** a writ to give the plaintiff in a real or mixed action possession of the freehold. **Habere facias visum:** a writ to cause the sheriff to take a view of the lands in question.

Habilis, *l.* Able; fit; suitable; good, sound.

Habit and repute, *sc.* Held and reputed.

Habitus, *t.* Habit; apparel; garb; manners.

Hæc est conventio, *l.* This is an agreement. **Hæc est finalis concordia:** this is the final agreement; words commencing the foot of a *fine.*

Hæredipeta, *l.* (An inheritance seeker.) The next heir.

Hæreditamentum, *l.*, **Hæreditament.** v. *Hereditament.*

Hæreditas damnosa, *l.* A burdensome inheritance. **Hæreditas jacens** (a prostrate inheritance): an inheritance not yet accepted and entered upon by the heir. **Hæreditas nihil aliud est quam successio in universum jus quod defunctus habuerit:** an inheritance is nothing but the succession to all the rights the deceased had. **Hæreditas luctuosa:** a mournful inheritance, as of a parent to a child. **Hæreditas nunquam ascendit:** an inheritance never [lineally] ascends. **Hæreditas paterna:** an inheritance from the father.

Hæres, *pl.* **hæredes,** *l.* Heir. **Hæres actu:** an heir by appointment. **Hæres astrarius:** an heir in possession. **Hæres de facto:** an heir in fact; from the wrongful act of his ancestor. **Hæres factus:** an heir by will, a testamentary heir. **Hæres est alter ipse et filius est pars patris:** an heir is another self and a son is part of the father. **Hæres est eadem persona cum antecessore:** an heir is the same person with the ancestor. **Hæres est quem nuptiæ demonstrant:** he is the heir whom the marriage indicates [the heir is determined by a lawful marriage]. **Hæres est aut jure proprietatis aut jure representationis:** the heir is either by right of property or right of representation. **Hæres est nomen collectivum:** heir is a collective name. **Hæres est nomen juris, filius est nomen naturæ:** heir is the name of the law, son the name of nature. **Hæres fiduciarius:** an heir in trust, or trustee. **Hæres hæredis mihi est meus hæres:** the heir of my heir is my heir. **Hæres natus:** a born heir. **Hæredes proximi:** next heirs, children. **Hæredes remotiori:** heirs more remote. **Hæres rectus:** a right heir. **Hæres suus:** a proper heir, a child or grandchild. **Hæredi magis parcendum est:** the heir is to be more favored. **Hæredum Deus facit, non homo:** God makes the heir, not man. **Hæredum appellatione veniunt hæredes hæredum in infinitum:** under the name of heirs come the heirs of heirs indefinitely.

Hæretico comburendo. v. *De.*

Hafne courts. Haven courts; old courts in English seaports.

Haia, *l.*, **Haye,** *fr.* A hedge.

Haimsucken, *sc.* Assaulting a person in his own house.

Half-blood. Descent from one lineal ancestor only of a pair. v. *Full blood.* **Half-proof**: in the civil law, proof by only one witness, or a private instrument. **Half-tongue**: a jury *bilinguis.*

Halywercfolk, *sax.* People who held lands by the service of defending or repairing a church.

Ham, *sax.* A home; house. **Hamesecken**; v. *Haimsucken.* **Hamsocne**: the privilege of a man's house, or the breach thereof.

Hanaper office. An office on the common law side of the Court of Chancery, in which the writs of private persons and returns, or the fees arising from them were kept, as those relating to the Crown were kept in the *Petty-bag office.*

Handborow. A hand-pledge; a name given to the nine ordinary frank-pledges of a decennary, the tenth or chief being the **head-borow.** v. *Tithing.*

Handhabend. Having in the hand; a thief caught with the goods in his possession. v. *Bacberend.*

Handsale. A sale confirmed by striking hands; the price.

Hangwite, *sax.* A fine for hanging a thief without trial.

Hanse towns. A commercial association of German cities, formerly existing, chief among which were Bremen, Lubec, and Hamburg, having a peculiar code of maritime laws.

Hariot. v. *Heriot.*

Harth-penny. A penny tax on every house. v. *Peter's pence.*

Hat-money. An allowance made the master of a ship for the purchase of winter clothing; *primage.*

Haubert, *fr.* A coat of mail; haubergeon.

Hault, haut, *fr.* High. **Haut chemin, vey**: highway. **Haut estret**: high street.

Haustus, *l.* Drawing; the servitude of entering and drawing water.

Haw. A house; a bit of land by a house.

Hawgh, howgh. A valley; a green plot in a vale.

Hay, Haya, *l.* A hedge; an enclosure.

Hayward. An officer who keeps the common cattle of a town and sees to the preservation of hedges.

Headborow. The chief pledge of a *tithing.* v. *Handborow.*

Hearth-money. A tax of two shillings on every hearth in England; *fuage.*

Heir One who takes the ancestor's property by descent. **Heir**

apparent: one certain to be heir if he outlive the ancestor; **heir presumptive**: the person who would be heir if the ancestor died to-day, but whose right of inheritance may yet be defeated by some contingency. **Heir by custom**: heir by special custom, as *gavelkind*, etc. **Heir by devise**: a person to whom lands are devised by will. **Heir general**: the ordinary heir by blood of all the lands. **Heir special**: the heir in tail, *per formam doni*, under the form of the gift; who may or may not be the heir general.

Heirloom. A chattel, personal property, which descends to the heir with the inheritance; such as the best bed, the doves, the fishes in the pond, the deeds and charters, etc.

Henghen, *sax.* A prison, gaol.

Hengwyte. v. *Hangwite.*

Heralds' college. An English corporation, founded 1 Rich. III., empowered to grant arms and preserve pedigrees, consisting of three **kings at arms,** six **heralds,** and four **pursuivants,** together with the Earl Marshal of England.

Herbagium, *l.* Herbage; the right of pasture. **Herbagium anterius**: the first crop of hay.

Herbergare, *l.*, **Herberger,** *fr.* To lodge; to harbor.

Hereditament. That which may be inherited. **Corporeal hereditaments**: such as are tangible, visible, material, and may pass by livery of seisin, as distinguished from **incorporeal hereditaments,** which lie only in grant and are not capable of manual delivery or feoffment.

Hereditas, Heres, etc. v. *Hæreditas,* etc.

Heriot. 1. A tribute in arms, horses, or money, due the lord on the death of a knight tenant. 2. The best or second-best beast, or, in copyhold tenure, other personal chattel, seized by or due to the lord on the death of the tenant.

Heritable and movable rights, *sc.* Real and personal. **Heritable bond**: a bond accompanied by the conveyance of an inheritance as security. **Heritable jurisdiction**: grants of criminal jurisdiction bestowed on great Scottish families.

Herus, *l.* A lord; master. **Herus dat ut servius faciat**: the master gives [wages] that the servant may do [the work].

Heybote. Hedgebote. v. *Bote.*

Hidage. A royal tax imposed on land by *hides.*

Hide. As much land as one plough could work; from sixty to a hundred and twenty acres; as much land as would support one family; a ploughland; a mansion-house.

Hide (hyde) and gain. Arable land.

High sea. Begins at low-water mark, excluding the *fauces terræ.* **High treason:** *treason* to the King or State. **Highway:** a foot, bridle, road, or water way open to the public. **High Court of Justice, of Appeal:** v. *Court*, 20, 26.

Hiis testibus, *l.* (These witnesses.) The attestation clause in deeds.

Hilary term. In England, began on the 11th and ended on the 31st of January.

Hinc inde, *l.* In Scotch law, on either side, reciprocally.

Hind, hine, *sax.* A servant in husbandry, a domestic.

Hirst, hurst. A wood.

Hoc intuitu, *l.* With this expectation. **Hoc loco:** in this place. **Hoc nomine:** in this name. **Hoc paratus est verificare per recordum:** this he is ready to verify by the record. **Hoc per quam durum est, sed ita lex scripta:** this is indeed hard, but so the law is written. **Hoc vobis ostendit:** this shows to you. **Hoc titulo:** under this title. **Hoc voce:** under this word.

Hogenhyne, Agenhyne, *sax.* A domestic servant; a member of the household; a guest on his third night or afterwards.

Holm. An island in a river; grassy ground by water.

Holograph. A deed or will written entirely by the grantor or testator, in his own hand.

Holt, *sax.* A wood, grove.

Homage, Homagium, *l.* An humble submission, an acknowledgment by the tenant in knight service that he was the lord's vassal, reserving only his faith to the King. **Liege homage:** such as is due the King independent of tenure, without any reservation. **Homage ancestral:** where a man and his heirs had held immemorially by homage; and the lord was bound to warranty. **Homagium reddere:** to renounce homage.

Home, homme, *fr.*, **Homo,** *pl.* **homines,** *l.* A man; men. **Homines de fief, feodaux, Homines ligii:** feudal tenants.

Homestead. The place of a home. In America, a dwelling-house, and land about it, exempted from execution for debts.

Homicidium, *l.* Homicide. The killing a man. **Homicidium**

per infortunium, per misadventure : accidental homicide, committed while doing a lawful act. **Se defendendo** : in self-defence; v. *Excusable homicide*. **In rixa** : homicide in a quarrel.

Hominatio, hominium, *l.* Homage.

Homine replegiando. v. *De.*

Homo, *l.* A man ; a vassal. **Homo potest esse habilis et inhabilis diversis temporibus** : a man may be capable and incapable at divers times. **Homo francus, ingenuus, liber** : a freeman.

Homologation. Approbation ; confirmation.

Honesti vivere, alteri non lædere, suum cuique tribuere, *l.* To live honestly, injure not another, render to each his own.

Honour, *fr.*, **Honor,** *l.* Honor. A nobler sort of seigniory. v. *Challenge, Acceptance.* **Honorary service** : those incident to *grand serjeanty.*

Honorarium, *l.* An honorary or free gift, which cannot be exacted.

Hope. A valley.

Horæ juridicæ, *l.* Hours in which the court sits.

Hore, ore, *fr.* Now.

Horn tenure. *Cornage.* **Horn geld** : a tax on horned beasts in a forest.

Hors, *fr.* Out ; without ; out of. **Hors de son fee** : out of his fee, an old plea to an action to recover rent on services. **Hors pris** : except. **Hors de temps** : out of time.

Hospes, *pl.* **hospites,** *l.* Guest ; host.

Hospitia curiæ, *l.* Inns of court. **Hospitium** : household.

Hospitelarius, *l.*, **Hostelier,** *fr.* An innkeeper.

Hostes, *l.* Enemies. **Hostes humani generis** : pirates.

Hotchpot. A mixing together, throwing into a common stock ; as of a child's *advancement,* when an inheritance is to be divided.

Housebote. v. *Bote.*

House of Lords. v. *Court,* 13.

How, howe. A hill.

Hue and cry. The alarm, and pursuit of a felon, in which all were bound to join.

Huis, huy, *fr.* A door.

Hundred. A portion of a county usually containing ten *tithings* and a hundred *frank-pledges,* in which all were liable, in case of an offence within the district, to produce the offender or make good the damage.

Hundred court: v. *Court*, 30. **Hundred gemote:** v. *Court*, 31.

Hurst. A little wood.

Huscarle, *sax.* A domestic; a vassal. **Husfastene:** a house-holder. **Husgablum:** house rent or tax.

Hustings. The principal court of the city of London. The raised place from which candidates for Parliament address the electors. v. *Court*, 58, 60.

Hutesium et clamor, *l.* *Hue and cry.*

Hypotheca, *l.* A pledge for a debt without delivery of the property pledged; hypothecation.

Hythe, *sax.* A wharf or haven.

I.

Ibi, *l.* There; in that place. **Ibi semper debet fieri triatio, ubi juratores meliorem possunt habere notitiam:** a trial ought always to be held where the jury can get the best information.

Ibid., for **Ibidem,** *l.* In the same place.

Icel, iceluy, icelle, iceux, *fr.* This; him; these; those.

Id, *l.* That; v. *Certum.* **Id est** (abb. i. e.): that is. **Id possumus quod de jure possumus:** we can do [only] that which we can do lawfully.

Idem, *l.* The same. **Idem agens et patiens esse non potest:** the same person cannot be both agent and patient. **Idem est non esse et non apparere:** not to appear is the same as not to be. **Idem sonans:** sounding the same.

Identitate nominis, *l.* A writ that lay for him who upon a *capias* or an *exigent* was taken and committed to prison for another man of the same name.

Idiota inquirendo, *l.* An old writ to inquire whether a man was an idiot or not, by a jury of twelve men; if so found, the profits of his land and the custody of his person might be granted by the sovereign to any subject who had interest enough to obtain them.

Ideo quære, *l.* Therefore inquire. **Ideo consideratum est:** therefore it is considered.

Ignitegium, *l.* Curfew.

Ignorare, *l.* To be ignorant. **Ignoramus:** v. *Bill*, I. 6.

Ignorantia eorum quæ quis scire tenetur non excusat, *l.* Ignorance of those things which any one is held to know is no excuse. **Ignorantia fact excusat, ignorantia juris non excusat** : ignorance of fact is an excuse, not ignorance of law.

Ignotum per ignotius, *l.* A thing unknown by something yet more unknown.

Il, *fr.* It, he. **Il covient** : it is proper. **Il est communement dit** : it is commonly said.

Illugne, illongues, etc., *fr.* There.

Illusory appointment. The appointment by a person having a power to appoint real or personal property among a class, of a merely nominal share to one of that class, practically excluding him ; frequently forbidden by statute. v. *Power.*

Immemorial. v. *Time.* Before the time of Richard I., before A. D. 1189.

Immobilis, *l.* Immovable. **Immobilia situm sequuntur** : things immovable follow [the law of] their site.

Impanel. To enter the names of the jurymen on the *panel,* a bit of parchment attached to the *venire facias.* In America, to choose the names of jurors for a particular case.

Imparlance. Leave given to the defendant to talk with the plaintiff and settle the suit amicably ; an extension of time for pleading ; a *continuance ;* a stay of execution. v. *Continuance.*

Imparsonee. Inducted and in possession of a benefice. v. *Induction.*

Impeachment of waste. Liability for waste ; also, a demand or suit for waste committed.

Impediens, *l.* One who hinders ; a defendant, deforciant. **Impeditor** : the disturber in *quare impedit.*

Imperitia, *l.* Unskilfulness. **Imperite** : unskilfully. **Imperitia culpæ adnumeratur** : want of skill is reckoned a fault [culpable negligence].

Imperium, *l.* Power, command ; authority.

Impetere, *l.* To impeach, command ; to sue. **Impetitio vasti** : impeachment of waste.

Implacitare, *l.* To implead ; to sue.

Implied. v. *Assumpsit, Colour, Condition, Consideration, Covenant, Malice, Trust, Warranty.*

Importer, emporter, *fr.* To carry away.

11

Impositio, *l.* Imposition; a tax or tribute.

Impossibilis, *l.* Impossible. **Impossibilium nulla obligatio est**: there is no obligation of [to do] impossible things.

Impotentia excusat legem, *l.* Inability excuses the law. [Impossibility or inability is an excuse for not doing what the law requires.]

Impound. 1. To put in a *pound.* 2. To retain in the custody of the law; as of a forged or suspicious document produced at a trial.

Imprimatur, *l.* (Let it be printed.) A license to publish.

Imprimis, *l.* In the first place; first of all.

Imprisonment. Confinement of any description. v. *False.*

Improbare, *l.* To disapprove; disallow.

Improbation. In Scotch law, an action to annul an instrument by proving it false or forged.

Improper feud. A feud held otherwise than by military service. v. *Feud.*

Impropriation. Appropriation of benefices to other than the proper spiritual uses; a living held by a layman or lay corporation.

Improve. Scotch, to disprove, invalidate, impeach.

Improviare, *l.* To improve land. **Improviamentum**: the improvement of land.

Impunitas semper ad deteriora invitat, *l.* Impunity always encourages greater faults. v. *Maleficia.*

Impuris manibus nemo accedat curiam, *l.* Let no one come to court with unclean hands.

Imputation of payments. *Application of payments.*

In, *l.* In; into; in possession. **In adversum**: against an adverse or unwilling party. **In æquali jure, melior [potior] est conditio possidentis [defendentis]**: in equal right, the possessor [defendant] has the better condition [position]. **In æquali manu** (in equal hand): in the hands of a third person. **In alieno solo**: on another's land. **In alio loco**: in another place; v. *Cepit.* **In ambigua voce legis ea potius accipienda est significatio quæ vitio caret**: in an ambiguous expression of law, that meaning should be taken which works no wrong. **In Anglia non est interregnum**: in England there is never any interregnum. **In antea**: henceforth. **In aperta luce**: in open daylight. **In arbitrio alieno**: in the discretion of another. **In arbitrio judicis**: in the discretion of the judge. **In arcta et salva custodia**: in close and safe custody. **In articulo mortis**: at the point of death. **In banco**: in *banc*. **In bonis defuncti**: among the goods of the deceased. **In capita**: to the polls. **In capite**: in chief; v. *Caput*. **In casu consimili**: in like case; v. *Action on the case*. **In casu consimili, proviso**; v. *Casu*. **In casu extremæ necessitatis omnia sunt communia**: in cases of extreme necessity, all is common property. **In commendam**: in commendation; v. *Commendam*. **In communi**: in common. **In consideratione inde**: in consideration thereof. **In consideratione legis**: in contemplation of law, in abeyance. **In consimili casu consimile debet esse remedium**: in like case the remedy should be similar. **In consuetudinibus non diuturnitas temporis sed soliditas rationis est consideranda**: in customs, not the length of time, but the strength of the reason should be considered. **In continenti**: immediately. **In contractibus tacite insunt quæ sunt moris et consuetudinis**: in contracts matters of custom and usage are tacitly implied. **In conventionibus contrahentium voluntatem potius quam verba spectari placuit**: in agreements it is better to regard the will of the parties than the mere words. **In corpore**: in body, in substance. **In crastino animarum**: on the morrow of All Souls'. **In criminalibus sufficit generalis malitia intentionis cum facto paris gradus**: in criminal cases a general malice [of intention] is sufficient [if coupled] with an act of equal degree [of wrong]. **In cujus rei testimonium**: in testimony whereof. **In curia**: iu court. **In custodia legis**: in custody of the law. **In damno**: in damage. **In defenso**: in prohibition; enclosed. **In delicto**: in fault; guilty. **In descendu**: by descent; v. *Formedon*. **In diem**: for a day. **In disjunctivis sufficit alteram partem esse veram**: in disjunctive [conditions] it is enough that either part be true [happen, be performed]. **In dominico**: in demesne. **In dominico suo ut de feodo**: in his demesne as of fee. **In dorso**: on the back. **In dubio, in dubiis**: in doubt, in uncertainties. **In dubiis benigniora præferenda sunt**: in doubt the more favorable views are to be preferred. **In dubio pars mitiora est sequenda**: in doubt the milder course is to be preferred. **In dubiis non præsumitur pro**

testamento: in cases of doubt there is no presumption in favor of a will. **In duplo, in duplum**: in double, for the double value. **In duriorem sortem** (to the harder lot): to the most burdensome debt. **In eo quod plus sit semper inest et minus**: in that which is greater the less is always contained. **In esse**: in being. **In essentialibus**: in the essential parts. **In excambio**: in exchange. **In exitu**: in issue, at the end. **In extenso**: in its .full extent. **In extremis**: in the last extremity. **In facie curiæ**: before court. **In facie ecclesiæ**: in the face of the church. **In faciendo** (in doing): for the performance. **In facto**: in fact, in deed. **In favorem libertatis**: in favor of liberty. **In favorem vitæ omnia præsumuntur**: all things are presumed in favor of life. **In feodo**: in fee. **In fictione juris semper subsistit æquitas**: in a fiction of law there always remains [must exist some] equity. **In fieri**: in becoming, in being done; imperfect, incomplete. **In flagrante delicto**: in the heat of the offence. **In forma pauperis**: in the character of a pauper. **In foro**: in the tribunal, court; v. *Forum*. **In fraudem legis**: in fraud of the law. **In futuro**: in future, at a future time. **In genere**: in kind. **In gremio legis**: in the bosom of the law, in abeyance. **In hac parte**: in this behalf. **In hæc verba**: in these words. **In hunc modum**: after this manner. **In individuo**: in distinct form, in the piece. **In initio, initialibus**: in the beginning, the preliminaries. **In integrum**: anew, to the original or complete state. **In invitum**: against an unwilling party. **In itinere**: on the way; v. *Assize*. **In judicio**: before a judge, in court. **In judicio non creditur nisi juratis**: in court belief is only given to persons sworn. **In jure**: in law. **In jure non remota causa sed proxima spectatur**: in law the nearest, not the remote, cause is regarded. **In jure alterius**: in the right of another. **In jure proprio**: in one's own right. **In jus vocare**: to summon to court. **In lecto**: on the death-bed. **In libera eleemosyna**: in *frankalmoign*. **In libero soccagio**: in free *socage*. **In limine**: on the threshold, at the outset. **In linea recta**: in the direct line. **In loco parentis**: in the place of a parent. **In majore summa continetur minor**: in the greater sum is contained the less. **In maleficiis voluntas spectatur non exitus**: in crimes the intent, not the result, is regarded. **In maleficio ratiha-bitio mandato comparatur**: in a wrongful act a ratification is held as a command. **In mero jure**: of mere right. **In misericordia**: *in mercy*. **In mitiori sensu**: in the milder sense. **In mora**: in default, in delay. **In mortua manu**: in dead hand, *mortmain*. **In nubibus** (in the clouds): in *abeyance*. **In nullius bonis**: in the property of no one. **In nullo est erratum** (in nothing has there been error): the name of the plea of joinder in error. **In octavis**: on the octave, an ancient return-day. **In odium spoliatoris**: to the hatred [prejudice] of the despoiler. **In odium spoliatoris omnia præsumuntur**: every presumption is made against a wrong-doer. **In omnibus**: in all things, in all points. **In omnibus pœnalibus judiciis et ætati et imprudentiæ succurritur**: in all penal judgments youth and want of understanding are favored. **In ore**: in the mouth. **In pace Dei et regis**: in the peace of God and the King. **In pari casu**: in a similar condition. **In pari delicto potior est conditio possidentis [defendentis]**: where the fault is equal the party in possession [defendant] shall prevail. **In pari materia**: upon the same sub-ject. **In patiendo**: in permitting, in suffering. **In pendente**: in suspension. **In perpetuum**: forever. **In perpetuam rei memoriam**: in perpetual memory of a matter. **In perpetuum rei testimonium**: for perpetual testimony of the thing. **In personam**: against the person. **In pios usus**: for religious purposes. **In plena vita**: in full life. **In pleno comitatu**: in the full county court. **In pœnalibus causis, benignius interpretandum est**: in penal cases the more favorable inter-pretation should be made. **In posse**: in possibility. **In pos-terum**: hereafter. **In potestate parentis**: in the power of a parent. **In præsenti**: at the present time. **In præsentia majoris cessat potentia minoris**: in the presence of the superior the power of the inferior ceases. **In principio**: at the beginning. **In propria persona**: in proper person, in one's own person. **In proximo gradu**: in the nearest degree. **In quantum lucratus est**: in so far as he has profited. **In quindena**: in fifteen days, an old return-day. **In quo quis delinquit, in eo de jure est puniendus**: in that in which he offends, he may lawfully be punished. **In quovis**: in what-

ever. **In re**: in the matter, in the affair; v. *Ad rem*. **In re
aliena**: in the affairs of another, in another's property. **In re
propria**: in one's own affairs. **In rebus**: in matters, in cases.
In rem: against the thing; v. *Ad rem*. **In rem suam**: in
one's own affairs. **In rem versum**: employed in one's own
profit, actually used in one's own affairs. **In rerum natura**:
in the nature of things. **In retentis** (in things held back): to
be kept back until wanted, taken and preserved secretly. **In
rigore juris**: in the rigor of the law. **In rixa**: in a quarrel.
In scaccario: in the exchequer. **In solido** (in the whole):
for the full amount, the entire obligation; jointly and severally.
In solidum: for the whole; as a whole, exclusively. **In solo
proprio**: in one's own land. **In solutum**: in payment. **In
spe**: in hope, in expectation. **In specie**: in kind; in the
same form; specific. **In statu quo ante bellum**: in the
state in which [the matter was] before the war. **In stipulationibus id tempus spectatur quo contrahimus**: in
agreements the time in which we contract is regarded. **In
stipulationibus quum queritur quid actum sit, verba
contra stipulatorem interpretanda sunt**: in contracts
where there arises a question as to what was done, the words are
to be taken against the (stipulator) person to whom the promise
is made. **In stirpes**: according to roots, or stocks; v. *Stirps,
per stirpes*. **In stricto jure**: in strict law. **In subsidium**:
in aid. **In substantialibus**: of a substantial nature. **In
summa**: in sum, on the whole. **In suo genere**: of their own
kind. **In superficie**: in the surface. **In suspenso**: in suspense. **In tantum**: insomuch; forasmuch. **In terminis ter-
minantibus**: in terms of determination. **In terrorem** (in
terror): by way of threat. **In totidem verbis**: in so many
words. **In toto**: entirely, as to the whole. **In toto et pars
continetur**: in the whole is contained the part also. **In tra-
ditionibus scriptorum, non quod dictum est, sed quod
gestum, inspicitur**: in the delivery of deeds, not what is said,
but what is done, is regarded. **In transitu**: in transit, during
conveyance; v. *Stoppage*. **In tuto**: in safety. **In utero**: in
the womb. **In vadio**: in gage or pledge. **In vinculis**: in
chains. **In vita**: in life.

In, *fr.* v. *En, En prender, render*, etc.

In action. Recoverable by action; not in possession. **In bank, banc:** a full court, all the judges; *Full Bank.* **In blank:** an indorsement simply of the indorser's name, without restricting it to any indorsee, whereby the note becomes payable to bearer. **In chief:** 1. Tenure *in capite,* directly of the chief. lord or of the Crown, is so called. 2. The first examination of a witness, before the *cross-examination.* **In mercy:** a phrase in the record of old judgments, denoting that the defendant was *in mercy* of the King, liable to amerciament, for his delay; or the plaintiff and his pledges, **pro falso clamore suo,** for his false claim. **In prender:** in taking, a term applied to such incorporeal hereditaments as the person might take for himself, in distinction from such as were **in render,** in yielding or paying, which the party liable, or the tenant, had to offer.

Incerta pro nullis habentur, *l.* Uncertain things are held as void.

Inchoate. Begun, incipient. **Inchoate dower:** a woman's interest in a husband's land during his lifetime.

Incipitur, *l.* It is begun: a term applied to an abbreviated entry on the record, as of a judgment or other proceeding.

Incivile, *l.* Irregular; against due course of law; improper.

Inclosure. The extinction of rights of common in land.

Inclusio unius est exclusio alterius, *l.* The inclusion of the one is the exclusion of the other.

Incorporalis, *l.,* **Incorporeal** v. *Hereditament.*

Incrementum, *l.* Increase. **Incrementa:** additions, increase of land by the sea.

Incumbent. A clergyman resident on his benefice.

Inde, *l.* Thence; thereof; therefrom; thereupon. v. *Et.*

Indebitatus assumpsit, *l.* Being indebted, he undertook. v. *Assumpsit.* **Indebitatus nunquam:** never indebted.

Indebiti solutio, *l.* The payment of something not due.

Indefeasible. That which cannot be defeated or made void.

Indefinite failure of issue. A failure of issue to a person at any time, before or after his death. v. *Dying.*

Indemnity. v. *Bill,* II. 2.

Indenture. A deed indented. v. *Deed, Fine.*

Independent. v. *Covenant, Condition.*

Index animi sermo, *l.* Speech is the indicator of intention.

Indicavit, *l.* A writ of prohibition which lay for the patron of a church whose parson was sued in the ecclesiastical court in an action of tithes by another clerk, when the tithes in question amounted to a ·fourth part of the value of the living; in which case the suit was cognizable in the "King's court," i. e. the common law courts.

Indicium, *pl.* **Indicia,** *l.* Sign; mark; badges; tokens; evidence.

Indictare, *l.* To indict. **Indictment.** v. *Bill,* I. 6.

Indorsement. The writing of his name on the back by a payee, drawer, or holder of a note or bill, whereby the property in it is transferred. A writing on the back of an instrument. v. *In blank.* An **Indorsement in full,** or **special indorsement,** has added the name of the person to whom the note or bill is assigned. An **indorsement without recourse** is a kind of **qualified indorsement,** effected by writing the words "without recourse," or words of like meaning, after the indorser's name. The indorser·thereby passes the title without incurring an indorser's liabilities for non-acceptance or non-payment.

Inducement. A preliminary statement of facts in the declaration of slander. v. *Colloquium.*

Induciæ, *l.* A truce; delay or indulgence.

Induction. The ceremony of giving a clergyman actual possession of the temporalities of a benefice, after the *institution;* as by holding the ring of the door, tolling the bell, or the like; when he becomes *imparsonee.*

Inest de jure, *l.* It is implied in the right, implied by law.

Infamia facti, *l.* General bad character, as distinguished from **infamia juris,** infamy arising from a legal conviction for crime.

Infangthefe, *sax.* A privilege of a lord of a manor to judge any thief taken in his fee. v. *Outfangthefe.*

Infans, *l.* A child under the age of seven.

Infant. A person under twenty-one.

Infantia, *l.* The age from birth to seven years.

Infeft, *sc.* To give seisin, enfeoff.

Infeodare, *l.* To give a fee, give seisin, enfeoff. **Infeodatio:** enfeoffment.

Infeodation, infeudation. Enfeoffment. **Infeodation of tithes:** the granting of tithes to laymen.

Infinitum in jure reprobatur, *l.* That which is endless is disapproved of in law.

Infirmative. Having a tendency to render infirm, to weaken.

Information. A complaint against a person for some criminal or penal offence, filed by the proper officer, on behalf of the Crown or people, at his own discretion, on the relation or information of some private person; resembling in criminal cases an indictment, but not founded on the oath of a jury, and in civil cases like the bill or declaration; in each class the subsequent proceedings being as usual. An **information in Chancery** is a bill instituted by the Attorney-General on behalf of the Crown. An **information in the Exchequer** has its object to recover money due the Crown, or damages for an *intrusion* upon Crown lands. An information on a penal statute gives the informer a share in the penalty. v. *Quo warranto, Quitam.*

Informatus non sum. v. *Non sum informatus.*

Infortunium, *l.* Misfortune; misadventure. v. *Homicide.*

Infra, *l.* Below; underneath; 'within. **Infra ætatem:** under age. **Infra annos nubiles:** under marriageable years. **Infra annum:** within a year. **Infra annum luctus:** within the year of mourning. **Infra brachia:** within [her] arms. **Infra corpus comitatus:** within the body of a county [where the jurisdiction of Admiralty ceases]. **Infra dignitatem curiæ:** beneath the dignity of the court. **Infra hospitium:** within an inn. **Infra præsidia:** within guards, under protection. **Infra quatuor maria:** within the *four seas;* in England. **Infra regnum:** within the realm. **Infra sex annos:** within six years. **Infra tempus semestre:** within six months.

Ingenuus, *l.* A freeman, yeoman.

Ingressus, *l.* Entry; ingress. A relief paid by an heir to the head lord. **Ingressu, De ingressu:** a writ of entry.

Ingressus et egressus, *l.* Freedom of entry and exit.

Inherent. v. *Condition, Covenant.*

Inheritable blood. Blood capable of transmitting an inheritance; as that of a legitimate son unattainted.

Inheritance. An estate or interest in property which may pass by descent from one person to another.

Inhibition. A writ from a higher ecclesiastical court to restrain proceedings in a lower.

Iniquum est aliquem rei sui esse judicem, *l.* It is unjust for any one to be judge in his own cause.

Initiate. Begun. **Initiate curtesy**: the interest of a husband, during his wife's life, in her lands, after the birth of a child capable of inheriting. v. *Curtesy*.

Initium, *l.* The beginning.

Injunction. A prohibitory writ issuing from a court of equity forbidding a party to do or suffer a certain act. A **mandatory injunction** forbids a party to allow a thing now existing to continue, and amounts to a direction to him to remove it. A **preliminary** or **provisional** injunction is granted at the outset of a suit, or **pendente lite**, to restrain the party's action until the suit has been determined; a **final** or **perpetual** injunction prohibits the party forever from doing the action or continuing the existence of the thing, and is granted as a means of permanent relief upon the end of the suit. **Common injunction**: one granted on default.

Injuria, *l.* Injury; legal wrong; tortious action. **Injuria non præsumitur**: tortious action will not be presumed; v. *Damnum*. **Injuria non excusat injuriam**: one tort does not excuse another.

Inlagare, *l.* To restore to law; to take back an outlaw.

Inland bill of exchange. One drawn and payable within Great Britain and Ireland, and the adjacent islands which are part of the British dominions.

Innocent. (v. *Conveyance*.) Not *tortious*.

Innotescimus, *l.* We make known; words used in *letters patent*.

Innovation. *Novation*.

Inns of Chancery. Clifford's Inn, Clement's Inn, New Inn, Staple Inn, and Barnard's Inn; formerly also Furnival's Inn, the Strand Inn, Lyon's Inn, and Thavies' Inn, with Serjeant's Inn, which consisted of serjeants only. They were formerly preparatory colleges for students, inhabited by clerks in chancery, attorneys, etc.; but performed no public functions, and are now sunk into insignificance.

Inns of Court. The four law societies of the Middle Temple, Inner Temple, Lincoln's Inn, and Gray's Inn, which in England are privileged to confer the degree of barrister at law.

Innuendo, *l.* Meaning; the clause in a declaration explaining slanderous matter. v. *Colloquium*.

Inofficiosum. Undutiful. **Inofficiosum testamentum**: an un-
natural will; one disinheriting a child.

Inops consilii, *l.* Destitute of counsel.

Inquest. A judicial inquiry; especially by a coroner's or sheriff's
jury. The finding of a jury. **Inquest of office**: the inquest
of a king's officer, coroner, or escheator, either by writ or commission, or *virtute officii*, into a matter in which the King is interested; the escheat of lands on attainder, etc. The verdict was
called **office found.**

Inquiry, Writ of. v. *Writ.*

Inquisitio post mortem, *l.* Inquest after death; an inquest of
office held on the death of a tenant in chivalry.

Insidiatores viarum, *l.* Highwaymen.

Insimul computassent, *l.* (They accounted together.) An action
upon an *account stated:* one of the *common counts.*

Insinuatio, *l.* Suggestion. **Ex insinuatione**: on the information of.

Inspection, Trial by. The trial of some issue in a suit by the decision of the judges upon the testimony of their own senses; as
of the *nonage* of one of the parties, an appeal of *mayhem,* etc.

Instance Court. The ordinary Court of Admiralty, as distinct
from the Prize Court. v. *Court,* 91.

Instar, *l.* Likeness; equivalent. **Instar dentium**: like teeth.

Instituta, *l.,* **Institutes.** 1. Elements of the Roman law compiled
under Justinian. 2. Coke's Institutes.

Institutio, *l.,* **Institution.** The investiture of a clerk by the
bishop; the ceremony of ordaining him as rector of a parish.
v. *Induction.*

Insula, *l.* An island.

Insultus, *l.* An assault.

Insuper, *l.* Moreover; over and above.

Insurance. A contract of indemnity against certain risks for a
pecuniary consideration. v. *Assurance.*

Integer, *l.* Entire; untouched; fresh. **Res integra**: a new matter, hitherto undecided.

Intendment of law. The true meaning of the law. A *presumption.*

Intentio, *l.* 1. The plaintiff's demand, count, or declaration.
2. Intention; purpose. **Intentio cæca mala**: if the purpose
is obscure, it is ineffectual. **Intentio debet inservire legibus**

non leges intentioni: the intention should accord with the laws, not the laws with the intention.

Inter, *l.* Between; among. **Inter alia:** among others. **Inter alios acta:** things done between other persons [than the parties.] **Inter amicos:** among friends. **Inter arma leges silent** (among arms): when appeal is made to arms the laws are silent. **Inter canem et lupum** (between dog and wolf): twilight. **Inter partes:** between parties. **Inter rusticos:** among illiterate persons. **Inter virum et uxorem:** between husband and wife. **Inter sese:** among themselves. **Inter vivos:** between persons living.

Intercommoning. A mutual privilege of common, enjoyed by two townships or manors in each other's land.

Interdict. 1. An injunction. 2. An ecclesiastical censure, prohibition of divine services, *interdiction.* 3. In Scotch law, a legal restraint from executing deeds, imposed on persons of weak mind.

Interesse, *l.* Interest; an interest in lands or money. **Interesse termini** (the interest of a term): the state of a lessee for years in the land before his entry.

Interest, *l.* It concerns; it benefits. **Interest reipublicæ,** it is of public importance, **ne maleficia remaneant impunita,** that crimes should not remain unpunished; **ne sua quis male utatur,** that no one make bad use of his property; **quod homines conserventur,** that the [lives of] men be preserved; **res judicatas non rescindi,** that things once adjudged should not be rescinded; **suprema hominum testamenta rata haberi,** that men's last wills be held valid; **ut carceres sint in tuto,** that prisons be secure; **ut finis sit litium,** that there should be an end of suits.

Interlocutio, *l. Imparlance.*

Interlocutor. Scotch, an order or decree of court.

Interlocutory. Immediate; temporary. v. *Decree, Costs.*

Intern. To restrict a person within a certain territory as a political prisoner.

International law. Customs and precedents affecting intercourse between nations, or persons of different nations, and sanctioned by usage or approval of nations generally. **International private law,** or **Private international law:** the law of the application of the laws of one nation, as to civil or private rights, within the courts of another nation; the rules of the "conflict of laws." So **International public law**, when applied to public or criminal cases.

Intérpleader. v. *Bill,* I. 7.

Interpret. v. *Construe.*

Interpretatio chartarum benigne facienda est ut res magis valeat quam pereat, *l.* The interpretation of deeds is to be liberal, that the thing may rather have effect than fail.

Interrogatories. Questions in writing administered to a party or a witness.

Interruptio, *l.* Interruption, interference; as of a prescription.

Intestate. A person deceased without a valid will.

Intra, *l.* Within. **Intra mœnia:** within the walls, domestic. **Intra parietes** (between the walls): among friends, out of court. **Intra quatuor maria:** within the *four seas.*

Intromission. Assuming authority over another's property, whether lawfully or not.

Intrusion. The entry of a stranger on land, at the death of a freehold tenant, to the prejudice of him in remainder or reversion. v. *Writ of Entry, Information.*

Intuitu matrimonii, mortis, *l.* In contemplation of marriage, death.

Invadiare, *l.* To pledge or mortgage. **Invadiatio:** a gage, pledge.

Invecta et illata, *l.* Things brought and carried in; a tenant's furniture.

Inveniendo, *l.* Finding; a word used in reserving rent. **Inventus:** found.

Investiture. Giving possession, whether of a fee or benefice.

Invito, *l.* Unwilling. **Invito beneficium non datur:** a benefit is not [may not be] given to a man against his will. **Invito domino, debitore:** against the will of the lord, the debtor.

Ipse, *l.* He; himself; the same. **Ipsissimis verbis:** in the very words. **Ipso facto:** by the fact itself. **Ipso jure:** by the law itself, by the same law.

Ire ad largum, *l.* To *go* at large.

Irritancy. Scotch, a becoming void, null.

Irritus, *l.* Void; invalid; in vain.

Irrotulatio, irrotulamentum, *l.* An enrolment, roll, record.

Is qui cognoscit, *l.* The cognizor. **Is cui cognoscitur**: the cognizee.

Issint, *fr.* So; thus.

Issuable. Traversable; producing an issue.

Issue. 1. A single point, developed by the pleadings, on which an action turns, which may be of **fact** or **law**. 2. Descendants, in general; [in a will] heirs, children. 3. v. *General Issue.* 4. Issues, profits.

Ita, *l.* So, thus. **Ita lex scripta est**: so the law is written. **Ita quod**: so that. **Ita semper fiat relatio ut valeat dispositio**: let the reference be always so made that the disposition may be valid. **Ita te Deus adjuvet**: so help you God.

Item, *l.* Also; a single charge in an account.

Iter, *l.* Way; path; right of way; journey; the circuit of a judge; v. *Assize, Eyre.* **Itinera**: eyres, circuits. **In itinere**: on the way. **Itinerantes**: travelling, in eyre.

J.

Ja, *fr.* Yet; now. **Ja demains**: furthermore. **Ja soit que**: although.

Jacere, *l.* To lie. **Jacens**: lying, in abeyance; v. *Hæreditas.* **Jacet in ore**: it lies in the mouth.

Jactitation of marriage. A boasting of marriage. v. *Causa.*

Jactura, *l.* *Jettison,* loss by *jettison.*

Jactus, *l.* *Jettison;* thrown, cast, defeated; *ject.*

Jail. v. *Gaol.*

Ject, *fr.* Cast; overthrown; defeated; cast, computed.

Jeo, *fr.* I. **Jeo ay, done, soy, guarantise**: I have, give, am, warrant.

Jeofail, *fr.* An oversight or mistake in pleading.

Jeofails, Statute of. A statute giving liberty to amend errors in pleading; and particularly the 14 Edw. III., st. 2, c. 6.

Jetsom, jettison. v. *Flotsam.* Part of the cargo thrown over to lighten the ship.

Jocus partitus, *l.* A divided hazard; an old method of settling a case upon a chance.

Joinder. A uniting together, meeting. **Joinder in demurrer,**

or of issue: the pleading answering and accepting a demurrer or issue, a *similiter*.

Joint. United; combined; shared; the reverse of *several*. **Joint action**: one in which two or more parties are joined as plaintiffs. **Joint bond**: one entered into by two or more obligors, which can be enforced only by action against them all together. **Joint stock company**: a kind of extended partnership, formed by voluntary association without a charter or patent, in which the capital is divided into shares which may be assigned without the express consent of the other members.

Joint tenants. When two or more persons acquire land at the same time by the same title, other than by descent, they hold it in a joint tenancy. Each is seised of the whole, *per my et per tout*, as well as the half; there is right of survivorship, but no dower or curtesy; and there must be the four unities of possession, title, time, and interest. v. *Coparcenary, Common.*

Jointure. An estate settled before marriage upon the husband and wife jointly; or limited to the wife after the death of the husband, to be enjoyed by her in lieu of dower.

Jour, *fr.* A day. **Jour en banc**: a *day in bank.*

Journée, *fr.* A court day.

Journeys accounts. The name of a writ sued out of Chancery as soon as possible after the abatement of a former writ, and which had effect as a continuance of the first.

Judex, *l.* A judge. **Judex a quo, ad quem.** v. *A quo.* **Judex æquitatem semper spectari debet**: a judge ought always to regard equity. **Judex est lex loquens**: a judge is the law speaking. **Judex non reddit plus quam quod petens ipse requirit**: a judge does not give more than the plaintiff himself demands. **Judici officium suum excedenti non paretur**: a judge exceeding his office is not to be obeyed. **Judicis est jus dicere, non dare**: it is the duty of a judge to expound law, not to make it.

Judgment debt. A debt due under a judgment. **Judgment note**: a promissory note, containing, in addition to the usual contents, a power of attorney authorizing confession of judgment against the maker, upon default of payment. **Judgment nisi**: a judgment to become absolute *unless* the court shall within the first four days of the next term order otherwise; giving the defeated party four days to move against the judgment. **Judgment paper**: in English practice, a sheet containing an *incipitur* of the pleadings in an action at law, upon which final judgment is signed by the master. **Judgment record** or **roll**: a formal systematic transcript or parchment of the proceedings in an action at law leading up to the judgment, and the judgment; the authentic official *record*, composed of the various entries in order, signed and filed and docketed in the treasury of the court.

Judicandum est legibus, non exemplis, *l.* Judgment is to be given according to laws, not precedents.

Judicature Acts. The statutes regarding the Supreme Court of Judicature, and particularly the 36 & 37 Vict. c. 66, changing the entire organization of the English courts. v. *Court*, 29. See also 37 & 38 Vict. c. 83; 38 & 39 Vict. c. 77; 39 & 40 Vict. c. 59; 40 & 41 Vict. c. 9; and, for Ireland, 40 & 41 Vict. c. 57.

Judicia posteriora sunt in lege fortiora, *l.* The later judgments are in law the stronger.

Judicial admission or **confession**. One made voluntarily in court or before a magistrate. **Judicial Committee of the Privy Council**: v. *Court*, 14, 89. **Judicial sale**: a sale by order of court; under judicial authority, by an officer legally authorized. **Judicial separation**: a kind of limited divorce, in which the parties are not allowed to marry again. **Judicial writ**: v. *Writ*.

Judicio sisti, *l.* A *caution*, or security, given in Scotch courts for the defendant to abide judgment within the jurisdiction.

Judicium, *l.* A court; an action; legal authority; a verdict; a judgment. **Judicium a non suo judice datum nullius est momenti**: a judgment given by one not the proper judge is of no authority. **Judicium capitale**: judgment of death. **Judicium Dei**: judgment of God, a term applied to the *ordeals*. **Judicium aquæ, ferri, ignis**: the *ordeal* by water, iron, or fire. **Judicium parium**: judgment of peers, by one's peers. **Judicium redditur in invitum in præsumptione legis**: judgment in presumption of law is given against an unwilling party.

Juge de paix, *fr.* In France, an inferior, or police, judge. **Juge d'instruction**: an officer who receives the complaint, examines the witnesses, and draws up the accusation in criminal cases.

Jugum terræ, *l.* A yoke of land, half a ploughland.

Jura, *l.* Rights; laws; v. *Jus.* **Jura ad rem**: rights to a thing, **in personam**, against a person. **Jura eodem modo destituuntur quo constituuntur**: laws are abrogated in the same manner in which they are enacted. **Jura publica anteferenda privatis**: public rights are to be preferred to private. **Jura summi imperii**: rights of sovereignty. **Jura in re**: rights in a thing, either partial rights or ownership; v. *Jus.* **Juria regalia, regia**: royal rights.

Juramentum, *l.* An oath.

Jurare, *l.* To swear, make oath. **Jurat** (he swears): the memorandum at the foot of an affidavit showing when, where, and before whom it was sworn.

Jurata, *l.* A jury.

Jurator, *l.* A juryman. **Juratores sunt judices facti**: the jurymen are the judges of fact.

Jure, *l.* In right; by right; in law; v. *Jus, Jura.* **Jure belli,** **civili,** etc.; v. *Jus.* **Jure uxoris**: in the right of the wife.

Juridical. Belonging to law; of law.

Juris, *l.* Of law; of right; v. *Jus, Jura, Jure.* **Juris præcepta sunt hoc**: the precepts of law are this. **Juris et de jure** (of law and by law): a term applied to conclusive, irrebuttable presumptions. **Juris et seisinæ conjunctio**: the union of legal right and seisin. **Juris utrum**: "a parson's writ of right" to recover lands alienated by his predecessor; v. *Assize.*

Jurisdictio, *l.* Jurisdiction; authority to judge or legislate. **Plea to the jurisdiction**: v. *Plea.*

Juristic act. One intended to have a legal effect.

Jury. 1. A number of men appointed by judicial or official authority to determine a question of fact. 2. A jury of twelve appointed by the sheriff, to try civil and criminal cases in court; the **petit** or **petty** *jury.* **Grand jury**: a body of from twelve to twenty-three men convened by the sheriff at all assizes or courts to inquire into the evidence against accused persons, and see that there is a just probability of their guilt; v. *Bill,* I. 6. **Common jury**: the ordinary *petty jury,* as distinguished from a **special jury,** a jury composed of members of a certain degree, as freeholders, merchants, etc.; or a **struck jury,** a jury chosen from a selected list of forty-eight, of which twelve names are struck out by each party. **Sheriff's jury**: a jury summoned by a sheriff for trial of an inquiry, or making an inquest or inquest of office. **Coroner's jury**: a jury appointed by a coroner to inquire into a sudden death. **Jury process**: the process of summoning a jury by *venire facias*, and compelling their attendance by *distringas* or *habeas corpora juratorum*. **Jury of matrons** was impanelled to judge of a woman's pregnancy in cases where she was condemned to death, and pleaded pregnancy; or on a writ *de ventre inspiciendo*. **Jury de Medietate Linguæ**: v. *De, Bilinguis*.

Jus, *l.* Right; justice; law. v. *Jura, Jure, Juris*. **Jus abutendi** (the right to abuse): the right to use as one likes, absolute ownership. **Jus accrescendi**: the right of survivorship [as in joint property, on the death of one owner, when the other has the whole]. **Jus accrescendi inter mercatores, pro beneficio commercii, locum non habet**: for the benefit of commerce, the right of survivorship has no existence among merchants. **Jus accrescendi præfertur oneribus**: the right of survivorship is preferred to incumbrances, or **ultimo voluntati**, to the last will. **Jus ad rem**: a right to a thing (in the civil law); a personal right, a right founded on contract. A right to the possession of a thing (in the canon law); an inchoate or imperfect right. A right to a thing (in the common law) as distinguished from *jus in re*, a right without possession. **Jus æsneciæ**: the right of primogeniture. **Jus angariæ**: v. *Angaria*. **Jus aquam ducendi**: the right of leading water [over another's land]. **Jus banci** (the right of bench): the right of having a high seat of justice, allowed only to the King's justices. **Jus belli**: the law of war. **Jus canonicum**, the *canon* law; **civile**, the *civil* law; v. *Corpus juris, Canon law, Civil law*. **Jus civitatis**: the right of citizenship. **Jus commune**: the common law; common right. **Jus cudendæ monetæ**: the right of coining money. **Jus curialitatis**: the right of *curtesy of England*. **Jus dare**: to make law. **Jus deliberandi**: the right of deliberating. In Scotland, the right of the heir to consider for a year whether he will take up the succession. **Jus dicere**: to declare the law. **Jus disponendi**: the right of disposing, of disposition. **Jus duplicatum**: a double right, *droit droit*. **Jus et fraus nunquam cohabitant**: justice and fraud never dwell together. **Jus ex injuria non oritur**: a right cannot arise from a wrong. **Jus fiduciarium**: a right in trust, a moral right. **Jus fodiendi**: a right of digging. **Jus gentium**: the *law of nations*. **Jus habendi et retinendi**: the right to have and retain the profits, tithes, and offerings of a rectory or parsonage. **Jus hauriendi**: the right of drawing water. **Jus in re**: in Roman law, a right in a thing; a right of property availing against all the world, and particularly of an easement or servitude; *droit droit,* a right of property coupled with possession. So also **Jus in rem**: a real right, a right in the thing itself; v. *Ad rem, Jus ad rem.* **Jus in personam**: a right against a person or particular class of persons; a personal right, a right founded on contract, or the act of another person. **Jus legitimum**: a legal right; enforceable at law. **Jus mariti**: the right of a husband; as, to his wife's movables. **Jus merum**: bare right [without possession or right thereto]. **Jus naturæ**: the law of nature. **Jus naturale**: natural law. **Jus non scriptum**: the unwritten law. **Jus pascendi**: right of pasture. **Jus patronatus**: 1. The right of patronage or *presentation* to a benefice. 2. A commission from the bishop awarded when two rival presentations are made to him upon the same *avoidance,* and directed to the bishop's chancellor and others of competent learning, who are to summon a jury of six clergymen and six laymen to determine who is the rightful patron. **Jus possessionis**: right of possession. **Jus postliminii**: the right of the owner to reclaim property after recapture in war. **Jus precarium**: a right existing only in curtesy, precarious. **Jus presentationis**: v. *Jus patronatus*, 1. **Jus proprietatis**: the right of property. **Jus publicum privatorum pactis mutari non potest**: a public right cannot be altered by the agreements of private persons. **Jus relictæ**: the right of a widow in her deceased husband's personal goods; anciently, one half, or one third if there were children. **Jus scriptum**: the written law. **Jus tertii**: the right of a third party. **Jus utendi**: the right to use a thing, the opposite of *jus abutendi.*

Jusjurandum, *l.* An oath.

Justice. A judge of a law court. **Justices of assize**: appointed to try writs of *assize.* Judges of the superior courts in England,

sent twice every year to try causes in their respective counties.
Justices of the Bench: justices of the *Common Pleas*. *Jus-*
tices in Eyre: v. *Eyre*. **Justice of the Forest**: appointed
to hold the court of *justice-seat*; v. *Court*, 78. **Justices of**
the Peace: county magistrates of limited civil and criminal
jurisdiction; v. *Quorum, Court*, 100, 112. Justice of *Gaol*
Delivery, Assize, Nisi Prius, Oyer and Terminer: see those
titles; v. *Assize, Commission*. **Lord Justice**; v. *Lord*.

Justiciar. Justice. The **Chief Justiciar**, in ancient times the second person in the kingdom; later, the Chief Justice of the K. B.

Justiciary Court. v. *Court*, 96.

Justicies. An ancient special writ, empowering the sheriff to try
a matter in a county court, although over 40 *s.* were involved.

Justifying bail. Showing the sufficiency of *bail*.

Justitia nec differenda nec neganda est, *l.* Justice is not to
be denied or delayed.

Justitiarius, *l.* Justiciar, justice. **Justiciarii itinerantes**: justices in *eyre*. **Justiciarii residentes**: justices resident at
Westminster.

Juxta, *l.* According to. **Juxta formam statuti**: according to
the form of the statute. **Juxta tenorem sequentem**: according to the following tenor.

K.

K. B. The King's Bench. v. *Court*, 8.

Keelage. The right of exacting a toll from ships in a harbor; the
money so paid.

Keeper of the Forest. The warden or chief officer of a *forest*.
Keeper of the Great Seal; v. *Lord*.

Kenning to a terce, *sc.* The assignment of a dower by a sheriff.

Kiddle. A dam or wear with a fish-way cut in it.

Kin. Relations or relationship by blood.

King's Bench. v. *Court*, 8. **King's Bench Division**: v. *Court*,
22. **King's Council**: v. *Court*, 6. **King's Court**: v. *Court*,
2, 115. **King's silver**: money formerly paid in the C. P. for
the *licentia concordandi* in levying a *fine*. **King's counsel**:
v. *Queen's Counsel*.

Kirby's quest. The record of a survey of all the lands in England made in the reign of Edward I.

Knight-service. Tenure in chivalry; v. *Tenure, Feud.* Tenure by military, uncertain services; or by paying *escuage.*

Knight's fee. So much land as was considered sufficient to maintain a knight (twelve ploughlands); the possessor of such an estate was formerly obliged to be knighted and attend the King in wars or pay *escuage.*

Knights of the shire. Two members of Parliament, elected to represent each county at large.

L.

L. S., Locus sigilli, *l.* The place for a seal.

La, *fr.* There. **La ou:** whereas.

Label. A narrow strip of paper or parchment affixed to an instrument for an appending seal. In the Exchequer, the copy of a writ.

Laborers, Statutes of. The 23 Edw. III., 12 Rich. II., 5 Eliz. c. 4, and 26 & 27 Vict. c. 125, making regulations as to laborers, apprentices, beggars, servants, etc.

Lacerta, *l.* A fathom.

Laches. Negligence.

Lading, Bill of. v. *Bill,* III., 5.

Læsa majestas, *l.* High treason (injured majesty).

Læsione fidei, pro, *l.* Suits for breach of contract, brought anciently in the ecclesiastical courts, but forbidden by the Constitutions of Clarendon.

Lag, *sax.,* **Laga,** *l.* Law.

Lagan, *sax.* Goods found floating in the sea at a distance from the shore.

Lage. Law. **Lageman:** a good and lawful man.

Laicus, *l.,* **Lai,** *fr. Lay,* layman. **Lais gents:** laymen, a jury.

Laisser aller, *fr.* (To let it go.) Let it alone, let things take their course.

Laity. The lay part of the people. v. *Lay.*

Lancaster. v. *County Palatine, Court,* 69.

Landboc, *sax.* A charter or deed by which lands are given or held.

Landcheap. A fine paid by custom on the alienation of land within certain manors and liberties.

Land-gable. A land tax or rent; a quitrent.

Langemanni, *l.* Lords of manors.

Languidus in prisona, *l.* Sick in prison; a sheriff's *return* to a *capias*.

Lapse. A slip, omission; the forfeiture of a right to present to a benefice by the patron's negligence. The failure of a testamentary disposition by reason of the death of the legatee before the testator; **a lapsed devise or legacy.**

Larceny. The forcible or fraudulent taking and carrying away the goods of another, with intent to convert them to one's own property. If the taking be lawful, the carrying away was formerly *embezzlement;* but is now made by statute, in some cases, larceny. If openly, from the person, by force or fear, it is **robbery.** If money be taken under color of office, or by official oppression and threats, it is **extortion.** If from the person, in a dwelling-house (in the daytime, v. *Burglary*), or on a wharf, it is **compound or mixed larceny;** as distinguished from **simple larceny,** which covers ordinary cases of theft. There was formerly also a distinction between **grand** and **petit larceny,** turning on the value of the goods stolen. If the owner intend to part with the entire right of property, it is **obtaining goods under false pretences;** if he merely intend to relinquish possession, it is still larceny; the goods in both cases being obtained by fraud.

Larcyn, *fr.* Larceny; robbery.

Large, à, *fr.* At large. **Mettre à large:** to set at liberty.

Laron, *fr.* A thief.

Last heir. He to whom lands escheat for want of lawful heirs, that is, the chief lord or the King.

Lata culpa dolo æquiparatur. Gross fault is put on a level with fraud.

Latens, *l.* Latent; not apparent. **Latens ambiguitas:** an ambiguity not evident, not on the surface.

Lathe. A division of a county, containing several *hundreds.*

Latitare, *l.* To lie hid. **Latitat;** v. *Bill,* I. 8.

Latori præsentium, *l.* To the bearer of these presents.

Latro, *l.* A thief. **Latrocinium:** larceny.

Latu sensu, *l.* In a wide sense.

Laudibus Legum Angliæ, de. v. *Fortescue.*

Law. For *Abnormal, Adjective, Agrarian, Brehon, Canon, Civil, Codes Napoléon and Civile, Consolato del Mare, Crown, Ecclesiastical, Ex post facto, International, Marque, Martial, Military, Municipal, Normal, Oleron, Positive, Private, Public, Rhodian, Salic, Spiritual, Substantive law,* see those titles. **Law borgh,** *so.* : a pledge for a party's appearance. **Law-burrows,** *sc.* . security to keep the peace. **Law day:** a day of open court; a day fixed for the payment of a bond debt. **Law lords :** peers who have held high judicial office, or have been distinguished in the legal profession. **Law merchant, commercial law, the law of merchants, law of the staple:** the law prevailing generally as to commercial matters, mercantile paper, etc., among merchants throughout the civilized world. **Law of the land:** due process of law. **Law of nations :** 1. The *Jus gentium* of the Romans; laws common to the civilized world. 2. *International* law. **Wager of Law:** v. *Compurgatores, Wager.*

Lawe. A hill.

Lawful. Legal, having the qualifications prescribed by law. **Lawful man :** a man free and capable of bearing oath, unattainted.

Lawing of dogs. Expedition; cutting out the ball or claws of a dog's foot, that he might not chase deer.

Lawless Court. A court held on King's-hill, Rochford, Essex, on Wednesday after old Michaelmas day, at cock-crowing. They speak in whispers, have no candle, nor pen and ink, but a coal; and he that owes suit and service forfeits double rent for each hour that he is missing. The court still exists.

Lawnde, lounde. A plain between woods.

Lay. 1. Not clerical, not ecclesiastical. A layman. **Lay corporation:** v. *Corporation.* **Lay fee:** a fee held by secular, not religious services. **Lays gents :** laymen, a jury. **Lay impropriator:** v. *Impropriation.* 2. To state or allege in pleading.

Lay days. Days allowed in charter-parties for loading or unloading.

Le, Les, *fr.* The. **Lesquel:** the which. **Le roi le veut** (the King wills it) : the form of royal assent to a bill in Parliament.

Le roy s'avisera (the King will consider): the form of dissent to a bill. **Le salut du peuple est la suprême loi**: the public welfare is the highest law.

Lea, ley. A pasture.

Leading a use. v. *Deeds to lead a use.* **Leading question**: one so framed as to suggest the answer.

Leal, *fr.* Loyal. **Lealte**: legality, loyalty.

Lease. A conveyance of an estate in lands or hereditaments, less than that possessed by the grantor, for life, years, or at will.

Lease and release. A species of conveyance in England, based upon the Statute of Uses, and evading livery of seisin and enrolment.

Leet. v. *Court*, 32.

Legacy. A bequest of goods or chattels; v. *Bequeath;* a gift by last will. A **general legacy** is one payable out of any assets; a **specific legacy** is a legacy of a particular piece of property; a **demonstrative legacy** is one directed to be paid out of a particular fund. A **cumulative legacy**: one given in addition to, not in lieu of, one given before. A **lapsed legacy**: v. *Lapse.* A **residuary legacy**: a bequest of all the testator's personal estate not otherwise disposed of by the will.

Legal assets. v. *Assets.* **Legal estate**: one held by legal title, enforceable in a court of common law; not *equitable.* **Legal memory**: runs back to the beginning of the reign of Richard I.

Legalis homo, *l.* A lawful man.

Legem amittere, *l.* To lose one's law, one's privilege of being admitted to oath. **Legem facere**: to make oath; to wage law; v. *Wager.* **Legem habere**: to have law, to be capable of giving evidence upon oath.

Leges, *l.* Laws. **Leges figendi et refigendi consuetudo est periculosissima**: the practice of making and remaking law is most dangerous. **Leges posteriores priores contrarias abrogant**: later laws abrogate prior laws which are contrary to them. **Leges scriptæ, non scriptæ**: written, unwritten laws. **Leges sub graviori lege**: laws under a weightier law. **Leges vigilantibus non dormientibus subveniunt**: laws are for the aid of those who are diligent, not those who sleep upon their rights.

Legibus solutus, *l.* Not bound by the laws, released from law, above law. **Legis constructio non facit injuriam**: the construction of law works no wrong.

Legisperitus, *l.* Learned in the law.

Legit vel non? *l.* Does he read or no? **Legit ut clericus**: he reads like a clerk. A question to, and answer of, the ordinary, when a prisoner claimed benefit of clergy.

Legitim. In Scotch law, the children's share in the father's movables.

Legitima potestas, *l.* (Lawful power.) *Liege pouslie.*

Lei, leie, *fr.* Law.

Leonina societas, *l.* The lion's partnership, a partnership where one party gets all the advantage.

Les lois ne se chargent de punir que les actions extérieures, *fr.* Laws only attempt to punish outward acts.

Lese majesty. High treason.

Lessor of the plaintiff The real plaintiff in *ejectment*.

Let. 1. To demise, lease. 2. To deliver. 3. Hindrance, interruption.

Letter-missive. 1. A letter from the King to a dean and chapter containing the name of the person whom he would have them elect as bishop. 2. A letter sent by the Lord Chancellor to a peer who is made the defendant to a bill in Chancery, to request his appearance.

Letters. An instrument giving authority: a written appointment or authority by, and under the seal of, a court. Letters of **administration, attorney, marque and reprisal, close** or **clause, patent**: see those titles. Letters of **credit, of exchange**; v. *Bill*, III. 2, 4. **Letters of request**: a mode of beginning a suit originally in the *Court of Arches*, instead of the *Consistory Court*. **Letters testamentary**: the instrument of authority and appointment, given an executor by the proper court.

Levandæ navis causa, *l.* For the purpose of lightening the ship.

Levant et couchant, *fr.*, **Levantes et cubantes,** *l.* (Rising up and lying down.) A term applied to trespassing cattle who have been long enough on the land to have lain down and risen up to feed, — one night, or a night and day, — until which time they could not, in certain cases, be distrained.

Levari facias, *l.* An old writ directing the sheriff to levy execution against a judgment debtor out of his goods and the profits of his land; superseded by *fieri facias* and *elegit*.

Levis culpa, *l.* Slight negligence or fault.

Levitical degrees. Those degrees of kindred set forth in the eighteenth chapter of Leviticus, within which marriage is forbidden by the English and American law.

Levy. 1. To raise. 2. To execute. 3. To collect, take or seize.

Lex, *l.* Law. **Lex agraria:** an *agrarian* law. **Lex aliquando sequitur æquitatem:** the law sometimes follows equity. **Lex Angliæ, anglicana:** the law, or curtesy, of England. **Lex Angliæ non patitur absurdum:** the law of England will not suffer an absurdity. **Lex Angliæ sine Parliamento mutari non potest:** the law of England cannot be altered without Parliament. **Lex apparens** (manifest law): trial by ordeal or battel. **Lex citius tolerare vult privatum damnum quam publicum malum:** the law will rather suffer a private loss than a public ill. **Lex communis:** the common law. **Lex contractus:** the law of [made by] the contract. **Lex deficere non debet in justitia exhibenda:** the law ought not to fail in showing justice. **Lex domicilii:** the law of the domicil. **Lex est ab æterno:** law is from everlasting. **Lex est norma recti:** law is a rule of right. **Lex est ratio summa, quæ jubet quæ sunt utilia et necessaria, et contraria prohibet:** law is the highest reason, which ordains what is useful and necessary, and forbids the contrary. **Lex et consuetudo Parliamenti:** the law and custom of Parliament. **Lex favet doti:** the law favors dower. **Lex feudi:** the law of the fee. **Lex fingit ubi subsistit æquitas:** the law feigns [makes a fiction] where equity exists [in a case where equity requires it]. **Lex fori:** the law of the court [where the remedy is sought]. **Lex judicat de rebus necessario faciendis quasi de re ipsa factis:** the law judges of things necessarily to be done as if done in fact. **Lex ligeantiæ:** the law of [the country to which one owes] allegiance. **Lex loci:** the law of the place. **Lex loci contractus, delictus, actus:** the law of the place where the contract, crime, act, took place. **Lex loci rei sitæ:** the law of the place where the thing is situated. **Lex loci solutionis:** the law of the place of payment. **Lex manifesta:** manifest law; *v. Lex apparens*. **Lex mercatoria:** the *law* *merchant.* **Lex necessitatis est lex temporis**: the law of necessity is the law of the moment. **Lex neminem cogit ad vana seu inutilia**: the law compels no one to do vain or useless things. **Lex neminem cogit ostendere quod nescire præsumitur**: the law forces no one to show what he is presumed not to know. **Lex nemini operatur iniquum**: the law works injustice to no one. **Lex nil frustra facit**: the law will do (does) nothing in vain. **Lex non cogit ad impossibilia**: the law does not force [one to do] impossible things. **Lex non curat de minimis**: the law takes no account of trifles. **Lex non favet votis delicatorum**: the law does not consider the wishes of the fastidious. **Lex non patitur fractiones et divisiones statutorum**: the law suffers not fractions and divisions of statutes. **Lex non requirit verificari quod apparet curiæ**: the law does not require proof of that which is apparent to the court. **Lex non scripta**: the unwritten law. **Lex patriæ**: the law of one's country. **Lex plus laudatur quando ratione probatur**: the law is most worthy of praise when consonant with reason. **Lex posterior derogat priori**: a prior statute shall give place to a later one. **Lex rejicit superflua, pugnantia, incongrua**: the law rejects things superfluous, contradictory, incongruous. **Lex reprobat moram**: the law reproves delay. **Lex respicit æquitatem**: the law regards equity. **Lex scripta**: the written law. **Lex semper dabit remedium**: the law will always give a remedy. **Lex semper intendit quod convenit rationi**: the law always intends what is agreeable to reason. **Lex spectat naturæ ordinem**: the law regards the order of nature. **Lex succurrit minoribus**: the law aids [favors] minors. **Lex talionis**: the law of retaliation. **Lex terræ**: the law of the land, due process of law.

Ley, *fr.* Law; an oath. **Ley gager**: wager of law.

Libel. 1. A little book. 2. The first pleading in an ecclesiastical or admiralty cause. 3. Written defamation. **To libel**: 1. To seize under admiralty process. 2. To defame by published writing.

Libellus, *l.* A *libel*. **Libellus famosus**: a defamatory publication.

Liber, *l.* 1. A book; a part of a book. **Liber Assisarum** (the

Book of the Assizes): a collection of cases in assizes, the fourth volume of the reports of the reign of Edward III. **Liber Feudorum** (the Book of Fiefs): a code of feudal law compiled under Frederic Barbarossa at Milan in 1170. **Liber judicialis**: the *Dome book; v. Dombec.* **Liber niger**: the *Black-book.*

2. Free. **Liber bancus**: *free bench.* **Liber et legalis homo**: a free and *lawful* man; a juror. **Liber homo**: a freeman. **Libera chasea**: free *chase.* **Libera eleemosyna**: free alms, *frank-almoign.* **Libera falda**: *frank-fold.* **Libera lex**: v. *Lex terræ, frank law.* **Libera piscaria**: free *fishery.* **Libera warrena**: free *warren.* **Liberum corpus æstimationem non recipit**: the body of a freeman does not admit of valuation. **Liberum maritagium**: *frank-marriage.* **Liberum servitium**: *free service.* **Liberum soccagium**: *free socage;* v. *Socage.* **Liberum tenementum**: frank tenement, *freehold.*

Liberare, *l.* 1. To free, set free. 2. To deliver, tender.

Liberate, *l.* (Deliver ye.) An old original writ to the Exchequer for the payment of a pension or grant; or to a sheriff for lands taken on forfeit of a recognizance; or to a gaoler for the delivery of a prisoner. v. *Extent, Statute Merchant, Statute Staple, Recognizance.*

Libertas, *l.* Liberty; a privilege, exemption, franchise. **Libertas non recipit æstimationem**: liberty does not admit of valuation.

Liberty. A privilege, held by royal grant or prescription. A place or district wherein certain privileges may be enjoyed; an extension of a gaol; an exclusive jurisdiction.

Licentia concordandi, *l.* Leave to agree; v. *Fine.* **Licentia loquendi**: leave to speak; v. *Imparlance.*

Licet, *l.* 1. Although. **Licet dispositio de interesse futuro sit inutilis, tamen potest fieri declaratio præcedens quæ sortiatur effectum, interveniente novo actu**: although the grant of a future interest is invalid, yet a declaration precedent may be made which will take effect on the intervention of some new act. **Licet sæpe requisitus**: although often requested.

2. It is allowed. **Licere**: to be lawful. **Licitum**: lawful. **Licita bene miscentur, formula nisi juris obstet** (lawful acts are well when mingled, unless some form of law forbid):

the several acts may be done by different parties, and yet the entire transaction take effect.

Lidford law. Lynch law.

Lie. To lie. To be available, proper. **To lie in:** to be capable of, to consist in; v. *Corporeal, Render.* **Lie in franchise.** Waifs, wrecks, estrays, and the like, which the persons entitled thereto may seize without the aid of a court, are said to lie in franchise. Property which passes, and must pass, by deed or charter, such as incorporeal hereditaments, is said to **lie in grant;** as opposed to fees and freeholds in the land itself, which **lie in livery.**

Liege. Bound in fealty; in simple fealty, without services; sovereign. v. *Homage.* **Liege poustie,** *sc.*: a state of health which gives one lawful power of disposition; the reverse of death-bed.

Lien. The right of a possessor or bailee to hold the property of another until some demand is satisfied; a **special** or **particular lien,** if the demand arise from the property itself, as by labor or service upon it, and the lien is thus confined to that property; a **general lien,** if the demand is general and indefinite, as for a balance of accounts. In equity, a vendor has a **vendor's lien** for the unpaid purchase money; a **vendee** has a lien for purchase money paid before the conveyance is complete. A **mechanic's lien,** on land and houses for labor done upon them. **Maritime liens:** for wages, damages by collision, goods supplied a ship, etc. Equitable, mechanics', and maritime liens exist independently of possession.

Lieu-conus, *fr.* A place well known, of notoriety, as a castle or manor. **In lieu:** in place of. **Lieu-tenant:** a substitute, deputy.

Life-estate. v. *Estate.*

Ligan. v. *Flotsam.*

Ligiantia, *l.,* **Ligeance.** Allegiance; the bond of *fealty,* fidelity between subject and sovereign.

Ligius, *l.* Bound to *fealty; liege;* subject; *sovereign.*

Lignum, *l.* Wood; dead wood, fuel. v. *Arbor.*

Limitatio, *l.* **Limitation.** Setting a bound or limit; a restriction. Words of **limitation:** words which define or limit the estate a grantee is to take, as distinguished from words of **pur-**

chase, which name the grantee or grantees to whom the conveyance is made. Thus, those who take by consent take under the
words of limitation; those who take by purchase, under the words
of purchase; v. *Descent, Purchase*. **Limitation of actions**:
a fixing of a term by law within which actions must be brought,
or the right of action will be barred. The principal English
Statutes of Limitation are the 21 Jac. I. c. 16 and 3 & 4
Will. IV. c. 27. See also 37 & 38 Vict. c. 57. **Limitation of
estates**: a limiting or determining an estate by an event, as to
A so long as he remained unmarried. If there be a limitation
over, which derogates from, or cuts short, the first estate granted,
it is a **conditional limitation**; as, to A and his heirs, but if
he marry, to B. If there be no limitation over, but the estate is
cut short upon the happening of the event, it is an **estate upon
condition**; as, to A and his heirs so long as he remain unmarried; v. *Conditional limitation*.

Limited company. A *joint-stock company* with **limited liability**,
where each person cannot be called on to contribute beyond the
amount of his shares, except as under § 4 of the 30 & 31
Vict. c. 131, providing that the liability of the directors or man-
agers may be unlimited. Limited *Divorce, Partnership:* see
those titles.

Linea, *l.* A line; a line of descent. **Linea recta semper præfertur transversali**: the direct line is always preferred to the
collateral.

Lineal. In a direct line; from parent to child. **Lineal warranty**:
a warranty of land made by a person in the line of title, or who
might have been heir. v. *Collateral*.

Liquere, *t.* To be clear. **Liquet satis**: it is sufficiently clear.

Liquidated. Cleared away; settled; v. *Damages*. **Liquidation**:
the winding up of an insolvent firm or company.

Lis, *t.* A dispute, controversy; a suit. **Lis mota**: a controversy
begun [before suit]; suit brought. **Lis pendens**: a suit pending; that legal process, in a suit regarding land, which amounts
to legal notice to all the world that there is dispute as to the
title; in equity, the filing of the bill and serving a subpœna
creates a *lis pendens*, except when statutes require some record.

Litera, *l.* A letter; the letter [as distinguished from the spirit of
a document]. **Litera acquietantiæ**: a letter of *acquittance*.

Litera excambii: a *bill* of exchange. **Litera scripta manet**: the written letter lasts. **Literæ clausæ**: *close* writs. **Literæ patentes**: open writs; letters *patent*. **Literæ procuratoriæ**: letters of *attorney*. **Literæ recognitionis**: a *bill* of lading. **Literæ sigillatæ**: sealed letters; the *return* of a sheriff.

Litigious right. One which can only be asserted by a suit.

Litis contestatio, *l.* In civil and canon law, the issue, the coming to an issue, in pleading. In ecclesiastical courts, the general answer and denial of the defendant.

Littleton. A judge of the reign of Edward IV. who wrote a treatise upon tenures, upon which Coke, C. J. wrote an extensive comment.

Littoral. Belonging to the shore; on the sea-shore.

Littus maris, *l.* The sea-shore.

Livery. Delivery. A writ for the heir in knight-service to recover his lands; v. *Ousterlemain*. **Livery of seisin**: the ceremony of delivery of corporeal possession of lands and tenements by the grantor to the grantee. The grantor or his attorney went upon the land and there delivered a twig, latch, key, or other symbol, in the name of the seisin. **Livery in law** was when they did not enter, but performed the ceremony in sight of the laud.

Livre, *fr.* A book; a pound.

Lloyd's. An association in the city of London, the members of which underwrite each other's policies. **Lloyd's bonds**: admissions of indebtedness, issued under the seal of a company, with a covenant to pay at some future time.

Local action. v. *Action.*

Locare, *l.* To let for hire. **Locatio**: a letting. **Locatio-conductio**: a letting and hiring, a compound word expressing the transaction on both sides. **Locatio custodiæ**: a bailment for reward for safe-keeping. **Locatio rei**: the letting of a thing. **Locatio operarum**: a letting of services. **Locatio operis faciendi**: a letting of a thing for the purpose of having work performed upon it. **Locatio operis mercium vehendarum**: a bailment of goods to be transported.

Location. The designation of the boundaries and position of land from a point of survey. **Locative calls**: v. *Calls.*

Locator, *l.* A lessor ; a lender.

Locus, *l.* A place. **Loco:** v. *In loco.* **Locum tenens:** a *lieu-tenant,* substitute. **Locum tenere:** to hold place; to be appli-cable. **Locus contractus:** the place of the contract. **Locus delicti:** the place of the crime. **Locus in quo:** the place in which [the trespass was committed]. **Locus partitus:** a di-vision between two towns or counties to determine where the land in question lies. **Locus pœnitentiæ** (room for repent-ance): opportunity to retract. **Locus regit actum:** the place [the law of the place] governs the act. **Locus rei sitæ:** the place where the thing is situated. **Locus sigilli:** the place for the seal. **Locus standi:** a right to be heard.

Loi, *fr.* Law. **Loial:** lawful. **Loisible:** lawful.

Loier, *fr.* Reward; fee; rent.

London Court of Bankruptcy. v. *Court,* 50. **London and Westminster Sittings:** v. *Court,* 28.

Longa possessio est pacis jus, *l.* Long possession is [gives] a right of peace. **Longa possessio parit jus possidendi et tollit actionem vero domino:** long possession is equal to right, and deprives the true owner of his action. **Longum tem-pus, et longus usus qui excedit memoria hominum, suffi-cit pro jure:** long time and usage beyond the memory of man suffices for right.

Loquela, *l.* A plaint; declaration; plea; suit; imparlance.

Loquendum ut vulgus, sentiendum ut docti, *l.* Speak like the common people; think like the learned.

Lord. 1. A feudal superior, one of whom the tenant holds lands. 2. A title of honor applied to peers. 3. A title of office. Lord *Admiral, Advocate, Chancellor, Chief Justice, Paramount, Privy Seal, Treasurer :* see those titles. **Lords spiritual:** the bishops and archbishops in the House of Lords. **Lords temporal:** the peers having seats in the House of Lords. **Lord Cham-berlain, of England,** has the government of the palace at Westminster; **of the King's House,** has authority over the King's wardrobe; also to license theatres and plays. **Lords Justices:** two judges appointed under the 14 & 15 Vict. c. 83, to assist the Lord Chancellor in hearing appeals from the Mas-ter of the Rolls and the Vice-Chancellors. They are now judges of the Court of Appeals; v. *Court,* 18, 26. **Lord Keeper of**

the **Great Seal**: *ex officio* lord and privy-councillor, an office now fused with that of Lord Chancellor. **Lord Lieutenant.** 1. The Viceroy of the Crown in Ireland. 2. The principal military officer of a county, appointed by the Crown. **Lord Mayor's Court**: v. *Court*, 62. **Court of Lord Steward, Treasurer, Comptroller of the King's Household, Lord Warden of the Stannaries**, etc.: v. *Court*, 54, 53, 46, 67, 72.

Lord Cranworth's Act. The 23 & 24 Vict. c. 145, conferring certain general powers upon trustees and mortgagees.

Lord Denman's Act. The 6 & 7 Vict. c. 85, removing the disability of witnesses not parties on ground of interest.

Lord Ellenborough's Act. The 43 Geo. III. c. 58, for punishing with death various assaults upon and offences against the person.

Lord Langdale's Act. The Wills Act, 7 Will. IV. & 1 Vict. c. 26.

Lord Lyndhurst's Acts. The 5 & 6 Will. IV. c. 54, making marriage within the prohibited degrees void *ab initio ;* the 7 & 8 Vict. c. 45, concerning meeting-houses.

Lord St. Leonards's Acts. The 22 & 23 Vict. c. 35, and 23 & 24 Vict. c. 38, for amending the law of property, relieving trustees, etc.

Lord Tenterden's Act. The 9 Geo. IV. c. 14, for the amendment and extension of the Statute of Frauds, etc.

Lords' Act. The 32 Geo. II. c. 28, for the relief of insolvent debtors.

Lors, *fr.* Then. **Lorsque** : at the time when.

Loy, *fr.* Law. **Loyal** : lawful.

Lucrative succession. Scotch, the conveyance to the heir, without valuable consideration, of a part of his inheritance, whereupon he is liable for all previous debts of the grantor.

Lucri causa, *l.* For the sake of gain.

Luctuosa, *l.* Mournful. v. *Hæreditas.*

Lunatico inquirendo. v. *De.*

Lupinum caput, *l.* A wolf-head ; an outlaw.

Lutosa, *l.* Miry ; impassable as a road.

Lui, luy, *fr.* Him ; her ; he ; it.

Lying in livery, in grant. v. *Lie,* etc., *Hereditament.*

Lyttelton. v. *Liltleton.*

M.

Mæremium, maremium, *l.*   *Timber ;* wood for building.

Magis, *l.*   More.   **Magis dignum trahit ad se minus dignum:** the more worthy draws after itself the less worthy.

Magister rerum usus, *l.*   Usage is the master of things [usage determines].   **Magister cancellariæ:** a *master in chancery.* **Magister navis:** the master of a ship.

Magistralia brevia, *l.*   Special writs.   v. *Writ.*

Magistrate.   A public civil officer; a person intrusted with the commission of the peace.

Magna assisa, *l.*   The *grand assize.*   **Magna Charta:** the Great Charter.   It was granted by John at Runingmede in 1215, at the same time with the Carta de *Foresta,* and confirmed by Henry III. in the ninth year of his reign, and also by the 25 Edw. I.   This latter charter, the *Confirmatio chartarum,* is the one commonly referred to as the Great Charter, the basis of the English constitution.   Magna Charta contained thirty-seven chapters, for the most part concerning landed estates and the rights of freemen.   **Magna culpa:** gross negligence.   **Magna componere parvis:** to compare great things with small.   **Magna serjeantia:** grand *serjeanty.*   **Magnum cape:** v. *Cape.*   **Magnum concilium** (the great council): Parliament.

Maiden assize.   One during which there is no capital conviction.   **Maiden rents:** a fine paid the lord by a copyhold tenant on marriage, for omitting the *marcheta.*

Maihemium, *t.,* **Mayhem, maim,** etc.   Violently depriving another of a member used in fighting; such an injury to a man as diminishes his power of self-defence.

Mail, Maille, *fr.*   Rent; tribute.

Main, *fr.*   Hand, a hand.   **Main à main:** immediately.

Mainbour, *fr.* & *sax.*   A *handborow ; mainprise.*

Mainour, meynour, etc., *fr.*   A thing stolen; especially when found in the thief's possession.   v. *Handhabend.*

Mainoverer, mainovre, *fr.*   Labor of the hands.   To cultivate, manure.

Mainpernours.   Sureties for the appearance of a person, who is arrested and delivered to them out of prison. They had no right to imprison him or surrender him up, like *bail*, and were bound to produce him in answer to all and any charges; v. *Mainprise.* **Mainpernable**: capable of being bailed.

Mainprise. The release of a man arrested, into the custody of his friends, who became bound for his appearance. A **writ of mainprise** directed to the sheriff ordered him to take *mainpernours*, and set the prisoner at large.

Mainsworn. Perjured by oath of hand upon the book.

Maintenance. Officious intermeddling in another's suit; aiding a party with money or otherwise. v. *Champerty.*

Maintenant, *fr.* Now; presently.

Maintes fois, *fr.* Many times.

Mais, *fr.* But. More. **Maisne**: younger.

Major, *l.* Greater. **Major hæreditas venit unicuique nostrum a jure et legibus quam a parentibus**: a greater legacy comes to every one of us from right and the law than from our parents. **Majora regalia**: the higher royal prerogatives. **Majoræ summæ minor inest**: the greater sum includes the less. **Majus dignum**, etc.; v. *Magis.* **Majus jus**: more right.

Make law, To. To deny under oath. v. *Wager of law.*

Mal, *fr.*, **Malum,** *l.* Ill; wrong; evil. **Mal de venue**: v. *Essoin.* **Mal grée**: of bad grace; against the will of.

Mala fides, *l.* Bad faith. **Mala grammatica non vitiat chartam**: bad grammar does not vitiate a deed. **Mala in se**: evils bad in themselves, natural wrongs. **Mala prohibita**: wrongs prohibited (by law). **Mala praxis**: malpractice. **Mala tolta**: an oppressive tax. v. *Malum.*

Male, *l.* Ill; unfavorably. **Male creditus**: of bad repute.

Maledicta est expositio quæ corrumpit textum, *l.* Cursed the interpretation which corrupts the text.

Malfeasance, *fr.*, **Maleficium,** *l.* Wrong-doing, crime. **Maleficia non debent remanere impunita; et impunitas continuum affectum tribuit delinquenti**: crimes ought not to remain unpunished; and impunity gives a continual impulse to the criminal [to commit another crime]. **Maleficia propositis distinguuntur**: crimes are distinguished by the purposes which prompted them.

Malice. **Express** or **actual malice** is necessary to establish certain degrees of criminal liability in certain cases, and may be defined as the'intent of one person to injure any other. But in certain other cases of heinous or reckless action, where the law dispenses with proof of actual malice, but affixes similar penalties or punishment, there is said to be **implied** or **constructive malice.** Actual malice, resulting in the crime of murder, is specially named **malice aforethought** or **malice prepense.**

Malicious prosecution. One brought without probable cause, and with intent to injure the defendant. The action for **malicious prosecution** is an action on the case for damages, brought after the fruitless termination of the suit complained of.

Malitia supplet ætatem, *l.* (Malice supplies age.) Proof that a child between the ages of seven and fourteen has "mischievous discretion" will render him *doli capax*, and criminally liable.

Malum, *l.* Evil; wickedness; ill. v. *Mal.* **Malo animo:** with evil intent. **Malum non præsumitur:** evil [intent] is not to be presumed. **Malum lecti, veniendi;** v. *Essoin.* **Malus usus abolenda est:** a bad custom ought to be abolished.

Manbote, *sax.* A compensation for homicide, due the lord for killing his vassal, the amount of which was regulated by the *were*.

Mandamus, *l.* (We command.) A writ, formerly *prerogative*, issuing out of a superior court to an inferior court, a public or private corporation, or an officer, directing them to perform some public, ministerial, or official duty, or to restore the complainant to his rights and privileges. If **peremptory**, it directed the defendant to perform its orders absolutely; if **alternative**, to do so, or show cause to the contrary.

Mandans, Mandator, *l.*, **Mandant.** A person commanding or committing; the employing party in a contract of *mandate*.

Mandare, *l.* To command. To commit to, to intrust with.

Mandatarius, *l.*, **Mandatary.** The party to whom a charge is given; the party employed in a *mandate*. **Mandatarius terminos sibi positos transgredi non potest:** a mandatary cannot exceed his instructions. **Mandavi ballivo** (I have commanded the bailiff): an old sheriff's *return* to an execution made in a *liberty*.

Mandatum, *l.*, **Mandate.** A command; a contract by which one man employs another gratuitously in the conduct of his affairs.

Manerium, *l.* Manor; a *manor.*

Manifest. A *sea-letter;* one of a ship's papers, specifying the cargo, port of departure, and destination.

Manor. A feudal estate granted to a lord or great personage with the right to hold a *court-baron.* It consisted of **terræ tenementales, bocland,** lands held of the manor in freehold; and the **demesne lands, terræ dominicales,** reserved for the lord's own use; which again were divided into lands held by tenants in *copyhold* (*folcland*), lands held by the lord for his own use, and the **lord's waste,** used for pasture and common.

Manorial Court. v. *Court,* 34.

Manrent. A bond between the lord and vassal; the vassal promising fidelity in consideration of the lord's protection.

Manslaughter. Homicide without malice, but not *excusable;* as, voluntarily, upon a sudden affray; or involuntarily, while performing an unlawful act, or when attended with criminal negligence.

Mansuetæ naturæ, *l.* Tamed; of a domestic nature.

Manucapere, *l.* To become surety, *mainpernor.* **Manucaptio:** *mainprise.*

Manus, *l.* A hand. An oath; a person swearing, a *compurgator.* **Manu brevi:** with a short hand, briefly. **Manu forti:** with strong hand. **Manus mortua** (a dead hand): *mortmain.*

Manure. To occupy, labor upon.

Marca, *l.,* **March.** A border; boundary line. **Marchers:** noblemen formerly living on the borders of Wales and Scotland in a state of semi-sovereignty, with laws of their own.

Marcheta, Mercheta, *l.* 1. In Scotch law, the right of the lord to pass the first night with the bride of his tenant. A fine for remitting such right. 2. In England, a maid's fee; a fine paid the lord by a tenant on the marriage of his daughter.

Mare, *l.* Sea. **Mare altum:** the high sea. **Mare apertum:** the open sea.

Maritagium, *l. Marriage.*

Market overt. A place, market, or shop, for the public sale of goods, where the innocent purchaser took a perfect title, except as against the Crown, whether the goods were stolen or rightfully sold.

Marksman. A person who cannot write his name.

Marleberge, Marlbridge. The statute passed 52 Hen. III., A. D. 1267, confirming the Great Charter and the Charter of the Forest, providing penalties for wrongful distress, introducing writs of *entry in the post*, providing as to guardians and wards in socage, etc.

Marque and Reprisal, letters of. A commission issued by a sovereign or state to its subjects, authorizing the seizure of the property of an offending nation, as reparation for the injury. It is now usually issued to privateersmen in time of war. **Law of Marque**: the law governing such reprisals.

Marriage. The feudal right enjoyed by the lord or guardian in chivalry of disposing of his ward in marriage. If the infant ward refused, he or she forfeited the **value of the marriage** (**valor maritagii,** *l.*), as much as a jury would assess, or the suitor would in good faith give for the alliance; and double the value of the marriage (**duplex valor maritagii**) was forfeited if the ward married without the lord's consent. **Marriage articles**: articles of agreement for a marriage settlement to be drawn after marriage. **Marriage brokage**: negotiating a marriage for a consideration. **Marriage license**; v. *Ban*. **Marriage settlement**: a settlement of the estate of a husband and wife, in consideration of the marriage, upon the wife, or the husband and wife, in a certain way.

Marshalling of Assets, Securities. v. *Assets*.

Marshalsea. A prison in London, formerly belonging to the K. B. An old court; v. *Court*, 55.

Martial law. The rule imposed on a conquered or occupied country by the commander of an army during the suspension of the civic authority. **Courts martial**: v. *Court*, 93.

Masters in Chancery. Officers of the Court of Chancery, who took accounts, oaths, affidavits, and acknowledgments, made inquiries concerning facts, and discharged other ministerial duties. They were formerly the chief clerks, or *præceptores*. **Master of the Crown Office**: the Queen's coroner and prosecuting attorney in the K. B. **Master of the Rolls**: originally the chief of the Masters in Chancery, had the custody of the records and the rolls which pass under the great seal. Later, an assistant judge, holding a court of his own next inferior to that of the Lord Chancellor; v. *Court*, 16.

Materfamilias, *l.*   The mother of a family.

Materna maternis, *l.*   The goods acquired through the mother descend to those connected with her.

Matrimonia debent esse libera, *l.*   Marriages ought to be free [not forced].

Matrons, Jury of. v. *Jury.*

Matter in deed. Writing under seal. **Matter in pais**: matter of fact [not in writing]. **Matter of record**: matter entered on the rolls of a court of record, which were formerly always parchment.

Maugre, *fr.* v. *Mal gré.*

Maunder, *fr.*   To command; to return [to a writ].

Mauveise, mauveys, *fr.*   False; bad; defective.

Maximus, *l.*   The greatest. **Maxime**: chiefly, most of all. **Maximus erroris magister populus**: the people is the greatest master of error.

Mayhem. v. *Maihemium.*

Mayn, *fr.*   A hand. v. *Main.*

Mayor.   The head of a municipal corporation. **Lord Mayor**: a title of the Mayors of London, York, and Dublin.

Medical jurisprudence.   The science of medicine as applied to legal questions.

Medietas linguæ, *l.*   Half-tongue. v. *Bilinguis.*

Medio tempore, *l.*   In the mean time.

Meditatio fugæ, *l.*   Intention of flight.

Medletum, *l.*   A medley; a *chance-medley.*

Meindre age, *fr.*   Minority; lesser age.

Mein, meyn, *fr.*   A hand. v. *Main.*

Melior est conditio possidentis, et rei quam actor, ubi neuter jus habet, *l.*   The position of the party possessing is the stronger (better), and of the defendant than the plaintiff, when neither has the right. **Meliorem conditionem suam facere potest minor, deteriorem nequaquam** (a minor can make his condition better, but never worse): the contracts made by a minor are only valid if beneficial to him.

Melius est petere fontes quam sectari rivulos, *l.*   It is better to seek the fountains than to follow out the streamlets.

Melius inquirendum, *l.*   A writ directing the sheriff to make further inquiry as to the lands, etc. of a person outlawed or attainted; after *office found* or a *diem clausit extremum.*

Memoria, *l.*, **memorie,** *fr.* Memory; mind; understanding. **Time of memory, memory of man** (v. *Legal memory*): extends back to the reign of Richard I.

Mens, *l.* Mind; intent; intention; meaning; will. **Mens testatoris in testamentis spectanda est:** in wills the intention of the testator is to be considered.

Mensa et thoro, *l.* (v. *A, Divorce.*) From bed and board.

Mensura domini regis, *l.* The King's measure; the standard.

Mercator, *l.* A merchant. **Mercatum:** a market.

Mercenlage, *sax.* The Mercian laws, which were observed in many of the midland counties and those on the Welsh border.

Mercy. The arbitrament of the judge. v. *Amerciament.*

Mere, *sax.* A fenny place.

Mere droit, *fr.*, **Merum jus,** *l.* Mere right, right without possession.

Meremium, *l.* (*Mæremium.*) Timber.

Merger. The sinking of one estate or interest in another; as by consolidation, or union in the same person.

Merton, Statute of. Passed 20 Hen. III., A. D. 1253, concerning dower, usury, legitimacy, lord's right in parks, etc.

Merx est quicquid vendi potest, *l.* Merchandise is whatever can be sold.

Mese, mais, *fr.* But.

Mesaventure, *fr.* Mischance; accident. v. *Homicide.*

Mese, meas, meason, etc., *fr.* A house.

Mesne, *fr.* Middle; mean. An intermediate lord standing between the *chief* lord and the tenant *paravail.* **A writ of mesne** in the nature of a writ of right lay for the tenant paravail against the mesne lord who suffered the tenant to be distrained for rent or services due from the mesne lord to the lord paramount. **Mesne process:** v. *Process.* **Mesne profits:** intermediate profits; profits while the land was occupied by a person having no right, or before a writ of ejectment was brought.

Mesprendre, *fr.* To do amiss, offend. **Mesprision:** a mistake.

Messis sementem sequitur, *l.* The crop follows [belongs to] the sower.

Messuage. A dwelling-house with outbuildings, garden, and *curtilage.*

Mester, mestre, *fr.* Need; •occasion.

Mestier, *fr.* (Mystery.) Handicraft, trade.

Meta, *l.* A butt; a boundary line.

Metegavel, *sax.* Rent payable in victuals.

Metes and bounds. *Butts and bounds.*

Mettre, *fr.* To put, fix. **Mis en escript:** put in writing. **Mettre à large:** to set free.

Meum et tuum. Mine and thine.

Metropolitan. The archbishop of a province.

Metus causa, *l.* By reason of fear.

Meyn, *fr.* Hand. v. *Main.*

Mi, my, *fr.* Half; middle. An atom, a smallest part of a thing.

Michaelmas Term. In England, begins on the 2d, and ends on the 25th of November.

Michelgemote. The great assembly of the people; the *Wilenagemote.* v. *Court,* 1.

Middlesex, Bill of. v. *Bill,* I. 8.

Miles, *pl.* **milites,** *l.* A soldier, knight.

Milieu, *fr.* Middle. **Juste milieu:** the happy mean.

Military Court. v. *Court of Chivalry, Court,* 93. **Military feuds:** genuine or original feuds, held in *chivalry,* by *knight service;* v. *Tenure.* **Military law:** regulations for the government of the army. **Military tenures:** by *knight service* and *escuage;* v. *Tenure.*

Minas, per, *l.* By threats. v. *Duress.*

Minatur innocentibus qui parcit nocentibus, *l.* He threatens the innocent who spares the guilty.

Minimus, *l.* The smallest. **Minime:** in the least. **Minima poena corporalis est major qualibet pecuniaria:** the smallest corporal punishment is greater than any pecuniary one. **Minime mutanda sunt quæ certam habuerunt interpretationem:** those things which have [once] had a certain interpretation are not to be altered.

Minor, *l.* Less; younger; an infant. **Minor jurare non potest:** a minor cannot make oath. **Minor 17 annis non admittitur fore executorem:** a person under seventeen is not admitted to be executor. **Minor ætas:** infancy. **Minora regalia:** the lesser prerogatives of the Crown.

Minus. Less; not. **Minus solvit qui tardius solvit:** he who pays too late does not pay at all.

Misa, *l.* *Mise;* the *issue* in a real action. **Misæ**: costs; expenses.

Misadventure. v. *Mesaventure.*

Miscontinuance. Continuance by faulty process. Discontinnance.

Misdemeanor. An indictable offence not amounting to felony.

Mise, *fr.* 1. Expenses, costs. 2. The issue in a writ of *right*, the *general issue.*

Misera est servitus, ubi jus est vagum aut incertum, *l.* Obedience to law is a hardship where the law is vague or uncertain.

Misericordia, *l.* *Mercy;* an *amerciament.*

Misfeasance. A misdeed, trespass; the improper performance of an act otherwise lawful. v. *Nonfeasance.*

Misjoinder. The improper joining of parties in a suit; or of different causes of action.

Misnomer. Misnaming; making a mistake in a person's name.

Mispleading. The use of a wrong plea, or the omission of an essential part; not curable by verdict.

Misprision. A neglect, oversight; a contempt. The concealment of a crime; as **of treason** or **felony.**

Mitiori sensu, *l.* In the milder sense.

Mitter à large, *fr.* To set free. **Mitter avant**: to set before. **Mitter le droit**: to pass the right. **Mitter l'estate**: to pass the estate; words used to distinguish different kinds of *releases.*

Mittere, *l.* To send, put. **Mittere in confusum**: to put into hotchpot. **Mittimus** (we send): 1. The warrant of a justice committing a prisoner to gaol. 2. A writ to transfer records from one court to another.

Mittomus, *l.* Let us suppose; put the case.

Mixed action. v. *Action.* **Mixed jury**: v. *Bilinguis.* **Mixed larceny**; v. *Larceny.*

Mobilia sequuntur personam, immobilia situm, *l.* Movable things follow [the law of] the person; immovable, of the place.

Modo et forma, *l.* In manner and form. Old words in a plea, not usually material, putting in issue concomitant matters such as time, place, etc.

Modus, *l.* Manner, mode. The manner in which an estate conveyed is to be held. **Modus dat legem donationi**: manner gives law to a gift; the mode of conveyance determines the character of the grant. **Modus decimandi**: a manner of tithing, a partial exemption from tithes, or a pecuniary composition prescribed by immemorial usage, and of reasonable amount; for it will be invalid as a **rank modus**, if greater than the value of the tithes in the time of Richard I. **Modus de non decimando**: a modus of entire exemption, a prescription to be discharged from tithes, **non valet**, is not valid. **Modus et conventio vincunt legem**: the form of agreement and the consent of the parties overrule the law. **Modus operandi**: the method of operating.

Moindre, moins, meins, *fr.* Less; the least.

Molendinum, *l.* A mill.

Molliter manu, *l.* With gentle hand. **Molliter manus imposuit**: he gently laid hands upon; old words in pleas of justification of trespass.

Molt, *fr.* Much; many; very.

Molutus, *l.* Ground; sharpened. v. *Arma.*

Molyn, *fr.* A mill. **Molyn ventresse**: a windmill.

Moneta, *l.* Money.

Money counts. The *common counts* in *assumpsit,* founded on an implied promise to pay money; including the counts for money had and received to the plaintiff's use, money lent, money paid, and money due on *insimul computassent.*

Monition. A summons to the defendant to appear and answer, issued on filing the libel in ecclesiastical and admiralty courts.

Monstrans de droit, *fr.* Showing of right; a common-law method of obtaining restitution of real or personal property, before the Chancery or Exchequer, the record title to which was in the Crown, as after an *inquest of office.* The plaintiff, if successful, obtained a judgment of *amoveas manus* or *ousterlemain.*

Monstrans de faits, *fr.* A showing of deeds; a *profert,* where a man pleaded a deed; whereupon the other party might claim *oyer.*

Monstravit, monstraverunt, *l.* A writ for tenants in *ancient demesne* who were distrained for duties or services contrary to their liberties.

Moot. A meeting or court; an argument. A subject for argument.

Mora reprobatur in lege, *l.* Delay is disapproved of in law.

Morandæ solutionis causa, *l.* For the purpose of postponing payment.

Morari, *l.* To delay. **Moratur in lege:** he demurs.

Morganatic marriage. A marriage between a woman and a man of higher rank, in which it is stipulated that neither she nor her children shall share his rank or enjoy the ordinary civil consequences of legal marriage.

Morier, mourir, etc., *fr.* To die. **Mourant:** dying.

Mors, *l.* Death. **Mors dicitur ultimum supplicium:** death is called the extreme penalty. **Mors omnia dissolvit:** death dissolves all things.

Mort, *fr.* Death. **Mort d'ancestor:** v. *Assize.*

Morte donantis donatio confirmatur, *l.* A gift is complete by the death of the donor [applied to revocable gifts].

Mortgage, Mortuum vadium, *l.* A dead pledge; one where the rents and profits did not go to the discharge of the debt. A conveyance of land defeasible on the performance of a certain condition; usually the payment of money.

Mortis causa, *l.* By reason, in contemplation, of death. v. *Causa, Donatio.*

Mortmain. (Dead hand.) A term applied to conveyances to a corporation; particularly a religious corporation, when it was held, without possibility of alienation or change, by persons dead in law. **Statute of Mortmain:** 7 Edw. I.; 9 Geo. II. c. 36.

Mortuary. Originally, a gift left by a man on his decease to the parish church, a *corse present;* later, it was claimed as a due, a sort of ecclesiastical *heriot.*

Mortum, *l.* Dead. **Mortuum vadium:** a mortgage. **Mortuus exitus non est exitus:** a dead issue is no issue.

Mos pro lege, *l.* Custom instead of law.

Mote, *sax.* A court or assembly; a meeting of the people.

Motion. An application made to the judge *viva voce* in open court.

Moult, mult, *fr.* v. *Molt.*

Movable. v. *Heritable.*

Moy, *fr.* Me; I.

Moyen, *fr.* Meau; intermediate; middle. **Pur moyen:** by means of.

Mulier, *l.* A woman, wife. A lawful son. **Mulier puisné**

(v. *Bastard eigné*) : the eldest legitimate son. **Multa conceduntur per obliquum quæ non conceduntur indirecto**: many things are allowed indirectly which are not allowed directly. **Multa in jure communi contra rationem disputandi, pro communi utilitate introducta sunt**: many things have been introduced into the common law for the public good, which are inconsistent with sound reason.

Multifarious. In equity pleading, putting distinct subjects in the same bill.

Multiplepoinding. A proceeding in Scotch law like *interpleader*.

Multiplicity of suits. This is discouraged by equity ; as if a bill be brought for a part of a single cause of action, or an heir seek to redeem one of two mortgages made by the ancestor. And see *Bill*, I. 12.

Multitudo errantium non parit errori patrocinium, *l.* The multitude of those who err does not amount to a protection of error.

Multure. The grinding of grain ; the toll paid therefor.

Municipal corporation. A public corporation, administering local government. **Municipal law**: the law of a particular state or nation. **Municipal court**: v. *Court*, 112.

Muniments, Miniments. Deeds or written evidences of title.

Munus, *pl.* **munera,** *l.* Grants made under the early feudal system, revocable at the lord's pleasure.

Murder. 1. Malicious homicide ; v. *Malice*. 2. Anciently, secret homicide ; the homicide of a Norman as distinct from that of an Englishman ; v. *Englecery, Murdrum.*

Murdrum, *l.* Murder. A fine imposed on a hundred where a person was found slain, *Englecery* not being proved.

Murorum operatio, *l.* The service of repairing castle walls or city walls ; which was commuted into a money payment by the tenants, called **murage** ; which name was also given to a toll for the same purpose, taken of every cart or horse passing through the town.

Mutatis mutandis, *l.* Those things changed which ought to be changed ; making the necessary changes. **Mutato nomine de te fabula narratur**: the story is told of you, under a different name.

Mutus et surdus, *l.* Deaf and dumb.

Mutuum, *l.* A loan of fungible goods, to be consumed and returned in kind.

My, *fr.* Half; middle.

Mys, *fr.* (*Mitter.*) Put; set; inserted.

N.

N. L., *Non liquet.* **N. P.,** *Nisi Prius.* **N′,** *Ne.*

Na, Nad, Navera, *fr.* He has not, shall not have; there is not.

Naam, nam, *sax.,* **Name,** *fr.,* **Namium,** *l.* A taking; a distress. **Namium vetitum**: *withernam.*

Nadgayers, Naidgaits, etc., *fr.* Lately; not long since.

Naif, *fr.* A villein, a born slave; a woman slave.

Naifté, *fr.,* **Naivitas,** *l.* Villeinage.

Nailours, *fr.* (*Nailleurs.*) Not elsewhere.

Nam, *l.* For. (For maxims beginning with *nam*, see under second word.)

Nappent, *fr* Does not belong.

Narr., for **Narratio,** *l.,* **Narragon,** *fr.* A count; a declaration. **Narrare,** *l.,* **Narrer,** *fr.*: to declare, to count. **Narrator,** *l.*: a countor, advocate.

Nastre, *fr.,* **Nasci,** *l.* To be born. **Nati et nascituri,** *l.*: born and (to be born) unborn.

Nativus, nativa, *l.* A villein, a female slave. **Nativitas**: v. *Naifté.*

Natura Brevium, *l.* (The nature of writs.) A collection of original writs, with brief comments upon them, compiled in the reign of Edward III., called **Old Natura Brevium** (O. N. B.), to distinguish it from the *Natura Brevium* of *Fitzherbert.* **Natura non facit saltum ; ita nec lex**: nature makes no leap [moves gradually]; so neither does law.

Naturale est quidlibet dissolvi eo modo quo ligatur, *l.* It is natural for a thing to be dissolved as (in the manner in which) it is created.

Naturalization. Admitting an alien to full rights of citizenship, for which an Act of Parliament was formerly necessary. v. *Denizen.*

Naufragium, *l.* Shipwreck.

Naulum, *l.* Freight.

Nautico fœnere, *l.* With *fœnus nauticum,* marine interest.

Navigable. A river is navigable at common law as far as the tide ebbs and flows.

Navigation Act. The 12 Car. II. c. 18, forbidding foreign ships and seamen to trade with British colonies.

Navis bona, *l.* A "good ship."

Ne, *fr.* Not. **Ne baila pas** (he did not deliver) : an old plea to *detinue.* **Ne disturba pas** (he did not hinder) : the general issue in *quare impedit.* **Ne dona pas** (he did not give) : the general issue in *formedon.* **Ne disseise pas** : not disseised. **Ne gist en le bouche** : it does not lie in the mouth. **Ne relesse pas** : not released. **Ne unques accouple** (never married) : a plea in *dower unde nihil habet.* **Ne unques executor** : never executor. **Ne unques receivour** (never receiver) : a plea in *account.* **Ne unques seise que dower** (never so seised that dower [ensued]) : the general issue in *dower unde nil habet.*

Ne, *l.* Lest; that not. **Ne admittas** : a writ to forbid the admission of a clerk pending a *quare impedit.* **Ne deficiat justitia** : lest justice should fail. **Ne exeat regno** : a prerogative writ issuing from Chancery to prevent a person from leaving the kingdom or state ; formerly political, but now used by the plaintiff in a civil suit ; called in America **ne exeat republica.** **Ne injuste vexes** : an old writ prohibiting a lord from demanding more services from the tenant than were justly due by the tenure under which his ancestors held. **Ne quis plus donasse præsumatur quam in donatione expresserit** : lest any one be presumed to have given more than he expressed in the grant. **Ne recipiatur** (that it be not received) : a caveat or warning to an officer, filed by a party, and directing him not to receive some process or record of the adverse party. **Ne varietur** (that it be not changed) : words written by a notary on a bill or note for purposes of identification.

Nec, neque, *l.* Nor; neither.

Necessitas est lex temporis et loci, *l.* Necessity is the law of time and place. **Necessitas facit licitum quod alias non est licitum** : necessity makes that lawful which is otherwise not lawful. **Necessitas inducit privilegium quoad jura pri-**

vata: necessity [of self-preservation, obedience, or resulting from acts of God or a stranger] creates a privilege as to private rights [is an excuse for the violation of them]. **Necessitas publica major est quam privata**: the public necessity overrules the private one [e. g. a man must die for his country]. **Necessitas quod cogit defendit**: necessity excuses what it compels. **Necessitas vincit legem**: necessity overrules the law.

Née, né, *fr.* Born. **Née vife**: born alive.

Nefas, *l.* Wrong; impious action. **Dies nefasti**: not court days.

Negare, *l.* To deny. **Negatum**: denied.

Negative pregnant. One which implies a possible affirmative; a denial not full, not covering the entire assertion.

Negligentia semper habet infortunium comitem, *l.* Negligence always has misfortune for a companion.

Negotiable. A term applied to an evidence of debt which may be so transferred that the transferee may sue in his own name. Transferable by indorsement. **Negotiable words**: the words "order" or "bearer" in a note, bill, or check.

Negotiate. To arrange; to sell, to discount; to indorse and deliver.

Negotiorum gestor, *l.* A person who manages the affairs of another in his absence, without his knowledge or mandate.

Neife, neif, niefe. v. *Naife.*

Neint, *fr.* None; not; v. *Nient*. **Neint contristeant**: notwithstanding. **Neint meins**: none the less.

Nem. con., Nemine contradicente, *l.* No one dissenting. **Neminem oportet esse sapientiorem legibus**: no one should be wiser than the laws.

Nemo, *l.* No one. **Nemo admittendus est inhabilitare seipsum**: no one is to be allowed to prove himself incapable. **Nemo agit in seipsum**: nobody can (act upon himself) sue himself, or be judge in his own cause. **Nemo allegans suam turpitudinem est audiendus**: no one should be heard to allege his own infamy. **Nemo bis punitur pro eodem delicto**: no one is punished twice for the same offence. **Nemo cogitur rem suam vendere, etiam justo pretio**: no one is forced to sell his own property, even for a fair price. **Nemo contra**

factum suum venire potest: no one can contravene his own deed. **Nemo cogitationis pœnam patitur**: no man suffers a punishment for thought. **Nemo dat qui non habet**: no one who has no title can make a grant. **Nemo dat quod non habet**: no one can give what he does not possess. **Nemo de domo sua extrahi potest**: no one can be forcibly taken from his house. **Nemo debet bis vexari pro una et eadem causa**: no one ought to be twice troubled for one and the same cause. **Nemo debet esse judex in propria causa**: no one ought to be judge in his own cause. **Nemo debet ex alieno damno lucrari**: no one ought to benefit by the loss of another. **Nemo debet locupletari aliena jactura**: no one ought to be enriched by another's loss. **Nemo est hæres viventis**: a person living has no heir. **Nemo enim aliquam partem recte intelligere possit antequam totum iterum atque iterum perlegerit**: for no one can rightly understand any part before having again and again gone over the whole. **Nemo ex alterius facto prægravari debet**: no one ought to be burdened in consequence of another's act. **Nemo ex consilio obligatur**: no man is bound by his advice. **Nemo ex proprio dolo consequitur actionem**: no man acquires a right of action from his own wrong. **Nemo in porpria causa testis esse debet**: no one ought to be witness in his own cause. **Nemo inauditus condemnari debet, si non sit contumax**: no one ought to be condemned unheard, unless he be contumacious. **Nemo invitus compellitur ad communionem**: no one can be forced into a partnership against his will. **Nemo patriam in qua natus est exuere, nec ligeantiæ debitum ejurare possit**: a man cannot abjure his native country nor his due allegiance. **Nemo plus juris ad alium transferre potest quam ipse haberet**: no one can transfer to another a greater interest than he himself possesses. **Nemo potest contra recordum verificare per patriam**: no one can disprove a record by an issue to the jury. **Nemo potest esse dominus et tenens, hæres**: no one can be [both] lord and tenant, heir. **Nemo potest esse simul actor et judex**: no one can be both judge and suitor. **Nemo potest facere per alium quod per se non potest**: no one can do by another what he cannot do himself. **Nemo potest**

14

mutare consilium suum in alterius injuriam: no one can change his purpose to another's injury. **Nemo præsumitur alienam posteritatem suæ prætulisse**: no man is presumed to have preferred another's posterity to his own. **Nemo præsumitur esse immemor suæ æternæ salutis, et maxime in articulo mortis**: no one is presumed to be unmindful of his salvation, most of all at the point of death. **Nemo præsumitur malus**: no one is presumed guilty. **Nemo prohibetur pluribus defensionibus uti**: no one is forbidden to use several defences. **Nemo prudens punit ut præterita revocentur, sed ut futura præveniantur**: no one punishes to undo what is done, but to prevent what may be done. **Nemo punitur pro alieno delicto**: no man is punished for the fault of another. **Nemo sibi esse judex, vel suis jus dicere debet**: no one ought to be judge in cases where himself or his family are concerned. **Nemo tenetur ad impossibilia**: no one is held to [perform] impossibilities. **Nemo tenetur,** no one is bound; **divinare,** to divine [foresee]; **edere instrumenta contra se,** to show instruments against himself [his own interest]; **jurare in suam turpitudinem,** to swear to his own infamy; **seipsum prodere,** to betray himself; **seipsum accusare,** to accuse himself; **seipsum infortuniis et periculis exponere,** to expose himself to misfortunes and dangers.

Nemy, *fr.* Not.

Nestre, *fr.* To be not. **Nest**: it is not, there is not.

Never indebted, plea of. The common traverse or general issue in actions of debt on simple contract.

New assignment. A restatement of a cause of action with more particularity, in answer to the defendant's plea; as when the defendant answered only one of several trespasses; or if he pleaded a justification, and the plaintiff grounded his action on excess. **New trial**: a rehearing of a case, after verdict, before another jury.

Next friend. A person, usually a relative, not appointed by court (v. *guardian ad litem*), in whose name an infant or married woman sues, and who becomes responsible for costs.

Next of kin. 1. A person's nearest relatives according to the civil law; v. *Degree.* 2. The relatives of a decedent entitled to his personal estate under the statute of distributions.

Niefe, *fr.* v. *Naif.* A female villein.

Nient, *fr.* Not; nothing; v. *Neint.* **Nient comprise**: not included. **Nient culpable**: not guilty, the general issue. **Nient dedire** (to deny nothing): to suffer judgment by default. **Nient le fait**: not the deed; v. *Non est factum.* **Nient seisi**: not seiscd.

Nihil, nil, *l.* Nothing; not. **Nihil aliud potest rex quam quod de jure potest**: the King can do nothing else than what he can do by law. **Nil capiat per breve** (that he take nothing by his writ): words of judgment for the defendant on an issue on a plea in bar or abatement. **Nil debet** (he owes nothing): the general issue in debt on a simple contract. **Nil dicit** (he says nothing): words in a judgment against the defendant for default in failing to answer. **Nihil consensui tam contrarium est quam vis atque metus**: nothing is so unlike consent as force and fear. **Nihil facit error nominis cum de corpore constat**: an error in the name has no effect when it is clear as to the person meant. **Nihil habet** (he has nothing): the name of a *return* made by a sheriff upon a *scire facias*, or other writ, which he has been unable to serve. **Nil habuit in tenementis** (he had nothing in the tenements): a plea in an action of debt upon a lease indented, setting up that the person claiming to be landlord had no title. **Nihil perfectum est dum aliquid restat agendum**: nothing is perfect while anything remains to be done. **Nihil præscribitur nisi quod possidetur**: there can be no prescription in that which is not possessed. **Nihil tam conveniens est naturali æquitati, quam voluntatem domini volentis rem suam in alium transferre, ratam haberi**: there is nothing so consistent with natural equity as to hold good the wish of an owner desiring to transfer his property to another. **Nihil tam naturale, etc.**: v. *Naturale.*

Nimia subtilitas in jure reprobatur et talis certitudo certitudinem confundit, *l.* Excessive subtlety is disapproved of in law, and such nicety confuses certainty.

Nisi, *l.* Unless; if not. **Rule, decree nisi**; v. *Absolute.* **Nisi feceris** (shouldst thou not do it): the name of a clause commonly occurring in the old manorial writs, commanding that, if the lords failed to do justice, the King's court or officer should do it. By virtue of this clause, the King's court usurped the jurisdiction of the private, manorial, or local courts. **Nisi prius**: unless before, a term applied to trials of fact before a single judge; to the ordinary court, the court of a judge on his circuit, as distinguished from the full bench, or the courts at Westminster; v. *Assize*. **Nisi prius court**; v. *Court*, 27. A trial before a single judge with jury. **Nisi prius record, roll**: the parchment roll containing the pleadings, issue, and jury process of an action, made up for the use of the judge at *nisi prius*. **Nisi prius writ**: the old name of the writ of *venire facias*, which directed the sheriff to bring the men impanelled as jurors to the courts at Westminster *unless before* that the justices of assize came into his county.

Nocere, *l.* To hurt, damage. **Nocent**: guilty. **Nocumentum**: nuisance, damage.

Nolle, *l.* To be unwilling. **Nolens volens**: willing or not. **Nolle prosequi**, **Nol. pros.**: a formal entry of the plaintiff, or prosecuting officer, on the record, that he *will not further prosecute* his suit as to some of the counts, or as against some of the defendants; or, less frequently, that he will wholly discontinue the action.

Nolo contendere, *l.* (I do not wish to contend.) The name of a plea in an indictment or criminal case, upon which the accused may be sentenced.

Nomen, *l.* Name. **Nomen collectivum**: a collective name, a singular noun of multitude. **Nomen generalissimum**: a most general name, the most comprehensive term. **Nomen juris**: a term technical in law. **Nomen universitatis**: the name (of the whole together), the entire thing, from all points of view, with all its rights. **Nomina sunt notæ rerum**: names are the marks of things. **Nomine pœnæ** (in the name of a penalty): a penalty fixed by covenant in a lease for non-performance of its conditions. **Nomine damni**: in the name of damage; by way of damages.

Nominal partner. v. *Partner*.

Nominatim, *l.* By name; each named in turn.

Nomination. v. *Presentation*.

Non, *l.* No, not. [For many phrases beginning with *non*, see under second word.] **Non acceptavit** (he did not accept):

a plea to an action against the drawee of a bill of exchange. **Non accipi debent verba in demonstrationem falsam, quæ competunt in limitationem veram**: words ought not to be taken for a mistaken description, when they may serve as a good limitation; v. *Falsa demonstratio*. **Non accrevit infra sex annos** (it did not accrue within six years): a plea of the statute of limitations. **Non age**: v. *Nonage*. **Non aliter a significatione verborum recedi oportet quam cum manifestum est aliud sensisse testatorem**: the literal meaning of words ought not to be departed from except when it is clear that the testator meant something else [in using them]. **Non assumpsit** (he did not promise): the general issue in *assumpsit*. **Non assumpsit infra sex annos** (he did not promise within six years): a plea of the statute of limitations in *assumpsit*. **Non cepit** (he did not take): the general issue in *replevin*. **Non claim**: v. *Nonclaim*. **Non concessit** (he did not grant): the plea of a defendant, a stranger to a deed or patent relied upon by the plaintiff, denying that it was granted as alleged. **Non consentit qui errat**: he who mistakes does not consent. **Non constat**: it does not appear, it is not clear. **Non cul'** (**culpabilis**): not guilty. **Non damnificatus** (not damnified): a plea of performance to an action of debt on a bond of indemnity; v. *Bond*. **Non dat, etc.**: v. *Nemo dat*. **Non debet adduci exceptio, etc.**: v. *Exceptio rei*. **Non debet cui plus, etc.**: v. *Cui licet*. **Non debet fieri**: v. *Fieri*. **Non decimando**: v. *De, Modus*. **Non decipitur qui scit se decipi**: a person is not deceived who knows he is being deceived. **Non dedit**: *Ne dona pas*. **Non demisit** (he did not demise): a plea to an action for rent, denying a *parol* lease; v. *Nil habuit in tenementis*. **Non detinet** (he does not detain): the general issue in *detinue*. **Non distringendo**: an old writ to prevent a distress. **Non entia**: things not existent. **Non efficit affectus nisi sequatur effectus**: the intent amounts to nothing unless the effect follow. **Non est arctius vinculum inter homines quam jusjurandum**: there is no closer bond among men than an oath. **Non est disputandum contra principia negantem**: there is no disputing with one who denies principles. **Non est factum** (it is not his deed): the general issue in debt on a specialty. **Non est inventus** (he is not found): the *return* made by the sheriff to a *capias* requiring him to arrest the person of the defendant, when he is not found within his bailiwick; and see *Bill*, I. 8. **Non facias malum ut inde fiat bonum**: you should not do evil that good may result. **Non feasance**; v. *Nonfeasance*. **Non fecit** (he did not make it): a plea to an action on a promissory note, etc. **Non habuit ingressum nisi per**, etc.: he had no entry except through, etc. **Non impedit clausula derogatoria quo minus ab eadem potestate res dissolvantur a qua constituentur**: a derogatory clause in an act does not prevent its being dissolved by the same power which created it. **Non impedivit**: *ne disturba pas*. **Non infregit conventionem**: he did not break the covenant. **Non joinder**: v. *Nonjoinder*. **Non juror**: v. *Nonjuror*. **Non jus sed seisina facit stipitem**: it is not the right, but the seisin, that determines the root of descent; i. e. an estate descends from the person last actually seised, not seised in law merely. **Non liquet**: it is not clear [I am undecided]. **Non memini**: I do not remember. **Non observata forma, infertur adnullatio actus**: where due form is not observed, the annulling of the act follows. **Non obstante**: notwithstanding, in spite of anything to the contrary. **Non obstante veredicto**: a judgment for the plaintiff entered by order of court after a verdict for the defendant. **Non omittas** (that you do not omit): a writ or clause in a writ authorizing a sheriff to enter a *liberty* in serving process. **Non omne damnum producit injuriam**: not every damage produces a legal wrong. **Non omne quod licet honestum est**: not everything that is lawful is honorable. **Non omnium quæ a majoribus constituta sunt ratio reddi potest**: a reason cannot be given for everything established by our forefathers. **Non plevin**: v. *Nonplevin*. **Non possessori incumbit necessitas probandi eas ad se pertinere**: the burden does not lie on a possessor of proving his possessions his own. **Non potest adduci**, etc.; v. *Exceptio*. **Non potest probari quod probatum non relevat**: that cannot be proved which would not be relevant if proved. **Non potest quis sine brevi agere**: no one can sue without a writ. **Non potest rex gratiam facere cum injuria et damno aliorum**: the King cannot confer a benefit to the damage and wrong of others. **Non pros', prosequitur** (he does not pursue) : an entry by, and judgment for, the defendant, when the plaintiff fails to proceed with his suit, or to file any necessary process in due time. **Non quod dictum, sed quod factum est, inspicitur**: not what was said, but what was done, is regarded. **Non refert an quis assensum suum præfert verbis, an rebus ipsis et factis**: it matters not whether he give his consent by words, or by the things themselves and deeds. **Non refert quid notum sit judici, si notum non sit in forma judicii**: it matters not what may be known to the judge, if it be not known judicially. **Non refert verbis an factis fit revocatio**: it does not matter whether the revocation be in words or deeds. **Non sequitur**: it does not follow; v. *Nonsuit*. **Non solent quæ abundant vitiare scripturas**: superfluous expressions do not usually vitiate instruments. **Non submisit** (he did not submit to arbitration) : a plea to an action on an award. **Non suit**: v. *Nonsuit*. **Non sum informatus** (I am not instructed): a species of judgment by default, entered for the defendant's attorney; usually in pursuance of an agrecment between the parties. **Non tenuit** ([the plaintiff] did not hold): a plea in bar in replevin to an *avowry* for arrears of rent. **Non tenure**: v. *Nontenure*. **Non term**: v. *Nonterm*. **Non-user**: v. *Nonuser*. **Non valet exceptio**, etc.: v. *Exceptio*. **Non videntur qui errant consentire**: they who consent under a mistake do not consent at all. **Non videtur consensum retinuisse si quis ex præscripto minantis aliquid immutavit**: if he changed anything at the dictate of a person threatening, he is not held to have continued his consent.

Nonability. Incapacity; as, to sue, etc.

Nonage. Infancy; under age; v. *Age*.

Nonclaim. A neglect to challenge another's right within the time limited by law, by which the claimaut was barred of his right or entry.

Nonfeasance. A not doing; a non-performance. v. *Malfeasance*.

Nonjoinder. A failure to join in an action all the necessary parties. A plea in abatement on that ground.

Nonjuror. A person refusing to take an oath imposed by the government; particularly the oath of allegiance to William III. and his successors, after the abdicatlon of James II.

Nonsuit. A judgment given against a plaintiff when he cannot prove his case, or when he abandons it after issue joined and before verdict. Nonsuits are commonly voluntary, and were effected by the plaintiff's not answering when *called* to hear the verdict.

Nontenure. An *exception* to the *demandant's count* in a real action, denying that he was *tenant* of the freehold.

Nonterm. The time of vacation between term and term.

Nonuser. Omission to assert a privilege, franchise, easement, or right.

Normal law. The law affecting persons *sui juris* and *compos mentis*, when they are in a *normal* condition; the *law of things*, as distinct from the *law of persons*.

Noscitur a sociis, *l.* [He] it is known by [his] its companions. The meaning of a word may be determined by the meaning of the words associated with it.

Not found. v. *Bill*, I. 6. **Not guilty**: a plea of the general issue in *trespass, case*, and criminal causes. **Not possessed**: a plea of specific traverse in trover, denying that the plaintiff was possessed of the goods at the time of action brought. **Not proven**: a Scotch verdict in criminal cases, having the legal effect of a verdict of not guilty, but leaving the prisoner under suspicion.

Nota, *l.*, **Note.** A note, a memorandum; a preliminary memorandum of a deed or charter; v. *Fine*. A **promissory note**: a *negotiable* unconditional promise, written and signed by the maker, for the payment of a certain sum of money to some certain person, his order, or bearer. He is called the **payee**.

Notary. A public ministerial officer, before whom many acts are required to be done; as the attestation of deeds or writings, the protesting of negotiable paper, etc.

Notice, Notitia, *l.* 1. Knowledge. **Actual notice**: when a third person has actual knowledge of a fact or transaction affecting his interests. **Constructive notice**: when such an act is done or state of things exists as would put a reasonable man on his inquiry, or where a legalized form of notice [such as record or advertisement] is complied with; in both of which cases, as to the rights of a third party, the legal consequences of *actual notice* will follow. 2. A written notification, dated, addressed, and signed by the party or his attorney.

Nova, *l.* New. **Nova constitutio futuris formam imponere debet, non præteritis :** a new statute ought to prescribe form to future acts, not past [ought to be prospective, not retrospective, in its operation]. **Nova custuma:** v. *Custuma.* **Novæ Narrationes** (new counts) : a book of forms of pleadings published in the reign of Edward III. **Nova statuta** (new statutes) : the English statutes from 1 Edward III.

Novatio, *l.,* **Novation.** The substitution of a new debt or obligation for an old one, which latter is thereby extinguished. It is novation if either the debtor, the creditor, or the obligation be changed.

Novel, *fr.* New. **Novel disseisin:** v. *Assize.*

Novels. The New Constitutions of Justinian and his successors.

Noverint universi per præsentes, *l.* Know all men by these presents.

Noviter ad notitiam perventa, *l.* Matters lately come to the knowledge of a party.

Novum judicium non dat jus novum, sed declarat antiquum, *l.* A new judgment does not give new law, but declares the old.

Nuda pactio obligationem non parit, *l.* A bare promise does not create an obligation.

Nudus, nudum, *l.* Naked; bare. **Nuda patientia:** mere sufferance. **Nuda possessio:** mere possession. **Nudum pactum:** an agreement without a consideration; v. *Ex.*

Nuisance. Annoyance, damage, especially if to or from real property. v. *Common, Private, Assize.*

Nul, *fr.* No; no one. **Nul agard, nul fait agard, nul tiel agard:** a plea denying the award in an action on an arbitration bond. **Nul assets ultra:** no further assets. **Nul disseisin:** the general issue in a real action, or assize of novel disseisin. **Nul prendra avantage de son tort demesne:** no one shall take advantage of his own wrong. **Nul tiel record:** a pleading denying the existence of a record as alleged; the general plea in an action of debt on a judgment. **Nul tort** (no wrong) : an old general issue in a real action, like *Nul disseisin.* **Nul wast fait:** the old general issue in an action of *waste.*

Nullus, nullum, *l.* No one; none; null; void. **Nulla bona** (no goods) : a sheriff's return to a *fieri facias,* when the defendant had no goods within the county on which a levy could be made. **Nulla⁴ pactione effici potest ut dolus præstetur** (by no agreement can it be effected that a fraud should be maintained) : no possible contract can prevent the agreement from being invalidated by fraud. **Nullius filius**: nobody's son, a bastard. **Nullius in bonis**: the property of no one. **Nullius juris**: of no legal force. **Nullum arbitrium**: no award ; v. *Nul agard*. **Nullum iniquum est præsumendum in jure** : nothing unjust is to be presumed in law. **Nullum simile est idem**: nothing similar is the same. **Nullum tempus occurrit regi** (no time runs against the King) : no lapse of time is a bar to a right of the Crown. **Nullus commodum capere potest de injuria sua propria**: no one can take advantage of his own wrong. **Nullus idoneus testis in re sua intelligitur** : no one is understood to be a fit witness in his own case. **Nullus jus alienum forisfacere potest**: no one can forfeit another's right. **Nullus recedat e curia cancellaria sine remedio**: let no one leave the Court of Chancery without a remedy. **Nullus videtur dolo facere qui suo jure utitur**: he is not to be esteemed a wrong-doer who avails himself of his legal rights.

Numerus certus pro incerto ponitur, *l.* A definite number is put for an uncertain one.

Nunc pro tunc, *l.* Now for then, retroactive.

Nuncupative will. Oral directions as to the disposal of the testator's property, made before witnesses, and not immediately reduced to writing.

Nundinæ, *l.* A fair; fairs.

Nunq, nunques, *fr.* Never.

Nunquam indebitatus, *l.* *Never indebted.* **Nunquam crescit ex post facto præteriti delicti æstimatio**: the character of a past offence is never aggravated by a subsequent matter. **Nunquam præscribitur in falso**: there never can be prescription in a case of forgery.

Nuper, *l.* Late. **Nuper obiit** (lately died) : an old writ for a co-heiress who was kept out of possession by her coparcener.

Nuptiæ, *l.* Marriage. **Nuptias non concubitus sed consensus facit**: the consent, not the consummation, makes the marriage.

O.

O. N. B. *Old Natura Brevium.*

Ob, *l.* For; about; on account of. **Ob turpem causam**: for an immoral consideration.

Obit, *l.* (He dies.) A funeral solemnity; the anniversary office; **Obiit sine prole**: he died without issue.

Obiter, *l.* By the way, in passing. v. *Dictum.*

Oblata, *l.* Gifts or offerings to the Crown; formerly a regular source of royal revenue. Old debts, in the Exchequer, *Oblations.*

Oblations. Gifts or offerings to God or the Church; *mortuary* presents, *soulscot;* payments or gifts for masses, funerals, etc. Formerly the principal source of church revenues.

Obligation. A bond; a sealed writing by which a person is legally bound.

Obligor. The party bound. **Obligee**: the party to whom a promise is made in a bond.

Obsta principiis, *l.* Withstand the beginnings.

Obstupare, *l.* To stop up. **Obstupavit et obstruxit**: stopped up and obstructed.

Obtemperandum est consuetudini rationabili tanquam legi, *l.* A reasonable custom is to be obeyed like law.

Obtulit se, *l.* (He offered himself.) An entry on the record when the other party did not appear.

Obventio, *l.* Obvention; rent; revenue of a spiritual living.

Occupant. A person who takes possession of a thing in default of an owner. **General occupant**: the first person who entered on lands held *pur auter vie* after the death of the tenant, and who might hold them until the death of the *cestui que vie.* If he entered under the original grant, as heir of the tenant, or otherwise, he was termed a **special occupant.**

Occupatio, *l.* The taking of what previously belonged to no one; an original method of acquiring property.

Occupavit, *l.* An old writ for one ejected from his land in time of war.

Octave. The eighth day after a feast; one of the old *return-days.*

Octo tales, *l.* Eight such. v. *Decem tales.*

Odio et atia. v. *De.*

Œps, œs, *fr.* Use.

Office, Office found. v. *Inquest of Office.* **Office copy**: 1. The copy of a record or filed document made by the officer having it in charge, or by him sealed or certified. 2. A copy written at pleasure ; v. *Close copy.*

Officina justitiæ, *l.* The workshop of justice. v. *Court,* 15.

Officium, *l.* Office. **Ex officio** : by or from office, by virtue of office, officially. **Officium nemini debet esse damnosum** : an office ought not to be an occasion of loss to any one [holding it].

Oie, oiez, oir, *fr.* v. *Oyer.*

Oil, oyel, *fr.* 1. Yes ; yca. 2. The eye.

Old Bailey. v. *Court,* 48. **Old Natura Brevium.** A list and treatise of the writs most in use, compiled in the reign of Edward III. ; v. *Natura Brevium, Fitzherbert.* **Old Statutes**: v. *Vetera Statuta.*

Oleron. A code of maritime laws was published at Oleron, an island off the French coast, in the twelfth century, under Richard I. or his mother, Queen Eleanor.

Olograph, olographic. A deed or instrument written entirely by the person making it, a *holograph,* autographic.

Om, on, *fr.* Man ; one ; any one.

Omissio eorum qui tacite insunt nihil operatur, *l.* The omission of those things which are tacitly implied has no effect.

Omissis omnibus aliis negotiis, *l.* Laying aside all other business.

Omne crimen ebrietas et incendit et detegit, *l.* (Drunkenness both instigates and discloses every crime.) Drunkenness aggravates the offence. **Omne jus aut consensus fecit, aut necessitas constituit, aut firmavit consuetudo** : every legal right was either created by consent, enacted by reason of necessity, or confirmed by custom. **Omne majus continet in se minus** : every greater contains in itself the less. **Omne majus dignum,** etc. : v. *Magis dignum.* **Omne quod inædificatur,** etc. : v. *Inædificatum.* **Omne sacramentum debet esse de certa scientia** : every oath [every statement sworn to] ought to be upon certain knowledge. **Omne testamentum morte consummatum est** : every will is made complete by the death [of the testator.] **Omnes licentiam habere his, quæ pro se indulta sunt, renunciare** : all have liberty to renounce such privileges as are conferred for their own benefit. **Omnes sorores sunt quasi unus hæres de una hæreditate**: all sisters are, as it were, one heir of one inheritance. **Omni exceptione majores** : beyond all exception ; above suspicion. **Omnia delicta in aperto leviora sunt**: all faults committed openly are less heinous. **Omnia performavit**: he hath performed them all. **Omnia præsumuntur contra spoliatorem**: every presumption is made against a despoiler [one who destroys or withholds evidence]. **Omnia præsumuntur rite, legitime, solemniter esse acta**: all things are presumed to have been properly, lawfully, formally done, **donec probetur in contrarium**, until proof be made to the contrary. **Omnia quæ sunt uxoris sunt ipsius viri**: all things which are the wife's are the husband's. **Omnibus ad quos præsentes literæ pervenerint, salutem**: to all to whom these letters shall come, greeting. **Omnis actio est loquela**: every action is a complaint. **Omnis definitio in lege periculosa**: any definition in law is dangerous. **Omnis innovatio plus novitate perturbat quam utilitate prodest**: every innovation disturbs more by its novelty than it benefits by its utility. **Omnis nova constitutio futuris formam imponere debet, non præteritis**: every new enactment ought to prescribe form for future things, not past. **Omnis privatio præsupponit habitum** : any deprivation implies former possession. **Omnis ratihabitio retrotrahitur et mandato priori æquiparatur**: every ratification works backward, and amounts to a previous command. **Omnium bonorum**: of all the goods; of one's entire estate.

Oneris ferendi, *l.* The servitude of support; as by a party wall or other structure to a neighbor's house.

Onerous. Not *lucrative;* with good consideration.

Onomastic. A signature to an instrument written by another hand; not *holographic.*

Onus probandi, *l.* The burden of proving.

Ope et consilio, *l.* By aid and counsel.

Open law. Manifest law ; trial by *ordeal* or *battel.* **Open policy**: v. *Policy.* **Open theft**: v. *Furtum manifestum.*

Operarius, *l.* A tenant by bodily labor.

Operatio, *l.* A day's work by the tenant.

Opinio quæ favet testamento est tenenda, *l.* The opinion which favors the will is to be held.

Oportet, *l.* It behoves. **Oportet quod certa res deducatur in donationem, in judicium :** it is necessary that a thing certain be brought into the gift, to judgment.

Opp'. For *Obtulit se,* he offered himself; an entry on the record when one party made default.

Optima est legis interpres consuetudo, *l.* Custom is the best interpreter of laws. **Optima est lex quæ minimum relinquit arbitrio judicis, optimus judex qui minimum sibi :** that law is best which leaves least to the judge's discretion; that judge, who leaves least to himself. **Optimus interpres rerum usus :** usage is the best interpreter of things.

Option. The prerogative of an archbishop on appointing a bishop to have the latter provide a living for a clerk named by the former. **Optional writ :** a writ framed in the alternative, to do a thing or show cause.

Opus, *l.* Work, labor. Benefit, advantage. **Opus manificum :** manual labor. **Opus novum :** a new structure.

Orator. A petitioner ; a plaintiff in equity.

Ordeal. An old method of trial *by the judgment of God.* The fire or **iron ordeal,** where the accused took a piece of red-hot iron in the hand, or stepped blindfold and barefoot over red-hot ploughshares. The **water ordeal,** where he either plunged his arm into boiling water, or was thrown into a pond. If he escaped unhurt, or sank in the latter case, he was acquitted. The *campfight* or *duellum* was also a sort of ordeal; so the *corsned.*

Order. In Chancery, a decision upon an interlocutory matter. The acts of a judge in chambers. v. *Rule.*

Ordinary. The judge having the ordinary, original, ecclesiastical jurisdiction in a diocese; generally the bishop. In some American States, the judge of probate and administration. **Ordinary's court :** v. *Court,* 82, 110.

Ordine placitandi servato, servatur et jus, *l.* When the order of pleading is observed, the law is also.

Ore, *fr.* Now.

Ore tenus, *l.* Orally; by word of mouth.

Original Bill. v. *Bill,* I. 10. **Original writ, conveyance, process ;** v. *Writ, Conveyance, Process.*

Origo rei inspici debet, *l.* The origin of the thing ought to be examined.

Orphan's Court. A Court of Probate. v. *Court,* 110.

Oster, Oter, *fr.* v. *Ouster.*

Ostendit vobis, *l.* Shows to you.

Ostensible partner. v. *Partner.*

Ou, *fr.* Or; where; whither; whereas; with; within.

Oultre le mer, *fr.* Beyond the sea.

Ouster, oster, oter, *fr.* To put out; take away; dispossess; to oust, deprive of. Dispossession of a freehold or chattel real, or an hereditament corporeal or incorporeal; the most general term for exclusion from the possession of land; whereby the party ousted can only regain possession by employing legal remedies. **Ousterlemain** (to remove the hand): 1. The *livery,* or delivery of the ward's lands out of the hands of the guardian on the former's arriving at the proper age; a writ against the lord for this purpose. 2. A delivery of lands out of the King's hands by judgment for the petitioner on a *monstrans de droit.*

Ouster, *fr.* Over; further; beyond. **Ouster le mer:** beyond sea; v. *Essoin.*

Outer bar. The junior barristers. v. *Queen's Counsel.*

Outfangthefe, *sax.* Either a tenant taken for theft outside the manor, or a strange thief taken within it. The privilege enjoyed by a lord of a manor of trying one of his tenants taken elsewhere for theft.

Outlaw. A person out of the protection of the law; whose property is thereby forfeited, and who has, in general, no legal rights. In early times he bore a *caput lupinum,* and might be killed at sight.

Outlawry. A process by which a defendant or person in contempt on a civil or criminal process was declared an outlaw. If for treason or felony, it amounted to conviction and attainder. v. *Exigent, Capias utlagatum.*

Outre, *fr.* Beyond.

Outstanding term. *Attendant term.*

Ove, *fr.* With, for. **Ovesque:** with.

Overt. Open, evident. v. *Market.*

Ovel, owel, *fr.* Equal. **Owelty:** equality. **En owel main:** in equal hand.

Owling. The offence of transporting wool or sheep out of the kingdom.

Oxgang, oxgate. As much land as an ox could till; fifteen acres.

Oyel, oyl, oil, *fr.* Yes.

Oyer, *fr.* To hear; hearing. **Oyez:** hear ye. The hearing a deed read in court, to which a defendant was entitled in actions based upon the deed or record where the plaintiff had to make *profert.* To **crave oyer:** to demand that the instrument be read, or that the party may be furnished with a copy.

Oyer et terminer, *fr.* To hear and determine. 1. A special commission to judges or others to inquire into a treason or felony on a sudden outbreak or public outrage. 2. The general commission of the same nature; v. *Assize.* 3. In New York, the title of a criminal court. v. *Court,* 111.

P.

P. C. For Parliamentary Cases, Privy Council, Pleas of the Crown.

P. P. *Per procurationem.*

Pactum, *l.* A pact; compact, agreement. **Pacta dant legem contractui:** the stipulations of the parties constitute the law of the contract. **Pacta privata non derogant juri communi:** private agreements cannot derogate from public right. **Pactum corvinum de hæreditate viventis:** a crow-like bargain for the inheritance of a living person. **Pactum de non petendo:** an agreement not to sue.

Paine forte et dure, *fr.* A punishment for a person accused of felony who stood mute and refused to plead. It was not administered until after threefold warning (**trina admonitio**), and consisted of being crushed with weights and starved.

Pais, *fr.* The country. The jury. **In pais:** open, in the country; v. *Matter in pais.* Trial **per pais:** by the jury.

Paix, *fr.* Peace. The concord of a *fine.*

Palace court. v. *Court,* 56.

Palam, *l.* Openly. **Palam populo:** before the people.

Palatine. Pertaining to a palace, possessing royal privileges. v. *County.*

Pandects. The Code Justinian, or Digest, the chief compilation of the *corpus juris civilis* under Justinian.

Panel, panell. A parchment schedule containing the names of the jurymen returned by the sheriff, annexed to the *venire facias.* v. *Impanel.*

Paper-book. A formal collection, copy, or file of the pleadings and proceedings in a cause, prepared for the judges upon the hearing; the transcript of the record.

Par, *l.* Equal, like. **Par in parem imperium non habet:** an equal has no authority over an equal. **Par delictum:** equal guilt.

Parage. Equality of condition, blood, or dignity. v. *Disparage.*

Paramount. Above, over all. The **lord paramount:** the chief lord, of whom the *mesne* lords held.

Paraphernalia, Parapherna. Movable goods which a widow is allowed to retain besides her dower; jewels, apparel, etc.

Paratum habeo, *l.* (I have him in readiness.) A sheriff's *return,* upon a *ca. resp.,* that he had taken the defendant, and had him ready to bring into court.

Paratus est verificare, *l.* He is prepared to verify. v. *Et hoc.*

Paravail. The lowest tenant of land was so called, he who held of the *mesne* lords, and was supposed to occupy the land.

Parceners. Coparceners. v. *Coparcenary.*

Parchemin, *fr.* Parchment; a record.

Parco fracto. v. *Poundbreach.*

Parens patriæ, *l.* The father of the country; in England, the King; in America, the State; having guardianship of the poor and incapable.

Par, *l.* Equal. **Pares:** peers. The freeholders of a neighborhood. **Pares curiæ:** the tenants of a manor in attendance on the court. **Pares de vicineto:** the freeholders of the neighborhood, the *venue.* **Pares regni:** peers of the realm.

Pari delicto, *l.* Of equal guilt. **Pari materia:** of the same matter, on the same subject. **Pari passu:** in equal degree, by equal steps. **Paribus sententiis reus absolvitur:** when the opinions are equally divided, the defendant is acquitted. **Parium judicium:** judgment of the peers, trial by jury.

Parish Court. v. *Court,* 112.

Park. A piece of enclosed land privileged for the keeping of beasts of chase.

Parler, *fr.* To speak. **Parlance:** speech.

Parmy, *fr.* By; through, throughout.

Parol, *fr.* A word. Oral; not written, not under seal. **Parol contract:** a contract, written or otherwise, but not under seal or of record. **Parol demurrer:** v. *Age-prier.* **Parols de ley:** the technical words of law.

Pars, *l.* A part, party. **Pars enitia:** v. *Enitia.* **Pars ejusdem negotii:** part of the same transaction. **Pars fundi:** part of the soil. **Pars judicis:** the duty of the judge. **Pars rationabilis:** v. *De rationabili parte bonorum.*

Parson imparsonee. v. *Induction, Imparsonee, Rector.*

Part and pertinent. Scotch, for *appurtenances.*

Parte, *l.* v. *Pars.* **Parte inaudita:** one side unheard, *ex parte.* **Partes finis nil habuerunt** (the parties to the fine had nothing): an old pleading in answer to a fine of land, set up in an action, but which had been levied by a stranger.

Particeps criminis, *l.* A party to the crime, an accomplice.

Particular average, lien. v. *Average, Lien.* **Particular estate:** an estate for life or years preceding a *remainder.*

Partition. The division of land held by more than one owner, as in common, joint tenancy, or coparcenary, into several shares.

Partnership. An association of persons for the purpose of profit, in which the members (**partners**) are mutually principal and agent, and share in the profits or losses; a **general partnership.** **Limited partnership:** one which contains one or more *special partners.* **Dormant partner:** one who partakes of the profits, but has no power in the partnership, and whose name does not appear in the firm. **Nominal partner:** one whose name appears in the firm, but who has no real interest. **Ostensible partner:** one who holds himself out as a partner, by interfering in partnership affairs, assuming authority, or allowing his name to appear in the firm. **Special partner:** one who is only liable for losses to the extent of his capital invested, and has no authority in partnership affairs.

Partus, *l.* Birth, offspring. **Partus sequitur ventrem:** the offspring follows the womb [belongs to the owner of the mother].

Party-wall. A wall erected on the line between two lots of land, belonging to the owners iu common. **Party-jury**: v. *Bilinguis*. **Party-witness**: v. *Witness*.

Parva proditio, *l.* Pctty *treason*. **Parva serjeantia**: petty *serjeanty*. **Parvum cape**: *petit cape* ; v. *Cape*.

Pas, *fr.* Not; no. A step.

Pascha, *l.,* **Paques,** *fr.* Easter.

Pateat universis per præsentes, *l.* Kuow all meu by these presents.

Patent. Open; unsealed. v. *Clause, Ambiguity, Writ.* **Letters patent**: a grant of some privilege, title, property, or authority madc by the sovereign to one or more subjects. **Patent**: the grant of an exclusive privilege to make, use, or sell an invention for a term of years ; a grant by the state or government of public lands.

Pater, *l.* Father. **Pater-familias**: the father of a family. **Pater est quem nuptiæ demonstrant**: the father is he whom the marriage indicates. **Pater patriæ**: father of the realm; v. *Parens*. **Paterna paternis**: paternal estates [go to the] heirs on the father's side; v. *Materna*.

Patiens, *l.* The passive party to an act; the patient. v. *Agent*.

Patria potestas, *l.* In civil law, the authority of a father over his family.

Patron. He who has an *advowson,* the gift of a benefice. **Patronage**: the *advowson*.

Patroon. In New York, the lord of a manor.

Pawn. A bailment of personal property as security for a debt; a *pledge*.

Pax, *l.,* **Paix,** *fr.* The peace: **Pax ecclesiæ**: the peace of the church, sanctuary. **Pax regis**: the King's peace; lawful order, quiet. The **verge of the court,** a privileged district or sanctuary around the King's palace.

Payee. v. *Note, Bill,* III. 4.

Payments, Appropriation, Application, Imputation of. The application of a payment to one of several debts existing between the same parties. If the debtor say nothing about it, the creditor may apply the payment to whichever debt he choose.

Pays, *fr.* Country. v. *Pais*.

Peace, Bill of. v. *Bill,* I. 12. **Commission of**: v. *Assize*.

Peas, *fr.* Peace ; the concord of a *fine*.

Peccatum, *l.*, **Peche,** *fr.* A fault; a sin.

Pecia, *l.* A piece.

Peculiar. In ecclesiastical law, a parish exempt from the *ordinary's* jurisdiction, and subject only to the *metropolitan*, or to him who holds the benefice. v. *Court of Peculiars, Court*, 84.

Peculium, *l.* Such private property as was allowed a wife, child, or slave in the Roman law. *Paraphernalia.*

Pecunia, *l.* Cattle; property; personal property; fungible goods; money. **Pecunia numerata**: counted money. **Pecunia non numerata**: money not paid. **Pecunia trajectitia**: a loan of money on a ship or cargo; *bottomry, fœnus nauticum.*

Pecus, *pl.* **pecora,** *l.* A beast; cattle.

Pede pulverosus, *l.* Dusty foot; a huckster attending fairs. v. *Court of Piepowders, Court*, 36.

Pedem ponere, *l.* To place the foot; enter on lands. **Pedis positio**: actual possession.

Pee, *fr.* The foot; the foot of a *fine.*

Peer. An equal. The vassal of a lord who sat in his court to judge his co-vassals. A lord temporal, having a seat in Parliament; a baron or higher nobleman.

Pees, *fr.* v. *Peas.*

Peine, *fr.* Punishment. v. *Paine.*

Penal. Punishable; with a penalty annexed. v. *Action, Bill*, III. 7.

Pendente, *l.* Hanging. **Pendente lite**: during the suit, **nihil innovetur**, nothing should be changed. v. *Fructus.*

Pendre, *fr.* To hang. **Pendu**: hanged.

Pensa, *l.* A weight. **Pensata**: weighed.

Per, *l.* Through; by; during. **Per ambages**: by evasive methods. **Per annulum et baculum**: by ring and staff; v. *Annulus.* **Per annum**: by the year. **Per auter vie**: for the life of another; v. *Pur.* **Per aversionem**: a sale by bulk, in a lump. **Per capita**: per head; by heads, as distinguished from **per stirpes**, by roots of descent, by families. **Per consequens**: consequently. **Per considerationem curiæ**: by the judgment of the court. **Per contra**: on the other hand. **Per corpus** (by the body): by *battel*, as distinguished from trial by jury. **Per, per and cui**: v. *Entry, writ of.* **Per cur', curiam**: by the court. **Per defaltam**: by default. **Per diem**: per day. **Per**

equipollens: by an equivalent [word]. **Per expressum**: expressly. **Per fas aut nefas**: by right or wrong. **Per formam doni**: by the *form* of the gift, which governed descent in estates tail. **Per fraudem**: by fraud. **Per incuriam**: by mistake. **Per infortunium**: by misadventure. **Per legale judicium parium**: by the lawful judgment of his peers. **Per legem Angliæ, terræ**: by the law of England, of the land. **Per medietatem linguæ**: by *half-tongue*; v. *Bilinguis*. **Per metas et bundas**: by metes and bounds. **Per minas**: by threats. **Per misadventure**: by mishap. **Per my et per tout** (*fr.*): of the half and of all; v. *Joint tenants*. **Per omnes**: by all [the judges]. **Per pais**: by the country; v. *Pais*. **Per pares curtis**: v. *Par*. **Per patriam**: by the *country*. **Per proc', procurationem**: by appointment; as agent. **Per quæ servitia** (by which services): a writ judicial issuing from the *note* of a *fine* of lands, which lay for the cognizee of a manor, seigniory, etc., to compel the tenant of the land to attorn to him. Abolished by the 3 & 4 Will. IV. c. 27. **Per quod actio accrevit**: whereby an action accrued. **Per quod consortium amisit** (whereby he lost the society [of his wife]): an action by the husband for trespass to the wife. **Per quod servitium amisit** (whereby he lost the service): an action for injury to, or seduction of, a child or servant. **Per saltum**: by a leap, at one step. **Per se**: by himself, in itself. **Per stirpes**: by stocks; v. *Capita, Per capita*. **Per subsequens matrimonium**: by a subsequent marriage. **Per tant**: v. *Pur*. **Per testes**: by witnesses; v. *Common form*. **Per totum tempus prædictum**: during all the time aforesaid. **Per totam curiam**: by the full court. **Per usucaptionem**: by possession, by uninterrupted enjoyment. **Per vadium**: by gage, by way of pledge. **Per verba de futuro**: by words of the future [tense]; **de præsenti**, of the present; a distinction made in contracts of marriage. **Per visum ecclesiæ**: by the supervision of the church. **Per visum juratorum**: by a view of the jury. **Per vivam vocem**: by the living voice, *viva voce*.'

Per, *fr.* v. *Pur*. **Peramount**: above. **Peravaile**: below.

Perdre, *fr.* To lose. **Perdu, pert**: lost.

Peremptory. v. *Mandamus*. **Peremptory challenge**: a *challenge* to a juror without cause or reason given, usually allowed in criminal cases. **Peremptory plea**: not *dilatory*, one impeaching the right.

Perfecting bail. To *justify bail* after exception.

Pergamenum, *l.* Parchment; a *record*.

Periculum, *l.* Danger, peril. **Periculo petentis**: at the risk of the suitor. **Periculum rei venditæ, nondum traditæ, est emptoris**: the risk of a thing sold, not yet delivered, is the buyer's.

Perjury. False swearing, under oath lawfully administered in a judicial, legal, or political proceeding, to a material point.

Permissive waste. Waste resulting from omission. v. *Waste.*

Pernancy. Receiving; actual taking of rents or profits.

Pernor, pernour, *fr.* A taker, receiver.

Perpetua lex, etc. v. *Clausula.*

Perpetual curate. v. *Rector.*

Perpetuating testimony. v. *Bill,* I. 13.

Perpetuity. An estate unalienable for a long time; for time longer than that allowed by law. Such limitation, if for a time which may be longer than lives in being at the time it takes effect and twenty-one years nine months after, is **void for remoteness**.

Perquirere. *l.* To gain, acquire. **Perquisitio**: purchase.

Persona conjuncta æquiparatur interesse proprio, *l.* (A united person is equivalent to one's own interest.) Nearness of blood is as good a consideration as personal profit. **Persona impersonata**: a parson *imparsonee.* **Persona prædilecta**: a person particularly favored.

Personable. Able to maintain a plea, capable of suing.

Personal. Of the person, following the person, not real. **Personal replevin**: v. *Replevin.* **Personal estate, assets, property**: those which go to the executor, not the heir, on the death of the owner; usually things movable. **Personal action, chattels, replevin**: v. *Action, Chattels, Replevin.* **Personal representative**: the executor or administrator; sometimes, the next of kin.

Personalty. Personal property. **Mixed personalty**: chattels real; for they are subject to the statutes of *Mortmain,* which pure personalty is not.

Perspicua vera non sunt probanda, *l.* Plain truths need not be proved.

Pertinens, *l.* Appendant, appurtenant. **Pertinentiæ:** appurtenances.

Pescher, *fr.* To fish. **Pescherie:** fishery.

Petere, *l.* To beg, demand; to sue. **Petens:** a demandant, a
plaintiff in a real action. **Petit judicium:** he prays judgment.

Peter's pence. A tax of a penny on each house in England;
formerly paid the Pope.

Petit, *fr.* Petty; small. **Petit Cape, Jury, Larceny, Serjeanty, Treason:** see those titles.

Petitio, *l.* A demand; a *count.* **Petitio principii:** a begging of
the question.

Petition de droit, *fr.* The modern name for a *monstrans de droit;*
a petition of right filed in Chancery, by which a subject recovers
lands or goods in possession of the Crown. Upon being indorsed by the King, *Soit droit fait al partie* (let right be
done to the party), a commission of inquiry issued; and judgment for the petitioner was by *amoveas manus.*

Petition. A written motion to a court. **Petition of Right:**
1. v. *Petition de Droit.* 2. A parliamentary declaration of the
liberties of the people, assented to by Charles I. in 1629. **Petitioning creditor:** the one who institutes proceedings for the
adjudication of a bankrupt.

Petitory Suit. A suit in admiralty to determine the title to property, not the possession. *Droitural,* not *possessory.*

Peto, *l.* I demand; the first word of the demandant's count in a
real action.

Petty. v. *Petit.* **Petty average:** v. *Average.* **Petty-bag
office:** an office on the common-law side of the Court of Chancery whence issued writs in Crown matters, or for or against the
officers of the court; v. *Hanaper.* It succeeded to the duties of
the *Cursitors.* **Petty sessions:** a court of summary jurisdiction
held by one or more justices of the peace.

Peu, *fr.* Few; a little. **A peu près:** almost.

Peut, *fr.* Can. **Ne peuvent:** they cannot.

Piccage. Money paid for setting up booths at fairs.

Pickery, *sc.* Petty theft.

Pie, *fr.* A foot. **Piepoudre:** v. *Pede pulverosus.* **Pied poudre:**
v. *Court of Piepowders, Court,* 36.

Pightel. A little close; a hedged bit of land.

Pignus, *l.* A pledge. **Pignori acceptum :** a bailment in pledge.

Pin-money. An allowance made by a husband to his wife for her apparel and personal expenses, which remains his property until expended.

Piperolla. The great rolls of accounts in the Exchequer.

Pipowders. v. *Court,* 36.

Piscary. Fishery; a liberty of fishing in another man's waters.

Pixing the coin. Testing coin by a jury of the Goldsmiths' Company.

Place. Pleas. Place where : v. *Locus in quo.*

Placita, *l.* Pleas; suits; pleadings. The title of a judgment record The old public assemblies at which the King presided. **Placita communia coronæ :** v. *Communis.* **Placita juris :** rules of law, arbitrary legal principles.

Placitamentum, *l.* The pleading of a cause. **Placitabile :** pleadable.

Placitum, *l.* v. *Placita.* A plea, suit, cause; an assembly, court; a day in court; a mulct or fine; a judicial proceeding; a legal principle. **Placito debiti, detentionis, etc. :** in a plea of debt, detinue, etc.

Plaga, *l.,* **Plaie,** *fr.* A wound; an incised wound.

Plaideur, *fr.* A pleader, advocate.

Plaint. The first process in an inferior court.

Plaintiff. The party suing in a personal action, whose name appears on the record. The party really interested as suitor in any judicial proceeding. **Equitable plaintiff :** one who, although really interested, sues in the name of another having the legal claim. **Plaintiff in error :** the party who brings a writ of error. **Calling the plaintiff** [to hear the verdict] : v. *Calling the plaintiff, Nonsuit.*

Plea. 1. A suit or action. 2. A pleading. 3. The pleading of the defendant. 4. A defendant's pleading setting up matter of fact. 5. In equity, a short answer in bar of the suit without giving discovery, stating facts which, if inserted in the bill, would render it demurrable. Pleas in **abatement, avoidance, bar, confession and avoidance, dilatory, equitable, peremptory, puis darrein continuance, special:** see those titles. In good order of pleading, a person ought to plead, — 1st. **To the jurisdiction of the court:** a foreign plea,

showing some other court in which the matter should be tried.
2d. **To the person of the plaintiff**, and next **of the defendant**: pleas of disability, privilege, etc. 3d. **To the writ**:
pleas of variance, death of parties, misnomer, misjoinder, nonjoinder, etc. 4th. **To the action of the writ**: showing the
plaintiff had no cause to have that writ brought, though he
might have another on the same cause of action, as if he mistook his action. 5th. **To the count or declaration**: variance, specialty of record, incertainty, etc. 6th. **To the action
itself**: in bar thereof. The first five are *dilatory pleas ;* the
sixth is *peremptory*, and includes pleas in *confession and avoidance*, which are *special pleas* par excellence, usually called **special pleas in bar**, or **special pleas** ; pleas of *traverse*, which
include the *general issue*, the *specific traverse*, and the *special
traverse ;* and pleas of *estoppel*, which are sometimes also called
special pleas in bar, as well as the specific traverse and the special plea proper. All *dilatory* pleas may be called pleas in *abatement ;* but the latter term more properly includes only the third,
fourth, and fifth classes. *Demurrers* properly take order at the
head of the sixth division. *Age-prier* was called a plea **in suspension**. In criminal law, the prisoner should plead, — 1st. To
the jurisdiction. 2d. In abatement. 3d. Special pleas in bar,
as *autrefois, acquit, convict, attaint*, and *pardon*. 4th. The general issue of not guilty. **Common pleas** : civil actions between
subject and subject, as distinct from **pleas of the Crown**,
criminal actions. **Court of Common Pleas** : v. *Court*, 10.
v. *Pleading*. **Plea side** : v. *Court*, 8, 11.

To Plead. 1. To litigate ; v. *Plea*, 1. 2. To conduct the *pleadings*, that part of a suit which contained the allegations of the
parties, formerly oral, by which they came to an issue ; v. *Plea*, 2.
3. To make an allegation of fact in conducting the pleadings ;
as distinct from to *demur ;* v. *Plea*, 4. 4. To put in a special
plea or plea in bar in answer to the declaration ; v. *Plea*, 3.
5. (Colloquial.) To appear in a cause, to act as advocate. **To
plead over** : v. *Pleading*.

Pleader. An advocate. **Special pleader** : a person (whether
admitted to the bar or not) employed to draw up pleadings, particularly *special pleas*, and to give legal opinions ; v. *Special
pleading*.

Pleading. The process of making the series of allegations in a cause which terminated in an *issue*. These allegations were formerly made orally in court, and are now termed **pleadings**, consisting of the *declaration, plea* (v. *Plea,* 4), *replication, rejoinder, surrejoinder, rebutter, surrebutter,* etc.; v. *Replevin.* **Special pleading**: v. *Pleader.* **Pleading over**: to go on pleading without noticing a defect in the last pleading of the other party, whereby such defect may be *cured*.

Pledge. 1. A bailment of personal property as security for some debt or engagement, the debtor retaining the title while the creditor has actual or constructive possession. 2. A thing pledged. 3. A surety. **Pledges to prosecute**: persons who become sureties for the plaintiff in a civil action, and were liable with him to be amerced **pro falso clamore suo**, for his false claim, if he deserted or lost his suit. Later they became fictitious persons, as John Doe and Richard Roe.

Plee, *fr.* An action; a plea.

Plegii ad prosequendum, *l.* *Pledges to prosecute.*

Plegii de retorno habendo: sureties for a *return* in replevin.

Plein, *fr.* Full. **Pleine age**: full age. **Pleinement administre**: fully administered.

Plenary. Full, complete; done formally and at length; not *summary.*

Plenus, plena, *l.* Full. **Plena ætas**: *full age.* **Plena fides**: good credit (full faith). **Plena probatio**: *full proof.* **Pleno jure**: with perfect right. **Plenarie**: fully. **Plene administravit** (he has fully administered): a plea by an executor or administrator that he has no assets of the deceased remaining in his hands; **plene administravit præter**, a similar plea excepting a specified balance which is not sufficient to satisfy the plaintiff's demand. **Plene computavit**: he has fully accounted, a plea in an action of *account.* **Plenum dominium**: v. *Dominium.* **Plenum rectum**: full right.

Plenarty. A full benefice, not a vacancy.

Plevina, *l.,* **Plevine,** *fr.* Security; a pledge's liability.

Pleyn, *fr.* v. *Plein.*

Pleynte, *fr.* A *plaint*, complaint.

Ploughbote. v. *Bote.* Plough-land; one hundred and twenty acres; a *carucata.*

Pluries, *l.* Many times. A writ issued after the first writ and an *alias* writ have failed of effect; the third writ. **A second pluries** is a fourth writ, etc.

Pluris petitio, *l.* A claim for more than is due.

Plus, *l.* More. **Plus peccat author quam actor:** the instigator sins more than the actor. **Plus valet unus oculatus testis quam auriti decem:** one eyewitness is of more weight than ten earwitnesses.

Plus, pluis, *fr.* More, most. **Au pluis:** at the most. **Plus tost:** rather; sooner. **Plus tost que:** rather than, as well as.

Pocket sheriff. One appointed by the sole authority of the Crown, without being nominated by the judges of the Exchequer.

Poer, *fr.* Power; to be able. **Poet:** v. *Peut.*

Pœna, *l.* Punishment, penalty; damages. **Pœna corporalis:** corporal punishment. **Pœnalis:** penal.

Pœnitentia, *l.* Repentance; change of mind.

Poinding, *sc.* Distress; a diligence, process of attachment.

Police Court. v. *Court,* 112.

Policies of Assurance Court. v. *Court,* 64.

Policy. An instrument embodying the contract of insurance, which is **open** if the value is to be proved by the insured, in case of loss; and **valued** where the value is inserted in the policy in the nature of liquidated damages.

Poll. Cut; shaved, even. v. *Deed.* **Polls:** v. *Challenge.*

Pollicitation. A promise before acceptance, without mutuality.

Ponderantur testes, non numerantur, *l.* Witnesses are weighed, not counted.

Pondus regis, *l.* The king's weight; the standard.

Pone, *l.* (Put.) 1. An original writ issuing to remove a cause from an inferior, or county court, to a superior, or to the C. B. 2. **Pone per vadium et plegios:** a writ issuing after the non-appearance of the defendant to the original writ, commanding the sheriff to attach him and take security or pledges. **Ponit se super patriam:** he puts himself on the *country.*

Pontage. A toll on, or tax for, a bridge.

Popular action: v. *Action.* **Popular Court:** v. *Court,* 116.

Porter, *fr.,* **Portare,** *l.* To bear; bring.

Portgreve. The chief officer of a seaport town.

Poser, *fr.* To put a question.

Positive law. Law enforced by a sovereign political authority, as distinct from laws of honor, laws of nature, etc.

Posse, *l.* To be able. **Posse comitatus:** the force of a county, the entire population above the age of fifteen, except peers and clergymen. **In posse:** in possibility, not *in esse.*

Possessio fratris facit sororem esse hæredem, *l.* The possession of the brother makes the sister heir. If a man die, and leave two sons by different wives, and the one brother be seised in possession of the father's estate and die, the estate shall not pass to his brother, but to his sister of the whole blood in preference. A maxim when descent was traced from the person last seised, not, as now, from the *purchaser.*

Possessory. About the possession, not *petitory.* v. *Action.*

Possibility. An uncertain event, a contingency. **Possibility coupled with an interest:** an expectation recognized in law as an estate or interest; as where the person who is to take an estate on the happening of the contingency is named or ascertained; not a **bare possibility,** as the expectation of an heir apparent. **Possibility on a possibility:** a double contingency, as an estate limited to a man's unborn son John; it is bad in law. **Possibility of reverter:** the estate of the grantor of an estate upon *condition.*

Post, *l.* After, afterwards; v. *Entry, writ of.* **Post diem, disseisinam:** after the day, the disseisin. **Post-factum:** an after act. **Post-fine:** the *king's silver;* v. *Fine.* **Post litem motam:** after the suit was begun; after the dispute arose. **Post mortem:** after death. **Post-natus:** after born. **Post-obit bond:** a bond in which the obligor agrees to pay a sum *after the death* of a third person, usually a person from whom the obligor expects to inherit. **Post prolem suscitatam:** after issue born. **Post terminum:** after the term.

Postea, *l.* Afterwards. The entry on the record of the proceedings at the trial of an action, stating what happened after the issue joined, at which the *nisi prius* record ends.

Post-note. A bank-note payable at a future time. **Post-obit:** v. *Post.*

Potentia, *l.* Power. **Potentia propinqua:** a near possibility.

Potior est conditio defendentis, *l.* The defendant has the better position [where both are in fault]. **Potior est conditio possidentis**: the possessor has the stronger position.

Potwallers, Potwallopers. Persons who cooked their own diet in a fireplace of their own, and were therefore, by the custom of some boroughs, entitled to vote.

Poundage. An allowance made the sheriff for his services in a levy.

Pound breach. The offence of breaking into a pound, and taking out the cattle impounded.

Pour, *fr.* For; v. *Pur.* **Pour compte de qui il appartient**: for account of whom it may concern. **Pour seisir terres**: a writ for the King to *seize lands* of a widow, held in dower, and *in capite*, if she married without his permission.

Pourparty, *fr.* Partition; division among coparceners.

Pourpresture, *fr.* The wrongful enclosure of another man's land; encroaching on Crown or common lands.

Poustie, *sc.* Power. v. *Liege poustie.*

Power. Authority. An instrument conferring authority upon another. A **power of appointment**: authority vested in a person called the **donee**, by deed or will, to appoint a person to the enjoyment of property of the grantor or testator. If the donee have no interest in the property himself, it is a **power collateral.** If he has an interest, it is a **power coupled with an interest**; and these may be either **appendant (appurtenant)**, as when the appointment is made out of, or in derogation of, his own estate, or **in gross**, when the appointment is to take effect on the termination of his estate. If the donee can appoint any one, it is a **general power**; if the appointment must be to one or all of a certain class of persons, it is **particular**; and in this latter case, if the power is to appoint to *all* of a certain class, the appointment must not be *illusory.* **Power of attorney**: the instrument giving authority to an agent, an attorney in fact, to make contracts or perform legal acts.

Practice Court. v. *Court,* 9.

Præceptores, *l.* Masters in chancery.

Præcipe, *l.* (Command.) An original writ commanding the defendant to do something or show cause to the contrary. **Præcipe in capite**: a præcipe or writ of *right* for a tenant *in capite.* **Præcipe quod reddat** (command that he return): a writ directing the defendant to restore the possession of land, employed at the beginning of a common *recovery*. **Præcipe quod teneat conventionem**: a writ of covenant employed at the beginning of a *fine* of lands. **Tenant to the præcipe**: the person against whom a præcipe was brought; v. *Recovery*.

Præco, *l.* A herald; the crier of a court.

Præd', *l.* For **prædictus**, aforesaid.

Prædium, *l.* Land; an estate. **Prædia belli**: *booty*. **Prædium dominans**, the dominant, **serviens**, the servient, estate in a **prædial servitude**, an *easement* enjoyed by the owners of one estate over another.

Prædial tithes. Such as arise from land. v. *Tithes, Great tithes.*

Præf', *l.* For **præfatus**, aforesaid.

Præmissa, *l.* The premises.

Præmium, *l.* Reward. **Præmium pudicitiæ**: the price of chastity.

Præmunire, *l.* To forewarn, summon. The offence of obeying or furthering other authority in the realm than that of the Crown, particularly that of the Pope; Papal usurpation.

Præpositus, *l.* A person placed in authority; a provost, sheriff. **Præposita negotiis vel rebus domesticis**: set over household matters, a term expressing a wife's authority to bind her husband for necessary purchases.

Prærogativa regis, *l.* The King's prerogative.

Præscriptio, *l.* Prescription. **Præscriptio fori**: an *exception* to the jurisdiction.

Præsens in curia, *l.* Present in court.

Præsentia corporis tollit errorem nominis, *l.* The presence of the body [the person meant] cures an error in the name.

Præstare, *l.* To pay; perform; make good.

Præsumitur pro legitimatione, *l.* The presumption is in favor of legitimacy.

Præsumptio juris, *l.* (Presumption of law.) A presumption of fact, rebuttable. **Præsumptio juris et de jure**: a presumption of law, irrebuttable. To the latter applies the maxim, **Præsumptio juris plena probatio**: a legal presumption of law is full proof; to the former, **Præsumptio valet in lege**: a legal presumption is of weight.

Pratum, *l.* A meadow.

Prava consuetudo, *l.* A bad [illegal] custom.

Praxis judicum interpres legum, *l.* The practice of judges is the interpreter of the laws.

Pray in aid. v. *Aid-prier.*

Prebendary. A stipend (not a benefice or dignity) paid a **prebend,** a member of a collegiate or cathedral church.

Precariæ, preces, *l.* Day's-works, performed for the lord in harvest time by the tenants of certain manors.

Prece partium, *l.* v. *Dies datus;* or prayer of the parties.

Precedent. v. *Condition.* An adjudged case; a recognized method of procedure.

Precept. An order; a written direction in minor process to a sheriff or other officer; a precept of a justice of the peace for the bringing of a person or records before him.

Precludi non debet, *l.* (He ought not to be barred.) The beginning of a replication to a special plea.

Predial. v. *Prædial.*

Pree, *fr.* A meadow.

Premises. (Things put before.) The part of a deed preceding the *habendum.* The place in question; the land or houses granted.

Premium. The money paid by the insured in the contract of insurance. v. *Præmium.*

Prender, *fr.* To take, taking; the power or right of taking a thing before it is offered. Thus a *heriot* is said to lie *in prender* because the lord may seize the identical thing itself; but he may not distrain for it.

Prerogative. A privilege, a royal privilege. v. *Court,* 85; *Writ.*

Pres, *fr.* Near. v. *Cy-près.*

Prescribe. To claim title to incorporeal hereditaments, on grounds of long usage, in one's self, one's ancestors, or grantors, by **prescription** [which differs from **custom,** a local usage not annexed to any particular person]. This prescription is **acquisitive** or **positive prescription,** as distinct from **restrictive** or **negative prescription,** which is the loss of a remedy by lapse of time; outlawry of actions.

Present. 1. To offer a clerk to the bishop for institution in a benefice; v. *Presentation.* 2. To find judicially; v. *Presentment.*

Presentation. The offering of a clerk by the patron to the ordinary for institution in a living; v. *Advowson*. **Nomination** is the appointment of a clerk to the patron to be by him *presented*. A person may have the right of nomination by virtue of a manor, by grant or mortgage of the entire advowson or of the **prochein avoidance**, the next presentation. **Presentative**: v. *Advowson*.

Presentment, presentation. The notice taken by a grand jury of an offence from their own knowledge, without an indictment.

Prest, prist, pret, *fr.* Ready.

Presumptio, *l.*, **Presumption.** v. *Præsumptio*.

Presumptive heir. v. *Heir*.

Pretium, *l.* Price; cost; value; reward. **Pretium affectionis** (the price of affection) : a fancy price. **Pretium periculi**: remuneration for risk. **Pretium succedit in loco rei**: the price succeeds in place of the thing [sold].

Prima facie, *l.* At first appearance, first sight. **Prima tonsura**: the first mowing. **Primæ impressionis** (of first impression) : without precedent; *res nova*.

Primage. A small extra allowance made to the master of a ship for his care and trouble; or to master and mariners for loading and unloading, use of cable, etc. v. *Hat-money*.

Primer, *fr.* First. **Primer fine**: v. *Fine*. **Primer seisin**: a feudal right of the King, when any of his tenants *in capite* died seised of a knight's fee, to receive from the heir, if he were of full age, one year's profits if the lands were in immediate possession, or half a year's profits if they were in reversion expectant on a life estate.

Primitiæ, *l.* The *first fruits*.

Primo venienti, *l.* To the one first coming. An executor anciently paid debts as they were presented, whether the assets were sufficient to meet all debts or not.

Primus inter pares, *l.* First among equals.

Princeps legibus solutus est, *l.* The emperor is unbound by laws.

Principal. Chief, the one commanding; as opposed to *Accessory, agent*. **Principal challenge**: v. *Challenge*.

Principia probant, non probantur, *l.* Principles prove, and are not [to be] proved. **Principiis obsta**: v. *Obsta*. **Principium**: the beginning.

Prior in tempore, potior in jure, *l.* v. *Qui prior,* etc. The one earlier in time has the better right.

Pris, *fr.* Taken. **Prise, prisa,** *l.* : a seizure.

Prisage, *fr.* 1. An ancient right of the Crown to take two tuns of wine out of every ship importing twenty or more. 2. The share of the Crown in prizes captured at sea.

Prisal en auter lieu, *fr.* A taking in another place.

Prist, *fr.* Ready ; an old word in oral pleading expressing a tender or joinder of issue.

Private act, statute. A statute affecting private concerns, of which the courts are not bound to take notice. **Private corporation:** v. *Corporation.* **Private law:** law affecting rights between subject and subject ; v. *Public law, International law.* **Private nuisance:** a nuisance affecting a private person or his estate ; v. *Nuisance.*

Privatum commodum publico cedit, or **Privatum incommodum publico bono pensatur,** *l.* Private advantage must yield to public ; or, the private inconvenience is made up by the public good. **Privatorum pacta,** etc.: v. *Pacta privata,* etc.

Privement enciente, *fr.* Privily [not visibly] pregnant.

Privies: v. *Privity.*

Privilege. A private right or franchise of some particular person or class, against or beyond the course of law. **Writ of privilege:** a writ for a member of Parliament, arrested on a civil suit, to obtain deliverance out of custody.

Privileged communication. 1. A defamatory statement made to another, in pursuance of a duty political, judicial, social, or personal, so that an action for libel or slander will not lie, though the statement be false, unless in the last two cases actual malice be proved in addition. 2. A communication protected from disclosure in a legal proceeding, as one from a client to his counsel. **Privileged debts:** debts which are first paid in full out of a decedent's or insolvent's estate, in preference to all others.

Privilegium clericale, *l.* *Benefit of clergy.* **Privilegium contra rempublicam non valet:** a privilege [excuse] does not avail against the public good.

Privity. Connection; mutuality of interest. The term **privy** is properly used in distinction from **party** ; but **privies to a contract** is used to mean the parties themselves. **Privity of es-**

tate: those interested, or who have been or might have been interested, in the same estate under the same title; as an ancestor, an heir, a grantor or grantee, etc.

Privy. v. *Privity.* **Privy council**: the English royal council, the judicial committee of which acts, or formerly acted, in lunacy, ecclesiastical, and admiralty cases as a court of last appeal; and has power of inquiring into offences against the government; v. *Court*, 6, 14. **Privy seal**: in England, grants and letters pass first under the **privy signet,** kept by a secretary of state; then under the **privy seal,** kept by the **Lord Privy Seal,** usually a baron and member of the Cabinet; and then, if necessary, under the *Great Seal.* **Privy verdict**: one formerly given to the judge out of court, when the jury had agreed after adjournment.

Prize Court. v. *Court*, 92.

Pro, *l.* For; in consideration of; on behalf of; in lieu of. **Pro bono et malo**: for good and evil. **Pro bono publico**: for the public good. **Pro confesso** (for confessed): a decree upon a bill in equity in favor of the plaintiff, when the defendant has not appeared and answered. **Pro consilio impedendo**: for advice to be given. **Pro convicto**: as convicted. **Pro defectu emptorum**: for want of purchasers. **Pro defectu exitus, hæredis**: for failure of issue, for want of an heir. **Pro defectu justitiæ**: for defect of justice. **Pro defendente**: for the defendant. **Pro derelicto**: as abandoned. **Pro diviso**: as divided, in severalty. **Pro domino**: as master. **Pro eo quod cum**: for that whereas. **Pro et durante**: for and during. **Pro falso clamore**: for his false claim; v. *In mercy.* **Pro forma**: as a matter of form. **Pro hac vice** (for this turn): for this particular affair. **Pro indefenso**: as making no defence. **Pro indiviso**: as undivided, in common. **Pro interesse suo**: to the extent of his interest. **Pro læsione fidei**: for breach of faith; v. *Læsione.* **Pro majori cautela**: for greater security. **Pro misis et custagiis**: for costs and charges. **Pro non scripto**: as if not written. **Pro omni servitio**: in lieu of all service. **Pro quer', querente'**: for the plaintiff. **Pro rata**: proportionately. **Pro re nata**: for the immediate occasion. **Pro salute animæ**: for the welfare of the soul. **Pro solido**: for the whole, in a lump. **Pro**

socio: for a partner. **Pro suo**: as one's own. **Pro tanto**: for so much, on the account of. **Pro tempore**: for the time being. **Pro termino vitarum suarum**: for a term of their lives.

Probate. The proof of, or proceedings in proving, a will before the proper authorities; v. *Court*, 25, 51, 79, 110.

Probatio viva, *l.* Proof by living witnesses. **Probatio mortua**: proof by deeds, writings, etc.

Probator, *l.* An *approver*.

Probus et legalis homo, *l.* A good and *lawful* man; free from all exception as a juror or witness.

Procedendo, *l.* 1. A writ to remove a cause, which has been taken to the superior court on *certiorari* or otherwise, back to the inferior court. 2. **Procedendo ad judicium**: a writ issuing from the common-law side of Chancery to a subordinate court which delayed judgment, directing it to give judgment for one side or the other. 3. **Procedendo in loquela**: a writ from the King authorizing the judges to proceed in an action concerning title after an *aid-prayer*. 4. A writ to revive the commission of a justice of the peace, suspended by a *supersedeas*.

Procedure. The formal steps in an action; the rules governing the *process, pleading,* and method of trial, judgment, and execution.

Proces-verbal, *fr.* An inventory; official minutes; a relation of what has been said or done in the presence of an officer, duly attested by him.

Process. 1. The *procedure* or method of getting a defendant into court, the summons, writs, and attachments for that purpose: **original process.** 2. **Mesne process** was formerly process not depending on the original writ, but on interlocutory or collateral matter; but now is commonly used to mean all process before judgment and **final process** [process of execution]; particularly, the *ca. resp.*

Prochein amy, *fr. Next friend.* **Procheyn heire**: next heir. **Prochein avoidance**: v. *Presentation.*

Proclamation. 1. An old writ issuing to the sheriff upon an *exigent* in process of *outlawry*, to make three proclamations to the defendant to yield himself or be outlawed. 2. In chancery practice, a public notice declaring a defendant, who had not appeared upon subpœna and attachment, a rebel if he failed still to appear by a certain day. 3. **Of a fine**: the public notice of a *fine* of lands, given by reading it sixteen times, — four times, within the year after its engrossing, at each assize of the county where the lands lay.

Proctor. The attorney in an admiralty or ecclesiastical court was so called.

Procul dubio, *l.* Without doubt.

Procuratio, *l.,* **Procuration.** Agency; administration of another's affairs on his behalf.

Procurations. Payments made by parish priests to bishops and archdeacons upon their visitations.

Proditorie, *l.* Traitorously; a word technical in indictments for treason.

Productio sectæ, *l.* Production of suit. In old English law, the production by a party of his witnesses; the tender of *suit* to prove his case, preceding the *medial* or proof judgment; the process referred to in the phrase *et inde producit sectam.* v. *Secta, Witness.*

Profert, Profert ad curiam. The production in court by a party of an instrument on which he relies; or the offer to produce, made in the pleading.

Profits à prendre. A right with a profit which one man has in another's land, such as rights of *common*, a right to enter and dig *sand*, etc. **Profits à rendre**: v. *Render;* v. *In prender, render.*

Prohibitio de vasto, *l.* A judicial writ to prohibit waste pending a suit.

Prohibition. A prerogative writ issuing from the King, or a superior court, or Chancery, to restrain proceedings in an inferior, or particularly an ecclesiastical court, for want of jurisdiction.

Proinde, *l.* Therefore.

Proles, *l.* Issue, progeny; lawful issue.

Promissory note. v. *Nota.*

Promoters. 1. Common informers, prosecutors in popular and penal *actions*. 2. The members of a company before its incorporation or charter.

Proof. v. *Half-proof, Full proof.*

Propinquus, *l.* Near; next of kin.

Proponent. In ecclesiastical law, a person propounding an allegation.

Propositus. The person proposed, taken as an example.

Propound. To offer in court; to present a will for probate.

Propre, *fr.* Own; proper. **En propre person:** in [his] proper person.

Proprietas, *l.* Property. **Proprietas plena:** full property, both the title and the beneficial interest. **Proprietas nuda:** naked property, the bare title.

Propria manu, *l.* By his own hand. **Propria persona:** in his own person. **Proprio jure:** by one's own right. **Proprio nomine:** in his own name. **Proprio vigore:** of its own force.

Proprietate probanda. v. *De.*

Propter, *l.* For; on account of. **Propter affectum:** on account of interest; v. *Challenge.* **Propter commodum curiæ:** for the advantage of the court. **Propter curam et culturam:** for care and cultivation. **Propter defectum sanguinis:** for failure of blood; v. *Escheat.* **Propter delictum:** on account of crime; v. *Challenge.* **Propter delictum tenentis:** for crime of the tenant; v. *Escheat.* **Propter honoris respectum:** for respect of rank; v. *Challenge.* **Propter majorem securitatem:** for greater security. **Propter sævitiam, adulterium:** for cruelty, adultery.

Prosecutor. In England, the person instituting a criminal proceeding on behalf of the Crown.

Prosternere, *l.* To throw down, abate. **Prostratus:** abated.

Protectio trahit subjectionem et subjectio protectionem, *l.* The protection [of a sovereign] draws after it subjection, and subjection, protection.

Protection. A prerogative writ granted by the King to a person in his employ, making the latter quit of all suits for a certain time.

Protest. The formal written declaration by a notary of the *dishonor* of a note or bill.

Protestando, *l.* By protesting; words in a *protestation.*

Protestation. A method of informally denying a fact in pleading, so that the pleader would not be estopped from denying it in another action or issue, but not so as to render the plea *double.*

Prothonotary. A chief clerk in the K. B., C. B., or other court.

Prout, *l.* As. **Prout moris est:** as the custom is. **Prout patet per recordum:** as it appears by the record.

Prover. An *approver.*

Provisione legis, *l.* By the provision of law. **Provisione viri:** by provision of the husband; v. *Dower.*

Proviso, *l.* Provided. **Trial by proviso** was where the plaintiff failed to proceed after issue joined; whereupon the defendant took the necessary steps to a trial, issuing the *venire,* etc.

Prox', for **Proximus,** *l.* The next. **Prox' seq', sequente:** next following. **Proximus hæres:** the next heir.

Public act. v. *Private act.* **Public corporation:** v. *Corporation.* **Public law:** the law as between the subject and the sovereign or state; criminal law; v. *International law.* **Public nuisance:** one affecting an indefinite number of persons, not the owner of a particular lot of land; v. *Nuisance.*

Publication. 1. The declaration of a testator that a given writing is intended to operate as his last will. 2. The opening of depositions, taken in Chancery, to the inspection of the parties. 3. The communication of a libellous statement to a third person.

Pueritia, *l.* Childhood; the age from seven to fourteen.

Puis, puys, puz, etc., *fr.* After; since. **Puis darrein continuance:** a plea of new matter arisen since issue joined, since the last *continuance;* a plea to the further maintenance of the action. **Puisne:** younger; junior; later in time; an ordinary judge in bank as distinguished from the chief justice. **Puis que:** after that. **Mulier puisne:** v. *Mulier.*

Puissance, *fr.* Power; authority.

Punctum temporis, *l.* A point of time.

Punica fides, *l.* "Punic faith"; treachery.

Pur, pour, *fr.* For. **Pur auter vie:** For the life of another; v. *Auter, Estate.* **Pur cause de vicinage:** by reason of neighborhood; v. *Common.* **Pur ceo que:** forasmuch as. **Pur tant que:** because; in order that.

Purchase. The acquisition of property by the act of the parties as distinguished from the act of law; by gift, grant, or devise, as distinguished from descent, escheat, or reverter; acquirement, not inheritance. **Words of purchase:** v. *Limitation.*

Purgation. The act of purging one's self of a fault or accusation;

clearing one's self of a crime. **Canonical purgation**: the purgation of a clerk by his own oath, with or without *compurgators*, or by the *corsned;* as distinct from **vulgar purgation**, purgation by the *ordeals* of fire, water, or *battel*.

Purlieu. A place (disforested) on the edge of a *forest*.

Purparty, Purprestura. v. *Pourparty, Pourpresture*.

Purq', purquoy, *fr.* Wherefore.

Pursue. *Sc.*, to prosecute. **Pursuer**: a plaintiff.

Purview (pourvu), *fr.* 1. Provided. 2. The enacting clause of a statute, the body; the scope of the act.

Q.

Q. B. The Queen's Bench. v. *Court of King's Bench, Court*, 8.

Q. C. *Queen's counsel.*

Q. V. (**Quod vide**), *l.* Which see; a reference to another title in a book.

Qua, *l.* As; in the capacity of. *Qua* executor; *as* executor, etc.

Quacunque via data, *l.* Whichever view be taken (way be given).

Quæ ad unum finem locuta sunt non debent ad alium detorqueri, *l.* [Words] which are spoken to one end ought not to be perverted to another. **Quæ est eadem** (which is the same): words used in pleas of justification of trespass, alleging that the trespass justified *is the same* as that of which the plaintiff complains. **Quæ fieri non debent, facta valent**: things which ought not to be done [may yet] be valid when done. **Quæ in testamento ita sunt scripta, ut intelligi non possint, perinde sunt ac si scripta non essent**: things which are so written in a will as not to be intelligible are as if not written at all. **Quæ nihil frustra**: which [requires] nothing [to be done] in vain. **Quæ non valeant singula, juncta, juvant**: [words] which, taken singly, are inoperative, are valid if taken together. **Quæ plura**: a writ like a *melius inquirendum*, but issuing when the escheator had proceeded *virtute officii*, not by *diem clausit extremum*.

Quælibet concessio fortissime contra donatorem interpretanda est, *l.* Every grant is to be interpreted most strongly against the grantor.

Quære, *l.* Inquire; question, doubt. **Quæritur:** it is doubted.

Quærens, *l.* [Properly *querens.*] A plaintiff; suitor. **Quærens nihil capiat,** etc.. v. *Nihil, Nil.* **Quærens non invenit plegium:** a return of the sheriff, that the plaintiff found no security, to a writ containing the *si fecerit* clause.

Quale jus, *l.* An old judicial writ that lay to inquire by what right a clerk had recovered a judgment for land, to see that the statutes of *mortmain* were not evaded.

Qualified fee. v. *Base fee,* 1.

Quamdiu, *l.* As long as. **Quamdiu se bene gesserit:** as long as he shall conduct himself well, during good behavior; like *ad vitam aut culpam,* a kind of tenure of office.

Quando abest provisio partis, adest provisio legis, *l.* When the provision of the party is wanting, the provision of the law is at hand.. **Quando acciderint** (when they shall fall in): a judgment for the creditor of a decedent on a plea of *plene administravit* by the administrator, to be satisfied out of assets which may afterwards come into his hands. **Quando aliquid mandatur, mandatur et omne per quod pervenitur ad illud:** when [the law] commands a thing, it also commands [authorizes] all [means] by which it may be accomplished. **Quando aliquid prohibetur fieri ex directo, prohibetur et per obliquum:** when anything is prohibited to be directly done, doing it indirectly is also forbidden. **Quando aliquis aliquid concedit,** etc.. v. *Cuicunque,* etc. **Quando duo jura concurrunt in una persona, æquum est ac si essent in diversis:** when two rights [titles] unite in one person, it [the law] is the same as if they were in different persons [i. e. he can assert either title separately]. **Quando lex aliquid aliqui concedit:** v. *Cuicunque,* etc. **Quando lex est specialis, ratio autem generalis, generaliter est intelligenda:** when a law is [applied to a] special [case], but its reason general, it should be [applied] understood generally. **Quando licet id quod majus, videtur licere id quod minus:** when the greater is allowed, it seems that the less should also be. **Quando plus fit quam fieri debet, videtur etiam illud fieri quod faciendum est:** when more is done than ought to be done, that which ought to be done is held as done [held good].

Quandocunque, *l.* At whatever time.

Quant, *fr.* When; as; how much. **Quantes fois:** how many times.

Quantum meruit, *l.* (As much as he deserved.) The *common count* for work and labor. **Quantum valebant** (as much as they were worth): the *common count* for goods sold and delivered. **Quantum damnificatus:** an issue to ascertain the amount of damages, directed by Chancery in a court of common law.

Quarantine. Forty days; the period during which dower was to be assigned a widow, and she was allowed to remain in the mansion-house.

Quare, *l.* Wherefore; why. **Quare clausum fregit** (because he broke the close): the action of trespass *vi et armis* for unlawful entry on the plaintiff's land. **Quare ejecit infra terminum** (because he ejected within the term): an action which lay for the ousted tenant of a term to recover it and damages from the feoffee of the wrong-doer, or person claiming under him. **Quare impedit:** a real action to recover an *advowson*, brought by a patron against a bishop or other person hindering his *presentation*. **Quare incumbravit:** a writ for the patron to recover the *presentation* and damages when the bishop had admitted a clerk to the living pending a *quare impedit*, and notwithstanding a *ne admittas*. **Quare non admisit:** a writ for the patron to recover damages from the bishop for not admitting his clerk, after a writ *ad admittendum clericum*. **Quare non permittit:** a writ for him who has the right of nomination against the patron for refusing to present his clerk. **Quare obstruxit:** a writ against a person obstructing a right of way.

Quarter days. In England, the 25th of March, Lady day; the 24th of June, Midsummer day; the 29th of September, Michaelmas day; the 25th of December, Christmas day. In Scotland, the 2d of February, Candlemas; the 15th of May, called Whitsunday; the 1st of August, Lammas day; the 11th of November, Martinmas. **Quarter sessions:** a minor criminal court held quarterly before two or more justices of the peace in each English county; v. *Court*, 40.

Quarto die post, *l.* The fourth day after. v. *Day*.

Quash. (*Casser, fr.*) To break; to annul, abate.

Quasi, *l.* As if; almost; as it were. **Quasi agnum committere lupo:** like handing the lamb over to the wolf.

Que, *fr.* That; who; which; than. **Que est le mesme**: *Quæ est eadem.* **Que estate** (which estate): the estate of whom; a term used in prescribing for easements enjoyed by former owners of the land, whose estate the person averring title now has.

Queen's Bench; *v. Court,* 8. **Queen's counsel**: a *barrister* called within the *bar,* appointed by letters patent to be her Majesty's counsel learned in the law, who has precedence over others, of the outer bar, cannot plead against the Crown without a license, and may wear a silk gown. **Queen's evidence, State's evidence**: evidence given by an accomplice, in capital cases, in the hope of pardon. The admission of Queen's evidence required the sanction, in England, of the justices of gaol delivery; and, if unsatisfactory, the witness was hanged, like the rest. v. *Approver.*

Quer', Querens, *l.* The complainant, plaintiff.

Querela, *l.* A *plaint, count;* a lawsuit.

Questus, *l.* (From *Quærere.*) Acquired, *purchased* land.

Questus est nobis, *l.* (From *Queror.*) He hath complained to us. An old writ of nuisance against him to whom the person levying [erecting] the nuisance had conveyed the land.

Qui, *i.* Who. **Qui approbat non reprobat**: one who approbates [ratifies] cannot reprobate [repudiate, as to a part]. **Qui concedit, etc.**: v. *Cuicunque,* etc. **Qui destruit medium destruit finem**: he who destroys the means destroys the end. **Qui ex damnato coitu nascuntur inter liberos non computantur**: those who are born of an illicit connection are not counted among children. **Qui facit per alium, facit per se**: he who does a thing by another does it himself. **Qui hæret in litera hæret in cortice**: he who sticks at the letter sticks at the rind [goes but skin-deep into the real meaning]. **Qui in jus dominiumve alterius succedit jure ejus uti debet**: he who succeeds to the right or property of another ought to enjoy the other's rights [be in the same legal position]. **Qui jure suo utitur neminem lædit**: he who but exercises his own right injures [legally] no one. **Qui jussu judicis aliquod fecerit non videtur dolo malo fecisse**: one who did a thing by a judge's command is not supposed to have acted from an improper motive. **Qui non habet, etc.**: v. *Nemo dat.* **Qui non habet in crumena [ære] luat in corpore**: he who has not in purse [money] must pay in person. **Qui non prohibet cum prohibere possit, jubet**: he who does not forbid when he can forbid, commands. **Qui peccat ebrius, luat sobrius**: he who sins while drunk must be punished while sober. **Qui per alium**, etc.: v. *Qui facit*, etc. **Qui prior in tempore, potior in jure**: he has the better title who was prior in time. **Qui sentit commodum sentire debet et onus**: he who feels the advantage ought to bear the burden. **Qui tacet consentire videtur**: he who is silent seems to consent. **Qui tam**: v. *Action*. **Qui tardius solvit minus solvit**: he who pays too late does not pay at all. **Qui vult decipi decipiatur**: let him who wishes to be deceived be deceived.

Qui, *fr.* Who. **Qui doit inheriter al père, doit inheriter al fitz**: he who would inherit from the father ought to inherit from the son.

Quia, *l.* Because. **Quia dominus remisit curiam** (because the lord has remitted his court): a phrase used in, and applied to, a writ of *right* brought originally in the King's court, and not in the manorial court. **Quia emptores**: the Statute of Westminster III., 18 Edw. I. c. 1, by which subinfeudation was abrogated; providing that owners of freehold land might freely sell their lands, but that the grantee should hold of the lord paramount, as did the grantor, and by the same services. **Quia erronice emanavit**: because it issued erroneously. **Quia timet**: v. *Bill*, I. 14.

Quicquid plantatur solo solo cedit, *l.* Whatever is planted in the soil belongs thereto. **Quicquid solvitur solvitur secundum modum solventis**: whatever is paid is to be applied according to the intention of the payer; v. *Application of payments*.

Quid, *l.* What. **Quid pro quo**: something for something.

Quietantia, *l.* An *acquittance*.

Quietus, *l.* Quit; an acquittance; a discharge. **Quieta clamantia**: quitclaim. **Quieti reditus**: quitrents; v. *Assize*. **Quietum clamare**: to quitclaim.

Quilibet potest renunciare juri pro se introducto, *l.* Any one may waive a right introduced for his own benefit.

Quinque portus, *l.* The *Cinque-ports*.

Quinto exactus, *l.* (Five times called.) A return of a sheriff after the fifth and last *proclamation* in *outlawry*.

Quitclaim. A deed of *release,* or discharge of claim; a deed without a *warranty.*

Quitrent: v. *Assize, Chief rents.*

Quivis præsumitur bonus donec probetur contrarium, *l.* Every one is presumed innocent until the contrary is proved.

Quo animo, *l.* With what intention, motive. **Quo jure** (by what title): a writ for one against another claiming common of pasture in his land. **Quo minus** (by which, not): words at the beginning of the old writs in Exchequer, suggesting the fiction that the plaintiff was the King's debtor. **Quo warranto** (by what warrant): an old prerogative writ of right for the King against one who usurped an office, franchise, or title, requiring him to show his authority. **Information in the nature of a quo warranto:** originally a criminal information for the wrongful use of a franchise, is now the usual civil method for trying the title to public or corporate offices.

Quoad hoc, *l.* As to this, as far as this is concerned.

Quod ab initio non valet, in tractu temporis non convalescet, *l.* What is void in the beginning does not become valid by lapse of time. **Quod ædificatur in area legata cedit legato:** things erected on devised land go to the devisee. **Quod approbo,** etc.: v. *Qui approbat.* **Quod breve cassetur** (that the bill be quashed): the form of judgment on a plea in *abatement.* **Quod computet** (that he account): the interlocutory judgment in an action of *account.* **Quod concessum fuit:** which was granted. **Quod contra legem fit pro infecto habetur:** that which is done contrary to law is held as not done at all. **Quod cum:** that whereas. **Quod curia concessit:** which the court granted. **Quod ei deforceat** (that he deforces him): a writ for the owner of a particular estate who had lost his lands by default on a *præcipe quod reddat.* **Quod fieri,** etc.: v. *Fieri,* etc. **Quod initio,** etc.. v. *Quod ab initio,* etc. **Quod meum est sine facto meo vel defectu meo amitti vel in alium transferri non potest:** what is once mine cannot be transferred to another without my act or default. **Quod non apparet,** etc.: v. *Idem est,* etc. **Quod non habet principium, non habet finem:** that which has not a beginning has not an end. **Quod nota:** which note [take note of]. **Quod nullius est,** that which has no owner, **est domini regis,**

belongs to the King; id ratione naturali occupanti conceditur, is by natural right yielded to the [first] occupant. Quod partes replacitent: that the parties plead over. Quod partitio fiat: that a partition be made. Quod permittat: a writ for the heir of one disseised of common of pasture against the heir of his disseisor. Quod permittat prosternere: an old writ of right commanding the defendant to *permit* the plaintiff to *abate* a nuisance. Quod pure debetur præsenti die debetur: what is due unconditionally is due to-day. Quod recuperet (that be recover): the ordinary form of judgment for the plaintiff. Quod redeat inde quietus in perpetuum, et querens in misericordia: that he go thence forever quit, and the plaintiff be *in mercy*. Quod remedio destituitur, ipsa re valet, si culpa absit: in matters where there is no remedy, a thing may become valid by a mere act, provided there be no wrong. The doctrine of *remitter* and other extra-judicial remedies. Quod respondeat, etc.: v. *Respondeat*, etc. Quod salvum fore receperint: which they received for safe keeping. Quod semel meum est amplius meum esse non potest: that which is once mine cannot be more fully mine. Quod semel placuit in electionibus amplius displicere non potest: election once made cannot be revoked. Quod si contingat: that if it happen. Quod stet prohibitio: that the prohibition continue. Quod voluit non dixit: whatever he meant, he did not express it. Quod vide: which see.

Quodque dissolvitur, etc., Quomodo quid, etc. v. *Eodem*, etc.

Quorum, *l.* Of whom, of which; whereof. Justices of the quorum: certain *justices of the peace* were so named, without the presence of one of whom no other justices could act, in certain cases.

Quoties in verbis nulla ambiguitas est, ibi nulla expositio contra verba fienda est, *l.* As long as there is no ambiguity in the words, no interpretation should be made contrary to them.

Quousque, *l.* Until, as long as.

Quovis modo, *l.* In whatever manner.

Quum, *l.* When. v. *Cum, Quando.*

R.

R. G., Regulæ Generales, *l.* General orders, rules.

Rack rent. A rent of the full value of the tenement.

Ran, *sax.,* **Rapina,** *l.* Open theft, robbery.

Raptus, *l.* Rape; abduction. **Rapuit:** he ravished.

Ratihabitio mandato æquiparatur, *l.* Ratification is held equal to a command.

Ratio, *l.* Reason. **Ratio decidendi:** the grounds of decision. **Ratio legis:** the reason [occasion] of the law. **Ratione contractus:** by reason of the contract; **impotentiæ,** inability, impotence; **tenuræ,** of tenure, etc.

Rationabilis, *l.* Reasonable; v. *Dos, De rationabili.*

Ratum, *l.* Held good, valid.

Ravishment de gard. v. *De raptu hæredis.*

Re, *l.* In the case [of]. In place of. v. *Rem, Res.* **Re. fa. lo.:** *Recordari facias loquelam.*

Re, *fr.* King. **Real:** royal.

Real. v. *Personal.* **Real action, chattels, contract:** v. *Action, Chattels, Contract.*

Reasonable part. One third share of a man's goods which went to his wife, another to his children, and another to his executor, at common law. v. *De rationabili parte bonorum.*

Reassurance. The insurance of property insured, made by the first insurer to protect himself.

Rebellion. v. *Commission,* 8.

Rebus integris, *l.* The circumstances complete [yet unchanged].

Rebutter. v. *Pleading.*

Recaption. 1. A retaking, reprisal; as of stolen goods. 2. A second distress upon one formerly distrained for the same cause. 3. A writ for the party so distrained, for damages.

Receipt. v. *Court,* 11. One side of the Exchequer. **Receipt,** in contracts of sale; the actual receipt of the goods, the transfer of possession; as distinguished from **acceptance,** which is the transfer of title, not necessarily of the goods.

Receiptor. A person, usually a friend of the debtor, to whose safe keeping a sheriff commits goods *attached.*

Receiver. 1. One who knowingly receives, and keeps or disposes of, stolen goods. 2. A managing trustee appointed by a court of equity to take charge of a railway or other property pending suit.

Recens insecutio, secta, *l.*   *Fresh suit.*

Recessus, *l.*   Egress.   **Recessus maris:** reliction of the sea.

Recognitio, *l.*, **Recognition.**   An inquiry, conducted by a chosen body of men, not sitting as part of the court, into the facts in dispute in a case at law; these **recognitors** preceded the jurymen of modern times, and reported their **recognition** or verdict to the court.   An *inquisition* was held by the court itself, as recognitors.

Recognizance.   1. A *recognition*, the verdict of an assize.   2. An acknowledgment of a past debt, made upon record, with or without sureties [or by sureties for a defendant's appearance], made to be void on the happening of a condition.   It existed at common law, and by the *Statutes Merchant* and *Staple.*

Recognize.   To make recognition; to examine as an *assize.*   To acknowledge.

Record.   1. A court having power to fine or imprison for contempt; a court of which the proceedings were entered in writing (formerly on parchment), a copy of which was conclusive evidence of the fact of such proceedings at another trial; a King's court as distinct from a subject's; v. *Court,* 117.   2. An enrolment or memorandum made in a court or registry, formerly necessarily on parchment.   3. Anciently, the proceedings of a court, although oral; or a plea thereof.   4. The official instrument containing an account of the proceedings in a court of justice, the history of the case; v. *Nisi prius.*   **Trial by record:** when the issue turns upon a record, and is tried by the inspection of the court without witness or jury.   Anciently (v. *Record,* 3), by the proceedings in a previous action as proved orally by witnesses.   **Matter of record:** matter evidenced by record, and which can therefore be proved and disproved only by the record itself or an authorized copy.

Recordari facias loquelam, *l.*   An old writ issuing for the plaintiff or defendant, in a suit brought in a county court, directing the sheriff to *cause the plaint to be recorded,* and to remove it to one of the courts at Westminster; v. *Court,* 29.

Recoupe, *fr.*   To defalk, discount, deduct.

Recoupment. A deduction made for a past claim in satisfying a present demand, both claims arising in the same matter, therein differing from *Set-off*. **Discount**: a present deduction made in satisfying a future claim.

Recourse, without. A qualified *indorsement ;* an assignment without assuming liability as an *indorser*.

Recovery. 1. A true recovery, the recovery of a thing or its value by judgment in court. 2. **A feigned recovery**, or **Common recovery**: a method by which a tenant in tail conveyed his estate in fee simple; the recoveror, the person to whom it was to be conveyed, bringing a *præcipe quod reddat* against the tenant, who defended his title by **vouching** [calling] a man of straw to warrant, asserting that the latter had conveyed to him; and upon the default of the **vouchee** (usually the court crier, the **common vouchee**), which always happened after leave was given the recoveror to **imparl** with him, the recoveror had judgment against the tenant, who in turn had a nominal remedy that he recover lands of equal value from the vouchee. A recovery by **double voucher** was where the estate was first conveyed to some indifferent person, the **tenant to the præcipe**, against whom the *præcipe* was brought, and who vouched the real tenant, who in turn vouched the common vouchee.

Recto, de. Of right; writ of *right*. **Recto sur disclaimer**: a writ of *right* issuing for the lord upon *disclaimer* by the tenant. **Rectum**: right. v. *De*.

Rector. A parson; a clerk having full possession of a living and tithes; as distinguished from a **vicar**, where there has been an *appropriation* or *impropriation* of the *prædial tithes*, and who is as it were the curate of the appropriator, though not removable at his caprice, by Stat. 4 Hen. IV. c. 12; and now commonly the vicarage is endowed. **Perpetual curate**: the minister of a parish exempted from the operation of 4 Hen. IV. c. 12. Now all parish priests, not *rectors*, are called *vicars ;* 31 & 32 Vict. c. 117; and a **curate** can mean only a vicar's or rector's salaried assistant.

Rectus in curia, *l.* Right in court, cleared of all charges or contempts.

Red Book of the Exchequer. An ancient collection of records and miscellaneous manuscripts in the Exchequer.

Reddendum, *l.* (Rendering) the clause in a charter of feoffment, deed, or lease, specifying the rents or services. **Reddere:** to render, yield, return. **Reddidit se:** he rendered himself [in discharge of his bail].

Redemption. v. *Equity of.* The process of defeating a mortgagor's title by fulfilment of the condition; or by a bill in equity after breach thereof.

Redeundo, *l.* Returning, while going back.

Redisseisin. A new disseisin by a person previously adjudged a disseisor, for which he was liable in double damages.

Reditus albi, nigri, *l.* White rents, black rents. v. *Black mail,* 2. **Reditus capitales:** *chief* rents, rents of *assize.* **Reditus quieti:** *quitrents.* **Reditus siccus:** *rent seck.*

Reduction into possession. 1. Of *choses in action.* 2. The taking possession by the husband of the wife's goods, so as to make them his. v. *Equity, wife's.*

Reeve, *sax. Gerefa.* A ministerial officer.

Referendo singula singulis, *l.* (Referring singles to singles.) Making proper application respectively.

Reg. gen. *Regula generalis.* **Reg. Jud.:** Register of Judicial *writs.* **Reg. lib.:** the Registrar's book in Chancery, containing all decrees. **Reg. Orig.:** Register of Original *writs.*

Regalia, *l.* Royal rights or prerogatives. **Regalia majora:** such as are part of the King's sovereignty, inseparable; **minora,** such as are created or conferred upon him.

Regard. v. *Court,* 76. One of the old *Forest* courts.

Regardant. Annexed to the land or manor. v. *Villein.*

Rege inconsulto, *l.* (The King not advised.) A writ directing judges not to proceed in a cause which might prejudice the King's interests, without advising him thereof.

Regia via, *l.* The royal [high] way.

Regiam majestatem, *l.* An ancient treatise on Scottish law resembling Glanvil.

Registrum brevium, *l.* A register of the original (*Reg. Orig.*) and judicial (*Reg. Jud.*) writs used in the law, first compiled in the reign of Edward I., and preserved in Chancery. v. *Fitzherbert.*

Regrating. Speculating in provisions. The offence of buying provisions at a market for the purpose of reselling them within four miles of the place.

Regula est, etc. v. *Ignorantia facti,* etc.

Regulæ generales, *l.* The general rules and orders issued from time to time by the judges of the English courts.

Regular clergy. Monks living in societies, as distinguished from the **secular** clergy, the parish priests.

Rehabere facias seisinam, *l.* A writ to cause the sheriff to re-deliver seisin, who ₁had seised the defendant of too much land under a *habere facias seisinam.*

Rei, *l.* v. *Res, Reus.*

Rejoinder. The defendant's second pleading. v. *Pleading.*

Relatio semper fiat ut valeat dispositio, *l.* Reference should be so made that the disposition may be valid.

Relaxare, *l.* To release. **Relaxavi:** I have released.

Relator. The person upon whose complaint an *information* or *quo warranto* is filed.

Release. A conveyance wherein the releasor yields his right or estate to a person already having some estate or possession in the lands. A *secondary* conveyance, which may enure either (1.) by passing the estate (**mitter l'estate**), where a fee-simple will pass without any words of *limitation,* as from one joint ten-ant or coparcener to another; (2.) by passing the right (**mitter le droit**), where words of limitation are not necessary, and there is no *privity* of estate, as from a disseisee to a disseisor; (3.) by extinguishment, as of a seigniorial right, or right of reversion; (4.) by enlarging a particular estate (**enlarger l'estate**); (5.) by entry and feoffment, as where one of two disseisors releases to the other.

Relicta verificatione. v. *Cognoscere, Cognovit.*

Reliction. The receding of the sea, whereby land is left dry.

Relevamen, relevium, *l.,* **Relief.** 1. A fine paid by the heir of a deceased tenant in chivalry for "taking up" the feud. 2. The specific assistance sought by a plaintiff in equity.

Rem. Thing. **Rights ad rem:** v. *Jura ad rem, Ad rem.*

Remainder. A future estate at common law, created to take effect after the end of a previous estate, which is called the **particular estate.** A **vested remainder** is a future estate given to some certain person or persons, which is to take effect immediately on determination of the particular estate, and must be ready at all times to take effect, (if not divested, as by death of the remainderman,) upon the determination of the particular estate in any way; and which must take effect at some time, if not divested. A **contingent remainder** is one which does not fulfil these conditions, because it depends upon an event which may never happen, or may not happen before the determination of the particular estate, or because the person to take the remainder is uncertain, or not in being. A **remainder limited by way of use** is when a future use is so limited that it might take effect as a *remainder;* in which case it is so considered; and the use becomes subject to the laws which govern remainders at common law.

Remanentia, Remanere, *l.* A remainder.

Remanet, *l.* A cause postponed to the next term. **Remanent pro defectu emptorum** (they remain for lack of purchasers): a sheriff's return to a writ of *fi. fa.* that he has been unable to sell the goods distrained.

Remitter. The doctrine by which a disseisee having good title, who acquires a later defective title and enters under it, is remitted to his original good title and deemed to hold thereby, free of incumbrances by the disseisor. v. *Quod remedio,* etc.

Remittit damna, *l.* The entry of the plaintiff on the record that he remits part of the damages awarded him by the verdict. **Remittitur**: the sending back of a record from a superior to an inferior court for entry of judgment, new trial, or other proceedings.

Remoteness. v. *Perpetuity.*

Remoto impedimento, emergit actio, *l.* The bar being removed, the action arises.

Render, *fr.* v. *Prender.* To yield; pay; return; used of rents, profits, or services which the tenant had to *render,* not the landlord to *take.*

Renounce probate. To refuse to act as executor under a will.

Rent. A certain amount of money, goods, or services rendered to the lord by the tenant in acknowledgment of tenure and compensation for his possession. If the **grantor** of the land have a reversion and may distrain, it is **rent service**; if he have no reversion, but may nevertheless distrain by special clause in the grant, it is **rent charge**; if he have no reversion nor right of distraint, it is **rent seck.** *Black* rent, *Chief* rent, *Fee-farm* rents, *Rack* rents, *White* rents, rents of *assize:* see those titles.

Reo absente, *l.* In the absence of the defendant.

Reparatione facienda, *l.* A writ to force the owner or part owner of property to make repairs.

Repellitur a sacramento infamis, *l.* An infamous person is (repelled from) refused the oath.

Repetitum namium, *l.* A repeated or counter distress, *withernam.*

Repleader. To plead the case over again, as when no satisfactory issue has been reached.

Replegiare, *l.,* **Replevir** *fr.* To take back on pledge; replevy. **Replegiare de averiis:** *replevin* of cattle. **Replegiari facias:** the original writ in replevin.

Replevin. An action for the specific recovery of cattle or goods distrained or taken. The **replevisor** or plaintiff gives pledges or bond to prosecute and return the goods if judgment be given against him; whereupon the sheriff seizes the goods, and the plaintiff brings his action, to which the defendant makes *avowry* or *conusance* in the nature of a declaration setting up his title; and the following pleading of the plaintiff is called the *plea,* and so on. This is replevin in the **detinuit;** replevin in the **detinet** was where there was no reseizure of the goods, as if they had been *eloigned.* v. *Capias in withernam.* **Personal replevin:** an action or writ to review an imprisonment and enforce rights of personal liberty, like the old writ *de homine replegiando.*

Replication. The plaintiff's second pleading. v. *Pleading.*

Reprobata pecunia liberat solventem, *l.* Money refused releases the payer [person tendering it].

Requests. v. *Court,* 63. **Letters of request:** v. *Letters.*

Res, *l.* Thing; case; matter; affair; subject; circumstance. **In re:** in a thing, in the matter of; v. *In re, Jura in re;* a real right, right of ownership or dominion. **Ad rem:** to a thing, a personal right; against the thing, an action determining property: v. *Actio, Ad rem, Jura.* **In rem:** like *ad rem;* v. *In rem;* against the thing, not against the person. **Res accessoria,** etc.: v. *Accessorium non ducit,* etc. **Res aliena:** the property of another. **Res caduca:** an escheat. **Res communes:**

things common [of common property]. **Res corporales:** corporeal things. **Res gestæ** (things done): the circumstances of the transaction. **Res integra** (an affair untouched): a new matter. **Res inter alios acta alteri nocere non debet:** a transaction between other parties ought not to injure one. **Res inter alios:** the acts of strangers. **Res ipsa loquitur:** the matter speaks for itself. **Res judicata:** an adjudged matter. **Res judicata pro veritate accipitur:** a judgment is taken for truth. **Res nullius:** the property of nobody. **Res nova:** a new matter. **Res perit domino** (the thing perishes to the owner): the loss falls upon the owner. **Res publica:** the common weal, the republic. **Res publicæ:** the commonwealth. **Res quotidianæ:** every-day matters. **Res sua nemini servit:** no man can have a servitude over his own property. **Res transit cum suo onere:** the thing passes with its burden [the incumbrance is transferred with it].

Resceit. The admission of a third party to defend his own interest, as the reversioner in an action against the tenant.

Rescissory. v. *Action*.

Rescous, *fr.* Rescue; the forcible taking of goods distrained, or delivery of a prisoner.

Rescript. The answer of a Roman Emperor when consulted on a difficult question of law. In American States, the written statement by the court of the grounds of the judgment on a point of law.

Rescutere, *l.* To rescue. **Rescussit:** he rescued.

Residuary. Of the residue. v. *Legacy*.

Resoluto jure concedentis, resolvitur jus concessum, *l.* When the assignor's right expires, the interest assigned comes to an end.

Resolutive, resolutory. Having the effect of ending. v. *Condition*.

Reson, *fr.* Truth; right; reason.

Respectus, *l.* Respite; delay.

Respondeat ouster, *l. & fr.* (Let him answer further.) The judgment for the plaintiff on a plea in abatement, that the defendant answer over. **Respondeat superior:** let the master answer.

Respondent. A defendant; an appellee.

Respondentia. A loan like *bottomry*, but secured upon the ship's cargo, and for which the borrower or master becomes liable personally if the goods are saved.

Respondes oustre, *fr.* Answer over.

Responsa prudentum, *l.* The opinions of Roman lawyers given as experts.

Responsalis, *l.* One who answered for another; an attorney.

Restitutio in integrum, *l.* Restitution to the original condition.

Restitution. A writ issued in favor of a successful plaintiff in error, to restore to him all he has lost by the judgment. **Restitution of conjugal rights**: a suit in the English ecclesiastical courts by one party to a marriage, to compel the other to live with him or her.

Rests. Periodical balancings of an account made for the purpose of converting interest into principal, and charging the party liable thereon with compound interest.

Resulting trust or use. One raised by equitable doctrines; or by implication, as on the expiration of a previous trust, or before the beginning of another. v. *Trust*.

Retainer. The payment by an executor of a debt due him from the estate, in preference to other debts of equal degree. The engagement of counsel by a party or attorney. A preliminary fee or honorarium.

Retorna brevium, *l.* (The return of writs.) The third day in the term.

Retour sans protêt, *fr.* A direction by the drawer to have a bill returned, if dishonored, without protest, and **sans frais,** without charges.

Retraxit, *l.* An open and voluntary renunciation by a plaintiff of his suit, differing from a *Nol. pros.* in that it is a bar to any other suit for the same cause.

Retro, *l.* Back; backward.

Rettare, *l.,* **Retter,** *fr.* To accuse, charge with a crime.

Rettum, *l.* An accusation, a charge.

Return. The act of a sheriff in returning a writ to the court issuing it, after execution or attempt to execute. The indorsement made upon the writ, stating how he has executed, or failed to execute it. **Return days**: fixed days in the term on which the return of writs was required to be made. v. *Replevin*.

Reus, *l.* A defendant; a person guilty.

Reve. v. *Reeve.* **Reve mote:** the sheriff's court.

Reversion. The returning of a feud to the Crown (now called *escheat*), or of a fee to the lord granting it; or, in modern times, of any property to the grantor of a common-law estate in it, after the determination of the estate. The residue of the estate, left in the grantor, to commence in possession after the determination of some particular estate granted out of it by him.

Review. v. *Bill,* I. 16; *Commission,* 9.

Revivor. v. *Bill,* I. 17.

Rex, *l.,* **Re,** *fr.* The King; a king. **Rex non potest peccare:** the king can do no wrong. **Rex nunquam moritur:** the King never dies. **Rex non debet esse sub homine, sed sub Deo et lege:** the King ought not to be subject to men, but to God and the law.

Rhodian law. The oldest collection of maritime law. Also, a name given to a more modern code, of later and spurious origin.

Rien, riens, *fr.* Nothing; not. **Rien culp.:** not guilty. **Rien dit:** says nothing, *nil dicit.* **Rien luy doit:** *nil debet.* **Riens en arriere:** nothing in arrear; a plea in *account* or *replevin.* **Riens lour deust:** not their debt; v. *Nil debet.* **Riens passa par le fait** (nothing passed by the deed): a plea against a person setting up a deed acknowledged or enrolled in court, where the plea of *non est factum* was not allowed. **Riens per descent:** nothing by descent, a plea by an heir sued for his ancestor's debt.

Right. Direct; lineal; next [heir].

Right, writ of. In general, a writ brought upon title to' recover the *full right* to a thing; a writ *droitural,* not *possessory.* Particularly, the writ for a tenant in fee to recover lands and tenements, counting upon his own title as superior to that of his adversary, the chief real action. This was a writ **patent** as, distinguished from a **writ of right close,** which lay either for a tenant *in capite;* or for tenants in *ancient demesne,* or their lords, about lands, rents, or services. So a **writ of right of advowson, dower** (where a widow endowed had been disseised), etc.: v. *Advowson, Dower, De dote, Search, Way, Bill,* II. 4.

Riot. A breach of the peace by three or more persons; v. *Affray, Assembly.* **Riot Act:** 1 Geo. I. st. 2, ch. 5.

Ripa, *l.* The bank of a river. **Riparia**: a river.

Rite, *l.* In due form; properly; legally.

Rixatrix, *l.* A scold.

Robaria, roberia, *l.* **Robbery.** v. *Larceny.*

Roigne, reine, *fr.* The Queen.

Roman law. The law as established by Justinian, the *civil law.* The law of the Romans.

Romescot. *Peter's pence.*

Roup, *sc.* An auction, a sale by auction.

Rout. An incipient *riot;* a meeting of three or more to do an unlawful act for a common grievance.

Roy, roi, re, *fr.* The King. **Roy n'est lié per ascun statute, si il ne soit expressement nosmé:** the King is bound by no statute unless he be expressly mentioned.

Royal court. v. *Court,* 115. The courts at Westminster. **Royal fish**: whales and sturgeons, which belonged to the King if cast ashore. **Royal mines**: mines of gold and silver.

Rule. An order of court. **Rule absolute, nisi:** v. *Absolute.* **Rule in Shelley's Case**: v. *Shelley's Case.* **Rules of a prison**: limits within which prisoners in civil suits might live, if they gave security not to escape.

Running with the land. v. *Covenant.* **Running days:** *lay days.*

Rusticum judicium, *l.* A rude judgment. The judgment of Admiralty, dividing the damages caused by a collision between the two ships.

S.

S. For *Salutem, Scilicet.* **S. C.:** same case. **S. P.:** *sine prole.* **S. V.:** *sub voce.*

Sac. The liberty of holding pleas and amercements; the jurisdiction of a franchise or manor court. **Soc:** the money paid therefor, or for exemption therefrom.

Sacaburth, saccabor, *sax.* A person from whom a thing had been stolen, and who freshly pursued the thief.

Sacher, *fr.* To know. **Sachent:** let them know. **Sachez:** know ye.

Sacramentum, *l.*   An oath ; a juror's oath.

Sacrilege.   Larceny or other trespass in a church.

Sæpius requisitus, *l.*   Often required, requested.

Sævitia, *l.*   Cruelty ; cruel treatment.

Safeguard.   A writ under the great seal, giving strangers license and protection in the realm.

Safe pledge.   A sufficient surety, *salvus plegius.*

Saisina, *l.   Seisin.*

Salic law.   The earliest barbarian code, dating from the fifth century, compiled under Pharamond, King of the Franks.

Salicetum, *l.*   A willow wood ; an osier bed.   .

Salina, *l.*   A salt-pit.

Salus populi suprema lex, *l.*   The welfare of the people is the supreme law.

Salutem, *l.*   Greeting ; a formal word beginning writs.

Salva gardia, *l.*   Safeguard.

Salvage.   A compensation allowed to persons who have saved or aided in saving ships or cargo from actual loss after wreck, or from impending danger, whether from fire, pirates, enemies, or the ordinary perils of the sea.

Salvo, *l.*   Saving, except ; safely.   **Salvo jure cujuslibet:** saving the rights of any and all.   **Salvo me et hæredibus meis:** except me and my heirs.   **Salvo pudore :** saving modesty.

Salvus plegius, *l.*   A satisfactory pledge ; a surety anciently required for the defendant's appearance.

Sanctio, *l.*   A sanction ; the part of laws prescribing a reward or penalty.   **Sanctio justa, jubens honesta et prohibens contraria :** a just sanction, authorizing what is right and forbidding what is not.

Sanctuary.   A consecrated or privileged place, wherein no arrest could be made.   v. *Abjuration of the realm.*

Sane, *fr.*   Sound.

Sanæ mentis, *l.*   Of sound mind.

Sanguis, *l.,* **Sang, sank,** *fr.*   Blood ; consanguinity.

Sans, *fr.*   Without.   **Sans ceo que:** without this, that ; v. *Traverse, special.*   **Sans jour:** without *day.*   **Sans nombre:** without number ; v. *Common.*   **Sans recours:** without recourse ; v. *Indorsement.*

Sapiens incipit a fine, et quod primum est in intentione

ultimum est in executione, *l.* A wise man begins with the end, and what is first in intention is last in execution.

Sart. A piece of woodland turned into arable. v. *Assartare.*

Satius est petere fontes quam sectari rivulos, *l.* It is better to seek the fountains than to follow out the streams.

Saunk, Sauns. v. *Sang, Sans.*

Saver default, *fr.* To excuse a default.

Sc. For *Scilicet,* to wit.

Scaccarium, *l.* Exchequer; the Exchequer. v. *Court,* 11.

Scan. mag., Scandalum magnatum, *l.* The slander of great men; as a peer, noble, or judge, which formerly made the slanderer liable to a special action on the case.

Scaver, Scavoir, *fr.* To know.

Sci. fa. *Scire facias.*

Sciant præsentes et futuri, *l.* Know all men present and to come. **Sciendum est:** it is to be known [understood].

Sciens et prudens, *l.* Wittingly; in full knowledge. **Scienti et volenti non fit injuria:** no legal wrong may be done to one who knows and wills it. **Scientia utriusque par pares contrahentes facit:** equal knowledge on both sides makes the contracting parties equal.

Scienter. Knowingly; a term used to express that the defendant was aware of circumstances, knowledge of which is necessary to make him liable; as that a dog was *ad mordendum assuetus.*

Scilicet, *l.* To wit; that is to say.

Scintilla, *l.* Spark. **Scintilla juris:** a particle of right.

Scire debes cum quo contrahes, *l.* You ought to know with whom you contract. **Scire facias** (that you cause to know); the name of a writ founded upon matter of record, and requiring the defendant to show cause why the plaintiff should not take advantage of it; most frequently brought to revive a judgment, or enforce a recognizance. Also, an interlocutory process, as to give notice in various cases. **Scire feci** (I have given notice): the return of a sheriff to a *scire facias.* **Scire fieri inquiry:** when a sheriff returned *nulla bona* to a *fieri facias de bonis testatoris,* without also returning *devastavit,* this writ issued to make inquiry as to what had become of the testator's goods.

Sciregemot, scyregmot, *sax.* The county *court.* v. *Court,* 29.

Scot. A tax, contribution. **Scot-ale:** *Gildale.*

Scribere est agere, *l.* To write is to act.

Scroll. An *escrow;* a rolled writing. A flourish or ornament.

Scutagium, *l.,* **Scutage.** *Escuage.* A payment in commutation of military services.

Scutum, *l.* A shield ; a pent-house.

Scutifer. An esquire.

Se, *fr.* If. **Se,** *l.* Himself; itself; themselves. **Se defendendo:** in defending himself ; v. *Homicide.*

Sea letter. A *manifest,* particularly in time of war ; a ship's passport.

Search, right of. The right of belligerent powers to search neutral vessels for contraband goods or enemy's property. **Search-warrant:** is granted by a justice of the peace for the searching of a house, shop, or other premises, for stolen or unlawful goods.

Sec, seck, *fr.* Dry; barren. v. *Rent.*

Second deliverance. A writ for the plaintiff in replevin, after judgment for a return on default or nonsuit, to have the goods again on his giving the same security as before. **Second surcharge:** a writ for surcharging a common against the same defendant against whom *admeasurement of pasture* has been had.

Secondary. v. *Conveyance, Evidence.*

Secta, *l.* Suit. Suit at court, attendance at court. The witnesses of a party in ancient procedure. v. *Witness, Compurgatores.* **Secta ad molendinum** (suit to a mill) : a writ against persons who were bound by tenure or custom to bring their corn to a certain mill to be ground. So **Secta ad furnum, torrale :** suit to a [public] oven, kiln, or malt-house. **Secta curiæ** (suit of court) : the attendance in the lord's court, to which a feudal tenant was anciently bound.

Sectator, *l.* A suitor ; one bound *ad sectam curiæ.*

Section. In American land law, one square mile, one thirty-sixth of a township.

Secundum, *l.* According to; in favor of; near. **Secundum æquum et bonum :** according to what is just and good. **Secundum allegata et probata :** according to what is alleged and proved. **Secundum consuetudinem manerii :** according to the custom of the manor. **Secundum formam chartæ, doni, statuti :** according to the form of the deed, gift, statute. **Secundum legem communem Angliæ :** according to the common law of England. **Secundum naturam, normam legis**: according to nature, the rule of law. **Secundum subjectam materiam**: according to the subject matter.

Securitate pacis, *l.* An old writ " for security of the peace " for one who was threatened by another.

Securus, *l.* Safe; sure. **Securitas**: surety.

Secus, *l.* Otherwise; contrary.

Sed, *l.* But. **Sed non allocatur**: but it is not allowed. **Sed per curiam**: but, by the court.

Sedato animo, *l.* With settled purpose.

Sedente curia, *l.* The court sitting; during the sitting of the court. **Sederunt**: in Scotland, the session of a court.

Sedes, *l.* A see; the dignity of a bishop.

Sedition. An offence, tending towards treason, but wanting the overt act.

See. A bishop's dignity or jurisdiction. **See**, *fr.*. seat.

Seigneur, seignior, *fr.* A lord; a master, owner.

Seigniory. A lordship; a manor. **Seigniory in gross**: a lordship independent of a manor; as the King's seigniory over tenants *in capite.*

Seised. Possessed of land under claim of a freehold interest. **Seisin**: seisin in fact, actual possession, investiture of a freehold. **Seisin in law**: the estate of a person having a freehold interest, while dispossessed or before entry. **Seised in his demesne as of fee**: holding a fee simple, in a corporeal hereditament, of the superior lord; v. *Livery, Feoffment.*

Seisina, *l.* Seisin. **Seisina facit stipitem** (seisin makes stock): the seisin determines the root of descent; v. *Possessio fratris*, etc. The old law by which descent was traced from the person last *seised in fact;* v. *Non jus*, etc.

Seized, seizin, etc. *Seised, seisin.*

Semb., Semble, *fr.* It seems. An expression applied to an *obiter dictum* by the judge, or a suggestion by the reporter.

Semblable, *fr.* Similar; like. **Semblement** (*Similiter*): likewise.

Semer, *fr.* To sow. **Seme**: sown.

Semi-plena probatio, *l. Half-proof.*

Semper, *l.* Always. **Semper in obscuris quod minimum est sequimur**: in things obscure we always follow the least obscure. **Semper paratus**: always (prepared) ready; v. *Tout temps prist*. **Semper præsumitur pro negante**: the presumption is always in favor of the one denying.

Senate. v. *Court*, 103.

Senatus consultum, *l.* A decree of the senate; one of the chief sources of Roman law.

Senescallus, *l.*, **Seneschal**, *fr.* A steward of a manor.

Sensus verborum est anima legis, *l.* The true meaning of the words is the soul of the law.

Sententia, *l.* Sense, meaning; sentence, decree.

Separatim, *l.* Severally.

Sequatur sub suo periculo, *l.* An old writ issued on a return *nihil* to a *summoneas ad warrantizandum*, after an *alias* and *pluries* had been issued.

Sequela, *l.* A suit; prosecution.

Sequestrari facias, *l.* A writ of execution against a beneficed clergyman, commanding the bishop to enter the rectory and church, and take and sequester the same until of the rents, tithes, and profits he have levied the plaintiff's debt.

Sequestration. In equity practice, the process of taking the property of a defendant in contempt, and holding it in the custody of the court.

Seriatim, *l.* In order, one after another.

Seriaunt, *fr.*, **Serjeant.** The highest degree in the profession of common law. Serjeants wore the coif, and had formerly the exclusive right to practise in the *Common Pleas*.

Serjeanty. A special kind of knight-service, held only of the King. **Grand serjeanty**: when the tenant was not bound to attend the King in wars, nor liable to aid or escuage; but performed some particular military duty or honorary service. **Petty serjeanty**: when the tenant held by annual render of some weapon or the like; in effect, like common socage. v. *Tenure*.

Serment, *fr.* Oath.

Sermo index animi, *l.* Speech is the index of the mind.

Serve. To legally deliver; as of a writ.

Service. The duty (whether of rents or services) which a tenant owed the lord for his fee. **Knight-service**: v. *Tenure*.

Serviens, *l.* A *serjeant*; a bailiff, officer.

Servient tenement. v. *Dominant*.

Servitium, *l.* Service. **Liberum servitium** : free service. **Servitium militare** : military service, knight-service. **Servitium regale** : royal service, granted by royal prerogative to the lord of a manor. **Servitium scuti** (service of the shield): knight-service. **Servitium sokæ** : socage, service of the plough. **Servitia solita et consueta** : the usual and customary services.

Servitus, *l.* A servitude; an easement. **Servitus servitutis esse non potest** : there cannot be an easement of [on] an easement. **Servitus non ea natura est, ut aliquid faciat quis, sed ut aliquid patiatur aut non faciat** : the nature of an easement is not that one should do anything; but that one should suffer, or refrain from doing something.

Servus, *l.* Slave, bondman. **Servus facit ut herus det** : the slave does [the work] that the master may give [the wages].

Session, Court of. The supreme civil court of Scotland. v. *Court,* 94. **Sessions** : v. *Court,* 27, 28, 40, 112.

Set-off. A claim for debt or damages set up by the defendant against the plaintiff in reduction of his claims. v. *Recoupment.*

Settlement. The rights and condition of a resident, as to parochial relief, etc. v. *Strict settlement.* **Act of Settlement** : v. *Act.*

Several. Individual; separate; entire. **Severalty** : an estate held entirely by one owner in his own right; v. *Joint.*

Severance. The dissolution or severing of parties to a suit; or of joint tenants or coparceners.

Shack. v. *Common.*

Shaw, *l.* A wood.

Sheriff's court, jury, v. *Court,* 33, 38, 39, 59, 97.

Shelley's Case. A case in which is stated the rule that you cannot limit an estate to a man for life, with a remainder to his children, or heirs in fee or tail. The latter words will be words of *limitation,* not *purchase,* and the man will take a fee. 1 *Coke,* 104.

Shifting use. v. *Use.*

Ship's-husband. The agent of the owners of a ship, who manages the affairs generally, sees to repairs, insurance, charter-parties, etc.

Shire-mote. The county court. v. *Court,* 29. **Shire-reeve** : the sheriff.

Si, *l.* If. **Si aliquid ex solemnibus deficiat, cum æquitas poscit, subveniendum est**: when any one of the proper forms is wanting, it will be aided if equity requires. **Si contingat**: if it happen. **Si fecerit te securum**: if he [the plaintiff] shall have made you secure [given sufficient sureties]. Words in the old writs which directed the sheriff to cause the defendant to appear in court, without any option given. **Si ita est**: if it is so. **Si non omnes**: if not all; an old writ authorizing two or more justices to proceed under the commission, if all were not present. **Si prius**: if before; *v. Nisi prius*. **Si recognoscat** (if he acknowledge): an old writ for a debt which had been acknowledged before the sheriff. **Si quis sine liberis decesserit**: if any one shall have died without issue.

Si, cy, *fr.* If; so. **Si comme**: so as.

Sic, *l.* So. **Sic hic**: so here. **Sic utere tuo ut alienum non lædas**: so use your own that you harm not another's. **Sic volo, sic jubeo, stet pro ratione voluntas**: so I will, so I order, stand my will for the reason.

Sicut, *l.* As. **Sicut alias**: as before, as at another time. **Sicut me Deus adjuvet**: so help me God.

Sier, scier, *fr.* To mow; cut.

Sigillum, *l.* Seal. **Sigillare**: to seal.

Sign manual. The royal signature, written at the top.

Significavit, *l.* A name for the writ *de excommunicato capiendo*, to imprison a person, during six months, for contempt of an order of the Ecclesiastical Court.

Signum, *l.* A sign; mark; seal. **Signare**: to sign, to seal.

Silent leges inter arma, *l.* The laws are silent among arms [in time of war].

Silva cædua, *l.* Wood which may be cut yearly; underwood; not *timber*.

Similiter, *l.* Likewise; a word used in *joinder of issue* or *demurrer*. A *joinder of issue*.

Simony. The corrupt presentation to an ecclesiastical benefice.

Simple. *v. Contract, Larceny*.

Simplex commendatio non obligat, *l.* Mere recommendation does not bind [the vendor]. **Simplex dictum**: mere averment. **Simplex loquela**: mere speech, the mere plaint of the plaintiff.

Simpliciter, *l.* Simply; of its own force.

Simul cum, *l.* Together with; words used in indictments or pleadings against a person who did a thing "with others" unknown. **Simul et semel**: together and at one time.

Sine, *l.* Without. **Sine animo remanendi, revertendi**: without intention of remaining, returning. **Sine assensu capituli**: an old writ for an ecclesiastical corporation to recover lands aliened by their collegiate head without their consent; so, for the successor of a bishop, against his alienee. **Sine cura**: without a *cure*, without any charge or duty. **Sine decreto**: without a decree or order of a judge. **Sine die**: without *day* [of meeting again], a final adjournment or dismissal. **Sine hoc quod**: without this, that; v. Special *traverse*. **Sine numero**: without number, without stint. **Sine prole**: without issue. **Sine quo non**: without whom (or *which*) not; the indispensable person or condition, without which nothing can be done; one of several trustees. **Sine vi aut dolo**: without force or fraud.

Single Bill. v. *Bill*, III. 7. **Single Bond**: a bond without a condition.

Singulariter, *l.* Singly; in the singular.

Singuli in solidum, *l.* Each for the whole.

Sist. In Scotch practice, a stay of proceedings.

Situs, *l.* Position, location, site; as for jurisdiction.

Sive tota res evincatur, sive pars, habet regressum emptor in venditorem, *l.* The purchaser who has been evicted in whole or in part has an action against the vendor.

Six Clerks. Clerks on the equity side of Chancery, who received and filed all bills, answers, replications, etc.

Slander. Defamation by words spoken. v. *Colloquium, Privileged communication, Libel.*

Soc, Socne, Socna, *sax.* v. *Sac.*

Socage, Socagium, *l.* Tenure by certain service, not military. **Free and common socage**: the general, and in modern times almost universal, tenure of English land; by free services, not military, as rents (farm produce or money). **Villein socage**: tenure by base, but certain, services; v. *Tenure.*

Societas, *l.* A partnership. **Socii mei socius meus socius non est**: the partner of my partner is not my partner.

Socman. A name applied to all kinds of tenants other than those in knight service.

Soi, *fr.* Him, her. **Soi mesme:** himself.

Soit, *fr.* Let it be. **Soit baile aux commons:** let it be delivered to the Commons. **Soit droit fait al partie:** v. *Petition de droit.*

Soka, soke, *l., fr.* 1. *Soc.* 2. A plough.

Solatium, *l.* (Consolation.) Compensation; sentimental damages.

Sold note. v. *Bought and sold notes.*

Sole. v. *Corporation, Feme.*

Solemnitas, *l.,* **Solempnité,** *fr.* Due form and ceremony.

Solicitors. The *attorneys* iu Chancery were so called.

Solidum, *l.* A thing undivided, entire; the whole.

Solum, *l.* The ground, soil.

Solutio, *l.* Payment; satisfaction. **Solutio indebiti:** paymeut of what is not due. **Solutio pretii emptionis loco habetur:** the payment of the price operates as a purchase.

Solutus, *l.* Loosed; freed; purged; released.

Solvendo, *l.* Paying. **Solvendum in futuro:** to be paid at a future time. **Solvit:** he paid. **Solvit ad diem, Solvit post diem** (he paid at the day, he paid after the day): pleas in an action of debt on a bond.

Son assault demesne, *fr.* His own assault; a plea in actions of trespass for assault. v. *De injuria,* etc.

Soub, soubs, sous, south, *fr.* Under.

Soul-scot. A mortuary offering; *corse-present.*

Sovent, souvent, *fr.* Often.

Sovereign. Of supreme civil, military, and political power; the person or body of persons in whom the ultimate authority of law rests.

Soy, *fr.* v. *Soi.*

Sparsim, *l.* Scattered, here and there.

Speaking demurrer. v. *Demurrur.*

Special Agent, Assumpsit, Bail, Case, Contract, Damages, Demurrer, Indorsement, Jury, Occupant, Partner, Plea, Pleader, Pleading, Tail, Traverse, Verdict: see those titles. **Special Counts:** v. *Common Counts.* **Special issue:** a plea of specific *traverse,* or the issue thereon. **Special pleading:** the art of drawing up pleas in confession and avoidance. In popular language, the adroit and plausible advocacy of a client's case in court. **Special property:** that of a bailec, or officer

18

in possession of the goods; such as is necessary to ground an action for trover. **Special sessions**: an extra session of the justices of the peace, held for special purposes, usually under acts of Parliament.

Specialty. A contract or obligation under seal.

Species facti, *l.* The character of the thing done.

Specific Legacy, Traverse: see those titles. **Specific Performance**: the execution of a contract as made, which can only be compelled by a court of equity.

Spes, *l.* Hope. **Spes accrescendi**: hope of surviving. **Spe recuperandi**: in the hope [expectation] of recovering.

Spiritual Courts. *Courts ecclesiastical, Christian.* v. *Court,* 79.

Spiritualities. The revenues of a bishop *as* bishop; his ecclesiastical receipts.

Spoliatio, *l.* Forcible deprivation; disseisin. **Spoliatus debet ante omnia restitui**: the party dispossessed ought first of all to be restored.

Spondet peritiam artis, *l.* [The workman engaged for hire] promises the skill of his craft.

Springing use. v. *Use.*

Spulzie, spuilzie, *sc.* Unlawful taking and carrying away of goods.

SS. A mark in a pleading or process indicating the *venue.*

Stabit præsumptio donec probetur in contrarium, *l.* The presumption shall stand until it be proved to the contrary.

Stable-stand. Standing ready with bow or hounds; one of the four evidences of intending to kill deer in a *forest.*

Stagnum, *l.* A pool, pond.

Stallage. The liberty of, or duty paid for, having stalls in a market.

Standing mute. A prisoner was said to *stand mute,* when, on being arraigned for treason or felony, he made no answer, answered foreign to the purpose, or, having pleaded not guilty, refused to put himself on the country. v. *Paine forte et dure.*

Stannary Courts. v. *Court,* 72.

Stapula, *l.,* **Staple.** A fair, market. v. *Statute.*

Starrum, *l.,* **Star.** A deed, contract.

Star Chamber. v. *Court,* 44.

Stare, *l.* To stand; be valid. **Stare decisis**: abide by the decisions.

State Courts. v. *Court*, 108.

State's evidence. v. *Queen's evidence.*

Statim, *l.* Immediately.

Stating part of a bill in equity. The part which states the case, the facts. v. *Charging part.*

Status, *l.* Estate; condition. **Status quo:** the state in which [it was before].

Statute-merchant. A bond or acknowledgment of debt entered into by a debtor before the chief magistrate of some trading town, by which the debtor's goods and lands might be seized and his body imprisoned; authorized by the statute *De Mercatoribus.* A **Statute-staple** is a similar bond acknowledged before the mayor of the *staple*, authorized by the 27 Edw. III. c. 9. For other **statutes,** see their titles.

Statutory release. A conveyance superseding the old *Lease and release*, created by 4 & 5 Vict. c. 21.

Statutum generaliter est intelligendum quando verba statuti sunt specialia, ratio autem generalis, *l.* A statute is to be generally interpreted, although the words be special, if the purpose be general.

Steelbow goods. In Scotland, cattle and implements of husbandry given by the landlord to the tenant, who is bound to return articles equal in value at the end of the lease.

Stet processus, *l.* (Let the process be stayed.) An entry by consent, made by the plaintiff on the record when he wished to stop the action without suffering a nonsuit; as if the defendant became insolvent.

Steth, Stede. The bank of a river.

Stillicidium, *l.* The servitude of suffering water to drip on one's land from the house of another.

Stint. Limit. v. *Common sans nombre.*

Stirps, Stipes, *l.* A stock; root of descent; family. **Per stipitem:** by stock, by families, by right of representation of an ancestor, not *per capita.*

Stipulation. In admiralty, an engagement in the nature of bail, or bond, to release from attachment.

Stoppage in transitu. The right of a vendor to rescind a contract of sale, and seize the goods while still in the hands of the carrier.

Stowe. A valley; a place.

Strata, *l.* A street, road.

Strict settlement. Popularly called **entail**; a settlement of lands by deed or will upon one for life, remainder to his first and other sons successively in tail, remainder to the daughters with cross remainders, remainder to the settlor or grantee in fee; with proper remainders to trustees to preserve contingent remainders interposed.

Stricti juris, *l.* In strict law, or right.

Striking a jury. v. *Jury, struck.*

Strip. Aggravated waste; *estrepement.*

Suapte natura, *l.* In its own nature.

Sub, *l.* Under; beneath; below; upon. **Sub-boscus:** under-wood. **Sub conditione:** under the condition. **Sub colore officii:** under color of office. **Sub cura mariti:** under the care of the husband. **Sub disjunctione:** in the alternative. **Sub judice:** under a judge, before court. **Sub modo:** under restriction, with a qualification. **Sub potestate viri, parentis, curiæ:** in power [under protection] of a husband, parent, the court. **Sub salvo et securo conducto:** under safe and secure conduct. **Sub sigillo:** under seal. **Sub silentio:** in silence, unnoticed. **Sub spe reconciliationis:** under the hope of reconciliation. **Sub suo periculo:** at his own risk. **Sub voce:** under the word [used in referring to another title].

Subinfeudation. The granting of a feud out of a feud, to be held of a mesne lord, forbidden by the statute *Quia emptores.*

Sublata causa, tollitur effectus, *l.* The cause removed, the effect is gone. **Sublato fundamento, cadit opus:** the foundation removed, the work falls. **Sublato principali, tollitur adjunctum:** the principal removed, the accessory is gone also.

Subletting. v. *Underlease.*

Subornation. Instructing or procuring another to commit an offence.

Subpœna, *l.* Under a penalty. A judicial writ commanding a party or witness to appear in court under a penalty. **Subpœna ad testificandum:** the common subpœna to a witness. **Duces tecum:** a subpœna commanding the person to bring with him certain documents or evidence. In **equity, the subpœna** is the first process; like the *writ* in law, and issues on filing the bill.

Subrogation. The substitution of one person for another; and particularly when one person, having discharged another's liability, or satisfied his claims, steps into his rights.

Subsequent. v. *Condition.*

Substantive law. That part of law which creates aud defines rights; not *adjective.*

Substituted service. Service of process authorized by the court to be made on some other person, when the party cannot be found.

Subtraction. Is where any person who owes any suit, duty, custom, or service to another, withdraws it or neglects to perform it.

Succurritur minori, *l.* A minor is to be aided [favored].

Sufferance. v. *Estate.* Tenure at sufferauce of the landlord, by a tenant holding over his term.

Suffragan. Assistant. A titular bishop, assistant to the bishop of the diocese.

Suggestio falsi, *l.* A false representation.

Suggestion. An entry on the record of a fact material to an action which cannot be pleaded.

Suus, sui, *l.* His; his own. **Sui generis:** of its own kind, the only one of its kind, peculiar. **Sui juris:** of one's own law, under no legal disability, not under guardianship.

Suit. 1. An action, prosecution. 2. Service; attendance by a tenant at the lord's court.

Suitors' fund. The moneys, and interest thereon, paid by litigants into court in the Chancery.

Summa ratio est quæ pro religione facit, *l.* (That is the greatest reason which makes for religion.) That rule of conduct is to be deemed most binding which religion dictates.

Summary. Hasty; provisional; without a jury; statutory; without an action at law.

Summoneas, *l.* A writ of **summons**; a general name for writs commanding a party's appearance in court; a writ judicial, by which all personal actions are in modern times commenced. **Summoneas ad auxiliandum:** a writ of summons on an *aid-prayer.* **Summoneas ad warrantizandum:** a writ of summons to a person who had been vouched to warranty.

Summum jus. Strict right, the rigor of the law. **Summum jus, summa injuria:** extreme right is extreme wrong.

Suo nomine, *l.* In his own name. **Suo periculo:** at his own risk.

Super, *l.* On; upon; above; over. **Super altum mare**: upon the high seas. **Super se susceperunt**: they undertook. **Super visum corporis**: upon view of the body.

Superficies, *l.* The surface.

Superflua non nocent, *l.* Things superfluous do no harm.

Superior. v. *Court*, 7, 15, 109.

Superonerare, *l.* To overburden; surcharge. **Superoneratio**: surcharge of common.

Supersedere, *l.* To supersede; stay: desist from; neglect. In Scotch law, a *sist*. **Supersedeas** (that you refrain): a writ granted to forbid the operation of another writ; a writ to stay proceedings or suspend jurisdiction.

Superstitious uses. Various bequests to Jews, Dissenters, and Papists for religious or quasi religious purposes, which in England were made void by several statutes; and the King might divert them to such uses as were "truly charitable."

Supplemental bill. v. *Bill*, I. 18.

Suppletory oath. An oath administered to a party himself where only one witness was offered, the object of which was to make *plena probatio* (in the civil law).

Supplicatio, *l.* In civil law, the rejoinder, the *duplicatio*.

Supplicavit, *l.* A writ to make a man find *sureties of the peace*.

Suppressio veri, *l.* Concealment of the truth.

Supra, *l.* Above; over. **Supra dictus**: aforesaid. **Supra protest**: upon protest; v. *Acceptance*.

Suprema voluntas, *l.* A last will.

Supremacy Act. v. *Act*.

Supreme. v. *Court*, 104, 108. **Supreme Court of Judicature**: v. *Court*, 19, 101.

Sur, *fr.* Upon. **Sur cognisance**, etc., **Sur done**, etc.: v. *Fine*. **Sur cui in vita**: v. *Cui in vita*. **Sur disclaimer**: a writ in the nature of a writ of right brought by the lord against a tenant who had disclaimed his tenure, to recover the land.

Surcesser, *fr.* To supersede; desist.

Surcharge. To overburden. In equity practice, to add an item to an account. v. *Falsify*. **Surcharge of common, pasture**: the commoning or pasturing of more beasts than the commoner is entitled to.

Surplusagium, *l.* Surplusage. v. *Superflua*, etc.

Surety. A pledge; a person who becomes answerable for the debt or default of another. He is not supposed to have actual custody of his principal, like *bail;* and may be sued immediately without a previous suit against the principal. **Surety of the peace**: a recognizance or bond to keep the peace, acknowledged before a justice of the peace, either on his own motion or on complaint of a third party who **swears the peace** against the one bound [makes oath that he is in bodily fear of him, and does not do it for malice or vexation].

Surrebutter. The plaintiff's fourth *pleading.*

Surrejoinder. The plaintiff's third *pleading.*

Surrender. The yielding up of a lesser estate to him who has a greater. **Surrender in deed,** surrender by conveyance, as the grant of a life estate to the remainderman; **in law,** implied by operation of law, as if a tenant for years accepts a new lease; **in copyholds,** the yielding up of a copyhold estate to the lord of the manor, usually in order that he may make a new grant; the method of alienating copyholds.

Surrogate. A bishop's chancellor, who usually presides in the diocesan court. A judge of matters of probate and guardianship. v. *Court,* 110.

Sursisa, *l.,* **Sursise,** *fr.* Neglect; default.

Sursum reddere, *l.* To render up, surrender.

Sus, *fr.* Upon; above. **Susdit**: aforesaid.

Sus. per coll., Suspendatur per collum, *l.* Let him be hanged by the neck.

Suspensive. v. *Condition.*

Suum cuique tribuere, *l.* To give to each one his own.

Suus, *l.* His; his own. v. *Sui, suo.*

Suzereign, *fr.* A crown vassal.

Swearing the peace. v. *Article, Surety of the peace.*

Swein. A freeholder; a freeman of a *forest.*

Sweinmote. v. *Court,* 77.

Syb and som, *sax.* Peace and security.

Sylva, *l.* Wood. **Sylva cædua**: coppice wood, cut annually.

Synod. A religious council or court.

Syngraph. A *chirograph; indenture.*

T.

T., Teste, *l.* Witness. **T., Termino,** *l.* Term.

T. R. E., Tempus regis Edwardi, *l.* In the time of Edward the Confessor.

Taberna, tabernaculum, *l.* A tavern ; inn.

Tabula rasa, *l.* A blank tablet.

Tacite, *l.* Silently, tacitly.

Tacking. The doctrine by which a mortgagee having liens acquired at different times may unite them and enforce them all with the earliest, to the exclusion of intermediate incumbrances.

Tail. 1. **Tail general :** an estate limited to a man and the lawful heirs of his body. **Tail male :** to a man and the male heirs of his body. **Tail female :** to a man and the female heirs of his body. **Tail special :** to a man and his heirs on a certain body begotten. 2. *Strict settlement;* v. *Fee.* **Tail after possibility of issue extinct :** the estate of a widower having no issue, holding lands under a grant in *tail special* or *frankmarriage.*

Tailzie, *sc.* An entail ; *tail.*

Taini, thaini. Freeholders.

Tale. A plaintiff's count.

Tales, *l.* Such ; so many. **Tales de circumstantibus :** so many jurors as may be necessary to make up the panel, selected from the bystanders, **talesmen.** v. *Decem tales, Octo tales.*

Talis qualis, *l.* Such as ; as much.

Taliter, *l.* In such manner. **Taliter processum est :** so it proceeded.

Tallagium, *l.* Tailage ; a tribute ; direct tax.

Talliare, *l.* To cut ; cut out ; abridge. **Tallia :** tail.

Tam, *l.* So. **Tam quam :** as well as. **Tam facti quam animi :** as much in act as in intention.

Tamen, *l.* Yet ; notwithstanding.

Taltarum's Case. The case which established the foundation of common *recoveries.* Y. B. 12 Edw. IV. 19–21.

Tanistry. An old Irish tenure by which lands descended to the eldest and worthiest of the blood and name.

Tanquam prescriptum quod possessum, *l.* Prescription can only go as far as possession [for what has been possessed]:

Tant, *fr.* As ; so ; as much. **Tantost:** forthwith ; as soon as.

Tantua, *l.* As much ; so much. **Tantum:** only. **Tantum bona valent quantum vendi possunt:** things are worth as much as they will bring.

Tard, *fr.* Slow ; late. **Tarde:** a return of a sheriff that a writ was delivered to him too late for execution.

Teinds, *sc.* Tithes. **Teind court:** v. *Court,* 96.

Teinland, *sax.* Land of a thane or noble ; not subject to the service of agricultural tenants ; held in knight-service.

Temere, *l.* Rashly ; inconsiderately.

Temple. v. *Inns of Court.*

Temporalities. The secular revenues, lands,. tenements, and lay fees belonging to a bishop.

Tempus, *l.,* **Temps,** *fr.* Time. **Temporis exceptio:** a plea of lapse of time. **Tempus utile:** available time ; v. *Annus utilis.*

Tenant. v. *Tenure.* 1. One holding lands. 2. One holding a lease for years. 3. The defendant in a real action. **Tenant in Capite, Chief, Common, Dower, Fee, Tail;** at **Sufferance ;** by the **Curtesy;** to the **Præcipe; Paravail:** see those titles. **Tenant for life,** v. *Life estate ;* **after possibility,** v. *Tail ;* **for years, from year to year, at will,** v. *Estate.*

Tenant-right. A kind of customary estate in the North of England and Ireland dependent on the right to renewal of leases.

Tender. An offer of money or other thing in satisfaction of a debt or claim ; a *plea* to that effect. **Tender of issue:** the part of a plea in traverse which offers to submit the dispute to the proper mode of trial.

Tenement. That which may be the subject of tenure ; any interest relating to land, or hereditament dependent on grant.

Tenendum, *l.* (To be held.) The part of a deed following the *habendum,* and stating the tenure by which the land was to be held.

Tenens, *l.* The *tenant.*

Tener, *fr.,* **Tenere,** *l.* To hold ; to keep. **Tenet, tenuit:** he holds, he has held ; v. *Waste.*

Tenor est qui legem dat feudo, *l.* The tenure regulates the law of the feud.

Tenths. 1. An ancient aid granted the King, being one tenth of each subject's personalty. 2. The tenth part of all spiritual benefices, formerly paid to the Pope, afterwards to the Crown, and applied by Queen Anne to make up the deficiencies of small benefices, called Queen Anne's bounty.

Tenure. I. **Allodial tenure** is not properly tenure at all, being absolute ownership, as distinct from (II.) **Feudal tenure**: where lands were held of some superior lord by services or rent; v. *Feudum, Fee.* Tenure differs, —

A. According to the nature of the service. 1. **Frank tenure** or **Freehold**: by *free services.* This includes (a.) *Knight-service,* (b.) *socage,* (c.) *spiritual service.* (a.) **Knight-service, military tenure, tenure in chivalry,** comprises knight-service proper, where lands were held by the service of attending the lord in war, furnishing armed men, horses, etc., or paying *escuage* in commutation therefor; **grand serjeanty,** a tenure of the Crown, by performing some special or personal service, which was not considered *base* because rendered to the King; and **cornage,** a kind of grand serjeanty, by winding a horn at the approach of the Scots or other enemies. All these tenures were abolished by the 12 Car. II. c. 24. (b.) **Socage,** service of the plough, comprising **Free and common socage,** by fixed, free agricultural services; usually rent, either in farm-produce or money; **petty serjeanty,** which was a socage tenure held of the Crown, by some small annual rent or render; **burgage,** a socage tenure in old boroughs, affected by local customs. In socage tenures the lands anciently descended to all the sons in common, which custom persisted in Kent; whence the Kentish socage tenure is called *Gavelkind.* (c.) **Spiritual service**; which included *Frankalmoign* and *Divine service;* v. *Frankalmoign.* 2. **Base tenure** or **Villenage**; which was either pure or privileged according as the services, though base, were certain or uncertain. This only survived in copyhold tenures; v. *Copyhold, Customary freehold, Ancient demesne.*

B. According to the lord of whom the land is held; as (a.) *in capite,* of the King, either *ut de corona* (as of the Crown) or *ut de honore,* in virtue of some honor, dignity, or manor of which the King was proprietor; (b.) of a mesne lord, the origin of one variety of *base fee;* (c.) of the lord of a manor, copyhold.

C. According to the duration of the interest; v. *Estate, Tenant.*

Terce. In Scotch law, dower; a widow's third.

Term. 1. An estate for years. 2. A time given, a limit of time. 3. The sitting of a court. **Term to attend the inheritance:** v. *Attendant term.*

Terminum qui præteriit. v. *Ad.*

Terminus, *l.* A bound, limit. **Terminus a quo:** the date or point of beginning; **terminus ad quem,** the time or point of ending. **Terminus juris:** the time of one or two years allowed in English ecclesiastical courts for appeals.

Terra, *l.,* **Terre,** *fr.* Land. **Terra culta:** tilled land; **frisca,** unploughed land. **Terra testamentalis:** devisable lands; hocland. **Terra vestita:** sown laud. **Terre-tenant:** a person occupying laud; v. *Use.* **Terræ dominicales, tenementales:** v. *Manor.*

Territorial courts. v. *Court,* 113.

Tertia, *l.* A third part, dower.

Tesmoyn, *fr.* An attesting witness; a witness.

Tesmoynage, tesmoynaunce, *fr.* Testimony.

Testate. A person deceased leaving a will. **Testator, testatrix:** the person whose will is in question.

Testatum, *l.* (Testified.) v. *Capias.*

Testis, teste, *l.* Witness. **Teste meipso:** witness myself.

Testimonia ponderanda sunt, non numeranda, *l.* Evidence is to be weighed, not measured (numbered). **Testimonium:** testimony; evidence; attestation.

Theft-bote. The receiving of money or goods from a thief to favor or aid him, or not to prosecute him.

Thegn. A chief lord, tenant *in capite.* **Thenningmannagemote, Thegnmen's court:** v. *Court,* 4.

Thellusson Act. The 39 & 40 Geo. III. c. 98, restricting accumulations to a term of twenty-one years from the testator's death. v. *Perpetuity.*

Theolonium, tholonium, *l.* Toll.

Thesaurus inventus, *l.* *Treasure-trove.*

Thirlage. Sc., a service or duty of *multure.*

Thrithing, *sax.* A riding; a third part of a county.

Tiel, tieulx, etc., *fr.* Such.

Tiers, tierce, *fr.* Third; a third part.

Tignum, *l.* A beam of a house; timber.

Timber. Large wood; building wood; oak, ash, and elm.

Time immemorial, Time out of memory. Before the reign of Richard I., A. D. 1189.

Tipstaff. An officer of the K. B. having custody of prisoners.

Tithes. The tenth part of the yearly increase or profits, from lands, stock, or personal industry, due the rector of a parish for his maintenance. Those from lands were **prædial**, those from stock **mixed**, and the last **personal**. The **great tithes** were corn, wood, hay, etc.; the **small tithes** included all others. Sometimes the latter were called **vicarage tithes**, as payable to the vicar, and the former **parsonage tithes**, as payable to the rector. **Tithe rent-charge:** the rent-charge established in lieu of all tithes by the 6 & 7 Will. IV. c. 71.

Tithing. An old Saxon division of a hundred, usually a tenth; and composed of ten *felawes, borghs, frank-pledges,* with their families, who were mutually responsible for one another by the *frank-pledge.* The **tithing-man**, or *head-borow,* was the chief; and had somewhat the duties of a constable.

Titulus est justa causa possidendi id quod nostrum est, *l.* Title is the just cause of possessing what is ours.

Toftum, *l.*, **Toft.** The site of a ruined or decayed house.

Toll. 1. A liberty to buy and sell within a manor. 2. A tribute paid for passage. 3. A liberty to take such tribute, or to be free therefrom. **Toll thorough:** *toll* (2.) over a highway or bridge. **Toll traverse:** a *toll* (2.) for passing over land of a private person. **Toll turn:** a *toll* (2.) on cattle returning from a market where they were not sold.

Toller, *fr.*, **Tollere,** *l.*, **Toll.** To lift up; take away; defeat. **Toll the entry:** to remove the right of entry; v. *Descent cast.*

Tolne, *fr.*, **Tolnetum,** *l.* Toll.

Tolta, *l.*, **Tolt.** An old writ or precept from the sheriff to remove a cause from a court-baron to the county court.

Tonsura, *l.*, **Tonsure.** The shaving of the crown of the head.

Tor, *sax.* A mount, hill.

Torcenouse, *fr.* Tortiously, tortious.

Torn. v. *Tourn.*

Torrale, *l.* A kiln; a malthouse.

Tort, *fr.* Wrong; legal wrong. A civil injury, for which an action may be maintained. A name given to that class of actions arising *ex delicto.* **Tort-feasor:** a wrong-doer, trespasser. **Tortious conveyance:** v. *Conveyance, Convey.*

Tot. A word written opposite an item in an account, indicating that it was good; when the item was said to be **totted.**

Tot, *fr.* v. *Tout.*

Tota curia, *l.* The whole court. **Toto cœlo:** by the whole heavens. **Toto genere:** in its whole nature.

Totidem verbis, *l.* In so many words.

Toties quoties, *l.* As often as; as many times as it shall happen.

Tourn. Sheriff's turn; v. *Court,* 33. The chief court-leet.

Toujours et uncore prist, *fr.* Now and always ready. **Tout temps prist:** all the time ready. French names for the plea of *tender.*

Tout un sound, *fr.* (*Idem sonans.*) The same in sound.

Tradas in ballium. v. *De odio et atia.*

Traditio, *l.* Livery; delivery. **Traditio brevis manus:** delivery by mere consent, not by act. **Traditio clavium:** delivery of the keys. **Traditio loqui facit chartam:** delivery makes the deed speak [gives effect to it]. **Traditio rei:** delivery of the thing.

Traditor, *l.* A traitor.

Traditur in ballium, *l.* He is delivered to bail.

Trahere, *l.,* **Trahir,** *fr.* To draw. **Trahens:** the drawer of a bill.

Trail-baston. (Draw-staff.) The name given to certain justices with extraordinary powers, appointed by Edward I. during his absence in the Scotch and French wars.

Transeat in exemplum, *l.* Let it pass into an example. **Transit in rem judicatam:** it becomes a matter adjudged. **Transit terra cum onere:** the land passes with the burden [the incumbrance is transferred with the land].

Transitus, Transitu, *l.* The transit, conveyance. v. *Stoppage.*

Traverse. A plea in denial, closing with a tender of issue. It may either be **general,** as denying the entire cause of action in general terms (*General issue*), or **specific, limited,** as denying one specified and particular, but essential fact. **Special traverse:** a plea of traverse, with an inducement alleging new matter in avoidance, and an *absque hoc* (without this) clause, traversing specifically some point in the declaration. The special traverse formerly concluded with a verification. v. *Pleading.*

Treason. In England, compassing or imagining the death of the

King, Queen, or their eldest son or heir; violating the King's consort, eldest daughter unmarried, or heir's wife; levying war against the King, or adhering to his enemies; counterfeiting his seal or money; slaying the chancellor, treasurer, or justices while sitting in office. In America, levying war against the United States; or adhering to their enemies, giving them aid and comfort. **Petit treason**: in old English law, the killing of a master by his servant, a husband by his wife, an ecclesiastical person by his inferior; or of any person by another, who owes him faith and obedience.

Treasurer, Lord High. Formerly, the chief treasurer of England, who had charge of the moneys in the Exchequer, the Chancellor of the Exchequer being under him. He appointed all revenue officers and escheators, and leased Crown lands. The office is obsolete, and his duties are now performed by the Lords Commissioners of the Treasury.

Treble costs. The common costs, half of them, and half of the latter; i. e. the costs and three fourths added.

Trebucket. A *castigatory, cucking-stool; v. Common scold.*

Tres, *l.* Three. **Tres faciunt collegium**: three [may] make a corporation.

Tres, *fr.* Very.

Tres, *fr.* Three; third. **Tresayle**: a grandfather's grandfather. v. *Aiel, Besail.*

Tresor trouvé, *fr.* Treasure-trove.

Trespass. 1. Any injury, misfeasance, or nonfeasance. 2. An injury or misfeasance to person or property, made "with force and arms" [force actual or implied in law], a breach of the King's peace. 3. An unlawful entry on land of another. 4. The action at law for any of these trespasses. This is either, A. **vi et armis**, brought for trespasses 2 and 3, the old action on a writ **de cursu**, issued by the clerks in Chancery according to established form, depending in the King's courts on a fiction of a breach of the King's peace, or contempt of royal authority (v. *Nisi feceris, Contra pacem*), whereby the King's courts anciently obtained jurisdiction, and consequently covering most cases of direct or intentional wrong; or, B. **on the case,** *super casum,* the action on special writs, adapted to special cases (*in casu consimili*) by the clerks in Chancery under au-

thority of the Statute of Westminster II., and covering most
cases of contract, or indirect or unintentional wrong, negligence,
etc. Class A. is usually called **Trespass** as distinct from B.
Case. Trespass **de bonis asportatis, de uxore abducto,
per quod servitium amisit, per quod consortium amisit,
quare clausum fregit**: see those titles.

Trespasser ab initio. Trespasser from the beginning; a term
applied to a tort-feasor whose acts relate back so as to make a
previous act, at the time innocent, unlawful; as if he enter peace-
ably, and subsequently commit a breach of the peace, his entry
is considered a trespass.

Trial. That part of an action which begins at the *joinder of issue,*
and ends at the judgment. Anciently, that part of an action
which began with the medial or proof judgment and ended with
the final judgment; as trial by *battel, ordeal,* and the like. Now
used to mean that part of the action which takes place in court.
Trial at *bar, nisi prius,* by *battel, ordeal, record, certificate, inspection :* see those titles.

Triare, *l.* To try. **Triatio**: trial. **Triatio ibi semper debet
fieri ubi juratores meliorem possunt habere notitiam :**
trial ought always to be had where the jury can have the best
information.

Triers, triors. Two indifferent persons selected by the court to try
a challenge of a juryman for favor. As soon as two good jurymen are sworn, the function of the triers ceases, and the jurymen take their place.

Trina admonitio, *l.* The third warning. v. *Paine fort et dure.*

Trinity term. Begins May 22, ends June 12.

Trinoda necessitas, *l.* (Threefold necessity.) The threefold
burden of repairing bridges, building castles, and service to re-
pel invasions, to which, by Saxon law, all lands were liable.

Triplication. In the civil law, the *surrejoinder.* In the canon
law, the *rejoinder.*

Trithing. v. *Thrithing.*

Tronage. A toll for weighing wool.

Trover, *fr.* To find. **Trove**: found.

Trover. An *action on the case* to recover the value of goods, brought
by a person having had possession against a person converting
them to his own use.

True bill. v. *Bill,* I. 6.

Trust. A beneficial interest in land, or other property, the legal title to which is in another, recognized and enforced by courts of equity. The person having the title is the trustee ; the person having the beneficial interest, the **cestui que trust,** or **beneficiary. Express trust** is one created by the words of a deed or will, as distinct from **implied trust,** one raised by operation of law. **Resulting trusts** are implied trusts, which arise upon the determination, or before the beginning, of a grant or express trust; **constructive trusts** are implied trusts which arise by equitable interpretation or extension of an express trust. **Voluntary trusts:** trusts created for a **volunteer,** a person who takes as a pure beneficiary, without consideration. **Trust-deed:** a kind of mortgage given to a trustee to secure a numerous class of creditors, with power to foreclose or sell if their bonds or notes are unpaid; usually employed in large railway or corporation mortgages. v. *Executed, Executory.*

Trustee process. The attachment of the defendant's debts while due from a third party. v. *Attachment, Garnishment.* A statutory process in some States, resembling one kind of foreign *attachment.*

Tuer, *fr.* To kill, slay.

Tulit, *l.* He brought, brought a writ.

Tumbrell. A *trebucket, castigatory.*

Tun, *sax.* A villa; a rural house or town.

Tunc, *l.* Then.

Turbary. The right of digging turf. v. *Common.*

Turnus, *l.,* **Turn.** *Tourn.* v. *Court,* 33.

Turpis, *l.* Base ; immoral ; illegal. **Turpis causa:** an illegal consideration. **Turpis contractus:** an immoral contract.

Turris, *l.* A tower. The Tower of London.

Tutela, *l.* Guardianship. **Tutor:** a guardian.

Tutius erratur ex parte mitiori, *l.* It is safer to err on the milder side.

Twyne's Case. The leading case on fraudulent conveyances, 3 *Coke,* 80.

Tyrrell's Case. Decided that you could not have a use upon a use. *Dyer,* 155 *a.*

U.

Uberrima fides, *l.* The most perfect good faith; required between partners.

Ubi aliquid conceditur, conceditur et id sine quo res ipsa esse non potest, *l.* Where anything is granted, that also is granted without which the thing itself cannot exist. **Ubi cessat remedium ordinarium, ibi decurritur ad extraordinarium:** where the usual remedy fails, recourse is had to the unusual. **Ubi eadem ratio ibi eadem jus:** like reason makes like law. **Ubi jus ibi remedium** (where there is a right there is a remedy): there is no wrong without a remedy. **Ubi major pars, ibi tota:** where the greater part is, there the whole [the majority rules]. **Ubi nullum matrimonium ibi nulla dos:** where there is no marriage, no dower. **Ubi revera:** where, in point of fact. **Ubi quis delinquit ibi punitur:** a man shall be punished where he sins. **Ubi verba conjuncta non sunt, sufficit alterutrum esse factum:** where words are not used in the conjunctive, it is enough if either be done.

Ubicunque fuerimus in Anglia, *l.* Wheresoever we shall be in England; the style of the return of original writs in the K. B. v. *Court,* 8.

Udal. *Allodial.*

Ulterius concilium, *l.* Further consideration.

Ultima voluntas testatoris est perimplenda secundum veram intentionem suam, *l.* The testator's last will is to be carried out according to his real intention. **Ultimum supplicium:** the extreme punishment, death. **Ultimum tempus pariendi:** the extreme period of gestation. **Ultimus hæres:** the last heir, to whom the escheat of an estate would fall; usually the Crown.

Ultra, *l.* Beyond; above. **Ultra fines mandati:** beyond the limits of the mandate, beyond his authority as agent. **Ultra mare:** beyond the sea. **Ultra petita:** beyond things demanded, a term applied to a judgment or decree awarding more than the plaintiff asked. **Ultra valorem:** beyond the value. **Ultra vires:** beyond their powers; the doctrine by which corporations cannot exceed the powers specially conferred by, or reasonably implied from, their charters.

Um, un, om, on, *fr.* A man; one; any one.

Un foitz, *fr.* Once; once upon a time.

Una cum, *l.* Together with. **Una voce**: with one voice. **Una cum omnibus aliis**: together with all other things.

Uncore, *fr.* Still; yet; again. **Uncore prist**: v. *Tout temps prist.*

Uncuth, *sax.* Unknown; a guest on his first night; *Agenhine.*

Unde, *l.* Whence; wherefrom; whereupon. **Unde rectatus est**: whereof he is accused. **Unde nihil habet**: of which he has nothing; v. *Dower.* **Unde petit judicium**: whereof he prays judgment.

Underlease. Where a lessee leases all the tenement for his entire term, it is properly an **assignment**; if all the tenement for a part of the term, it is an **underlease**; if part of the tenement, it is a **subletting.**

Undique, *l.* On all sides; from every quarter.

Unico contextu, *l.* In one transaction, in one connection.

Unilateral. One-sided. v. *Contract.*

Uniformity of Process Act. The 2 Will. IV. c. 39, establishing one and the same process of beginning actions in all the courts of law at Westminster.

United States Courts. v. *Court,* 102.

Unity. A similarity of estate among tenants of the same land; as, **Unity of interest,** where the estate of each is of the same duration; **Unity of title,** where acquired by the same title; **Unity of time,** when vested at the same period; **Unity of possession,** where each tenant is seised equally of the whole. v. *Joint tenants, Common, Coparcenary.*

Universitas, *l.* A thing complete, in its entirety. A *corporation aggregate.* **Universitas bonorum**: a man's entire estate. So, **Universum jus**: the entire right or estate.

Universities Courts. v. *Court,* 65.

Unlawful assembly. A riotous *assembly,* an assembly of three or more persons to do an unlawful act. v. *Affray.*

Uno absurdo dato, infinita sequuntur, *l.* One absurdity given, an infinite number follow.

Uno flatu, *l.* In one breath.

Unques, *fr.* Ever; always. **Unques prist**: always ready; v. *Tout temps prist.*

Unum quid, *l.* One thing, taken in a lump. **Unumquodque eodem modo quo colligatum est dissolvitur:** everything is dissolved by the same means by which it is constructed.

Ure, *fr.* Effect; practice. **Urer:** to enure.

Usage. The custom of a locality or trade.

Usance. The customary time allowed, as between different countries, for the payment of a bill of exchange, after its date.

Use. Originally a beneficial estate, like a trust; the **terre-tenant** or **feoffees to uses** having the legal title, and the **cestui que use** the beneficial interest. The **Statute of Uses,** 27 Hen. VIII. c. 10, converted the use into the legal estate, and gave rise to many new kinds of conveyances without livery of seisin. A **use upon a use,** as if land be conveyed to A to the use of B to the use of C, is not good, and B will have the legal estate; v. *Tyrrell's Case.* Uses are **present** (*executed*), which vest immediately, or **future** (*executory*), which vest at some future time. Executory uses may be either **springing** (**primary**), which are to arise at some future time, there being no previous use; or **shifting** (**secondary**), which take effect in derogation of some preceding use. A **contingent use** is one which may never take effect. Uses are also **express,** by act of the parties; or **implied**; which latter may be either **resulting** or **constructive**; v. *Trust.* Thus, an estate is granted by A (without consideration) to B and his heirs to the use of C and his heirs on A's death; but if C die without issue at his death, then to the use of D. Here B has the legal estate, A a resulting use, C a springing use, and D a shifting use, which is also contingent. A's use is executed; all the others are executory. A **constructive use:** one raised by the law in modification or extension of an express use; as if a *superstitious use* were diverted to a *charitable use.* A **charitable use:** such a use as is authorized by the 43 Eliz. c. 4, and other statutes, in spite of the *mortmain* acts and the rule against perpetuities; such as uses for the maintenance of schools, hospitals, public works, and other charities.

User. The actual enjoyment of property or a right. **User de action:** the pursuing or bringing an action.

Usque ad, *l.* As far as. **Usque ad medium filum aquæ, cœlum, inferos:** as far as the middle thread of the stream, the heavens, the centre of the earth.

Usucapio, *l.* Usucaption; the right of property in a thing or corporeal hereditament acquired by long possession; an acquisitive *prescription.*

Usufruct. The right to the use or profits of a thing, usually for the life of the usufructuary.

Usura, *l.* Interest; usury. **Usura manifesta**: open usury as distinct from **velata,** veiled usury, or **dry exchange,** where the interest was added to the principal of the bond given for the loan. **Usura maritima**: maritime interest; v. *Fœnus nauticum.*

Usury. 1. Interest. 2. Unlawful interest.

Usus, *l.* Use. **Usus bellici**: warlike uses. **Usus fori**: the practice of the court, of this jurisdiction.

Ut, *l.* That; as; so. **Ut antiquum**: as if ancient; v. *Feudum.* **Ut audivi**: as I heard. **Ut credo**: as I believe. **Ut currere solebat**: as it used to run. **Ut de feodo**: as of fee. **Ut res magis valeat quam pereat**: that the thing rather stand than fall. **Ut pœna ad paucos, metus ad omnes perveniat**: that the fear may reach all, but the penalty few. **Ut supra**: as above.

Utas, *l.* The octave; the eighth day after a feast.

Uterine. Of the same mother.

Utfangthefe. v. *Outfangthefe.*

Uti, *l.* As. **Uti possidetis** (as you possess): a phrase indicating that disputing parties or nations are to keep what they now have.

Utile per inutile non vitiatur, *l.* (The useful is not spoilt by the useless.) Surplusage does not vitiate what is otherwise good and valid.

Utitur jure auctoris, *l.* He enjoys the rights of his assignor. **Utitur jure suo**: he exercises his own rights.

Utlagatus, *l.,* **Utlagh,** *sax.,* **Utlage,** *fr.* An *outlaw.*

Utland, *sax.* Outland; the tenemental land without the demesne of a manor.

Utrum, *l.* Whether. v. *Assize.*

Utter. To publish; put in circulation.

Utter, *sax.* Outer. **Utter barristers**: the outer barristers, not Queen's counsel or serjeants; without the bar.

Uxor, Ux', *l.* Wife. **Uxor non est sui juris, sed sub potestate viri, cui in vita contradicere non potest**: a wife is not capable at law, but under the protection of her husband, whom she cannot contradict during his life.

V.

V. For **vide**, *l.*, see; aud **versus**, against.   **V. C.**: Vice-Chancellor.   **V. R.**: for **Victoria regina**, *l.*: Victoria, Queen.

Vacant. Empty, unclaimed.   **Vacant succession**: where the heirs are unknown, or have all renounced.

Vacantia bona, *l.*   Goods unclaimed, without an owner; escheated.   v. *Bona.*

Vacare, *l.*   To be vacant.   **Vacatur**: it is vacated, annulled.

Vacaria, *l.*   A piece of waste ground.

Vacca, *l.*, **Vache,** *fr.*   A cow.   **Vaccaria**: a dairy; cow-house.

Vadari, *l.*   To hold to bail, give bail.

Vades, *l.*   Pledges; sureties.

Vadia, *l.*   Wages.

Vadiare, *l.*   To wage; give security.   **Vadiare duellum**: to wage *battel.*   **Vadiare legem**: to *wage* law.   **Vadiatio legis**; *wager of law.*

Vadium, *l.*   A pledge; security, surety.   **Vadium mortuum**: a dead pledge, *mortgage.*   **Vadium vivum**: a vifgage, a pledge of property to hold until the profits or interests paid off the debt.

Vail' q' vail' purr', *fr.*, **Valeat quantum valere potest,** *l.*   Let it avail [take effect] as far as it can.

Valentia, *l.*, **Vaillance,** *fr.*   Value.

Valor maritagii, *l.*   The value of the *marriage.*

Valuable consideration.   Money, goods, lands, services, or marriage.   v. *Good consideration.*

Valued policy.   v. *Policy.*   **Value of the marriage**: v. *Marriage.*

Valvasour, *fr.*, **vavasor,** *l.*   1. A vassal; the chief vassal of a tenant in chief.   2. An old dignity below the peerage.

Vana est illa potentia quæ nunquam venit in actum, *l.*   That power is useless which never comes into action.   **Vani timores sunt æstimandi qui non cadunt in constantem virum**: those fears are to be deemed idle which do not affect a man of nerve.

Variance.   A discrepancy between the statement of the cause of action in the writ, and that in the declaration; or between a statement in a pleading and the evidence adduced in support of it.

Vassal. The tenant of a *fief;* a feudatory.

Vastum, Vastitas, *l.* *Waste.*

Vaut, *fr.* Is worth. **Rien ne vaut:** it is worth nothing.

Vectura, *l.* Maritime *freight.*

Veer, veier, *fr.* To see. **Ve:** seen.

Veer, *fr.* To go; refuse; forbid. **Vee:** refusal.

Vefue, Veif, *fr.* Widow. **Veffete, vefuage:** widowhood.

Veigner, *fr.* To come, happen.

Veisin, *fr.* Neighbor.

Vejours, *fr.* Viewers, *Visores.*

Vel, *l.* Or; as; whether.

Venaria, *l.* Animals of the chase. **Venatio:** hunting.

Venditioni exponas, *l.* (That you expose to sale.) A writ judicial commanding a sheriff to sell goods taken on execution.

Vendor's lien, Vendee's lien. v. *Lien.*

Vener, *fr.,* **Venire,** *l.* To come, appear. A name given the precept or other process for collecting a jury. **Venire facias** (that you cause to come): a judicial writ directing the sheriff to cause twelve good and lawful men to come before the court for a jury. In England long since supplanted by a *distringas juratores.* v. *Nisi prius.* **Venire facias de novo:** a writ to summon another jury for a new trial; the motion or order for a new trial. **Venire facias ad respondendum:** a writ to summon to answer any crime under felony or treason; the first process in *outlawry.*

Venison, *fr.* Animals of the chase.

Venit et defendit vim et injuriam, *l.* He comes and defends [denies] the force and injury. **Venit et dicit:** he comes and says.

Vente, *fr.* Sale.

Venter, *l.* The belly, womb. **Ventre inspiciendo:** v. *De.*

Venue, visne, *fr.,* **Visnetum, vicinetum,** *l.* (The neighborhood.) 1. The neighborhood whence the jury was to be summoned. 2. Hence, the place where the action arose or crime was committed. 3. The place or county where the action is tried. 4. In pleading, the statement of the county on the margin of the declaration.

Verba, *l.* Words, language. **Verba accipienda sunt,** words are to be taken, **secundum subjectam materiam,** according to the subject matter; **ut sortientur effectum,** so that they may take effect. **Verba artis ex arte:** technical words in their technical sense. **Verba chartarum fortius accipiuntur contra proferentem:** the words of a deed are taken the more strongly against him who sets it up. **Verba generalia,** general words, **generaliter sunt intelligenda,** are to be understood generally; **restringuntur ad habilitatem rei vel personam,** are limited according to the person or the capabilities of the thing. **Verba intentioni, et non e contra, debent inservire:** words ought to carry out the intention, and not run counter to it. **Verba illata inesse videntur:** words imported [into an instrument] by a reference are deemed to be included [in the instrument]. **Verba ita sunt intelligenda:** words are to be só understood; v. *Ut res,* etc. **Verba relata,** etc.; v. *Verba illata,* etc. **Verba precaria:** precatory words, words of request or trust.

Verd. The privilege of cutting green wood in a *forest.*

Verderor. An officer of a *forest.*

Verdict. The formal and unanimous·answer of a petit jury given in open court. **General verdict:** a verdict simply for the plaintiff or defendant upon the issue, as distinct from a **special verdict,** one finding particular facts. **Sealed verdict:** when the jury have agreed during the absence of the court, they are sometimes dismissed, after placing their written verdict in an envelope and sealing it.

Veredictum, *l.* A verdict. **Veredicto non obstante:** notwithstanding the verdict.

Verey, very, verray. True.

Verge. v. *Pax regis.*

Vergens ad inopiam, *l.* In declining circumstances.

Verification. The concluding part of a plea in confession and avoidance. An averment.

Veritas nominis tollit errorem demonstrationis, *l.* Truth in the name removes (obviates) error in the description.

Vers, *fr.,* **Versus,** *l.* Against.

Vert. Anything that grows and bears a green léaf in a *forest ;* cover.

Verus, *l.* True; very.

Vest. To clothe with possession; to deliver full possession. **Vested use, legacy,** or **estate** is when there is a fixed existing person in whom the right resides. To **vest in possession**: when an estate actually takes effect as a present interest. **Vested remainder**: v. *Remainder*. **Vesting order**: a decree of Chancery in trust cases vesting the legal title in the *cestui que trust*.

Vester, *fr.*, **Vestire,** *l.* To clothe; vest; invest; give seisin.

Vestimentum, vestura, *l.* Clothing; investiture; seisin. **Vesturæ terræ**: the things growing on the land.

Vetera statuta. The ancient statutes; from Magna Charta to the end of the reign of Edward II.

Vetitum namium, *l.* 1. A refused taking; withholding of things distrained. 2. *Withernam.*

Vexata quæstio, *l.* A doubtful question; vexed, unsettled.

Vey, *fr.* Way.

Vi aut clam, *l.* Forcibly or covertly, by force or fraud. **Vi, clam, aut precario**: forcibly, secretly, or doubtfully. **Vi et armis**: by force and arms; v. *Trespass.*

Via, *l.* A way, road. **Via alta**: the highway. **Via regia**: the King's highway. **Via amicabili**: in a friendly way. **Via trita via tuta**: the beaten path is the safe path.

Viagium, *l.* A voyage; journey.

Vic'. For **Vicecomes,** *l.*: sheriff.

Vicar. The incumbent of an *appropriated* benefice. v. *Rector, Parson, Tithes.*

Vice, *l.* In place of. **Vice-Chancellor**: there are three Vice-Chancellors in England, each holding a court, from which an appeal might be taken to the Chancellor; v. *Court,* 17. **Vicecomes** (viscount): the sheriff. **Vicecomes non misit breve**: the sheriff hath not sent the writ; v. *Continuance.* **Vice versa**: in inverse manner, in the opposite order.

Vicinetum, *l.* Vicinage; neighborhood; *venue.*

Vicontiel. Of a sheriff, or sheriff's court.

Vicus, *l.* A village; street.

Videlicet, *l.* (It is allowed to see.) To wit.

Vidimus, *l.* (We have seen.) An exemplification in charters, like *innotescimus.*

Vidua *l.* A widow. **Vidua regis** (a king's widow): the widow of a tenant *in capite.*

Vie, *fr.* Life. **Vief, vif:** living, alive.

View. Inspection; examination. 1. **View of frankpledge:** the office of a sheriff in seeing all the frankpledges of a hundred, and that all youths above fourteen belonged to some *tithing;* a function of the *Court-leet.* 2. The *Court-leet;* v. *Court,* 32, 33.

Vigilantibus non dormientibus jura subveniunt, *l.* Laws aid the waking, not the sleeping.

Vigilia, *l.* A watch, watch.

Vigore cujus, *l.* By force whereof.

Viis et modis, *l.* (By ways and means.) A citation against an absent defendant in admiralty practice, served by posting up in certain specified public places, as the Royal Exchange, the Market-cross at Edinburgh, etc.

Vill. A manor; tithing; town.

Villanus, *l.* A villein. **Villanum servitium:** villein service.

Villanous judgment. One by which the defendant lost his *law.*

Villein. A feudal tenant of the lowest class; at first a simple bondman; afterwards holding land by base and uncertain services. **Villein socage:** tenure in villeinage, but by certain services; v. *Tenure.* **Villein in gross:** a bondman, annexed to the lord's person, and freely transferable; **villein regardant,** a villein annexed to the manor, transferable only with the land.

Villeinage. v. *Villein, Tenure.*

Vinculum, *l.* A chain; a bond. **Vinculo matrimonii:** from the marriage tie; v. *Divorce.*

Vinum, *l.* Wine. **Vinum adustum:** brandy.

Violent presumption. A presumption of the truth of a fact founded on circumstances which are necessarily followed by it or attended with it. **Violent profits:** in Scotch law, double the rent; the extreme value of the land.

Vir, *l.* A man; a husband. **Vir et uxor censentur in lege una persona:** man and wife are deemed one person in law.

Virga, *l.* A rod; a staff; a yard.

Virga, virgata terræ, *l.* A yard-land; from twenty to forty acres.

Viripotens, *l.* Marriageable.

Virtus, *l.* Virtue; the substance, tenor, effect. **Virtute cujus:** by virtue of which. **Virtute officii:** by virtue of his office.

Vis, *l.* Force; v. *Vi.* **Vis armata:** an armed force. **Vis et metus:** force and fear. **Vis divina:** the act of God. **Vis**

fluminis: the force of the current. **Vis impressa**: the original force, first impulse. **Vis inermis**: an unarmed force. **Vis laica**: a lay force. **Vis major**: irresistible force. **Vis proxima**: the immediate force or impulse.

Visconte, *fr.* Sheriff.

Visne, *fr.*, **Vicinetus,** *l.* Neighborhood; *venue.*

Visores, *l.* Viewers. **Visus**: view. **Visus franci plegii**: *View of frankpledge;* v. *Court,* 33.

Vita, *l.* Life.

Vitium, *l.* Vice; fault; error. **Vitium clerici, scriptoris**: the mistake of a clerk or scribe.

Viva aqua, *l.* Living, running water. **Viva voce (vive voys,** *fr.***)**: by word of mouth. **Vivum vadium**: v. *Vadium.*

Vix, *l.* Scarcely; hardly; rarely.

Voc., *l.* For **Voce**. Under the name or title.

Vocabula artis, *l.* Technical terms.

Vocare, *l.* To call upon, vouch. **Vocans**: a voucher. **Vocat'**: called. **Vocatio**: voucher, vouching. **Vocatus**: a vouchee.

Vocher, *fr.* To vouch. **Voche**: a vouchee.

Vociferatio, *l.* Outcry; hue and cry.

Voco, *l.* I call; I summon; I vouch.

Voer, voir, *fr.* To see.

Void. Null. **Voidable**: that may be annulled at pleasure. **Void for remoteness**: v. *Perpetuity.*

Voidance. Vacancy; want of an incumbent for a benefice.

Voier, voir, *fr.* To see. **Voire dire** (to speak the truth): a name given to the preliminary oath of a witness, and examination as to his competency, interest, etc.

Volenti non fit injuria, *l.* (No injury is done to the willing.) What a person assents to he cannot afterwards complain of as an injury.

Volere, *l.* To wish, will. **Volo**: I will. **Volumus**: we will. **Voluit, sed non dixit**: he wished, but did not express it. **Volentes**: being willing.

Voluntarius dæmon, *l.* A voluntary madman; a drunkard.

Voluntary. Free; not compulsory; without consideration. v. *Trust;* not *contentious;* intended, not *permissive,* v. *Waste.*

Voluntas, *l.* Will; design; purpose; last will. **Voluntas donatoris in charta doni sui manifeste expressa, obser-**

vetur: the will of the grantor as openly expressed in the deed of feoffment should be observed. **Voluntas et propositum distinguunt maleficia**: the intent and purpose distinguish [the different grades of] crimes. **Voluntas reputatur pro facto**: the will is taken for the deed [in treason]. **Voluntas testatoris est ambulatoria usque ad mortem**: the will of the testator is revocable until death.

Volunteer. A grantee or beneficiary in a *voluntary* conveyance; without consideration.

Vouch. To call; to call to warranty. v. *Avoucher, Recovery*. To call upon a grantor or other warrantor to defend the title. v. *Ejectment*. **Vouchee**: the one vouched.

Voucher. An account-book; acquittance, receipt.

Vous avez cy, *fr.* You have here. **Vous voiez**: you see.

Vox, *l.* Voice; speech. **Vox Dei**: the voice of God. **Vox emissa volat, litera scripta manet**: the spoken word flies, the written letter remains.

Vs. For versus, *l.*, against.

Vulgaris opinio, *l.* Common opinion. **Vulgaris purgatio**: common purgation; the *ordeal*, as differing from canonical purgation by oath.

Vulgo concepti, *l.* *Filii populi;* bastards.

W.

Wacta, *l.* Watch; watch and ward.

Wadset, *sc.* A mortgage; a pledge of lands.

Wage. To give security for. To **wage battel**: to give security or pledges to try a cause by *battel*. To **wage law**: v. *Wager of law*.

Wager of law. A method of trial by the oath of the defendant, supported by the oaths of his neighbors, usually eleven, making his own oath the twelfth (*duodecima manu*). It was allowed in *debt* and *detinue*, and caused the discontinuance of these actions. v. *Witness*.

Wager-policy. A policy of assurance or insurance taken out by a party having no insurable interest.

Waif. A thing stolen and thrown away by the thief in his flight.

Wainable. That may be tilled. **Wainage**: carts and implements of husbandry.

Waive. To throw aside, as by a thief of goods stolen, in his flight. To renounce, abandon.

Waiviaria, *l.* The waiving, outlawry of, a woman.

Wales. v. *Court,* 71.

Walla, wallia, *l.* A bank of earth; a wall, a sea-wall.

Wapentake. A division of the northeastern counties in England answering to the hundred. A hundred court.

Waractum, *l.* Fallow ground. v. *Warectare.*

Warantia, *l.* Warranty. **Warantizare**: to warrant. **Warantus**: a warrantor.

Ward. Guard; the service of guarding a castle; wardship; an infant in guardianship. **Ward-holding**: the Scotch term for military service. **Ward-mote**: a court in each ward in London. **Ward-wit**: immunity from service of *ward*.

Warda, *l.* Ward, wardship. An award.

Warden. A guardian, keeper.

Wards and liveries. v. *Court,* 45.

Wardship. In military tenures, the right of the lord to have custody, as guardian, of the body and lands of the infant heir, without any account of profits, until he was twenty-one, or she sixteen. In socage, the guardian was accountable for profits; and he was not the lord, but the nearest relative to whom the inheritance could not descend, and the wardship ceased at fourteen. In copyholds the lord was the guardian, but was perhaps accountable for profits.

Warectare, *l.* To fallow; to plough in the spring for fallow. **Warectum**: fallow ground.

Warenna, *l.* A warren.

Warentare, warentizare, *l.* To warrant.

Warrandice. Scotch, for *warranty.*

Warrant. To defend, guarantee. In contracts, to engage the truth of certain facts as an essential condition. In land, to bind one's self by grant or collateral covenant that the title is good and the grantee shall be undisturbed in his possession.

Warrant. A written document, writ, or precept conferring authority; an official precept, authorizing arrest, distress, or search, issued under the seal of a justice or court. A *warranty.*

Warrantia, *l.*   Warranty.   **Warrantia chartæ, custodiæ, diei**: v. *De.*

Warranty. Anciently, the duty of a grantor and his heirs, implied in the word *dedi* in the grant, to warrant and defend the title and possession of the grantee, or give him other lands of equal value. In modern times, an express covenant by the grantor that he has good title, and for breach of which he is liable to the grantee in damages. **Absolute, collateral, lineal warranty**: see those titles. **Warranty deed**: a deed containing a covenant of warranty.

Warren. A place privileged for the keeping of beasts of warren, hares, conies, partridges, pheasants, etc.

Waste. Spoil or destruction done or permitted by the tenant to houses, lands, or tenements. **Voluntary** or **actual waste**: waste actually committed, as by cutting trees or pulling down a house. **Permissive** or **negligent waste**: by omission, as by neglecting to repair. **Equitable waste**: v. *Equitable.* **Writ of waste**: an old mixed action, which lay for him that had the next estate of inheritance against the tenant for life, years, in curtesy or dower, committing waste. By the Statute of Marlberge and at common law the plaintiff recovered only single damages; but by the Statute of Gloucester he recovered treble damages and the land or tenement wasted; and by Westminster II. the remedy was given to one tenant in common against another. This action long since gave place to the action on the case for waste, and the bill in equity to restrain waste. v. *Estrepement.* **Waste in the tenet** was when the particular estate still existed, and the writ was brought both for damages and the estate itself; **in the tenuit**, when the particular estate had determined and the writ was brought to recover damages for past waste. **Lord's waste**: v. *Manor.*

Water ordeal. v. *Ordeal.*

Way. The right of a man and his heirs, or of the owner of a certain estate, or of a certain class of individuals, to pass through another man's land; an incorporeal hereditament, a kind of easement.

Waygoing crop. The crop sown by a tenant whose term ends before it is harvested. v. *Emblement.*

Weald, *sax.* A wood, woody country.

Wear, weir. A place in a river for taking fish, made by dams; a fishway.

Welsh mortgage. An old *mortuum vadium*, where land was conveyed to the creditor, redeemable at any time on payment of the principal debt; the mesne profits going for the interest, like the *antichresis*.

Were, *sax.* A price; a fine for homicide paid the kin. v. *Æstimatio capitis.* **Weregild**: payment of the *were*, blood-money.

Westminster. The seat of the *superior courts.* v. *Nisi prius.* **Westminster I.**: a statute in 3 Edw. I. (1275), containing many provisions concerning *purgation* of clerks, felons, *paine forte et dure, marriage* of wards, *prescription* in writs, *vouching to warranty,* etc. **Westminster II.**: the 13 Edw. I. c. 1 (1285), containing the statute *de Donis,* matters concerning *formedon, second deliverance, cui in vita, advowsons* usurped, *vouching to warranty, mesne, waste, fieri facias, elegit,* etc. **Westminster III.**: the 18 Edw. I. (1290), the statute of *Quia emptores,* concerning alienations, *mortmain,* etc.

White rents. *Rents* payable in silver, money.

Whole blood. Kinship by descent from the same pair of ancestors. v. *Half-blood, Possessio fratris.*

Wic, wyk, *sax.* A house, castle, town.

Widow's chamber. The apparel and furniture of a widow's bedchamber, to which she was entitled by a London custom. **Widow's quarantine**: the period of forty days from the death of a man seised of land, during which the widow might remain in his chief mansion without paying rent, and during which her dower was to be assigned. **Widow's terce**: in Scotland, the right of a widow to a third part of her husband's rents.

Wife's equity. v. *Equity.*

Wild's Case. The *Rule in Wild's Case*: if A devises land to B and to his children or issue, and B hath no issue at the time of the devise, it is an estate tail; but if he has issue at the time, B and his children take joint estates for life. 6 *Coke,* 16 b.

Wills, Statute of. The 32 Hen. VIII. c. 1 (1540), by which persons seised in socage could devise all their lands except to bodies corporate; and persons seised in chivalry, two thirds.

Winchester, Winton, Statute of. The 13 Edw. I. s. 2 (1285), providing for duties of constables, watch and ward, etc.

Wisbuy, laws of. A code of maritime law compiled in the fourteenth century at Wisbuy in Gothland, Sweden.

Wite, *sax.* A penalty; payment, amerciament; or immunity therefrom.

Witenagemote. (The assembly of wise men.) The Saxon national council or Parliament. v. *Court,* 1.

Withdrawing a juror. A method of suspending an action by consent, and sharing the costs. **Withdrawing a record:** a method of suspending an action by withdrawing the nisi prius record, revoking the entry by the plaintiff.

Withernam, *sax.,* **Withernamium,** *l.* (Other taking.) A taking in reprisal; as when a distress has been made and the goods eloigned so that they cannot be replevied, the plaintiff may have a writ to take other goods in withernam. v. *Capias,* 5, *Replevin.*

Without day. Without adjournment or *continuance;* to go **without day,** to be finally dismissed the court. **Without impeachment of waste:** without liability for waste other than *equitable.* **Without recourse:** an assignment without assuming the liability of an indorser; v. *Indorsement.* **Without this, that:** words introducing the negative part of a special *traverse.*

Witness. A person called before a court to give evidence. **Party-witness:** a term applied to old methods of trying an issue by witnesses produced by the parties; as the plaintiff's *secta,* the witnesses *de visu et auditu* or *de vicineto,* and *compurgators.* The witnesses **de visu et auditu** (of sight and hearing) spoke to the fact itself, were **transaction witnesses,** the origin of the modern *jury;* the **secta** and the defendant's **compurgators** spoke to the plaintiff's or defendant's credibility only. In ecclesiastical causes the compurgators varied in number, and anciently might always be used instead of the other forms of trial. v. *Purgation, Compurgatores, Wager of law.*

Wold, *sax.* A down; a hilly tract without trees.

Wolfshead. An *outlaw, caput lupinum.*

Woodgeld. Money paid for taking wood from a *forest.*

Woodmote. The *court of attachments,* or *forty-days court,* a *forest* court. v. *Court,* 74, 75.

Woolsack. The seat of the Lord Chancellor in the House of Lords.

Worth, weorth, *sax.* A country-house or farm.

Wreck. Goods cast ashore from a wreck under such circumstances as to be forfeit to the Crown or State.

Writ. Originally, the written command of the King, or some member of his household, introduced into England from Normandy. Later, the written command or precept of any court or officer. v. *Breve, Action, Bill of Middlesex, Trespass.* **Prerogative writ:** a special writ issued by the royal authority or prerogative, as matter of favor; as distinct from the **writs de cursu,** writs of course, issued by the Crown or court, or person authorized by the Crown, as matter of right. The writs *de cursu* were at first vague in form, but by the time of Glanvill had assumed definite shape; they were **formed writs,** called later **original writs,** and by promulgation in the year 1258 no new writs could be issued. By the Stat. Westminster II. c. 24, it was enacted that new writs should be issued in similar cases (v. *Case, Action on the case*), whence these latter were termed **writs on the case,** as distinct from the original writs. Both the original writs, or writs *de cursu,* and writs on the case were **original writs,** as distinct from judicial writs; that is, they issued from Chancery under the seal of the King, as the fountain of justice, at the beginning of actions; **judicial writs** issues from a court, and include all writs issuing after the beginning of the action (v. *Bill, Process*). **Close writs, clause writs,** are sealed writs; grants of the King, sealed with his great seal, but directed to some particular person for particular purposes; not *letters patent.* **Writ of inquiry:** a proceeding by which the sheriff inquires by a jury into the amount of damages, after judgment by default. For other writs, see their respective titles.

Writer to the Signet. Anciently, clerks in the office of the Scotch Secretary of State, who prepared writs passing the King's signet, and various other processes; they are also attorneys or solicitors, and privileged to conduct causes in the Court of Session.

Wynton. v. *Winchester.*

Y.

Y, *fr.* There. **Y est:** there is.

Yalemaines, *fr.* At least, however.

Ycel, yceux, *fr.* It; them.

Yard-land. *Virgata terræ.*

Year books. The oldest English reports; from Edward II. to Henry VIII.

Year, day, and waste. A privilege of the Crown to have the lands of a person attainted for felony or petty treason for a year and a day, with the privilege of committing waste, before restoring them to the lord of the fee.

Year to year, from. v. *Estate.* **Years:** v. *Estate.*

Yeoman. A freeholder under the rank of gentleman, who had land to the value of 40 *s.* a year, and was thus a *good and lawful man.*

Yeven, yeoven. Given; dated.

York. A Yorkshire custom of dividing the goods of an intestate among the widow, children, and administrator in equal thirds.

THE END.

University Press: John Wilson & Son, Cambridge.